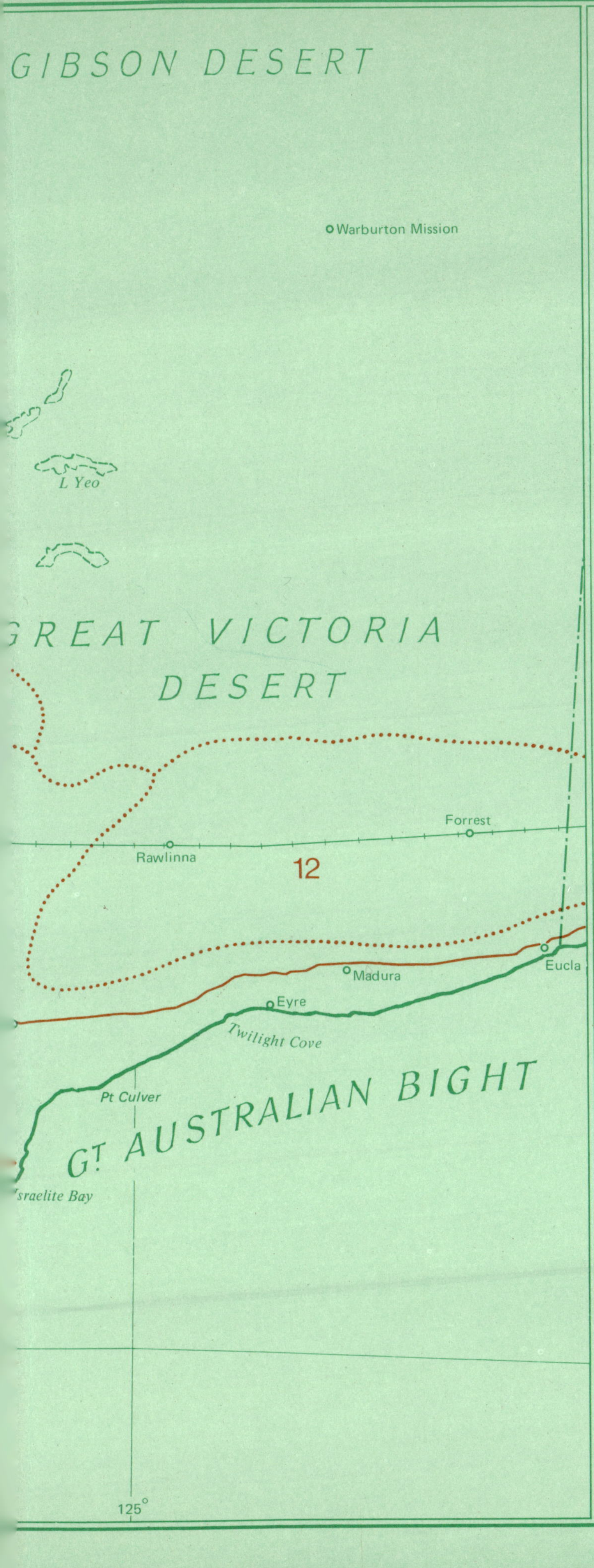

GUIDE MA

FLOWERS AND PLANTS OF WESTERN AUSTRALIA
SOUTH-WEST DIVISION

(See back Endpaper for N.-W. Division)

PLANT REGIONS

1 Swan Coastal Plain and Darling Scarp
2 Jarrah Forest
3 Karri Forest
4 Albany District
5 Stirling Range
6 Southern Sandplains & Heath
7 The Barrens
8 Northern Sandplains & Heath
9 Wheatbelt
10 Granite Outcrops (not shown individually)
11 Transitional Woodland
12 Nullarbor
13 Mulga, Wattle Scrub & Spinifex

Boundaries of Plant Regions
Roads
Railways
Rabbit Proof Fences
State Boundary

0 50 100 150 200 250 300 350 400
KILOMETRES

☆☆☆

LOCATION MAP

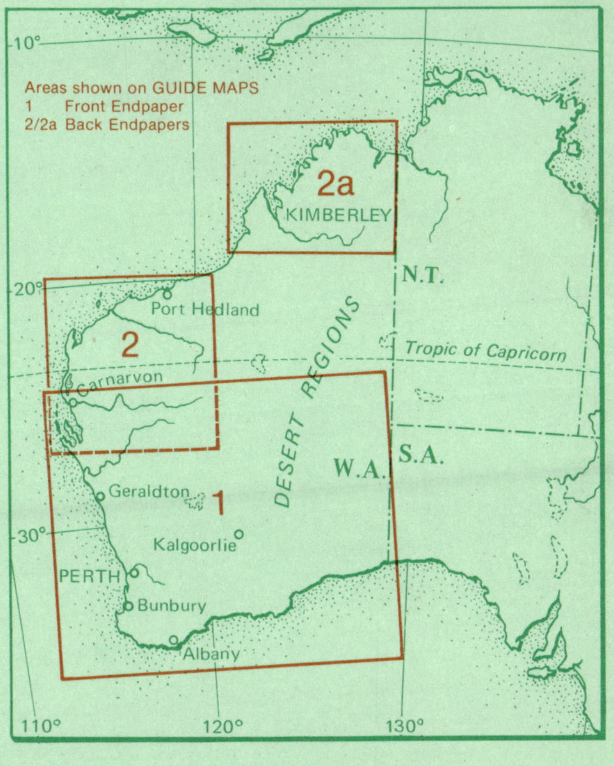

P. J. C. Trotter.
5.1.83

FLOWERS & PLANTS OF WESTERN AUSTRALIA

FLOWERS & PLANTS OF WESTERN AUSTRALIA

Rica Erickson ~ A.S. George
N.G. Marchant ~ M.K. Morcombe

REED

First published 1973
Revised edition 1979
Reprinted 1982

AH & AW REED PTY LTD
2 Aquatic Drive Frenchs Forest NSW 2086
68 Kingsford-Smith Street Wellington 3

National Library of Australia
Cataloguing-in-Publication Data
Flowers and plants of Western Australia.
Index
First published, Sydney: Reed, 1973.
ISBN 0 589 50116 X
1. Wild flowers — Western Australia. I. Erickson, Rica.
582.13'0994'1

Printed and bound by Kyodo-Shing Loong, Singapore

Contents

	PLATES	PAGES	TEXT
Preface			6
Introduction to First Edition			8
Introduction to Second Edition			10
Photographic Credits			11
References			11
Swan Coastal Plain and Darling Scarp	1–79	17–37	13
Jarrah Forest	80–143	38–55	16
Karri Forest	144–154	56–59	178
Albany District	155–188	60–69	181
Stirling Range	189–212	70–77	184
Southern Sandplains and Heath	213–256	78–89	186
The Barrens	257–277	90–95	189
Northern Sandplains and Heath	278–329	96–109	192
Wheatbelt	330–404	110–129	197
Granite Outcrops	405–425	130–135	199
Transitional Woodlands and Nullabor Plain	426–452	136–143	202
Mulga, Wattle Scrub and Spinifex	453–493	144–155	205
Ranges and Tablelands of the North-West	494–523	156–164	209
North-West Coast	524–538	165–168	212
The Kimberley	539–567	169–176	215
Glossary			220
Index			222

Preface

TO THE EYES OF the earliest European visitors the vegetation of the coast of what is now Western Australia was both disappointing and uninteresting. Only the Englishman William Dampier gave any hint of the unique character of the flora: it was he who after his second visit in 1699 remarked on the predominance of blue among the flowering plants.

Subsequent expeditions visiting this coast included among their members a number of scientists who carried back to Europe large collections of the plants and animals of the new land. These created great interest particularly among botanists, and following the establishment of the Swan River Colony in 1829 a number of botanical collectors visited the settlement to make further extensive collections. Men like George Maxwell, Ludwig Preiss, William Baxter and James Drummond travelled extensively throughout the south-west, and sent back to Europe so many new and unique plants that the Swan River Colony became renowned among scientists as the home of some of the most unusual wildflowers. In commenting on one of Drummond's collections from the south coast which had been sent to the Royal Botanic Gardens at Kew in England, the Director Sir W. J. Hooker wrote that he had 'rarely seen so great a number of fine and remarkable species arrive at one time from any country'.

Today the Western Australian flora is still renowned for the number of unique plant species which it contains. New species are constantly being discovered and as botanical research continues it is likely that many more species will be brought to light. While it is true that the flora exhibits a remarkable diversification at the species level it is also true that there is little of peculiar interest at the family level. This was pointed out by J. D. Hooker in an essay on the Australian flora. He stated:

> That it contains more genera and species peculiar to its own area, and fewer plants belonging to other parts of the world, than any other country of equal extent. About two-fifths of its genera, and upwards of seven-eighths of its species are entirely confined to Australia. On the other hand, if, disregarding the pecularities of the Flora, I compare its elements with those of the Floras of similarly situated large areas of land, or with that of the whole globe, I find that there is so great an agreement between these, that it is impossible to regard the Australian vegetation in any other light than as forming a peculiar, but not an aberrant or anomalous, botanical province of the existing Vegetable Kingdom. I find that all the Australian Natural Orders (families), with only two small exceptions, are also found in other countries; that most of those most widely diffused in Australia are such as are also the most widely distributed over the globe; and that Australia wants no known Order of general distribution.*

Sir J. D. Hooker, who succeeded his father as Director of Kew, was one of the most eminent of British botanists, and he made the above remarks after examining collections of Australian plants. They were authoritative opinions based on a sound knowledge of the floras of other lands as well. The same general principle is still very true today, and a full appreciation of the beauty and unique qualities of the flora is acquired only by a close study of the plants themselves.

More and more people in Western Australia and indeed in many other countries, are turning to nature for relaxation and enjoyment of their leisure time. Even the most casual association with wildflowers in the undisturbed bushland areas leads almost automatically to a greater awareness of their intrinsic beauty and an appreciation of their value to a commerce-weary world. Over the past decade there has been a very great increase in public interest in the native flora of the State and there is developing a great urge for their preservation and conservation both by the creation of National Parks and Nature Reserves, and by cultivation.

To some people the peace and quiet of the bush is what appeals most, but to others the individual plant species, their variety of colour and form, and their flowering periods throughout the year provide a source of endless study and enjoyment. To these people, as to the Hookers in England many years ago, the naming of the individual plants is of great importance and satisfaction. Names can be obtained by asking other people, but the maximum amount of pleasure is obtained by those who go to the trouble of examining the plants in detail and working out the names for themselves. At times this can be a difficult and perplexing operation, but as many have already found out, the more difficult the task, the greater the satisfaction at the conclusion of a job well done.

There are several methods by which plants can be identified although all of them may not be available to everyone who wishes to put a name on a plant. The first method, and one which is used universally by professional botanists is the use of a botanical key which is basically a sequential catalogue of certain of the characteristics of the group of plants concerned. The most commonly used is known as the dichotomous key since it provides at each step two contrasting characters. The choice of the correct character at each step is the basis of the successful use of the key and leads

*Botany of the Antarctic Voyage, etc., Part 3, Flora Tasmaniae, pp xxvii, xxviii (1859)

ultimately to the accepted botanical name for the plant. The botanical key can be rather frustrating for the beginner, not only because of the inherent difficulties involved in the dissection of flowers, but also because of the amount of variation which is common among the individual specimens of almost every known plant species. Despite these difficulties however, the key will always be the most important and reliable means of putting a name on a plant specimen.

Another method by which a plant can be identified involves a comparison of the unknown specimen with one which has already been named. However the use of this method requires a certain basic knowledge of the family and preferably also of the genus to which the plant begins.

Where a herbarium collection of named plants is available and the name of the genus to which the plant belongs is known, it can be compared with specimens of each of the species within the genus until ultimately the correct name can be found. With small genera this is a satisfactory technique, but it is a lot more difficult if the unknown plant belongs to a large genus such as Eucalyptus, Acacia or Grevillea. Furthermore the variation caused by the conditions under which the plant grew, or by inherited characters sometimes complicates the identification.

Still another method is one which involves the use of illustrations instead of preserved specimens. This is probably the best method for the beginner, and although it has some serious limitations, it serves as a very useful introduction to the techniques of plant identification. A great many books of wildflower illustrations have been produced, and most of them have met a steady demand from the public. However the number of species illustrated in these books is usually very small and they are seldom arranged in any way which is calculated to make the task of identifying a plant any easier.

This present volume, Flowers and Plants of Western Australia, is designed to overcome some of these difficulties. A large number of species has been selected to give a wide cover and to provide typical examples of as many genera as possible. By this means the beginner can be guided over the first hurdle—placing the unknown plant into the correct genus. If there is no illustration which precisely corresponds to the specimen in this book or in any other illustrated reference book available, the investigation can then proceed further, possibly to a key to the genus for final naming at the species level.

To simplify the matter even further thc book has been arranged in sections so that the field of investigation is narrowed down considerably. Thus the plants of the Stirling Range are grouped into one section and those of the Jarrah Forest into another, while two other sections deal with the plants of the North-West Ranges and the Southern Sandheath. There are fourteen such sections, and for each there is an accompanying description of the general plant ecology. This arrangement is a very useful aid to identification but it should be remembered that many plant species will be found in more than one district of the State. Despite its limitations it is hoped that this book will make a welcome and significant addition to the libraries of those naturalists who are sincerely looking for names for the wildflowers of this State.

R. D. ROYCE
Formerly Curator
Western Australian Herbarium
South Perth

Introduction to First Edition

THE PUBLICATION OF J. T. Salmon's *New Zealand Flowers and Plants in Colour* by A. H. & A. W. Reed commanded envy and admiration among naturalists in Australia. There was admiration for a fine production which could encompass the total flora of a country, and envy because it was felt that a similar publication illustrating the several thousands of Australian plants would be impossible to produce.

Nevertheless a number of Victorian naturalists were inspired to attempt to achieve the impossible. Although every species of wildflower in Victoria is not included, the resulting book *Flowers and Plants of Victoria,* published by the same firm in 1968, covers a very wide field. The superb photography and the concise, illuminating text make it a work of interest and value to wildflower lovers in all States of the Commonwealth.

Victorians in their turn were envied by other Australians, and when the publishers proposed that a similar book may be produced for Western Australia, the chosen committee were enthusiastic in their response, and were grateful to have such an excellent pattern to follow.

The committee appointed to produce *Flowers and Plants of Western Australia* were Mr M. K. Morcombe, as photographer, Mr A. S. George and Dr N. G. Marchant as botanists, and Mrs Rica Erickson, as chairman and co-ordinator.

Michael Morcombe, a professional naturalist and author of several fine publications, has a reputation for excellent photography in all branches of natural history. His extensive collection of wildflower photographs, made while caravanning around Australia assembling the material for his book on National Parks, was a deciding factor in favour of producing this work.

Alex George and Neville Marchant, botanists at the Western Australian Herbarium in South Perth, have an intimate knowledge of the wildflowers of the State and are accomplished in research and field studies. A tribute must be paid to Mr R. D. Royce, Officer in Charge of the Botany Branch of the Department of Agriculture, and Curator of the Western Australian Herbarium, for valuable assistance in planning the work in its initial stages, and for generous help given at all times.

Initially it was planned for the botanists to draw up an extensive list of species for the photographer to portray, but with the limited time in which to work it soon became evident that while attempting to find as many of the selected plants as possible, Michael Morcombe should be given a free hand to choose his subjects as he found them.

This arrangement was considered to be satisfactory, since those plants which catch the eye of a photographer as he travels along the highways and byways, and through the National Parks, would also attract the attention of other passersby, and therefore warranted inclusion in the book.

It was unfortunate that in the first of the two seasons during which Michael Morcombe was working on this project, the State suffered the worst drought on record, followed in the next year by a stormy springtime. It became necessary therefore to use some photographs from other sources, including a number from a bank of transparencies at the Western Australian Herbarium. Grateful thanks are offered to all who have lent photographs, and their names are recorded in the list of credits. In all, 509 species are illustrated as close-ups in 538 plates, and several other species as general views. Of these 432 are endemic (denoted by the † sign).

Approximately a quarter of the species shown in the Victorian book occur also in Western Australia. Although many of these plants are commonly seen here, they have not been included in the Western Australian book, and it is recommended that readers in this State refer to both books. In some instances, plates in the Victorian book have been cited, e.g. Vic. 191. One reason for avoiding duplication is that the number of photographs is limited, and only a small proportion of Western Australian wildflowers can be depicted. Because of this limitation the committee decided also to exclude the tropical flora of the State. It is hoped that another publication may be brought out in the future to illustrate the plants of Northern Australia. In the meantime a companion volume on the wildflowers of New South Wales is being produced, and in time a comprehensive coverage of the wildflowers of the whole continent may be achieved.

The regions of Western Australia which are covered in this book are the South-West and North-West divisions of the State, and some of the adjacent so-called desert lands. The area covers a thousand miles or more, from Port Hedland in the north to the far south, and inland for several hundred miles, offering a large variety of vegetation types.

These two divisions have been subdivided into loosely defined, but obviously different regions, which are discussed in turn in the general text. The main characteristics of each region are described and the predominating plants are named, including noteworthy species which may not be illustrated.

The flora of the North-West division has been little publicised, but the rapid development brought about by the mining boom in this part of the State has created an increasing interest in the wildflowers, which in good seasons are abundant in the interesting coastal region, the spectacular ranges, and the vast stretches of wattle scrub, mulga and spinifex of the inland.

The botanical regions of the South-West division have been more difficult to define. The subdivisions adopted by botanists since the turn of the century, namely the Irwin, Darling, Warren, Avon, Stirling and Eyre, although meaningful to botanists are of little value to the layman. A modification of these subdivisions has been introduced in this work, using titles more descriptive of the habitats, and recognising as distinct, some areas which had been united in former works. Some are well-known botanical districts and some are named for the predominating vegetation, which is readily recognised in the field. The boundaries are not easily marked on a map because of intrusions of some habitats into other regions. For instance, granite outcrops occur in jarrah forests and wheatbelt districts, while sandplains finger their way into forest areas.

A dominating factor is soil type. Soils may determine the members of a plant community more than rainfall or height above sea level. For example all sandplains are not alike. Some plants grow only in deep white sand, others in deep yellow sand, while many prefer shallow sand overlying hard gravel beds. Many different kinds of soil may occur within a small area.

The sandplains and heathlands north of the Moore River have interesting affinities with the sandplains and heathlands of the south, but each region has a high number of plants restricted to its own area and they are distinct entities.

Although the Swan coastal plain and the Albany region both include coastal dunes, swamps, heathlands and forest, they have been separated because the Albany district is especially rich in unusual species.

The jarrah forest, the karri forest, Stirling Range, the Barrens and the Nullarbor are all readily recognisable regions. Farther inland, the predominance of wheat farmlands precludes the use of any other term than wheatbelt for a region which extends from near the Murchison in the north almost to Esperance in the south. It includes a complexity of habitats defined roughly as forest, sandplain and mallee country. The innumerable granite outcrops with their isolated 'island communities', and the margins of the vast salt lakes, add variety to the wheatbelt flora. Inland from this region, beyond the farms, extend the transitional woodlands of eucalypts, mallee lands and wattle thickets of the goldfields districts and pastoral regions.

In the pictorial section of the book each region is dealt with separately and introduced by a view showing a typical habitat with its plant associations. Where plants occur in more than one region their pictures have usually been allotted to that in which they most commonly occur.

Each photograph is numbered, labelled with the common name of the plant, and the flowering season noted in brackets. The related caption headings are not numbered, but they repeat the common name in heavy type on the left, while on the right appears the scientific name. Some of these scientific names will be different from those in recent use, since the authors have updated the names of species which have been recently studied so that they are now accepted according to the internationally accepted rules governing nomenclature, by which in time it is hoped to bring order out of chaos.

The provision of common names has entailed a great deal of work and thought. Unlike Victoria, where a comprehensive list of common names for native plants has been in use since 1916, no such list has been made for Western Australian plants. Victoria has about 3000 species, while Western Australia has over 6000. The provision of common names for all these plants has hitherto been regarded as a colossal task, too formidable to begin. The authors decided to form a sub-committee to embark upon it, beginning with the plants in this book and continuing, family by family, in the future. Most Western Australian native plants have no common names, but there are a few which are known by several, and pose the problem of right selection. A number of sources of names have been consulted, including eastern Australian lists, to achieve unanimity if possible. Unfortunately, some names in use in other States are not applicable here.

The photographs will serve only as a guide for identification. With some plants it is not possible to show the specific differences in a picture. Also, in the limited space of a caption, full descriptions for positive identification cannot be given. Authoritative botanical works, or experts, should be consulted for this purpose.

An attempt has been made to include in each caption the particular property of the plant, its family, range, habitat, general appearance and size. Distribution in other States is indicated by the abbreviations NT, Qld, NSW, Vic, Tas and SA.

The captions were written by Alex George with the exception of the *Drosera* species, *Cephalotus*, and numbers 1–17 and 49–79 of the Swan Coastal Plain and Darling Scarp Section, all of which were written by Neville Marchant. The general text sections were written as follows: Neville Marchant—Swan Coastal Plain and Darling Scarp, Jarrah Forest, Karri Forest, Wheatbelt, Granite Outcrops; Alex George—Albany District, Stirling Range, Southern Sandplains and Heath, The Barrens, Northern Sandplains and Heath, Transitional Woodlands and Nullarbor, Mulga, Wattle Scrub and Spinifex, Ranges and Tablelands of the North-West, North-West Coast.

Pastoral, agricultural, mining, and even forestry activities, all take their toll of native flora. In recent years since tourism has become a major industry, a demand has grown for illustrated books on wildflowers to guide a traveller to areas where they may be seen, and to enable him to name the plants. The saddening progressive loss of wildflowers along the roadsides may mean that in the future the flora reserves and national parks will be the only places where wildflowers may be seen. It should be noted that the picking of all native flora is prohibited on all Crown lands, state forests, public reserves and roadsides in the South-West and Eucla Land Divisions. Permits which allow picking in certain circumstances may be obtained from the Department of Fisheries and Wildlife.

The Photographs

Photography by Michael Morcombe for this book commenced in May 1969 and was completed in the spring of 1971. During this time several thousand photographs were taken in order to provide a wide variety of illustrations to meet botanical requirements, and at the same time provide an adequate technical and artistic quality.

As far as possible natural light, mainly sunlight, was used. Although electronic flash gives very consistent results, and freezes any movement due to wind, it can tend to give too many dark and confused backgrounds, and it is much more difficult for the photographer to predict the final result. The effect of natural lighting can of course be seen through the camera, but flash gives a picture somewhat different from that seen through the viewfinder.

Electronic flash was used quite often, however, in very windy or dull weather.

For the majority of these photographs the film used was Agfacolor CT 18, which gave satisfactory rendering of most colours. For blue flowers it was found best to remove the skylight filter normally kept screwed onto the lens, as this warm-tinted filter weakens the rendering of most blues.

The camera used by Michael Morcombe for almost all of the small photographs in this book was a Konica Autoreflex T, a 35 mm single lens reflex camera which, as its name implies, features automatic exposure control by a through-the-lens light measuring meter. However for most photographs the automatic exposure device was disregarded and the shutter and lens aperture set according to the photographer's experience. The reason for this is that the flower usually covers but a small part of the total area of the picture, while the background, often of a different brightness, covers a larger area of the format. Therefore any automatic average exposure reading without some over-riding adjustment could be biased by the background illumination and be incorrect for the small but vital flower.

Lenses used on this camera were a Konica Hexanon 1.8/85 mm, with extension tubes, and a Schneider Xenar 4.5/105 mm short-mount lens on close-up focussing bellows.

For the larger habitat photographs at the beginning of each section several medium format cameras were used, principally a Plaubel Peco Junior and a Plaubel Profia; both are monorail or optical bench type cameras. These have the advantage of a swing-back device which permits tilting of the film plane, so that one may focus upon a flower very close to the camera, and simultaneously have in focus the distant background landscape. Usually an intermediate zone, not lying precisely in the plane of focus that extends from flowers to horizon, will be out of focus. These cameras provide a larger transparency, 6 × 9 cm, preferably for larger reproductions. The main drawback of such cameras is size and weight; the Profia, with lenses, film backs and carrying case weighs thirty pounds, which together with tripod must at times be carried quite a few miles.

The photographs by Alex George have been taken over the past ten years, though mostly since 1969. The 35 mm slides were all taken with a Zeiss Super Contaflex single-lens reflex camera with Tessar 2.8/50 mm lens, using Zeiss Proxar supplementary lenses for close-ups. In most cases natural lighting was used and the exposure set according to the built-in light meter, with some variation according to experience. A few were taken with electronic flash. The larger-format photographs were taken with a Rolleiflex twin-lens reflex with Tessar 3.5/75 mm lens, kindly loaned by Mr Kevin Richards. The film used in all cases was Agfacolor CT 18.

Introduction to Second Edition

The addition of a section on the Kimberley has expanded the coverage to include most of the settled regions of Western Australia, and provides an insight into the plants of one very different from the remainder. The Kimberley is yearly becoming more popular with visitors and there is little published information on the flora.

Indeed, much is still to be learned about it, for many areas of difficult access have not been examined, and few collections have been made in the wet season.

The Kimberley section has been written by Alex George and Neville Marchant, and the captions as follows: Neville Marchant: 542, 546, 548, 550, 557, 562-7; the remainder by Alex George.

Photographic equipment and techniques were the same as described in the first edition.

The original text has been corrected as necessary. Nomenclatural changes are few and follow improvements in the classification of the flora. Typographic errors have been corrected. We thank the many people who have assisted by pointing out errors.

In this edition, 538 species are illustrated as close-ups in 567 plates, of which 433 are endemic to Western Australia.

The number of new references added to the list reflects the increase in interest and publication about the flora not only of Western Australia but of the whole continent. There is also a greater awareness of the need to conserve our wildlife. A new Flora Protection Act protects native flora on all Crown lands, State forests, public reserves and road verges throughout the State. Requests for permits to allow picking in certain circumstances should be made to the Department of Fisheries and Wildlife.

PHOTOGRAPHIC CREDITS

E. M. BENNETT: 252.

R. ERICKSON: 10, 39, 47, 71, 173, 174, 239, 245, 328, 460, 461, 467, 484, 502, 508, 509, 513, 515, 517, 519, 520, 521, 522, 523, 531.

A. S. GEORGE: 2, 3, 4, 6, 15, 16, 17, 18, 21, 22, 24, 25, 27, 28, 39, 40, 44, 46, 48, 54, 59, 62, 63, 68, 69, 72, 73, 76, 77, 78, 81, 85, 86, 87, 90, 93, 94, 95, 96, 97, 98, 102, 104, 109, 111, 112, 118, 123, 125, 126, 129, 132, 136, 137, 138, 147, 151, 166, 175, 182, 187, 188, 194, 195, 201, 204, 205, 208, 210, 213, 217, 226, 227, 229, 230, 231, 232, 238, 242, 243, 244, 246, 248, 250, 251, 254, 257, 258, 260, 262, 270, 272, 274, 276, 277, 278, 280, 281, 285, 290, 291, 293, 295, 296, 304, 306, 309, 310, 311, 314, 322, 324, 327, 329, 330, 332, 335, 336, 349, 353, 357, 358, 360, 363, 376, 380, 382, 384, 389, 395, 396, 397, 407, 408, 409, 411, 413, 414, 415, 417, 418, 419, 421, 422, 423, 424, 431, 435, 440, 444, 445, 447, 449, 450, 451, 452, 454, 456, 458, 464, 466, 469, 470, 474, 475, 480, 483, 487, 496, 497, 498, 499, 500, 501, 504, 505, 511, 512, 514, 518, 524, 525, 526, 527, 529, 534, 537, 538, 540, 541, 542, 543, 544, 545, 546, 547, 548, 549, 550, 551, 552, 553, 554, 557, 558, 560, 561, 562, 563, 564, 565, 566, 567.

F. W. HUMPHREYS: 8, 31, 55, 100, 121, 152, 156, 177, 181, 190, 237, 253, 263, 279, 283, 301, 312, 319, 321, 339, 365, 369, 374, 381, 390, 402, 432, 459, 463, 510, 528.

B. M. J. HUSSEY: 455.

N. G. MARCHANT: 149.

I. MORCOMBE: 5, 472, 556, 559.

M. K. MORCOMBE: 1, 7, 9, 11, 12, 13, 14, 19, 20, 23, 26, 29, 30, 32, 33, 34, 35, 36, 37, 38, 41, 42, 43, 45, 49, 50, 51, 52, 53, 56, 58, 60, 61, 64, 65, 66, 67, 70, 71, 74, 79, 80, 82, 83, 84, 88, 89, 91, 92, 99, 101, 103, 105, 106, 107, 108, 110, 113, 114, 115, 116, 117, 119, 120, 122, 124, 127, 128, 130, 131, 133, 134, 135, 139, 140, 141, 142, 143, 144, 145, 146, 148, 150, 153, 154, 155, 157, 158, 159, 160, 161, 162, 163, 164, 165, 167, 168, 169, 170, 171, 172, 176, 178, 179, 180, 183, 184, 185, 186, 189, 191, 192, 193, 196, 197, 198, 199, 200, 202, 203, 206, 207, 209, 211, 212, 214, 215, 216, 218, 219, 220, 221, 223, 224, 225, 228, 233, 234, 235, 236, 240, 241, 247, 249, 255, 256, 259, 261, 264, 265, 266, 267, 268, 269, 271, 273, 275, 282, 284, 286, 287, 288, 289, 292, 294, 297, 298, 299, 300, 302, 303, 305, 307, 308, 313, 315, 316, 317, 318, 320, 323, 325, 326, 331, 333, 334, 337, 338, 340, 341, 342, 343, 344, 345, 346, 347, 348, 350, 351, 352, 354, 355, 356, 359, 361, 362, 364, 366, 367, 368, 371, 372, 373, 377, 378, 379, 383, 385, 386, 387, 388, 391, 392, 393, 394, 398, 399, 400, 401, 403, 404, 405, 406, 410, 412, 413, 416, 420, 425, 426, 427, 428, 429, 430, 433, 434, 436, 437, 438, 439, 441, 442, 443, 446, 453, 457, 462, 465, 468, 471, 473, 476, 477, 478, 479, 481, 482, 486, 488, 489, 490, 492, 494, 495, 503, 506, 507, 516, 530, 532, 533, 535, 536, 539, 555, and jacket.

R. D. ROYCE: 57, 75, 370, 375, 485.

R. A. SAFFREY: 491, 493.

SELECTED REFERENCE WORKS

Aston, H. I. (1973). *Aquatic Plants of Australia*. Melbourne University Press, Carlton, Vic.

Beard, J. S. (Ed.) (1970). *West Australian Plants*, 2nd ed. Society for Growing Australian Plants, Sydney, NSW.

Beard, J. S. (no date). *Wildflowers of the Northwest*. Westviews, Perth, WA.

Bentham, G. (1863-78). *Flora Australiensis*. Reeve, London.

Black, J. M. (1978). *Flora of South Australia*, 3rd ed. J. Jessop, editor. Government Printer, Adelaide—continuing.

Blackall, W. E. & Grieve, B. J. (1956-65). *How to Know Western Australian Wildflowers*. Parts 1-3. University of Western Australia Press, Nedlands, WA.

Breeden, S. & K. (1975). *Australia's North. A Natural History of Australia* 3. Collins, Sydney, NSW.

Burbidge, N. T. (1963). *Dictionary of Australian Plant Genera*. Angus & Robertson, Sydney, NSW.

Chippendale, G. M. (1973). 'Eucalypts of the Western Australian Goldfields and adjacent wheatbelt.' Australian Government Publishing Service, Canberra, ACT

Cochrane, G. R. et al. (1968) *Flowers and Plants of Victoria*. Reed, Sydney, NSW.

Cribb, A. B. & J. W. (1974). *Wild Food in Australia*. Collins, Sydney, NSW.

Erickson, R. (1958). *Triggerplants*. Paterson Brokensha, Perth, WA.

Erickson, R. (1965). *Orchids of the West*. 2nd ed. Paterson Brokensha, Perth, WA.

Erickson, R. (1968). *Plants of Prey in Australia*. Lamb Paterson Perth, WA.

Gardner, C. A. (1944). 'The Vegetation of Western Australia.' Presidential Address, 1942. *Journal of the Royal Society of Western Australia* Vol. 28 pp. xi-lxxxvii.

Gardner, C. A. (1952-66). 'Trees of Western Australia.' Bulletins from the *Journal of Agriculture of Western Australia*. Western Australian Department of Agriculture, South Perth, WA.

Gardner, C. A. (1973). Wildflowers of Western Australia. West Australian Newspapers, Perth, WA.

Gardner, C. A. (1972). *Western Australian Wildflowers,* Vols. A and B. Jacaranda, Brisbane, Qld.

Gardner, C. A. & Bennetts, H. W. (1956). *The Toxic Plants of Western Australia*. West Australian Newspapers, Perth, WA.

George, A. S. & Foote, H. E. (1969). *Orchids of Western Australia.* Westviews, Perth, WA.

Grieve, B. J. and Blackall, W. E. (1975). *How to Know Western Australian Wildflowers*. Parts 1-3. University of Western Australia Press, Nedlands, WA.

Harmer, J. (no date). *North Australian Plants*. Society for Growing Australian Plants, Sydney, NSW.

Jones, D. L. & Clemesha, S. C. (1976). *Australian Ferns and Fern Allies.* Reed, Sydney, NSW.

Jones, D. L. & Gray, B. (1977). *Australian Climbing Plants*. Reed, Sydney, NSW.

Kelly, S. (1969, 1978). *Eucalypts* Vols. 1 & 2. Text by G. M. Chippendale and R. D. Johnston. Nelson, Melbourne, Vic.

Main, Barbara York (1967). *Between Wodjil and Tor*. Jacaranda (Brisbane) and Landfall (Perth).

Morcombe, M. K. (1968). *Australia's Western Wildflowers.* Landfall, Perth, WA.

Mullins, B. and Baglin, D. (1978). *Western Australian Wildflowers in Colour*. Reed, Sydney, NSW.

Nuytsia (1970). *Bulletin of Western Australian Herbarium*. Continuing series containing papers on the Australian flora. Western Australian Department of Agriculture, South Perth, WA.

Rotherham, E. R. et al. (1975) *Flowers and Plants of New South Wales and Southern Queensland.* Reed, Sydney, NSW.

Royce, R. D. (no date). *Wildflowers of Western Australia*. Westviews, Perth, W.A.

Seddon, G. (1972). *Sense of Place. A Response to an Environment: The Swan Coastal Plain, Western Australia.* University of Western Australia Press, Nedlands, WA.

Semeniuk, V., Kenneally, K. and Wilson, P. G. (1978). 'Mangroves of Western Australia.' Handbook No. 12, WA Naturalists' Club, Perth, WA.

Sharr, F. (1978). *A Dictionary of Western Australian Plant Names.* University of Western Australia Press, Nedlands, WA.

Western Australian Herbarium Research Notes. Continuing series containing papers on WA flora and ecology. Western Australian Department of Agriculture, South Perth, WA.

Willis, J. C., (ed.) H. K. Airy Shaw (1966). *A Dictionary of the Flowering Plants and Ferns*, 7th ed. Cambridge University Press, England.

Swan Coastal Plain and Darling Scarp

THE SWAN COASTAL PLAIN is here regarded as extending from the Moore River to Busselton. It is characterised especially by extensive poor sandy soils. Along the coast is a narrow zone of sand dunes and inland from this is a limestone belt which in the metropolitan area is a definite ridge up to 75 metres above sea level. Estuarine and freshwater wetlands, sandy ridges and the rocky Darling Scarp provide further diverse habitats for the plants of this region.

The coastal sand dunes are a hostile environment with a characteristic flora. Only plants adapted to strong salt-laden winds, moving sand and the very high light intensity of summer are able to survive. This is the home of the true Spinifex, both *Spinifex longifolius* (Pl. 524) and the silvery-leaved *S. hirsutus* (Vic. 285), and many cosmopolitan species such as the Sea Rocket, *Cakile maritima*. Further from the beach the dunes are more stable and shrubs of *Acacia* and *Scaevola* can grow in sheltered spots. Further inland still, there is no moving sand, but strong winds prune shrubs to form a low heath of wattles such as Prickly Moses, *Acacia pulchella* (Pl. 11), Yellow Buttercup, *Hibbertia hypericoides* (Pl. 30), and a dull-flowered relative of the Blue Tinsel Lily *(Calectasia cyanea)*, *Acanthocarpus preissii* which is particularly common on Rottnest Island.

Low bluffs of coastal limestone which are buffeted by waves in winter storms, support a few small shrubs such as *Frankenia pauciflora*. In more sheltered areas such as rock crevices grow some of the coastal heath shrubs.

The higher ridges of coastal limestone also have a characteristic flora. The higher, more exposed areas support a dense heath of *Hakea, Dryandra, Melaleuca* and Cockies' Tongues, *Templetonia retusa* (Pl. 11). The lower, protected areas of deep soil have more luxuriant growth of the same species. These areas, particularly in the vicinity of Perth, are generally very much disturbed by Man's building and cultivating activities. In the market gardening areas to the east of the limestone ridge Man's influence is indicated by the prevalence of Mediterranean weeds. Masses of Wild Oats and Aniseed plants are seen along the roadsides. Fortunately many native plants still persist in these areas, for example the Swan River Daisy, *Brachycome iberidifolia* (Pl. 4), and Snakebush, *Hemiandra pungens* (Pl. 2).

An impression of the original vegetation of the metropolitan area is not difficult to obtain. Remnants of the limestone flora still exist at Buckland Hill, on the steep western banks of the Swan River and in Kings Park as well as on the off-shore islands. The sheltered limestone slopes and valleys support stands of Rottnest Tea-tree, *Melaleuca lanceolata,* and Rottnest Cypress, *Callitris preissii.* On deeper soils Tuart, *Eucalyptus gomphocephala,* occurs as a large tree, the height being determined by the salt-laden westerly winds. This fine tree which is always an indicator of limestone soils attains a height of 40 metres. It occurs between the Hill River and Busselton. At the southern end of its range it forms a magnificent forest, the Ludlow State Forest. Under the Tuart trees grow the W.A. Peppermint, *Agonis flexuosa* (Pl. 8), wattles and some species of *Grevillea.* In deep hollows such as those formed by collapsed caves, dense thickets of sedges and wattles provide a shaded habitat for moisture-loving species of mosses and a small delicate fern, *Anogramma leptophylla.*

Extensive estuaries and large cut-off sections of the sea are a feature of the Swan Coastal Plain particularly from Perth southwards to Bunbury. Salt-water-tolerant species such as samphires and the Berry Saltbush, *Rhagodia radiata* (Pl. 9), grow around the shores. At Bunbury a few stands of the White Mangrove, *Avicennia marina* (Vic. 190, 191), which is common in northern and eastern Australia, grow in the Leschenault Inlet. This is the only recorded western occurrence of this species south of the Abrolhos Islands.

The salt-water lakes and estuaries are usually surrounded by the Salt-Water Paperbark, *Melaleuca cuticularis*, with an undergrowth of sedges and a few herbs. The higher ground is sandy and consequently well-drained as is most of the coastal plain up to the foothills of the Darling Scarp. Where the water table reaches the surface there are permanent or ephemeral fresh-water lakes. In the permanent waters grow a few species of aquatic plants such as the Swamp Lily, *Ottelia ovalifolia* (Vic. 271). The wetlands surrounding these lakes are frequently very extensive in winter. They are covered by marsh-dwelling plants such as the Bulrush, *Typha domingensis* (Vic. 261), and the Jointed Rush, *Baumea articulata.* Another of the Paperbarks, *Melaleuca rhaphiophylla,* is able to withstand very long periods of inundation. This small tree is easily recognised by its soft, needle-like leaves which are 2–3 cm long. It frequently forms dense thickets with an undergrowth of semi-aquatic plants such as Water-ribbon, *Triglochin procera* (Vic. 266), grasses and sedges. In the ephemeral swamps where water lies for only a few months or less the number of plant species is greater. Another Paperbark with small, pointed, broad-based leaves, *Melaleuca preissiana,* along with many other species which prefer the heavier soil of depressions and can withstand the wet months, contribute to the diversity of the ephemeral swamps.

The ephemeral swamps, particularly those near the foothills of the scarp, are noted for the prevalence of endemic species. It is here that one finds many insectivorous plants such as the Southern Byblis, *Byblis gigantea* (Pl. 62), and five or six species of Sundew or *Drosera* such as the Pimpernel Sundew, *D. glanduligera* (Pl. 384). These plants have sticky glands on their leaves which act as 'flypapers', catching small insects and absorbing nourishment from their decaying bodies. Other carnivorous plants also grow in the winter-wet depressions. The ground-dwelling members of the Bladderwort family *(Lentibulariaceae)* such as Redcoats, *Utricularia menziesii* (Pl. 64), and the related genus *Polypompholyx*, have minute root bladders which trap tiny soil-water-dwelling animals. These plants are able to supplement their diet by their carnivorous habit and are thus able to live in the impoverished top layer of soil without extensive root systems.

Bulbous and rhizomatous plants abound in the winter-wet areas. The Hoary Twine Rush, *Leptocarpus canus* (Pls. 65, 66), and other members of the family *Restionaceae,* which have their nearest relatives in South Africa, are notoriously difficult to identify. The reason for this is that they are dioecious; that is, the male and female flowers are borne on different plants and sometimes these have a very different appearance making the collection of both sexes of a species difficult.

The most common shrub of the heavier swampy soils is the Swamp Tea-tree, *Leptospermum ellipticum,* with small scattered leaves and pink or white flowers. A few species of shrubby *Banksia* are also able to withstand seasonal flooding as is the White Myrtle, *Hypocalymma angustifolium* (Pl. 53). Slightly drier ground is the home of some members of the Kangaroo Paw family, *Haemodoraceae*, including the Green Kangaroo Paw, *Anigozanthos viridis* (Pl. 52), and some of its less spectacular relatives in the genus *Tribonanthes*. The Red Swamp Cranberry, *Astroloma stomarrhena* (Pl. 51), is also found on drier ground which only becomes very damp in the depths of winter.

Low undulating hills with well-drained sandy soils of a grey, white or yellow colour cover most of the Swan Coastal Plain. Only a few species of tree are very widespread on these soils. By far the most common is Jarrah, *Eucalyptus marginata.* On the gravelly soils of the Plateau and edge of the Darling Scarp this tree forms an extensive forest of tall, single-stemmed trees. On the sandy soils of the Coastal Plain the Jarrah trees are mixed with other species and are widely spaced, the crowns of neighbouring trees rarely touching. This vegetation type is known as a woodland. The Jarrah trees themselves rarely reach a great height and are frequently multi-stemmed.

Resembling Jarrah and common in some areas, especially in the north of the region, is the Pricklybark, *E. todtiana.* It has several stems with coarse, stringy bark, and the flowers and fruits are larger than those of Jarrah.

Marri, *Eucalyptus calophylla*, is common on the eastern part of the plain where it prefers the clay soils washed down from the plateau. This is also good farming land so very little of the undergrowth of the Marri woodlands is left. The trees themselves develop oak-like crowns when neighbouring trees have been removed and so provide ideal shade trees for stock.

Five species of *Banksia* occur as trees on the Coastal Plain. One is Menzies' Banksia, *B. menziesii* (Pls. 1, 20), which has toothed leaves 2–3 cm wide and generally has yellow and red flowering spikes. Another is *Banksia attenuata* which has narrower leaves and yellow flowers. The orange-flowered Acorn Banksia, *B. prionotes,* occurs on yellow soil pockets. It is still present in Kings Park, Perth, but is more common on similar soils further north. The grotesque Bull Banksia, *B. grandis,* which has leaves up to 40 cm long with wide triangular lobes, occurs on grey sand frequently in association with the common Sheoak, *Casuarina fraserana.* The fifth species is the Holly-leaved Banksia, *B. ilicifolia.* This tree prefers less-well-drained soils and has long, erect branches with very dark green holly-like leaves. The flowers are borne in short heads similar to those of Parrot Bush (Pl. 110).

The Sheoak *Casuarina fraserana* is found scattered in the woodland either singly or in groups. The main features of this genus are the very modified leaves and simple flowers. The leaves are reduced to whorls of small scales scattered along the generally drooping green branchlets. The branchlets are shed at the end of their functional life and as a result a very thick layer of litter may develop underneath each tree. This litter layer modifies the acidity of the soil so that few species of plant can survive. One species which frequently thrives under these conditions is the Bee Orchid, *Caladenia discoidea.*

The flowers of *Casuarina* are highly specialised for wind pollination. They are extremely reduced to very simple structures aggregated at the ends of special branchlets. The female flower consists of a single ovary with two long, red styles, surrounded by a few brown scales. At maturity the styles protrude from the branchlets to catch the wind-borne pollen grains from the male trees. The male flower consists of a single stamen surrounded by bracts, hundreds of flowers being aggregated at the ends of numerous branchlets. At maturity the male trees can easily be recognised by the rust-coloured branches which liberate clouds of pollen grains.

The only other widespread tree of the coastal plain is the Christmas Tree, *Nuytsia floribunda* (Pl. 25). This semi-parasite is a member of the Mistletoe family, *Loranthaceae*, and when flowering is probably one of the most spectacular flowering trees in the world. Biologically this tree is an oddity. It is considered the giant of all mistletoes because the other five hundred or so species of the family are shrubs either ground-dwelling or living on the branches of other trees or shrubs.

The Christmas Tree derives part of its nourishment

from many kinds of host plants through modified roots which clasp the roots or underground stems of the host. Carrots, grasses, shrubs and trees of very diverse species have been observed to help sustain the Christmas Tree. Even telephone cables with polyethylene covers have been attacked by the clasping roots.

The stem of the Christmas Tree is very different from most other tree trunks. Instead of a simple central cylinder of wood surrounded by bark, it has layers of wood and inner bark forming concentric cylinders. This means that the wood is very brittle and frequently unable to support the heavy branches in a storm. In nature the trees may also be severely pruned by fire. There is no doubt that the Christmas Tree is one of our many native species adapted to periodic burning. Even after an intense bush fire the number of flowers is greatly increased, these appearing before most of the leaves are replaced so that the vivid tangerine-coloured flowers stand out against the blackened stems.

In contrast to the tree flora the shrub flora of the coastal plain and Darling Scarp is very rich. Many different genera of the four most important South-Western families inhabit the various ecological niches described above. The most spectacular species are probably those belonging to the *Myrtaceae*. Always recognisable by the strong odour when a few leaves are crushed between the fingers, this family contains the Tea-trees, Bottlebrushes, Featherflowers and Honey-myrtles as well as the Eucalypts.

On the coastal limestone the flowers of the Chenille Honeymyrtle, *Melaleuca huegelii* (Pl. 7), make an attractive display. Further inland the most obvious plants of this family are the Swan River Myrtle, *Hypocalymma robustum* (Pl. 36), and one of the Starflowers, *Calytrix flavescens* (Pl. 23).

The sixteen species of *Beaufortia* in the South-West are represented on the coastal plain by the Sand Bottlebrush, *B. squarrosa* (Pl. 49), though the flowering spike of this species is not a true bottlebrush type like that of some other species of the genus. Apart from the Paperbarks and the Chenille Honeymyrtle mentioned earlier there are many shrubby species of *Melaleuca* which inhabit the winter waterlogged soils near the foothills of the scarp, for example the honeymyrtle, *M. polygaloides* (Pl. 50).

The genus *Darwinia* which is named in honour of Erasmus Darwin is largely a South-Western genus with about twenty eight species here. In contrast to most of the members of the family the main attraction of the flowers of *Darwinia* is the involucre of coloured bracts surrounding the aggregated flowers. In the Fringed Bell, *D. nieldiana* (Pl. 56), for example the flowers are typically myrtaceous with small petals and prominent stamens and style, but groups of these are surrounded by fringed bracts. Most of the other members of the Myrtaceae develop small colourful flowers, the main attraction being the staminal filaments. In *Calothamnus* and *Melaleuca* for example the petals are reduced to small lobes and the staminal filaments are joined together in groups. The colouring of the groups of filaments provides the main attraction for pollinating birds or insects. Other members of the family such as the well-known Geraldton Wax, *Chamelaucium uncinatum,* rely on their relatively large petals for their attraction.

A shrubby member of the *Banksia* family, *Proteaceae,* is the Common Woollybush, *Adenanthos cygnorum* (Pl. 54). This is a grey-green bush covered with soft, hairy leaves. It is particularly common on sandy rises. The flowers of this species are rather insignificant when compared with other species such as the Basket Flower, *A. obovatus* (Pl. 45).

Perhaps the most common shrub belonging to the *Proteaceae* is the Blueboy, *Stirlingia latifolia* (Pl. 39). This is characteristic of well-drained sands and is even able to withstand disturbance by man, especially frequent burning. The common name is derived from the fact that wall plaster made with sand from areas where it grows turns blue. Related to the Blueboy is the Common Smokebush, *Conospermum stoechadis* (Pl. 34). This species like some other smokebushes has the same general habit as the blueboy only with densely woolly flowers.

Nearly half of the species of *Proteaceae* in Australia belong to two closely-related genera, *Hakea* and *Grevillea.* These genera can be separated on the basis of their follicles. The generally thin-walled follicle of *Grevillea* splits along one side at maturity so as to resemble a short, opened pea pod. The follicle of *Hakea* which is generally woody and often quite large, splits along the upper and lower sides, the two halves opening away from each other. The Harsh Hakea, *H. prostrata* (Pl. 13), in the Perth region is a shrub or small tree which may reach 5 metres. The specific name of this species, *prostrata,* means growing close to the ground which is descriptive of the species on the windswept south coast, the site of the original collection by Robert Brown in 1801.

A favourite with beekeepers because of the quantity of nectar produced is the Parrot-bush, *Dryandra sessilis* (Pl. 110). On the coastal plain this species often forms dense thickets particularly in limestone areas which are not burnt regularly, since the plants are killed by fire and must regenerate from seed.

The Pea-flowered family *Papilionaceae* and the related *Mimosaceae* are also very well represented on the plain. The Common Hovea, *H. trisperma,* (Pl. 29), has intensely blue-purple flowers and is particularly common on the sandy soils. As with many of our blue-flowered native plants, white forms may occur though never frequently.

The most spectacular wattle of the coastal plain is the Prickly Moses, *Acacia pulchella* (Pl. 14). This is one of the relatively few W.A. species with true feather-like leaves rather than phyllodes. Masses of these bushes flower in winter, giving vivid golden splashes of colour to the coastal hills.

Darling Scarp

Along the eastern boundary of the Swan Coastal Plain rises the Darling Scarp, which at the same time marks the western edge of the Great Plateau of W.A. The large expanses of shallow soil on granite rocks and on laterite support a specialized and characteristic flora. The winter wetness allows the growth of algae, lichens, mosses and liverworts on the granite slopes. The deeper soils fringing the granite slopes receive extra watering from the rock and support a wealth of shrubs (Pl. 68). The Waxy Cryptandra, *C. arbutiflora* (Pl. 73), the Sticky Thomasia, *T. glutinosa* (Pl. 69), and the Spindly Grevillea, *G. endlicherana* (Pl. 79), often form dense shrub thickets. One of the characteristic scarp plants is the Fuchsia Grevillea, *G. bipinnatifida* (Pl. 71), which can flower at any month of the year.

Where the scarp soil is deep there are woodlands of white-barked Wandoo, and Marri. The Wandoo trees of this zone nearly always grow on the dark red soil over the epidiorite dykes. On the laterite especially where it is flat, Jarrah becomes the dominant tree.

Jarrah Forest

THE JARRAH FOREST IS one of the finest hardwood stands in the world. Covering some 1.6 million hectares, it stretches from the Perth-Toodyay Road in the north to near Albany in the south. Prime forests are developed on lateritic soils where the annual rainfall exceeds 1100 mm though the largest trees are usually found in the loam soils of deep river valleys.

Exploitation of Jarrah trees began in the early days of the Swan River Colony when the trees were called 'Swan River Mahogany'. The durability of the timber resulted in many thousands of tonnes being shipped to Europe before the turn of the century. Jarrah paving blocks, sleepers and cabinet woods gave Western Australia a considerable income for many years. This early exploitation has left only small areas of original undisturbed forest.

Unlike most of the world's hardwoods Jarrah occurs as an almost pure stand. Few other trees grow in association, and these have their specialized requirements and prefer soils other than pure laterites. The Marri, *Eucalyptus calophylla*, is most commonly associated with Jarrah though it generally prefers loam soils and is more common on the lower valley slopes.

Marri and Jarrah can be differentiated on bark characters as well as the large 'gum nut' fruits which litter the ground under Marri trees. Jarrah has red-grey, stringy bark with vertical fissures. Marri has a grey-brown, rough bark which does not break up into strips but remains as rough square or rectangular areas on the trunk. When burnt the bark of both species becomes charred, but the Marri usually exudes a dark red resin, hence the alternative common name Red Gum for this species. It is one of the very few bloodwoods found in the South-West.

Jarrah flowers from spring to early summer though the flowers are small and often inconspicuous among the foliage. However, the cream flowers of the Marri make an attractive display in mid- and late-summer. Red and pink-flowered variants occur sporadically through the forest. Usually referred to as *E. calophylla* variety *rosea*, this variety is often confused with the Red-flowering Gum, *E. ficifolia* (Pl. 173). Both Jarrah and Marri are important honey plants.

The second common associated tree of the forest is Wandoo, *Eucalyptus wandoo*. As mentioned in the previous section, Wandoo occurs in the western part of the Jarrah forest and on the Darling Scarp in soil developed from basic epidiorite dykes which have intruded the granitic country rock. Further east the Wandoo is restricted to the clay, valley soils. Where the rainfall is too low for Jarrah it becomes the dominant tree of the western edge of the Wheatbelt.

Another common Eucalypt in the Jarrah forest is the W.A. Blackbutt, *E. patens*. This tree prefers alluvial soil along creeks. The bark is very persistent and the trunk is usually blackened by fire, hence the name Blackbutt. It is distinguished from Jarrah by its more pointed, blue-green leaves and smaller fruits which have a narrower rim than the fruit of Jarrah.

The common Sheoak, *Casuarina fraserana* is a frequent understorey tree in the forest as well as in the woodland of the coastal plain. The female flowers, which have been described in the previous section as very highly reduced structures, develop into compound fruits commonly called 'cones'. These fruits consist of pairs of woody bracts arranged around the developing seeds. The seeds are winged and are wind-dispersed.

The only other trees common in the forest are tree members of the family *Proteaceae*. The Banksias are represented by four species. Only one of these grows in association with Jarrah, the others preferring sandy or riverbank soils. The Bull Banksia, *B. grandis*, is the only species which grows on laterite in the forest. The large saw-toothed leaves of this tree and the very long, yellow flower spike make this one of the most distinctive species of the genus. Menzies' Banksia, *B. menziesii* (Pl. 20), and Slender Banksia, *B. attenuata*, occur on the sandy soils of the forest. The River Banksia, a variety of *B. littoralis*, grows in the moist soil of river flats specially in the southern part of the Jarrah forest.

Patches of sandy soil with vegetation similar to that

(*continued on page 169*)

1 Woodland on the coastal plain near Perth, with Menzies' Banksia (*Banksia menziesii* R. Br.)

SWAN COASTAL PLAIN AND DARLING SCARP

The Swan Coastal Plain is here regarded as extending from the Moore River to Busselton, containing diverse habitats ranging from coastal limestone to clay and gravel of the Darling Scarp foothills. Most of the plain is covered by low, sandy hills and ridges with intervening winter-wet depressions. The well-drained sand supports Jarrah, Coastal Blackbutt and banksia woodlands. Extensive wetlands occur around the estuaries of the major rivers and around numerous permanent fresh-water lakes on the landward side of the coastal limestone. There are winter-wet areas near the Darling Scarp which are particularly rich in species. The Darling Scarp, which rises to over 300 m near Perth, but is lower to the north and south, forms a marked eastern boundary to the coastal plain. Its granitic and lateritic slopes carry a distinctive flora.

2 Snakebush (July–Dec)

Snakebush † *Hemiandra pungens* R. Br.
A spreading shrub to 80 cm with rigid, pungent leaves. The flowers which are up to 2 cm across vary from pale mauve with pink spots on the throat to white with brown and pink spots. It is common on sandy soils of the coastal plains from Dongara to Albany and in sandy heaths of the jarrah forest.
Family: Lamiaceae

3 Yanchep Rose (July–Oct)

5 Bronze Shell Orchid (June–Aug)

Bronze Shell Orchid *Pterostylis scabra* Lindl. var. *robusta* (Rogers) George
This delicate greenhood has translucent flowers 2–3 cm long, the linear, irritable lip being hidden within the flower. It grows under shrubs, especially on coastal dunes, between Geraldton and Albany, as well as in SA and Vic. The var. *scabra,* with a longer, protruding lip, occurs mainly in the wheatbelt.
Family: Orchidaceae

4 Swan River Daisy (All year)

Yanchep Rose † *Diplolaena angustifolia* Hook.
Related to *Boronia, Diplolaena* has five species all restricted to WA. The flowers are aggregated into dense pendant heads up to 3.5 cm across, surrounded by 3 or 4 series of bracts. The stamens, up to 3 cm long, range from crimson to pale orange. A shrub to 1 m on sand and limestone it extends from Dongara to Perth.
Family: Rutaceae

Swan River Daisy *Brachycome iberidifolia* Benth.
This very widespread, erect ephemeral growing up to 30 cm is common on limestone or sand extending to the NW and into NT and SA. The flower heads are 1.5 cm across with white or blue ray florets up to 1 cm long. Family: Asteraceae

WA Peppermint † *Agonis flexuosa* (Spreng.) Schau.
Commonly used as a street tree because of its weeping habit, the Peppermint ranges from Perth to Bremer Bay along the coast and in the karri forest. It is a tree to 15 m with flowers up to 1 cm across arranged in tufts so that the petals often appear crowded. Family: Myrtaceae

Rough Daisybush *Olearia rudis* F. Muell. ex Benth.
This is another widespread daisy which extends to SA, Vic and NSW. The heads, which are up to 4 cm across, have blue, mauve or white ray florets. In WA this variable species is common on the Swan Coastal Plain and extends to the goldfields and southern sandheaths.
Family: Asteraceae

6 Rough Daisybush (July–Dec)

8 Peppermint (Sept–Dec)

7 Chenille Honeymyrtle (Nov–Jan)

9 Berry Saltbush (Dec–Feb)

Berry Saltbush † *Rhagodia radiata* Nees
A species of coastal dunes and limestone, the Berry Saltbush extends from north of Perth to Esperance. It is a dioecious straggling shrub up to 3 m. The female flower has red or pink sepals which later surround the fleshy fruit up to 5 mm across. The male flowers are inconspicuous with small exserted stamens. Family: Chenopodiaceae

Chenille Honeymyrtle † *Melaleuca huegelii* Endl.
A shrub up to 4 m this has triangular leaves 2 mm long. The flowers, in spikes 10 cm long, have red petals which are hidden at flowering by the pink or white staminal bundles. A coastal limestone species, it ranges from Geraldton to Augusta. Family: Myrtaceae

Cowslip Orchid † *Caladenia flava* R. Br.
The only bright yellow *Caladenia*, this widespread species has a lanceolate leaf, and flowers 3–5 cm across. The red markings are variable. It extends from the Murchison River to Israelite Bay.
Family: Orchidaceae

10 Cowslip Orchid (Sept–Oct)

Cockies' Tongues *Templetonia retusa* (Vent.) R. Br.
This pea flower has a long, narrow standard bent back on the calyx and long wings giving the appearance of a cockatoo's head. The flowers, up to 6 cm long, are usually red or pink though cream flowers are not rare. It is usually a limestone-loving species, extending from Geraldton to the southern part of the Nullarbor Plain and to SA. Family: Papilionaceae

11 Cockies' Tongues (May–Sept)

12 Mangles' Kangaroo Paw (Aug–Nov)

Mangles' Kangaroo Paw † *Anigozanthos manglesii* D. Don
WA's floral emblem, this well known species is a tufted perennial herb with broad linear leaves and flowers 7 cm long on scapes up to 1 m high. It ranges from Shark Bay to Manjimup, northern populations often having branching scapes.
Family: Haemodoraceae

13 Harsh Hakea (Aug–Oct)

Harsh Hakea † *Hakea prostrata* R. Br.
Robert Brown, botanist of the Flinders expedition, collected this plant from the windswept south coastal heaths in 1801. In this habitat the Harsh Hakea is a low-growing shrub. Away from the coast it is a small tree up to 4 m. The axillary clusters of flowers are usually creamy white though sometimes reddish in inland areas. The perianth segments are up to 1.5 cm long. It is common in sand between Perth and Albany. Family: Proteaceae

Common Pin-heath † *Styphelia tenuiflora* Lindl.
There are 16 species of the Australian genus *Styphelia*, 5 endemic in WA. They differ from *Leucopogon* mainly in the prominently exserted stamens. This species is widespread in forests, woodlands and heaths, ranging from Gingin to Pinjarra and east to Lake Grace. It is a shrub to 50 cm with pungent leaves 10–15 mm long (shorter and broader on sandheaths) and flowers 2 cm long. Family: Epacridaceae

15 Common Pin-heath (May–July)

14 Prickly Moses (May–Oct)

Prickly Moses † *Acacia pulchella* R. Br.
One of the relatively few Australian wattles with true leaves, this variable, usually thorny plant, makes an attractive display on the coastal plains and the Darling Range. A diffuse shrub up to 2 m, it has bipinnate leaves with leaflets 5 mm long and flower heads up to 1 cm diameter. Family: Mimosaceae

16 Scrub Sheoak (Male) (Fls. Aug–Oct)

17 Scrub Sheoak (Female) (Fls. Aug–Oct)

Scrub Sheoak † *Casuarina humilis* Otto et Dietr.
Casuarina is a genus of 30 species all Australian except one which occurs on other tropical coasts. They are dioecious shrubs or trees with jointed almost leafless stems. The flowers are greatly reduced, the prominent parts being the ovary with two red styles of the female flower and the single, brown stamen of the male flower. The fruiting spikes have hard woody bracts which open when dried to release the winged fruit. This species is a shrub of 1–1.5 m, common on sand from Geraldton to Israelite Bay. The cones are 2–4 cm long and 1.5 cm across. Family: Casuarinaceae

18 Tiered Mat-rush (May–July)

Tiered Mat Rush † *Lomandra endlicheri* (F. Muell.) Ewart

There are about 30 species of *Lomandra* in Australia and a few in New Caledonia and New Guinea. Over 20 species occur in WA, being dioecious, grass-like perennial herbs with rhizomes and tough linear leaves. The small white, yellow or purple flowers are in spikes or racemes. This species, found in sandy woodlands from Perth to Albany, is 15–35 cm high with sweetly-scented flowers (♂ centre, ♀ left and right of photo). Family: Xanthorrhoeaceae

Winter Bell † *Blancoa canescens* Lindl.

Blancoa has only one species, differing from *Conostylis* in the racemose red flowers. It is a rhizomatous perennial herb with grey-pubescent leaves, and flowers 3–4 cm long, tomentose outside and golden-orange within. It inhabits sandy heaths and Banksia woodland between the Hill River and Perth. Family: Haemodoraceae

19 Winter Bell (June–Aug)

20 Menzies' Banksia (Mar–Aug)

Menzies' Banksia † *Banksia menziesii* R. Br.

One of the commonest trees between the Hill River and Pinjarra (with a few populations N to the Murchison), this usually has reddish-pink flowers. It is a tree to 10 m with crumbling bark and leaves 10–25 cm long. The prominent, mottled follicles usually shed their seeds about a year after flowering. The name commemorates Archibald Menzies who collected plants here on the Vancouver expedition in 1791. The genus is named after Sir Joseph Banks who in 1770 collected the first specimens at Botany Bay while on the Cook expedition. There are over 70 species, 60 being endemic in the South-West, the others occurring in eastern Australia and one across tropical Australia. The latter, *B. dentata* L.f., occurs also in New Guinea and on Aru Island in the S. Moluccas. The *Banksias* are shrubs or trees, very diverse in habit, leaves, flowers and fruit. They show strong adaptions to fire, the woody fruit of many species opening to shed the seed only after a fire. Many species are spectacular in flower and are becoming popular garden subjects. Family: Proteaceae

23 Summer Starflower (Dec–Jan)

Summer Starflower † *Calytrix flavescens* A. Cunn.
Brightening the bushland when few flowers are out, this small shrub has leaves 4–7 cm long and flowers with petals 5–7 mm long, the calyx tube being 8–12 mm with short bracteoles. It grows in sandy woodlands and heath from Eneabba to Busselton and E to Ongerup.
Family: Myrtaceae

21 Pipe Lily (Aug–Oct)

Pipe Lily † *Johnsonia pubescens* Lindl.
The 3 species of *Johnsonia* are endemic in the South-West. Tufted perennial herbs with narrow-linear leaves, they have small flowers hidden within papery bracts in a spike. This species is 10–20 cm high with spikes 2–3 cm long. It grows in sand from Dongara to Busselton. Family: Liliaceae

A Banjine † *Pimelea floribunda* Meisn.
Found in sandy woodlands between Geraldton and Perth, this glabrous shrub has rather soft leaves 2–3 cm long and silky-pubescent flowers 2 cm long in heads subtended by 4 broad, glabrous bracts. Family: Thymeleaceae

24 A Banjine (Aug–Oct)

22 Prickly Bitter-pea (July–Sept)

Prickly Bitter-pea *Daviesia pectinata* Lindl.
This shrub has many erect stems to 1 m tall with pungent leaves decurrent down the angular stems. The flowers, 5–6 mm across, are followed by triangular pods 1 cm across. It occurs in forests, woodlands and heaths from the Hill River to Collie and E to Esperance. Also in SA and Vic. Family: Papilionaceae

Bristle-daisy † *Athrixia pulverulenta* (Lindl.) Druce

This small genus occurs in South Africa and Australia, with 7 species in southern WA. They are ephemeral or perennial herbs with many bristle-like bracts around the flower heads. This species is a sparsely pubescent ephemeral 15–30 cm high with linear leaves to 6 cm long and heads 3–4 cm across. It grows in sandy woodlands between Gingin and Albany.

Family: Asteraceae

26 Bristle-daisy (Oct–Dec)

25 Christmas Tree (Nov–Jan)

Christmas Tree † *Nuytsia floribunda* (Labill.) R. Br. ex Fenzl.

One of the few arborescent mistletoes in the world, this endemic tree is a semi-parasite common in sandy soil from the Murchison River to Israelite Bay. The branches and thick, linear leaves are brittle, and the flowers are sweetly honey-scented. The dry, 3-winged fruit is 2–3 cm wide, maturing in autumn.

Family: Loranthaceae

27 Zamia (Male) (July–Aug)

28 Zamia (Female) (March–May)

Zamia † *Macrozamia riedlei* (Gaud.) Gardn.

There are 12 species of *Macrozamia*, all Australian, with 1 endemic in the South-West. It is found in various habitats from Eneabba to Israelite Bay. The bole is usually less than 1 m high but at the northern and eastern limits of the range it may reach 4 m. The male cones (Pl. 27), are 25 cm wide, the sporophylls tightly packed but loosening to release pollen in spring. Fertilisation occurs 4 months later, and the seeds are shed in autumn (Pl. 28), but their development continues until germination a year later. The seeds are toxic. Family: Zamiaceae

29 Common Hovea (June–Aug)

Common Hovea † *Hovea trisperma* Benth.
Widespread in coastal woodlands and the jarrah forest from Moora to Busselton and on heaths E to Esperance, this is a shrub to 50 cm with linear-lanceolate leaves to 5 cm long and flowers 1 cm across. The spherical pod contains 2–4 seeds.
Family: Papilionaceae

Yellow Pea † *Gompholobium capitatum* A. Cunn.
This small glabrous or hirsute shrub has pinnate leaves of 5–7 linear leaflets 1 cm long (longer around the flowers). The flowers are 10–15 mm across, and the globular pod contains less than 8 seeds. It occurs in sandy woodlands from Pinjarra to Busselton and E to Albany.
Family: Papilionaceae

31 Yellow Pea (Sept–Dec)

30 Yellow Buttercups (July–Sept)

Yellow Buttercups † *Hibbertia hypericoides* (DC.) Benth.
Distinguishing features of this shrub are the linear leaves 5–15 mm long, stellate-tomentose below; the pedicellate flowers with tomentose sepals and deeply notched petals; and the pubescent carpels with fertile stamens on one side and staminodes on the other. It is common on the coastal plain and in jarrah forest from Geraldton to Margaret River. Family: Dilleniaceae

Globe Heath † *Brachyloma preissii* Sond.
Restricted to sandy woodlands just S of Perth, this much-branched shrub of 1 m has crowded leaves 10–15 mm long and glabrous flowers 5 mm long, the calyx and corolla both coloured. *Brachyloma* is an Australian genus of 7 species, 2 being endemic in the South-West. Family: Epacridaceae

32 Globe Heath (May–Aug)

33 Southern Diplolaena (July–Oct)

Southern Diplolaena † *Diplolaena dampieri* Desf.
This is a tomentose shrub of 1–2 m. The aromatic leaves are oblong-obovate, up to 4 cm long, and the flowers in heads 2–2.5 cm long. It occurs on coastal dunes between Cape Leeuwin and Lancelin. Family: Rutaceae

Stirling's Mulla Mulla † *Ptilotus stirlingii* (Lindl.) F. Muell.
This prostrate or ascending perennial herb has striate stems, linear-lanceolate, undulate leaves 1.5–3 cm long and flower spikes 2.5 cm across. It grows in sandy woodlands and on heaths from the Kalbarri to Bunbury and from Walpole to Esperance. Family: Amaranthaceae

35 Stirling's Mulla Mulla (Nov–Jan)

Swan River Myrtle † *Hypocalymma robustum* Endl.
A many-stemmed shrub to 1 m high, this has opposite leaves 10–15 mm long and scented flowers 1 cm across. It is common in sandy woodlands and the jarrah forest between Perth and Albany. There are 12 species of *Hypocalymma,* all endemic in WA. Family: Myrtaceae

36 Swan River Myrtle (July–Sept)

34 Common Smokebush (Sept–Nov)

Common Smokebush † *Conospermum stoechadis* Endl.
Widespread on sandheaths and in sandy woodlands from Shark Bay to Bunbury and Ongerup, and E to Southern Cross, this many-stemmed shrub to 1.5 m has terete leaves to 10 cm long and woolly flowers 5 mm long in loose panicles. Family: Proteaceae

37 Purple Tassels (Aug–Sept)

Purple Tassels † *Sowerbaea laxiflora* Lindl.
Sowerbaea has only 4 species, 2 in the South-West, 1 in tropical NT and 1 from Qld to Vic. They have many linear leaves arising from a rhizome and long-pedunculate solitary umbels of purple flowers. This species has umbels 2.5–3 cm across. It occurs on sandheaths and in woodlands from Northampton to Augusta. Family: Liliaceae

39 Blueboy (Sept–Oct)

Blueboy † *Stirlingia latifolia* (R. Br.) Steud.
This is a common shrub of sandheaths and woodlands between Three Springs and Busselton, and E to the Stirling Range. It is a glaucous shrub to 1.5 m with leaves 20–30 cm long divided into linear lobes, and flowers 5 mm long in paniculate heads. Family: Proteaceae

Rose Banjine † *Pimelea rosea* R. Br.
This is the typical variant of this species, a shrub to 1 m with soft, linear-lanceolate leaves 1–2 cm long and flower heads 2–2.5 cm across, the flowers very spreading-hirsute. It is common on the coastal plain from Perth to Albany. (See also Pl. 117). Family: Thymeleaceae

38 Rose Banjine (Sept–Oct)

40 Snottygobble (Oct–Dec)

Snottygobble † *Persoonia saccata* R. Br.
Found in sandy woodlands from the Moore River to Cape Naturaliste, this shrub of 1 m has slender leaves 4–10 cm long and pubescent flowers 10–13 mm long. The short, thick style is curved into the 'pouch' on the lower side of the flower. The fruit is a 1 or 2-seeded drupe with a succulent outer layer. Family: Proteaceae

41 Pink Rainbow (July–Oct)

Pink Rainbow † *Drosera menziesii* R. Br. ex DC.
There are over 100 species of *Drosera* distributed almost throughout the world. Of these, 33 are in the South-West. The Pink Rainbow has erect, leafy stems 10–30 cm long, arising from an underground tuber. The flowers range from pink to reddish and are up to 2.5 cm across. This species inhabits wet sandy clay between the Murchison River and Esperance.
Family: Droseraceae

43 Red Ink Sundew

42 Red Ink Sundew (May–June)

Red Ink Sundew † *Drosera erythrorhiza* Lindl.
One of the rosetted Sundews, this species is noted for the bright red tuber, 1–1.5 cm across, up to 10 cm below the ground. During the first autumn rains a flowering stem enclosed by developing leaves arises from the tuber and pushes its way to the surface. By the time the inflorescence appears above ground, buds are well developed and soon expand into white or yellowish sweetly-scented flowers 8–10 mm across. At maturity there are 10–30 flowers on a scape 3–8 cm high. After flowering, the leaves expand up to 3–5 cm long, reaching full size after the scape has withered. This species commonly forms large colonies on sand where it flowers profusely after fire; it ranges from Three Springs to the southern sandplains near Ongerup.
Family: Droseraceae

Painted Sundew † *Drosera zonaria* Planch.
This *Drosera* apparently flowers only after summer fire followed by autumn rain. Few flowering specimens have been collected. The leaves, 2–3 cm long, are broadly spathulate with red distal margins. Development of the inflorescence is the same as in the Red Ink Sundew, the scape being 3–4 cm high and the white or yellowish sweetly-scented flowers 6–8 mm across. The species extends from Perth across the central wheatbelt to Esperance. Family: Droseraceae

44 Painted Sundew (April–May)

45 Basket Flower (May–Sept)

Basket Flower † *Adenanthos obovatus* Labill.
Adenanthos is an Australian genus of 20 species, mostly in the South-West. This species inhabits sandy swamp margins and woodlands from Gingin to Albany. It has many stems to 70 cm high, leaves 1–2 cm long and flowers 1.5–2 cm long, the styles 3–4 cm. Family: Proteaceae

Purple Flags † *Patersonia occidentalis* R. Br.
The most common *Patersonia* in WA, ranging from the Murchison River to Esperance, this perennial has tough leaves to 40 cm long and flowers 4–5 cm across opening for 1 day only. Family: Iridaceae

47 Purple Flag (Sept–Nov)

Curry Flower † *Lysinema ciliatum* R. Br.
There are 5 species of *Lysinema,* all endemic in the South-West. This is the most common, growing on sandheaths and in woodlands from Geraldton to Israelite Bay. It is a small slender shrub with ovate leaves 3–6 mm long and curry-scented flowers 12–20 mm long, often curved, with the brown sepals and bracts densely ciliate. Family: Epacridaceae

48 Curry Flower (July–Oct)

46 Pixie Mops (Sept–Nov)

Pixie Mops † *Petrophile linearis* R. Br.
This is a small shrub to 50 cm with curved leaves 3–8 cm long and softly-hirsute flowers 2–2.5 cm long. The upper part of the style is swollen, above which there is a dense brush, the stigma being small and terminal. It is common on the coastal plain between the Hill River and Busselton. Family: Proteaceae

49 Sand Bottlebrush (All year)

Sand Bottlebrush † *Beaufortia squarrosa* Schau.
A shrub of variable habit this has decussate leaves less than 5 mm long and flower spikes 3 cm across. On the Swan Coastal Plain it is a small shrub of sandy clay flats. On northern sand heaths it is a tall, open shrub often with orange and yellow flowers. It ranges from the Murchison River to Busselton.
Family: Myrtaceae

A honeymyrtle † *Melaleuca polygaloides* Schau.
One of many swamp-loving species, this small tree or shrub up to 3 m has a rough bark. It is particularly common in the swamps south of Perth and often forms dense thickets but extends from the Moore River to Albany. The flowers are usually yellow cream, in spikes up to 5 cm long and the leaves are 1.5 cm long.
Family: Myrtaceae

50 A honeymyrtle (July–Oct)

51 Red Swamp Cranberry (May–Sept)

52 Green Kangaroo Paw (July–Nov)

Green Kangaroo Paw † *Anigozanthos viridis* Endl.
Slightly smaller than Mangles' Kangaroo Paw, the Green Kangaroo Paw inhabits winter-damp clay depressions. The all-green flowers, 5–6 cm long are in racemes of up to 15 flowers. The basal, narrow linear leaves are up to 30 cm. This species is found only on the coastal plain between Moora and Busselton.
Family: Haemodoraceae

Red Swamp Cranberry † *Astroloma stomarrhena* Sond.
There are 20 species of *Astroloma,* all but a few found in the South-West. The Red Swamp Cranberry is a diffuse shrub to 40 cm which is common on low-lying sandy soils between the Hill River and Perth. The hairy, pungent leaves are 2–3 cm long, and the flowers are red or pink. Family: Epacridaceae

53 White Myrtle (June–Oct)

White Myrtle † *Hypocalymma angustifolium* Endl.
This differs from Swan River Myrtle in floral details as well as its preference for low-lying sandy clay soils. It is a many-stemmed shrub up to 1 m high. The flowers, 8 mm across are usually white but may have a reddish tinge. It is widespread mostly in coastal areas from Northampton to Albany but also occurs inland. Family: Myrtaceae

Semaphore Sedge † *Mesomelaena tetragona* (R. Br.) F. Muell.
Forming dense, dull green tussocks to 70 cm high, the Semaphore Sedge has narrow basal leaves up to 50 cm long. The long bracts forming the 'arms' of the semaphore are up to 15 cm long. It is widespread from the Perth area to east of Esperance, frequently on low-lying heath. Family: Cyperaceae

55 Semaphore Sedge (Aug–Dec)

Common Woollybush † *Adenanthos cygnorum* Diels
A very common grey-green shrub to 6 m on sandy soil in the Perth area, this is the tallest species of the genus. The flowers, 3–4 cm long, are inconspicuous among the leaves. The young shoots are red-tinged. Family: Proteaceae

54 Common Woollybush (Aug–Mar)

56 Fringed Bell (Sept–Dec)

Fringed Bell † *Darwinia nieldiana* F. Muell.
This genus was named in honour of Erasmus Darwin, grandfather of Charles. About 40 of the 45 species of *Darwinia* are restricted to the SW. Many species have colourful bracts around the flowers. This species has a number of fringed bracts forming an involucre 3–5 cm across. A shrub growing to 50 cm, it has leaves about 1 cm long and ranges from Dongara to Perth. Family: Myrtaceae

57 A Dodder (All year)

A Dodder *Cassytha*
The parasitic, twining stems of dodder often form dense masses especially over wattle thickets in coastal regions. There are nine species in WA all having small yellow, brown or white flowers only 2–4 mm diameter. The leaves are reduced to small scales. Family: Lauraceae

Platytheca † *Platytheca verticillata* (Hueg.) Baill.
The genus *Platytheca* has two species both endemic in the South-West. This is the more common one, ranging from Perth to east of Albany. A compact shrub to 50 cm it is usually found in moist areas. The pendant flowers are 1.5–2 cm across, and the leaves 1.5–2 cm long. The other species *P. juniperina* is a pungent-leaved shrub restricted to the peaks of the Stirling Range and the Barrens. Family: Tremandraceae

58 Platytheca (June–Nov)

60 Pepper & Salt (June–Dec)

59 A Beard-heath (July–Oct)

Pepper and Salt † *Eriostemon spicatus* A. Rich
Related to *Boronia,* Pepper and Salt is a spindly shrub up to 1.5 m with racemes up to 10 cm long. The flowers, 6 mm across, vary from deep pink to mauve and white. It is common on sandy and sometimes gravelly soils from Jurien Bay to the south coast. Family: Rutaceae

A Beard-heath † *Leucopogon pulchellus* Sond.
Over 100 of the 140 or so Australian species of *Leucopogon* are restricted to the South-West. The Beard-heath depicted here is a very common species in the Perth region extending south to Albany. It is a small shrub to 60 cm with leaves up to 1 cm long. The bearded flowers, which are characteristic of the genus, are 4–8 mm across. Family: Epacridaceae

Southern Byblis † *Byblis gigantea* Lindl.
The two species of *Byblis* are insectivorous plants. The Southern Byblis is the larger species with densely glandular leaves up to 30 cm, arising from an erect stem up to 10 cm long. The flowers are 3–4 cm across. Now rare in a few low-lying areas east of Perth, this species is fairly common on sandplain from the Moore River to Eneabba. The Northern Byblis, *B. liniflora*, is widespread across tropical Australia.
Family: Byblidaceae

Bacon and Eggs † *Oxylobium capitatum* Benth.
A close relative of some of the native toxic species, Bacon and Eggs is very common on the coastal plain between Moora and Busselton. It is a straggling shrub up to 1 m with leaves 6–10 cm long. The flowers, which vary from yellow to reddish with a red centre, are about 1 cm across. Family: Papilionaceae

61 Bacon & Eggs (June–Sept)

62 Southern Byblis (Aug–Jan)

63 Pink Fan Triggerplant (Oct–Dec)

64 Red Coats (May–Sept)

Pink Fan Triggerplant † *Stylidium utricularioides* Benth.
Over 100 of the 140 known species of *Stylidium* are recorded from WA. Many of them occur in masses in low lying areas. This species which has 2–6 flowers up to 1 cm across is up to 10 cm tall. The leaves, which are scattered along the lower part of the stem, are less than 3 mm long. It extends from Gingin to Bunbury. Family: Stylidiaceae

Redcoats † *Utricularia menziesii* R. Br.
A bladderwort with minute traps in the soil water, the Redcoat grows on wet sandy-clay soil or in moss beds on granite slopes. The flower is up to 1 cm across with a spur 2.5 cm long. The tiny spathulate leaves arise from a rootstock below soil level. It ranges from Perth to the south coast as far east as Esperance.
Family: Lentibulariaceae

65 Hoary Twine-rush (Female) (July–Oct)

Hoary Twine-rush † *Leptocarpus canus* Nees

About 30 species of *Leptocarpus* occur in Africa and a few also occur in South America and Asia. The Hoary Twine-rush is the most common of the 8 or 9 species in the South-West. It forms dense clumps with numerous erect culms to over 70 cm long. The leaves, as in other *Restionaceae*, are reduced to brown, stem-clasping scales. The plants are dioecious, the female flowers being borne in small groups of grey-coloured spikelets, each spikelet only a few mm long. The brown male spikelets are up to 1 cm long. This species forms extensive stands in low lying areas of sand over clay, ranging from Gingin to Busselton. Family: Restionaceae

67 Pink Bunny Orchid (July–Oct)

66 Hoary Twine-rush (Male) (July–Oct)

Pink Bunny Orchid † *Eriochilus scaber* Lindl.

Eriochilus is an Australian genus of 3 species, 1 widespread in eastern Australia, the other 2 endemic in the South-West. This species is found between Perth and Albany in low-lying or swampy areas, flowering mainly after bushfires. The small basal leaf is ovate-cordate and the flowers are 1 cm across and scentless. Late-flowering plants are more slender and less hirsute. The other WA species, *E. dilatatus*, has an ovate leaf up the stem and scented white flowers appearing in autumn. It is widespread from Shark Bay to Israelite Bay. Family: Orchidaceae

68 Darling Scarp

Darling Scarp
Spring on the Darling Scarp east of Perth. The drying, granitic slope is bordered by *Borya nitida, Calytrix glutinosa* (pink) and *Verticordia acerosa* (yellow). In the background is an open woodland of the white-barked Wandoo, with Jarrah and Marri on the ridges.

Granite Petrophile † *Petrolphile biloba* R. Br.
A showy species restricted to the Darling Scarp east of Perth, this is one of about 40 species of *Petrophile,* over 30 of which are restricted to the South-West. Masses of flowers occur in the upper axils. The shrub grows to 1.5 m high, the individual flowers being up to 2.5 cm long.
Family: Proteaceae

70 Granite Petrophile (July–Sept)

69 Sticky Thomasia (Oct–Nov)

71 Fuchsia Grevillea (All year)

Sticky Thomasia † *Thomasia glutinosa* Lindl.
All but one of the 27 species of Thomasia are restricted to the South-West Sticky Thomasia is a shrub to 1 m. The leaves vary from narrow linear to the lobed variant shown here. The calyx, 1–2 cm across, is the showy part of the flower, there being no petals. It extends from the Moore River to Perth.
Family: Sterculiaceae

Fuchsia Grevillea † *Grevillea bipinnatifida* R. Br.
The racemes of this sprawling shrub are up to 20 cm long, the perianth is 1–1.3 cm long and the styles up to 4 cm. The leaves, 15 cm long, are deeply dissected into rigid segments giving the whole plant a prickly aspect. It is a scarp species which ranges from Mogumber to Collie.
Family: Proteaceae

Winged Stackhousia † *Stackhousia brunonis* Benth.
About 24 species of *Stackhousia* are distributed between SE Asia and Australasia, half of them in WA. Winged Stackhousia is generally a small plant with few branches to 60 cm. The leaves which are only on the lower part of the stem are 1–2 cm long. The fragrant flowers vary from yellow to yellow-green and cream, and the fruits are broadly 3-winged. It is widespread from Wubin to Albany. Family: Stackhousiaceae

74 Slender Smokebush (July–Oct)

Slender Smokebush † *Conospermum huegelii* R. Br.
Named in honour of an Austrian who collected from the Swan River Colony in 1833, the Slender Smokebush is a perennial with a tuft of curly, narrow, basal leaves. The flowers, on leafless scapes up to 60 cm high, are 4–8 mm long and vary from blue to pale blue. It inhabits moist places of the eastern coastal plain and the Darling Scarp. Family: Proteaceae

72 Winged Stackhousia (Aug–Nov)

Silky Hemigenia † *Hemigenia sericea* Benth.
A shrub to 1 m high with velvety leaves 2–4 cm long, this plant is widespread in the South-West. The flowers, up to 1.5 cm long, vary from blue to pale mauve. Family: Lamiaceae

75 Silky Hemigenia (Aug–Nov)

Waxy Cryptandra † *Cryptandra arbutiflora* Fenzl.
Usually a spinescent shrub up to 1 m, the showy flowers of this plant are conspicuous along the Darling Scarp in late winter. The calyx tube, up to 5 mm long, is the showy part of the flower, the petals being reduced to small hoods enveloping the stamens. It is widespread south of the Murchison River. Family: Rhamnaceae

73 Waxy Cryptandra (July–Nov)

Strange Peppermint † *Agonis grandiflora* Benth.
This rare, slender shrub to 1.5 m with only 1–2 branches grows in rocky soil along the scarp between Lesmurdie and Harvey. The flowers, which may become pink with age, are about 1 cm across.
Family: Myrtaceae

76 Warrine (Male) (May–June)

78 Strange Peppermint (Oct–Nov)

Warrine † *Dioscorea hastifolia* Endl.
This is the only member in the South-West of a very large tropical genus. The Warrine or Native Yam is a common rock-loving, dioecious twiner of the Darling Scarp. The leaves, which are very variable in size and shape, are up to 8 cm long. The female flowers which are only 3–4 mm across are followed by hop-like winged fruits about 2 cm across. The yellow male flowers are 2–3 mm across and are borne in racemes similar to those of the female plant. The Warrine occurs mainly in coastal regions from north of the Murchison River to south of Perth.
Family: Dioscoreaceae

77 Warrine (Female) (June–Nov)

79 Spindly Grevillea (July–Nov)

Spindly Grevillea † *Grevillea endlicherana* Meisn.
Restricted to the Darling Scarp between Bindoon and Perth, this *Grevillea* takes its common name from the almost leafless flowering stems up to 1 m long. The silky leaves which are on the lower branches, are 5–6 mm long and 2–3 mm wide. The flower clusters, 1–2 cm across, vary from white to pink.
Family: Proteaceae

80 Early spring in the Jarrah forest with Wattle (*Acacia lateriticola* Maslin) and Prickly Bitter-pea (*Daviesia pectinata* Lindl.).

JARRAH FOREST

Extending from the south coast almost to New Norcia and bounded on the east by the 750 mm isohyet, Jarrah forms extensive, almost pure forests on lateritic soil. Few other tree species occur within the forest and they are usually restricted to deeper soils and river banks. Generally the trees are relatively widely spaced with an open crown allowing much light through to the forest floor. Here there is an understorey of many species of shrubs and herbs. Although the forest has been extensively worked for timber, much of it is still in an almost virgin state. Late winter and spring are the main flowering periods although the forest trees themselves are mostly summer flowering.

81 Fringed Leek Orchid (July–Oct)

Fringed Leek Orchid † *Prasophyllum fimbria* Reichb. f.
There are over 100 species of *Prasophyllum*, in Australia and New Zealand, WA having 18. This robust species up to 1.5 m tall has sweetly-scented flowers 10–15 mm across, varying from brown to green. It grows in various habitats within 100 km of the coast between the Murchison River and Esperance.
Family: Orchidaceae

Silky Yellow Banjine † *Pimelea suaveolens* (Endl.) Meisn.
A slender shrub to 70 cm, this species is distinguished by the very hirsute inflorescence bracts. The leaves are 1–3 cm long and the flower heads 3–4 cm across. It ranges through the forest from New Norcia to Albany.
Family: Thymeleaceae

83 Silky Yellow Banjine (Sept–Oct)

Couch Honeypot † *Dryandra nivea* (Labill.) R. Br.
Dryandra is a genus of over 60 species endemic in the South-West of WA, distinguished from *Banksia* by having flowers in heads surrounded by persistent bracts, and by the much thinner fruiting follicles. This ground-hugging species is widespread from Badgingarra to the south coast. The flower-heads are 4–5 cm long, surrounded by many short bracts.
Family: Proteaceae

82 Couch Honeypot (July–Sept)

84 Wilson's Grevillea (Sept–Jan)

Wilson's Grevillea † *Grevillea wilsonii* A. Cunn.
This vivid species is a many-stemmed shrub to 1.5 m with divaricately-divided leaves. The perianth is 12–15 mm long and the style 30–35 mm. It extends from Toodyay to Busselton.
Family: Proteaceae

85 Hooded Smokebush (Sept–Nov)

Hooded Smokebush † *Conospermum glumaceum* Lindl.

This is one of the most unusual smokebushes, with thin bracts 6–12 mm long concealing the tiny, glabrous, scented flowers. It is a shrub of 1–2 m with linear leaves 2–6 cm long, and grows in the open jarrah forest between New Norcia and Perth, with outliers north of Badgingarra on lateritic hills. Family: Proteaceae

86 Hooded Smokebush (Sept–Nov)

A Tetratheca † *Tetratheca hirsuta* Lindl.

Tetratheca is an Australian genus of about 40 species, 21 of them in the South-West of WA. They are perennial herbs with 5 small sepals, large petals and 10 stamens. Each anther has 4 cells (the name refers to this character) which are contracted upwards into a tube and shed the pollen through an apical pore. This species grows to 40 cm and has whorled leaves 5–15 mm long and flowers 1 cm long. It is widespread in the jarrah forest. Family: Tremandraceae

88 A Tetratheca (Aug–Nov)

Speckled Snakebush † *Hemiandra linearis* Benth.

This is a prostrate shrub with linear, pungent leaves 2–3 cm long. The calyx has 2 broad, pungent lobes and the corolla is 3 cm across with a slender tube. It occurs in the jarrah forest E and NE of Perth as well as on the coastal plain from Perth to the Moore River. There are about 8 species of *Hemiandra,* all endemic in the South-West. They have pungent leaves, and only one cell of each anther is fertile, the other being reduced to a small appendage. Family: Lamiaceae

87 Speckled Snakebush (Oct–Nov)

89 Drumstick Isopogon (Sept–Nov)

Drumstick Isopogon † *Isopogon sphaerocephalus* Lindl.
Isopogon is an Australian genus of about 35 species, 25 of them endemic in WA. This is a hirsute shrub to 1.5 m with leaves 5–10 cm long and flower heads 3–4 cm across. It extends from Perth to Pemberton, but a variant with broader leaves occurs on Mt. Lesueur. Family: Proteaceae

Pincushion Coneflower † *Isopogon dubius* (R. Br.) Druce
This shrub, up to 1 m tall, has leaves with broadly-linear, channelled, pungent lobes. The silky flowers are in heads 4–5 cm across, surrounded by many short, tomentose bracts. It is common in the jarrah forest between Moora, Perth and Pingelly. Family: Proteaceae

91 Pincushion Coneflower (July–Oct)

Bookleaf † *Daviesia cordata* Sm.
Common between Toodyay and the south coast, this shrub of 1.5 m has leaves 6–10 cm long. The pea flowers appear in October-November, and the bracts then enlarge to 3–5 cm across around the triangular pods. Family: Papilionaceae

90 Bookleaf (Fr. Nov–Dec)

92 Common Donkey Orchid (July–Oct)

Common Donkey Orchid *Diuris longifolia* R. Br.
Widespread across southern Australia, this variable species has channelled linear leaves 10–20 cm long and flowers 2.5–4.5 cm long. It grows in many habitats, ranging in WA from the Murchison River to Israelite Bay. About 35 species of *Diuris* occur in Australia, 6 of them in WA. Family: Orchidaceae

93 Pingle (July–Oct)

Pingle † *Dryandra carduacea* Lindl.
This is an erect shrub to 4 m with pungently-toothed leaves 4–8 cm long, longer and erect on young plants. The flowers are 2 cm long, with very short bracts around the heads. A good honey plant, it grows in laterite, often forming dense stands, between New Norcia, Busselton and Narrogin. Family: Proteaceae

95 Devil's Pins (July–Aug)

Devil's Pins † *Hovea pungens* Benth.
There are 12 species in the Australian genus *Hovea,* 6 of them endemic in southern WA. This species is an erect shrub of 1–2 m with pungent leaves 1–2 cm long and flowers 1 cm across. The fruit is a spherical pod containing 1 or 2 seeds. It occurs around granite outcrops through the jarrah forest and Darling Scarp, on coastal limestone and in a few areas of sandheath N to Geraldton and E to Ravensthorpe. Family: Papilionaceae

94 Crinkle-leaf Poison (Aug–Oct)

Crinkle-leaf Poison † *Gastrolobium villosum* Benth.
Gastrolobium is a genus of about 45 species, all endemic in the South-West of WA except one in central and tropical Australia (*G. grandiflorum* F. Muell.—Wallflower Poison). A number of species are toxic, the principle being monofluoroacetate. Crinkle-leaf Poison is a prostrate or ascending shrub with oblong, undulate leaves 2–5 cm long. It is common between Bindoon and Brookton, growing in jarrah forest and wandoo woodland. Family: Papilionaceae

Wiry Wattle † *Acacia extensa* Lindl.
Common in the jarrah forest, especially along creeks, this tall shrub has terete, angular phyllodes 10–15 cm long. The pods are linear, up to 7 cm long, constricted between the seeds.
Family: Mimosaceae

96 Candle Cranberry (June–Aug)

98 Wiry Wattle (Aug–Oct)

Candle Cranberry † *Astroloma ciliatum* (Lindl.) Druce
There are two variants of this species. One, shown here, is an erect, pine-like shrub to 70 cm, found in a few areas of the forest E of Perth. The other is prostrate and mat-like, occurring between Toodyay and Albany. The pungent leaves are up to 1 cm long and the flowers 2–2.5 cm long.
Family: Epacridaceae

Bristly Goodenia † *Goodenia fasciculata* (Benth.) Carolin
This perennial herb to 70 cm tall has clustered, linear leaves 5–10 mm long and flowers 5–7 mm long. It occurs along the Darling Scarp and nearby forest areas, especially near granite, ranging from Mogumber to Collie.
Family: Goodeniaceae

97 Bristly Goodenia (Sept–Nov)

99 Blue China Orchid (Aug–Oct)

Blue China Orchid † *Caladenia gemmata* Lindl. forma *gemmata*
The most intense blue of any *Caladenia*, the flowers of this species are 3–5 cm across, while the ovate leaf is 2–3 cm long. There are several rows of small calli on the lip. It grows in various habitats from the Murchison River to Esperance. Pale yellow-flowered plants are sometimes seen (forma *lutea* Clemesha).
Family: Orchidaceae

100 Yellow Flags (Sept–Oct)

Yellow Flags † *Patersonia xanthina* F. Muell.
The only yellow-flowered *Patersonia*, this is common in jarrah forest from Perth almost to the south coast. The flowers, 3–4 cm across, are on scapes up to 70 cm tall.
Family: Iridaceae

103 Slender Blackboy (Oct–Nov)

Slender Blackboy † *Xanthorrhoea gracilis* Endl.
Never forming a caudex, this has wiry leaves to 60 cm long and a flower spike 8–15 cm long on a slender scape up to 3 m tall. It is common in the forest from Perth to Collie.
Family: Xanthorrhoeaceae

101 Royal Robe (Sept–Nov)

Royal Robe † *Scaevola striata* R. Br.
The large genus *Scaevola* is mostly Australian but has species on Pacific islands and other tropical coasts. Royal Robe is a hirsute perennial herb with cuneate toothed leaves 3–5 cm long and flowers 2–3 cm long, the corolla wings striate. It is common in jarrah forest from New Norcia to the south coast.
Family: Goodeniaceae

102 Pom Poms (Oct–Dec)

Pom Poms † *Ptilotus manglesii* (Lindl.) F. Muell.
There are over 100 species of the Australian genus *Ptilotus*, mostly in the drier regions. This species has a perennial stock from which ephemeral stems arise. The flowers are 18–25 mm long. It is common in woodlands and forests from the Murchison River to Nannup and Kojonup. Family: Amaranthaceae

Urchin Dryandra † *Dryandra praemorsa* Meisn.
An attractive shrub with oak-like leaves 5–10 cm long, dark green above and white-tomentose below, this species has large flower-heads with styles 3–5 cm long. It occurs between Northam and Collie. Family: Proteaceae

105 Urchin Dryandra (Aug–Sept)

Bushy Kennedia † *Kennedia stirlingii* Lindl.
Named after the first Governor of WA, this is an erect perennial to 70 cm. The trifoliate leaves have leaflets 2–5 cm long with prominent stipules, and the flowers are 1.5 cm across. It grows in jarrah forest from Chittering to Donnybrook.
Family: Papilionaceae

106 Bushy Kennedia (Aug–Oct)

Bushy Everlasting *Helichrysum bracteatum* (Vent.) Andr. var. *albidum* DC.
Widespread over most of Australia, this scabrous perennial herb typically has gold and red-brown bracts around the flower heads which are 3–4 cm across. The var. *albidum* occurs in the jarrah forest and coastal areas of the South-West, as well as in Vic and Tas. Family: Asteraceae

104 Bushy Everlasting (Oct–Dec)

Broad-leaved Fanflower † *Scaevola platyphylla* Lindl.
This is a small shrub with broad, stem-clasping leaves 3–6 cm long and flowers 3–4 cm long, each subtended by 2 leafy bracts. It extends from New Norcia to Perth, with a few outliers in the nearby wheatbelt. Family: Goodeniaceae

107 Broad-leaved Fanflower (Oct–Dec)

108 Hairy Jugflower (July–Dec)

109 Blue Lechenaultia (Aug–Nov)

110 Parrot Bush (July–Nov)

Hairy Jugflower † *Adenanthos barbigerus* Lindl.
This is a many-stemmed shrub to 70 cm with scabrous leaves 3–5 cm long and flowers 2–2.5 cm long, the styles 3.5–4 cm. It is common in the forest from Perth to Augusta.
Family: Proteaceae

111 A Wattle (June–Sept)

A Wattle † *Acacia lateriticola* Maslin
This is a shrub to 1.5 m with hirsute stems and bipinnate leaves with leaflets 5–10 mm long, the margins recurved. The pod is oblong, 3 cm long, narrowed at each end and very hirsute, with thick margins. It grows in gravel in forests between Chittering and Pemberton. Family: Mimosaceae

Blue Lechenaultia † *Lechenaultia biloba* Lindl.
One of the State's best-known flowers, this small shrub has terete, rather soft leaves less than 1 cm long and delicate flowers 2–3 cm across, of various shades of blue. Widespread in the jarrah forest as far south as Manjimup, it also occurs on heaths N to Eneabba and E to Lake King.
Family: Goodeniaceae

Parrot Bush † *Dryandra sessilis* (Knight) Domin
Very common in the jarrah forest and on coastal limestone, this shrub, up to 6 m tall, has flowers 3 cm long in heads surrounded by short bracts. It extends from Geraldton to the south coast, and is an excellent honey producer.
Family: Proteaceae

Leaping Spider Orchid † *Caladenia macrostylis* R. Fitzg.
Found mainly in laterite in forests from Perth to Albany, this spider orchid has petals and sepals 25–30 mm long, each tipped with a small club. The shining black calli are tightly packed on the lip. Family: Orchidaceae

113 Leaping Spider Orchid (Sept–Oct)

Woodbridge Poison † *Isotoma hypocrateriformis* (R. Br.) Druce
Isotoma has 11 species in Australia and 1 widespread in tropical countries. It differs from *Lobelia* in having stamens inserted on the corolla which is tubular at the base. This species is an ephemeral with a semi-succulent stem which stores the nutrients for flower and fruit development. The linear leaves and stem base die as flowering commences but the flowers and fruit develop to maturity. Pink and mauve flowers also occur. The plants have an acrid taste and may be toxic. It is widespread in the jarrah forest and other habitats from Dongara to the south coast. Family: Lobeliaceae

112 Woodbridge Poison (Oct–Dec)

114 Little Kangaroo Paw (July–Oct)

Little Kangaroo Paw † *Anigozanthos bicolor* Endl.
Smaller than *A. manglesii* (Pl. 12), with flowers 4–5 cm long, this is common in winter-wet areas on the Darling Scarp, in the forest from Perth to Albany, and in scattered localities E to Esperance. Both leaves and flowers die down over summer, the plant surviving as an underground rhizome. The genus *Anigozanthos* contains 10 species, all endemic in the South-West. Their strange and vividly-coloured flowers covered with velvety hairs have always attracted attention, and most species are now popular in cultivation. The name is derived from Greek words meaning opened flower and apparently refers to the manner in which the perianth tube splits open, leaving all 6 lobes on one side. All species have perennial rhizomes from which linear leaves arise. In some these are ephemeral while in others they too are perennial. The floral scapes are produced annually. Family: Haemodoraceae

115 Coral Vine (Sept–Oct)

Coral Vine † *Kennedia coccinea* Vent.
Kennedia is an Australian genus of about 16 species, mostly endemic in the South-West. They provide some of the few creepers in our flora. Coral Vine is a vigorous climber with trifoliate leaves, the leaflets usually broadly oblong, 3–7 cm long. The flowers, in profuse umbels, are 10–12 mm across, followed by oblong, pubescent pods 3–5 cm long with up to 9 oblique seeds. It is widespread in forests and on coastal limestone from Perth to Albany, and on sandheaths E to Esperance where the leaflets are broader and often lobed. Family: Papilionaceae

116 Coral Vine (Sept–Oct)

117 Rose Banjine (Sept–Oct)

Rose Banjine † *Pimelea rosea* R. Br.
Typically a pink-flowered shrub on the coastal plain (Pl. 38), in the forest areas this species is always white-flowered. It is a shrub to 70 cm with linear-oblong leaves 1–2 cm long and flower heads 2–3 cm across. Family: Thymeleaceae

Honeybush † *Hakea lissocarpha* R. Br.
Hakea is one of the largest genera of Proteaceae with over 150 species, over 100 of them in WA. They have woody follicles which usually persist on the shrub until dried or burnt, when they open to release 2 winged seeds. Honeybush is a spreading shrub of 1–1.5 m with pungently-divided leaves and sweetly-scented flowers 3–4 mm long, providing much nectar. The fruit is a compressed ovoid follicle 10–15 mm long with 2 apical horns. It inhabits forests, woodlands and heath from the Murchison River to Donnybrook and E to the southern heaths.
Family: Proteaceae

119 Honeybush (June–Sept)

118 Blue Lady Orchid (Sept–Oct)

Blue Lady Orchid † *Thelymitra crinita* Lindl.
Thelymitra has over 50 species ranging from the Philippines to New Zealand and Australia. Over 40 species, known as Sun Orchids, occur in Australia. The flowers have similar petals and sepals, and usually open only on sunny days. This bright blue species has a broad, ovate leaf 3–10 cm long and flowers 2.5–4 cm across. The column has a crested apex with two hair tufts at the front. It is widespread in forests and woodlands from Perth to Cape Riche. Family: Orchidaceae

120 Bird Orchid (Aug–Oct)

Bird Orchid † *Pterostylis barbata* Lindl.
One of 2 species of this form, this leafy-stemmed plant has a single flower 3–4 cm long with a yellow-haired lip which is unusual for the genus also in being insensitive. It occurs mainly in forest between Perth and Albany with outliers in the central wheatbelt. The related *P. plumosa* has a narrower, bright green flower with dense hairs on the lip and occurs between Pemberton and Esperance, as well as in other States. Family: Orchidaceae

121 Mogumber Bell (Oct)

Mogumber Bell † *Darwinia carnea* C. A. Gardn.
A rare species known only from rocky hills near Mogumber and Narrogin, this is one of the few true bells outside the Stirling Range. It is a shrub to 40 cm tall with leaves 5–15 mm long and bells 3 cm long. Family: Myrtaceae

White Spider Orchid *Caladenia patersonii* R. Br. var. *longicauda* (Lindl.) Rogers
Widespread in various habitats from the Murchison River to Israelite Bay, this graceful orchid has flowers 10–20 cm across, often sweetly scented. The typical variety is common and variable in south-eastern Australia. Family: Orchidaceae

122 White Spider Orchid (Sept–Dec)

123 Orange Stars (Sept–Oct)

124 Winged Wattle (July–Sept)

Winged Wattle † *Acacia alata* R. Br.
A hirsute shrub of 1–3 m with stems up to 3 cm wide and flower heads 1 cm across, this leafless species is common along creeks in the forest from New Norcia to the south coast, with a few outliers N to Northampton. The pods are flat, curved and hirsute, 4–5 cm long, with thick margins. Family: Mimosaceae

Orange Stars † *Hibbertia stellaris* Endl.
This low shrub has linear leaves 1–2 cm long and profuse flowers 15 mm across on slender pedicels. It grows in open sandy areas among jarrah forest and on the coastal plain from Gingin to Busselton and E to Albany. Northern populations have yellow flowers. Family: Dilleniaceae

Orange Hibbertia † *Hibbertia miniata* C. A. Gardn.
One of the few orange-flowered species, this showy shrub is only 20–30 cm tall with broad-linear leaves 2–3 cm long and flowers 3 cm across, with many free stamens surrounding the carpels. It grows in a few small areas of the northern jarrah forest. Family: Dilleniaceae

Hairy Flag † *Patersonia rudis* Endl.
This is distinguished from the Common Flag (Pl. 47), by the hirsute inflorescence bracts. It is found in the jarrah forest E and NE of Perth, and on heaths near the Hill River.
Family: Iridaceae

126 Orange Hibbertia (Sept–Oct)

125 Hairy Flag (Oct)

127 Bushy Boronia (Oct–Nov)

128 Large Hibbertia (Aug–Sept)

Bushy Boronia † *Boronia fastigiata* Bartl.
A many-stemmed shrub to 50 cm with linear-obovate leaves 1–2 cm long, often toothed, and flowers 8–10 mm across, this species occurs in jarrah forest and on swampy flats between Perth and the south coast. Family: Rutaceae

Large Hibbertia † *Hibbertia lasiopus* Benth.
This glowing species is a small, prostrate shrub with broad, obtusely-toothed leaves 2–7 cm long. The flowers, on long hirsute pedicels, are 4–5 cm across. It is fairly common in the northern jarrah forest. Family: Dilleniaceae

129 Bristly Cottonheads (Sept–Oct)

Bristly Cottonheads † *Conostylis setigera* R. Br.
Conostylis is a genus of about 25 species endemic in the South-West. They are perennial herbs with tough, linear leaves and regular flowers in heads. This species has narrow leaves with bristly margins and flower heads 2–3 cm across. It is very common between Moora and Albany.
Family: Haemodoraceae

131 A Billardiera (Jan–Mar)

A Billardiera † *Billardiera variifolia* DC.
Billardiera is an Australian genus of creepers, 15 of the 24 species occurring in WA. This species has leaves 1–3 cm long and flowers 10–12 mm across, the sepals very hirsute. It extends from Perth to Augusta and E to Albany, growing in the forest, often in sandy areas. Family: Pittosporaceae

130 Pineapple Bush (Oct–Jan)

Pineapple Bush † *Dasypogon hookeri* Drumm. ex F. Muell.
This odd plant is one of the 2 species of *Dasypogon*, both endemic in the South-West. It has a caudex to 4 m tall, tough leaves 1 m long with rough margins, and flower heads 3 cm across. It is found in the jarrah forest between Donnybrook and Augusta. Family: Xanthorrhoeaceae

Mat Cottonheads † *Conostylis prolifera* Benth.
Forming dense mats or discrete tufts, this has few-flowered heads, each flower 10–12 mm long. It grows on damp flats in the northern jarrah forest and wandoo woodland, but is more common on sandheaths N to the Murchison River. Family: Haemodoraceae

132 Mat Cottonheads (Aug–Oct)

Yellow-eyed Flame Pea † *Chorizema dicksonii* Grah.
Seventeen of the 18 species of *Chorizema* are endemic in the South-West, the other occurring in Qld and NSW. They are shrubs with brightly-coloured flowers. This species grows to 70 cm, having ovate-lanceolate pungent leaves 1–2 cm long and flowers almost 2 cm across in terminal racemes. It inhabits open gravelly forests between New Norcia, Perth and Northam.
Family: Papilionaceae

134 Yellow-eyed Flame Pea (Aug–Sept)

Common Dampiera † *Dampiera linearis* R. Br.
Widespread in many habitats from Geraldton to the south coast, this perennial herb, up to 40 cm tall, has linear to cuneate leaves, often toothed, and flowers 12–16 mm across. The inflorescence is grey-hirsute. *Dampiera,* named after William Dampier, is an Australian genus of about 60 species, mostly blue-flowered. There are 40 species endemic in the South-West.
Family: Goodeniaceae

133 Common Dampiera (Aug–Oct)

135 Jug Orchid (Aug–Sept)

Jug Orchid † *Pterostylis recurva* Benth.
The intriguing genus *Pterostylis* has nearly 100 species, in Australia, New Guinea, New Caledonia and New Zealand. Generally known as greenhoods, they have delicate flowers banded with green or brown and most have a sensitive labellum. There are 15 species in WA. The Jug Orchid is unusual in having the 'horned' lateral sepals more prominent than the galea (hood). It is a leafy-stemmed plant to 40 cm with flowers 25–30 mm long. Found in various habitats, usually sheltered woodlands and forests, it extends from Wongan Hills to Augusta and E to Esperance.
Family: Orchidaceae

136 Banded Greenhood (June–Aug)

Banded Greenhood *Pterostylis vittata* Lindl.
Widespread in the South-West, this is typically green (left) but may also be brown. The large-flowered var. *subdifformis* Nicholls (right) has flowers 23–25 mm long with concave lateral sepals. The lip is very sensitive. Also in SA and Vic.
Family: Orchidaceae

137 Native Gerbera (Nov–Jan)

139 Silky Blue Orchid (Aug–Oct)

Silky Blue Orchid † *Caladenia sericea* Lindl.
Tallest of the blue *Caladenias*, reaching 40 cm, this has a softly hirsute, ovate leaf 2–5 cm long and flowers 3–4 cm across. It inhabits forests and woodlands from Perth to Albany.
Family: Orchidaceae

138 Black-eyed Sundew (Sept–Oct)

Native Gerbera † *Trichocline spathulata* (A. Cunn. ex DC.) J. H. Willis
This is the only Australian species of a genus otherwise South American. A small rhizome produces a rosette of petiolate, spathulate leaves up to 15 cm long and a scape to 60 cm tall. The single flower head has rays 2–2.5 cm long, red outside. It is a common forest-dweller from Gingin to Augusta.
Family: Asteraceae

Black-eyed Sundew † *Drosera platystigma* Lehm.
This pigmy sundew is distinguished by the orange and black flowers 1–2 cm across with club-tipped styles. The peduncle is only 3–5 cm tall. It frequently forms large colonies on gravel in the jarrah forest and also occurs more sparsely on the coastal plain.
Family: Droseraceae

Flying Duck Orchid *Paracaleana nigrita* (Lindl.) Blaxell
A small genus confined to Australia and New Zealand, *Caleana* has 1 WA species. It is an inconspicuous plant of the jarrah forest and swamp margins between Moora and Ravensthorpe. The boat-shaped column and narrow perianth are 1 cm long and the lip is very sensitive. It is also in S A.
Family: Orchidaceae

140 Morning Iris (Aug–Oct)

142 Flying Duck Orchid (Sept–Oct)

Morning Iris † *Orthrosanthus laxus* (Endl.) Benth.
A genus with 5 species in southern WA, SA and Vic, and 3 in tropical America, *Orthrosanthus* has flowers which open for 1 day only. They are tufted perennial herbs with grass-like leaves and loose panicles of flowers in short spikes. This species is common between Mingenew and Donnybrook.
Family: Iridaceae

Trumpets † *Conostylis androstemma* (Lindl.) F. Muell.
One of two *Conostylis* species with long, solitary flowers, this caespitose perennial has wiry leaves, and flowers with a tube 2–3 cm long, the lobes almost as long. It grows in open parts of the forest and on sandheath, ranging from the Murchison River to Perth.
Family: Haemodoraceae

143 Golden Rainbow (Aug–Sept)

141 Trumpets (June–Aug)

Golden Rainbow † *Drosera microphylla* Endl.
This is a slender plant up to 40 cm tall with cup-shaped glandular leaves 3–4 cm across. The golden, glabrous sepals are up to 1 cm long. The slightly shorter petals vary from deep pink to dark red. It grows in gravel or loam of heaths and forests between the Hill River and Albany.
Family: Droseraceae

144 Karri forest near Manjimup

KARRI FOREST

Karri, *Eucalyptus diversicolor,* is restricted to the wetter areas of the lower South-West on granitic or gneissic soils. The distinct layering of the forest and the density of the lower storey are reminiscent of a temperate rain forest. Though the Karri tree has an open, leafy crown, the large trunks and the dense understorey make the forest floor very shady and relatively cool and humid. Only a few shade-tolerant herbs, ferns, mosses and liverworts grow among the leaf litter and fallen trees, while the understorey, though dense, contains few species. There are three areas of distribution of Karri: one from Yallingup to Augusta, the main area from Manjimup to Denmark, and one in the Porongurups with a small outlier at Mt. Manypeaks.

Screw Fern *Lindsaea linearis* Swartz

Ferns are relatively scarce in WA, only 50 species being recorded for the whole State. This is the only species in WA of *Lindsaea*, a genus of over 200 species in Africa, Australia and New Zealand. The fronds, arising from an underground rhizome, are up to 30 cm tall with pinnae 5–10 mm wide. The indusia, containing the spores, are under the outer edge of the pinnae which, when fertile, are recurved and deflexed, giving the frond a screw-like aspect. It is common in forests and woodlands from Perth to Albany and in a few localities E to Esperance. Also in other States. Family: Lindsaeaceae

146 Screw Fern (All year)

Cutleaf Hibbertia † *Hibbertia cuneiformis* (Labill.) Gilg.

One of the tallest *Hibbertias* in WA, this glabrous shrub reaches 3.5 m tall. The cuneate, dentate leaves are 2–4 cm long and the flowers 2–3 cm across with the stamens united into 5 bundles. Common in the karri forest, it also inhabits coastal districts from Mandurah to Albany. The genus *Hibbertia* occurs in Malagasy, New Guinea, Australia, New Caledonia and Fiji, most of the 100 species being endemic in Australia. About 60 species are endemic in the South-West of WA, occurring in many habitats and mostly having yellow flowers. Two species are known from the Kimberleys and one from the Hamersley Range. Family: Dilleniaceae

145 Cutleaf Hibbertia (Sept–Dec)

147 Karri Wattle (Sept–Nov)

Karri Wattle † *Acacia pentadenia* Lindl.

This is a tall shrub to 5 m, common in the jarrah and karri forests from Nannup to Denmark. Near the coast it is also found in swamps where it has a lower habit and the leaflets have reflexed tips. The leaves are bipinnate with 2–5 pinnae, the rather soft leaflets 2–5 mm long. The flower heads are clustered in the leaf axils and are followed by linear pods 3–6 cm long with thickened margins. Family: Mimosaceae

148 Crowea (Sept–Oct)

Holly Flame Pea † *Chorizema ilicifolium* Labill.
A variable species, this is a shrub with narrow or broad leaves to 8 cm long and flowers 1 cm across. In the karri forest it is a straggling shrub to 3 m but elsewhere is a short erect shrub. It extends from Moora to Albany. Family: Papilionaceae

150 Holly Flame Pea (Aug–Nov)

Tassel Flower † *Leucopogon verticillatus* R. Br.
The largest species of *Leucopogon*, this is a shrub of 1–4 m with leaves 5–10 cm long, sometimes more, in false whorls. The flowers are scented, and less hirsute than in most species. It occurs in the karri forest, and in the jarrah forest as far N as Perth. Family: Epacridaceae

Crowea † *Crowea angustifolia* Sm.
This is a glabrous shrub to 3 m tall with leaves 2–4 cm long and flowers 15 mm across. The var. *angustifolia* has narrow leaves and pink flowers, while the var. *dentata* (Benth.) Wilson, shown here, has broader leaves and white flowers. Both occur between Pemberton and Albany, the var. *dentata* being common in karri forest. Family: Rutaceae

151 Tassel Flower (Sept–Nov)

149 Karri Dampiera (Sept–Dec)

Karri Dampiera † *Dampiera hederacea* R. Br.
This tomentose perennial herb scrambles over the ground and undergrowth in the karri forest. It has leaves 1–4 cm long and flowers 1 cm long. It also occurs in sheltered areas of the jarrah forest, ranging from Perth to Albany. Family: Goodeniaceae

Karri Boronia † *Boronia gracilipes* F. Muell.
A rather sparsely-flowered species, this is a slender, hirsute shrub 1 m tall with pinnate leaves of leaflets 5–10 mm long. The flowers are 8–12 mm across, on long pedicels. It is found in karri and jarrah forests from Margaret River to Denmark. There are about 70 species of *Boronia,* 45 of them in the South-West and the remainder in the wetter parts of eastern and northern Australia. All have foliage containing aromatic substances, but only a few have scented flowers. The Brown or Scented Boronia, *B. megastigma* Nees is best-known and is now widely cultivated. The genus is distinguished by the 4 petals and sepals and 8 stamens, often dimorphic, the anthers usually being appendaged. Family: Rutaceae

153 Karri Boronia (Sept–Nov)

152 Chorilaena (Sept–Dec)

Chorilaena † *Chorilaena quercifolia* Endl.
There is only 1 species of *Chorilaena,* endemic in the South-West. It is a stellate-tomentose shrub 1–3 m tall with oak-like leaves 2–4 cm long and compound heads of many flowers 15 mm long, surrounded by many linear bracts. The sepals and petals are very narrow and hirsute, while there are 10 stamens. Common in the karri forest, it also grows in coastal thickets between Augusta and Albany. The hairs often wear off the upper surface of the leaves. Family: Rutaceae

154 Tree Hovea (Sept–Nov)

Tree Hovea † *Hovea elliptica* (Sm.) DC.
This is the tallest species of *Hovea* in WA, reaching 3 m, with elliptic-lanceolate leaves 3–8 cm long. The flowers, in axillary racemes, are 12–14 mm across with rusty-pubescent calyxes. The fruit is a small spherical pod containing 1–2 seeds. It occurs in karri and jarrah forest from Margaret River to Albany. Family: Papilionaceae

155 Swampland and wooded hills near Mt. Gardner, east of Albany.

THE ALBANY DISTRICT

Following its discovery by George Vancouver in 1791, King George Sound, a natural haven for ships, was visited by many of the early expeditions to Australian shores and soon became known to European botanists for its new and fascinating flora. The hinterland, stretching from west of Walpole to Cape Riche and including the Porongurup Range, has perhaps the richest flora in the south-west, due largely to the great variety of landforms: precipitous headlands and sandy bays, inlets, fresh lakes and swamps, heaths, and lateritic and granite hills. The vegetation varies accordingly, from low heaths to tall forest. Swamplands are especially interesting for the number of small plants such as orchids, sundews and triggerplants. While spring is the time for the greatest profusion of flowers, there are some to be seen at any season.

156 Sticky Tail-flower (any month)

Sticky Tail Flower † *Anthocercis viscosa* R. Br.
Anthocercis is an Australian genus of about 20 species, of which 11 are endemic in WA. This species is a viscid shrub of 1–4 m which grows around granite rocks on or near the coast between Albany and Israelite Bay. The leaves are 2–5 cm long and the fragrant flowers 2.5–4 cm across.
Family: Solanaceae

Rose Cone Flower † *Isopogon formosus* R. Br.
A shrub to 1.5 m tall, this species has much-divided leaves with narrow pungent lobes. The flowers arise between the woolly bracts of the 'cone', forming heads 4–6 cm across. It is common in woodlands of the Albany district and Stirling Range, extending north to Perth and east to Esperance.
Family: Proteaceae

158 Rose Coneflower (Aug–Oct)

157 Scarlet Banksia (June–Oct)

159 Long-leaved Petrophile (Oct–Jan)

Long-leaved Petrophile † *Petrophile longifolia* R. Br.
This ground-hugging shrub has short stems with terete leaves 20–40 cm long. The silky flower heads, 4–6 cm across, are surrounded by many short, pointed bracts. The species is common in sandy or gravelly soils on heaths between Albany and the Stirling Range.
Family: Proteaceae

Scarlet Banksia † *Banksia coccinea* R. Br.
This striking inflorescence is borne on a slender shrub or tree 2–4 m tall, occasionally larger and more robust. The leaves are 3–6 cm long and the flower spikes up to 6 cm long. The fruit is small, with hirsute follicles 5–10 mm across. The species is common in deep sands on heaths between Albany and Hopetoun, including the Stirling Range.
Family: Proteaceae

160 Hooded Lily (Sept–Dec)

Hooded Lily † *Johnsonia lupulina* R. Br.

A wiry, tufted perennial herb to 70 cm with narrow leaves, the Hooded Lily has small flowers hidden among the papery bracts of a spike 3–6 cm long. It grows in sandy or gravelly soils of open woodlands between Busselton and Albany. (See also Pl. 207) Family: Liliaceae

162 Swamp Daisy (Sept–Jan)

Swamp Daisy † *Actinodium cunninghamii* Schau. ex Lindl.

This deceptive plant is not a true daisy but a myrtle. It is a monotypic genus endemic in WA and is also unusual in having flower parts in 4's instead of 5's. The white outer flowers are sterile and the red inner ones hermaphrodite, the whole 'head' 2–3 cm across. The plant is a slender shrub to 50 cm tall with small heath-like leaves. It prefers low-lying sandy areas between Albany and the Fitzgerald River, including the Stirling Range. Family: Myrtaceae

161 Climbing Triggerplant (June–Feb)

Hidden Featherflower † *Verticordia habrantha* Schau.

This is a shrub to 50 cm, often slender, with thick, linear leaves 2–4 cm long, or the lowest ones longer. The flowers are 7–10 mm across with the fringed calyx-lobes almost hidden by the petals. It occurs on sandheaths north of Albany, extending to Lake Grace and Ravensthorpe. Family: Myrtaceae

163 Hidden Featherflower (Sept–Nov)

Climbing Triggerplant † *Stylidium scandens* R. Br.

This glabrous perennial usually trails over shrubs to a height of 2 m, clinging by the recurved ends of the whorled leaves which are up to 5 cm long. Occasionally it forms an erect tufted herb to 50 cm tall. The flowers, pale to deep pink, are 1.5 cm across. It extends from Bunbury to Albany, including the Stirling Range. Family: Stylidiaceae

Spindle Heath † *Cosmelia rubra* R. Br.
The slender, little-branched stems of this shrub, up to 2 m tall, rise above the dense scrub of swamps between Albany and Margaret River. The flowers are about 2 cm long. *Cosmelia* is a monotypic genus endemic in WA, and often occurs in the same swamps as the Pitcher Plant.
Family: Epacridaceae

166 Spindle Heath (June–Feb)

164 Albany Pitcher Plant (Dec–Feb)

165 Albany Pitcher Plant

Albany Pitcher Plant † *Cephalotus follicularis* Labill.
This insectivorous plant grows among dense shrubs and sedges around swamps and along streams where water is continually moving through the soil. Two types of leaf are produced, flat ones and leaves modified into pitchers. The pitchers, up to 5 cm long, contain a watery liquid in which insects easily drown and later decompose. The lid usually does not close but may do so during hot weather to reduce evaporation. Sweetly scented flowers 4–5 mm across are borne on peduncles up to 60 cm long from December to March. Occurrence is sporadic in coastal areas from Mt. Manypeaks to the Donnelly River and at Yallingup. It is the only member of its family.
Family: Cephalotaceae

167 Baxter's Banksia (Dec–May)

168 Red Swamp Banksia (any month)

Rattle Pea † *Daviesia oppositifolia* Endl.

Like the Bookleaf (Pl. 90) this species has floral bracts which after flowering enlarge greatly around the triangular pods. It is a shrub to 50 cm with lanceolate-obovate leaves 3–7 cm long, opposite or scattered. It grows in gravelly soils of woodlands and heaths from Albany to Ravensthorpe.

Family: Papilionaceae

169 Rattle Pea (Oct–Dec)

Baxter's Banksia † *Banksia baxteri* R. Br.

A rather open spreading shrub of 2–3 m with leaves 6–14 cm long, this species has rounded flower spikes 7–8 cm across. The follicles are few, relatively large and surrounded by the persistent old flowers. It occurs between Albany and Hopetoun on sandy heaths.

Family: Proteaceae

Red Swamp Banksia † *Banksia occidentalis* R. Br.

This erect shrub of 1–4 m has relatively soft narrow leaves 6–12 cm long, sparsely toothed and arranged in false whorls. The flower spikes are 5–12 cm long, and the follicles small and hidden among the old flowers. It grows in swamps between Augusta and Cape Arid.

Family: Proteaceae

170 Baxter's Wattle (Dec–Jan)

Baxter's Wattle † *Acacia baxteri* Benth.

This is a spreading shrub to 70 cm tall with pungent, ribbed phyllodes 1–2 cm long and spiny stipules. The flower heads are 7–9 mm across and the pods are thick, terete and smooth, about 6 cm long. It grows in gravelly or swampy soil from Albany to the Stirling Range.

Family: Mimosaceae

171 Albany Synaphea (Sept–Nov)

172 Albany Bottlebrush (Sept–Dec)

Red-flowering Gum † *Eucalyptus ficifolia* F. Muell.
This spectacular tree, now widely cultivated, is restricted in the wild to a small area between Denmark and Walpole. A bloodwood to 8 m tall with rough bark, it has dark green foliage while the flowers, 3–4 cm across, vary from pale to deep red. The fruit is urn-shaped, 2–2.5 cm long, with winged brown seeds. Family: Myrtaceae

173 Red-flowering Gum (Jan-Feb)

Albany Synaphea † *Synaphea polymorpha* R. Br.
Synaphea is a genus of about 12 species endemic in WA. All have yellow flowers and most have variously-lobed leaves. Albany Synaphea is a shrub to 50 cm with reddish stems and oblong, undivided basal leaves 10–20 cm long, the upper leaves much shorter and divided into pungent lobes. The individual flowers are 4–5 mm long. It occurs in woodlands between Albany and the Stirling Range, and on sandheaths to the east. Family: Proteaceae

Synaphea † *Synaphea petiolaris* R. Br.
There are several *Synapheas* which are tufted shrubs with short stems, long-petiolate deeply-lobed leaves and elongated flower-spikes. They are separated by small differences in the flowers and leaves. This species occurs in woodlands between Albany and Perth, and on sandheaths of the south coast. Family: Proteaceae

174 Synaphea (July–Nov)

Albany Bottlebrush † *Callistemon speciosus* (Sims) DC.
The Australian genus *Callistemon* contains 20 species, 2 of them endemic in WA. This species is an erect shrub of 1–2 m with thick-margined leaves 6–12 cm long. The flower spikes are about 10 cm long and the axis always grows out before flowering. The species is common on swamp margins of the Albany district, and has been recorded from Busselton and Collie.
Family: Myrtaceae

Albany Cat's Paw † *Anigozanthos preissii* Endl.
Growing only within 30 miles of Albany, in sandy jarrah woodlands, this striking species has narrow leaves and only one or two stems to 50 cm tall. The inflorescence is once-forked just below the flowers, which are 5–6 cm long and the most claw-like of the genus.
Family: Haemodoraceae

175 Red Boronia (Oct–Nov)

177 Albany Cat's Paw (Sept–Nov)

Red Boronia † *Boronia heterophylla* F. Muell.
This is a glabrous shrub of about 2 m, with simple or pinnate leaves 3–5 cm long. The flowers are 6–8 cm long with alternating fertile and sterile stamens. It occurs on sandy swamp flats in the Albany-Denmark district, and also near Busselton. Family: Rutaceae

Tall Boronia † *Boronia molloyae* Drumm.
This hirsute spreading shrub up to 4 m tall has pinnate leaves 2–4 cm long and bell-like flowers 5–6 mm long. Four large fertile stamens alternate with 4 small sterile ones. It grows along creek banks and in swamps, being common near Albany and west to Margaret River, with a few outliers further north. Family: Rutaceae

178 Tall Kangaroo Paw (Oct–Jan)

176 Tall Boronia (Sept–Oct)

Tall Kangaroo Paw † *Anigozanthos flavidus* Red.
This species grows in large clumps with perennial, smooth strap-like leaves, and flowering stems 1–3 m tall. The flowers, 3–4 cm long, are usually yellowish-green, but around Margaret River red flowers are common. It extends from Busselton to Albany, and a few localities as far north as Pinjarra, growing in swamps. Family: Haemodoraceae

181 Pink Enamel Orchid (Sept–Nov)

179 Swamp Bottlebrush (Jan–April)

Pink Enamel Orchid † *Elythranthera emarginata* (Lindl.) A. S. George
There are two species of *Elythranthera,* both endemic in WA. They are characterised by the glossy perianth, the small membranous lip and the hooded column. This species has flowers 2.5–3.5 cm across, while *E. brunonis* has smaller, purple flowers. Both occur in a variety of habitats between the Moore River and Esperance. Family: Orchidaceae

Swamp Bottlebrush † *Beaufortia sparsa* R. Br.
In late summer many swamps of the south coast between Albany and Margaret River are ablaze with this brilliant bottlebrush. It is a shrub of 1–3 m with scattered leaves 1 cm long and flower spikes 6–7 cm across. The small woody fruit form dense spikes on the older stems. Family: Myrtaceae

Showy Flame Pea † *Chorizema reticulatum* Meisn.
This small shrub to 50 cm tall has linear to lanceolate net-veined leaves 1–2 cm long crowded on the lower stems, while the flowers are about 1 cm across. It grows in sand or gravel in jarrah woodlands between Busselton and Albany. Family: Papilionaceae

Southern Cross † *Xanthosia rotundifolia* DC.
Xanthosia is an Australian genus of about 20 species, half of them endemic in WA. Southern Cross is a perennial herb to 50 cm tall with ovate-cuneate, dentate leaves 3–6 cm long. The flowers, in terminal compound umbels 3–6 cm across, have conspicuous bracts. The species is common in sandy or rocky soil of woodlands and heaths from Albany to the Stirling Range. Family: Apiaceae

182 Showy Flame Pea (Sept–Oct)

180 Southern Cross (any month)

Crab-lipped Spider Orchid † *Caladenia plicata* R. Fitzg.
The flattened lip with its sharply reflexed tip and dense band of fleshy calli give this orchid its unusual aspect. The plant is 15–30 cm tall with a very hirsute leaf 8–15 cm long and 1 or 2 flowers. The clubbed sepals are 2–2.5 cm long. It grows in sandy or lateritic soils in jarrah-marri forest, between Pemberton and Albany. Family: Orchidaceae

183 Crab-lipped Spider Orchid (Sept–Oct)

Zebra Orchid † *Caladenia cairnsiana* F. Muell.
A very slender plant of 5–25 cm with a narrow hirsute leaf, the Zebra Orchid has 1 or 2 small flowers with the striped lip the most conspicuous feature. The ovate lip is 10–15 mm long and has a small dark flange at its tip. The species is widespread in the lower South West in woodlands and coastal scrub, while in the wheatbelt it prefers sandy loam under jam trees and sheoaks. It also occurs on the lower Murchison River and at Salmon Gums. Family: Orchidaceae

184 Clubbed Spider Orchid (Aug–Oct)

185 Zebra Orchid (Aug–Oct)

Clubbed Spider Orchid † *Caladenia longiclavata* Coleman var. *longiclavata*
This orchid has clubs to the petals as well as sepals, while the lip has a relatively short fringe and is unstriped in the lower half. It has 1 to 3 flowers 4–6 cm across on a stem of 20–40 cm, and grows in forests between Perth and Albany. The var. *magniclavata* has larger clubs, a smaller lip and is more deeply coloured, while the var. *rhomboidiformis* has no clubs to the petals.
Family: Orchidaceae

Pouched Leek Orchid † *Prasophyllum gibbosum* R. Br.

A swamp-dweller which flowers best after a bushfire, this sweetly-scented orchid is 3–25 cm tall with a leaf 5–15 cm long which is somewhat inflated where it leaves the stem. The broad white lateral sepals have a pouch at the base into which the claw of the lip fits. The species occurs in coastal areas between Perth and Albany and in the Stirling Range, with a few localities eastwards to Hopetoun. Family: Orchidaceae

187 Pouched Leek Orchid (Oct–Nov)

186 Hammer Orchid (Sept–Oct)

Hammer Orchid † *Drakaea elastica* Lindl.

Named after an English botanical artist, Miss Drake, *Drakaea* is a genus of 4 species endemic in WA. All are inconspicuous plants of sandy flats in dry swamps or woodlands. There is a single, thick, rounded leaf about 1 cm across lying flat on the ground, with a wiry stem 15–25 cm tall and a single flower. The narrow sepals and petals are about 1 cm long, while the curious hinged lip is not irritable but can be swung over so as to almost touch the column. Hammer Orchids are pollinated by male thynnid wasps which attempt to mate with the flower. The plants apparently emit the same pheromone as the female, flightless wasp. Family: Orchidaceae

188 King Leek Orchid (Oct–Nov)

King Leek Orchid † *Prasophyllum regium* R. S. Rogers

This is one of the largest and most robust Leek Orchids, reaching 2 m with up to 100 or more flowers. Distinguishing features of the flowers, 1.5–2 cm high, are the dark colours, the prominent smooth plate on the lip, and the curved obtuse column wings. Growing in swamps between Pemberton and Albany, it is at its best the first season after a bushfire. Family: Orchidaceae

189 Ellen Peak and Pyungoorup in the Stirling Range, with Black Gins (*Kingia australis* R. Br.).

THE STIRLING RANGE

Rising to over 1,100 metres, the Stirling Range is a magnificent line of peaks stretching for some 60 kilometres in an east-west direction. Hard, metasedimentary rocks of Proterozoic age, they are the highest peaks in the southern half of the State and are attractive for their scenery alone. However, the presence of a rich flora makes them outstanding among the National Parks of Australia. Apart from the many rugged bluffs and crags, they are covered with dense scrub, while on the surrounding plains, heaths and woodlands occur. Other than a few small springs there is no permanent water in the Range, but many creeks flow after winter rains. Over 550 species of plants are found in the Range, including many species endemic to the area. Flowering is at its best on the plain and lower slopes from August to October, and on the higher slopes in October-November.

Dwarf Kangaroo Paw † *Anigozanthos gabrielae* Domin
The smallest of the Kangaroo Paws, this grows in clumps and has linear leaves 4–7 cm long with flowers 2.5 cm long on scapes up to 15 cm high. It favours winter-damp flats of the Range and a few localities near the Kalgan River.
Family: Haemodoraceae

Cranbrook Bell † *Darwinia meeboldii* C. A. Gardn.
One of 8 species of *Darwinia* restricted to the Range, Cranbrook Bell is a shrub to 3 m tall with linear leaves 5–8 mm long. The tricoloured inflorescence bracts are up to 3 cm long, enclosing 7 flowers. It grows among thick scrub on the rocky slopes of Hamilla Hill.
Family: Myrtaceae

190 Cranbrook Bell (Sept–Nov)

191 Dwarf Kangaroo Paw (Sept–Oct)

192 Stirling Range Smokebush (Oct–Nov)

193 Mountain Kunzea (Oct–Dec)

Stirling Range Smokebush † *Conospermum dorrienii* Domin
This is an erect shrub to 70 cm tall with terete, incurved leaves 1–2 cm long. The flowers are 6–8 mm long with only a few, short hairs, followed by top-shaped silky fruit 3 mm across. It grows in sandy or rocky soil and is restricted to the Range.
Family: Proteaceae

Mountain Kunzea † *Kunzea recurva* Schau. var. *montana* Diels
Restricted to the higher rocky slopes of the Range, Mountain Kunzea is a shrub to 2 m tall with leaves 5–10 mm long and flower heads 1.5–2 cm across. Broad bracts cover the developing heads. It differs from the typical variety in the larger leaves and bracts and the larger, yellow flowers.
Family: Myrtaceae

194 Black Gin (any month)

Black Gin † *Kingia australis* R. Br.

Named after both Phillip King, commander of survey expeditions on Australian coasts from 1818 to 1822 and Philip King, Governor of New South Wales from 1800 to 1807, this relative of the Blackboys usually has a single trunk to 5 m tall with silky leaves up to 1 m long. The flower heads, ± 5 cm across, are on stout peduncles covered with silky bracts. It is widespread between Perth and Albany and east to Cape Riche, with outlying populations near the Hill River. The genus is monotypic. Family: Xanthorrhoeaceae

Scallops † *Hakea cucullata* R. Br.

An openly-branched shrub to 5 m, this species has cupped leaves 4–8 cm across supporting the racemes of flowers about 2 cm long. The buds are enclosed by broad silky deciduous bracts. Two winged seeds are held in a woody fruit 2–3 cm long which is swollen at the base and has a thick beak. It is common in the Stirlings, south to Albany and east to Cape Riche, with a few populations farther east, growing on sandy or gravelly heaths. Family: Proteaceae

196 Scallops (June–Oct)

195 Wedge-leaved Dryandra (May–Oct)

Wedge-leaved Dryandra † *Dryandra cuneata* R. Br.

This shrub, up to 1.5 m tall, has prickly leaves 4–7 cm long and flower heads 3–4 cm across surrounded by many tomentose bracts. It is frequent on heaths between Albany and Esperance, extending inland to the Stirlings and Lake Grace. Family: Proteaceae

Drummond's Wattle † *Acacia drummondii* Lindl.

This variable species is one of two bipinnate-leaved wattles in WA with the flowers in spikes. It is a shrub to 2 m, almost glabrous, with leaflets usually about 1 cm long and flower spikes 1–4 cm long. The pods are oblong, 2–3 cm long, pointed, with thick margins and oblique seeds. The variant shown, subsp. *elegans* Maslin, occurs in the Stirling Range—Albany region.

Family: Mimosaceae

198 Drummond's Wattle (July–Oct)

197 Painted Lady (Sept–Oct)

Painted Lady † *Burtonia scabra* R. Br.

Burtonia is an Australian genus of about 12 species, mostly in WA. This species is a shrub to 1 m tall with leaves of 3 narrow leaflets 6–10 mm long, a smooth or pubescent calyx and petals 10–15 mm long. The pod is almost spherical, 5 mm wide, with 1 or 2 seeds. It grows on sandheaths or in forests from the Moore River to Esperance. A related species which also occurs in the Stirlings is *B. villosa,* which has a woolly calyx.

Family: Papilionaceae

199 Stirling Range Coneflower (Aug–Oct)

Stirling Range Coneflower † *Isopogon baxteri* R. Br.

One of many plants named after the collector William Baxter who visited the south coast of WA in the 1820's, this species is confined to the Range. It is a shrub to 1.5 m tall with wedge-shaped, prickly-lobed leaves 2–3 cm long and flowers about 2 cm long. It grows in sandy or rocky soil among thick scrub.

Family: Proteaceae

200 Brush Starflower (Oct–Jan)

Brush Starflower † *Calytrix asperula* Schau.
This is a glabrous shrub to 50 cm tall with linear leaves ± 5 mm long. The calyx tube is 6–8 mm long, with 2 small, pointed basal bracts and aristate lobes 10–12 mm long, while the petals are 4–5 mm long. It grows in sand on heaths and in woodlands from the Stirling Range to Albany.
Family: Myrtaceae

Blue Hakea † *Hakea lehmanniana* Meisn.
Named after J. G. C. Lehmann (1792–1860), a German botanist at Hamburg, this is a shrub to 1.5 m tall with terete pungent leaves 2–5 cm long. The flowers are 1.5 cm long and are various shades of blue. The fruit is ovoid, 1.5–2.5 cm long, covered with spiny processes. It extends from Pingelly to the south Stirlings, growing on gravelly or sandy heaths and it is the only blue-flowered *Hakea*.
Family: Proteaceae

201 Blue Hakea (June–Aug)

202 Pink Mountain Bell (Oct–Nov)

Pink Mountain Bell † *Darwinia squarrosa* (Turcz.) Domin
This is a much-branched shrub to 1 m tall with oblong-elliptic ciliate leaves 5–8 mm long. The floral bracts, 1.5–2 cm long, are also ciliate and enclose 6 or 7 flowers. It grows on the steep rocky upper slopes of the eastern peaks of the Range.
Family: Myrtaceae

Tangled Honeypot † *Dryandra pteridifolia* R. Br.
This small tufted shrub has variable leaves up to 40 cm long with narrow lobes 3–5 cm long. The flower heads, mostly at ground-level, are 4–5 cm long and are surrounded by many tomentose bracts. It grows in sand or gravel, on heaths and in woodlands, ranging from Albany to Hopetoun and inland to Lake Grace. Family: Proteaceae

204 Tangled Honeypot (April–June)

Stirling Range Banksia † *Banksia solandri* R. Br.
A rather open shrub of 1–5 m, this species has oak-like leaves 10–20 cm long and woolly flower spikes 8–15 cm long of a brown or purplish colour. The fruit has many narrow follicles, partly concealed by the old flowers. It is restricted to the Range, growing in rocky soil among thick scrub on the slopes, extending almost to the summits. The name commemorates Daniel Solander, librarian to Joseph Banks on Cook's first voyage (1768–1771). Family: Proteaceae

203 Stirling Range Banksia (Sept–Nov)

205 Little Fringe-leaf (Sept–Oct)

Little Fringe-leaf † *Chamaexeros serra* (Endl.) Benth.
Chamaexeros is a genus of 3 species endemic in south-western WA. All three have membranous fringe-like leaf-margins. This species is a tufted perennial with leaves 10–15 cm long and flowers 6 mm across in umbels surrounded by papery bracts. It occurs in scattered localities between Perth and Albany, extending eastwards to Ravensthorpe, growing usually in clay or sandy-clay. Family: Xanthorrhoeaceae

206 Stirling Range Bottlebrush (Aug–Oct)

Stirling Range Bottlebrush † *Beaufortia heterophylla* (Turcz.) Domin

There are 17 species of *Beaufortia,* all endemic in south-western WA and distinguished from *Melaleuca* by the basifixed, not versatile, anthers. This species is a shrub to 1 m tall with often-ciliate leaves 5–10 mm long. The stamens, the most prominent part of the flower, are 2–2.5 cm long. The plant grows in gravelly soils of heaths and woodlands in the Range and in a few localities to the north-east. Family: Myrtaceae

208 Spiked Andersonia (July–Oct)

207 Hooded Lily (Oct–Nov)

Spiked Andersonia † *Andersonia simplex* (Stschegl.) Druce

Andersonia is a genus of about 22 species endemic in south-western WA. All are small or medium shrubs with sessile leaves, often stem-clasping. Many species have pink calyxes and blue or pink corollas, while others are red, white or cream. This species is an open shrub of 10–40 cm with spreading leaves 3–6 mm long. The corolla may be pink or blue. The species grows on sandy or gravelly heaths and woodlands from the Stirlings to Albany. Family: Epacridaceae

Hooded Lily † *Johnsonia lupulina* R. Br.

This deep-pink variant of the Hooded Lily is restricted to the Range where it favours sandy soil. (See also Pl. 160) Family: Liliaceae

Giant Andersonia † *Andersonia axilliflora* (Stschegl.) Druce
This, the largest of the *Andersonias,* is confined to the higher slopes of the eastern peaks of the Range. It is a shrub to 2 m with erect stems and rigid leaves 3–6 cm long. The floral leaves are creamy-white, enclosing cream flowers 1 cm long. Family: Epacridaceae

Mountain Pea † *Oxylobium atropurpureum* Turcz.
Restricted to the Range, this shrub of 1–2 m has broad, oblong-ovate leaves 3–8 cm long and pendulous flowers 1.5–2 cm long. It grows on the upper rocky slopes. Family: Papilionaceae

209 Mountain Pea (Oct–Nov)

211 Giant Andersonia (Oct–Dec)

Mountain Paper-heath † *Sphenotoma drummondii* (Benth.) F. Muell.
Sphenotoma is a genus of about 6 species endemic in south-western WA. The corolla-lobes are thin and wavy and become papery when old. This species is a small tufted shrub growing from rock crevices near the summits of the peaks in the Range. The basal leaves are 4–6 cm long, becoming shorter and less spreading on the scapes, while the flowers are 1 cm across and arranged in dense spikes 2.5 cm wide. Family: Epacridaceae

Red Andersonia † *Andersonia grandiflora* Stschegl.
This cushion-like perennial is less than 10 cm high with rather twisted leaves 10–15 mm long and flowers ± 10 mm long. It grows in shale under thick scrub on the lower slopes of the Range and in a few localities to the south. Family: Epacridaceae

210 Red Andersonia (Aug–Oct)

212 Mountain Paper-heath (Oct–Nov)

213 Low sandheath near Lake King, with white and yellow featherflowers (*Verticordia roei* Endl., *V. chrysantha* Endl.).

SOUTHERN SANDPLAINS AND HEATH

From Lake Grace and Ongerup to the western edge of the Great Australian Bight lie the southern sandplains and heath. These gently undulating plains consist of shallow sand and loam overlying laterite which in Tertiary times was deposited on the granitic basement of the Great Plateau of WA. In some places this basement is exposed as granite outcrops (Plates 405–425), while in others, especially near the coast, the sand deposits are deeper and often formed into moving or consolidated dunes. The vegetation is mainly low or tall scrub, but there is considerable diversity in its composition. The banksia, legume and myrtle families are well represented, and there are colourful displays in late winter and spring. Near the coast there are some flowers to be seen at any season.

Red-flowered Moort † *Eucalyptus nutans* F. Muell.
This smooth-barked mallee to 3 m tall has lanceolate leaves 4–7 cm long and flowers in groups of up to 7 on a thick recurved peduncle. The bud-caps are about 6 mm long, and the stamens may be red or yellow. It grows in clay or loam on mallee-heath between Bremer Bay and Ravensthorpe. Family: Myrtaceae

Four-winged Mallee † *Eucalyptus tetraptera* Turcz.
This mallee forms an open shrub 1–3 m tall. The leathery leaves are up to 18 cm long and the solitary flowers, on thick flattened peduncles, are 3–4 cm long, the fruit being slightly larger. It grows in sand on open heaths from the Stirling Range to Israelite Bay. Family: Myrtaceae

Pom-Pom Darwinia † *Darwinia vestita* Benth.
One of the *Darwinias* without large floral bracts, this slender shrub 30–70 cm tall has crowded, heath-like leaves 2–4 mm long and flowers in condensed racemes 1–2 cm across. It grows in sand on heaths from Albany to Esperance, including the Stirling Range. Family: Myrtaceae

215 Red-flowered Moort (Sept–Nov)

214 Pom-pom Darwinia (July–Oct)

216 Four-winged Mallee (Sept–Dec)

217 Warted Yate (Oct–Nov)

Warted Yate † *Eucalyptus megacornuta* C. A. Gardn.
A smooth-barked tree to 12 m tall, this has flowers in groups of 3 to 7 on strap-like peduncles. The strange bud-caps are 3–4 cm long. The typical form grows only on a few lateritic hillsides of the Ravensthorpe Range, but a smooth-budded form occurs on the Fitzgerald River. Family: Myrtaceae

Red Toothbrushes † *Grevillea hookerana* Meisn.
A variable species, this is typically a spreading shrub of 1–2 m with pinnate leaves 6–12 cm long. The racemes are 3–6 cm long and the perianths 1 cm, with styles ± 2 cm long. It is common on the southern sandheaths, extending north to the Great Eastern Highway. Family: Proteaceae

Red Combs † *Grevillea concinna* R. Br.
This sprawling shrub grows to 70 cm tall with simple leaves 2–6 cm long. The racemes are 1–2.5 cm long, and the flower styles 2–3 cm. It grows in clay or sand on open heaths from Ongerup to Israelite Bay. Family: Proteaceae

218 Red Toothbrushes (any month)

220 Red Combs (any month)

219 Ashy Hakea (Aug–Oct)

221 Nodding Coneflower (Sept–Oct)

Nodding Coneflower † *Isopogon teretifolius* R. Br.
The leaves of this rigid shrub, up to 1 m tall, are usually divided into terete lobes but are sometimes entire as shown here. The silky flowers are 10–12 mm long. It grows on open heaths and is common from the Stirling Range to Israelite Bay and north to Pingelly, with outliers near Manjimup and Moora. Family: Proteaceae

Ashy Hakea † *Hakea cinerea* R. Br.
This is a robust shrub to 2.5 m tall with stiff, pungent leaves 5–10 cm long. The styles of the flowers are 2–3 cm long, and the narrow, beaked fruit is 2 cm long. It grows in sand on heaths between Hopetoun and Esperance, and a variant with thicker fruits occurs to the north of Badgingarra. Family: Proteaceae

222 Teasel Banksia (any month)

Teasel Banksia † *Banksia pulchella* R. Br.
Teasel Banksia is a spreading shrub less than 1 m tall with leaves ± 1 cm long and flower spikes 5 cm across. The grey fruit has small follicles and sheds the old flowers. It grows in deep sand on coastal heaths from Hopetoun to Israelite Bay. Family: Proteaceae

Southern Plains Banksia † *Banksia media* R. Br.
Typically a robust shrub 3–6 m tall, this has leaves 4–10 cm long and flower spikes 6–7 cm across. The wrinkled follicles of the fruit are almost hidden by the old flowers. It is common on heaths from Cape Riche to Israelite Bay and inland to Lake King. On the coast it is kept low by wind-pruning. Family: Proteaceae

Showy Banksia † *Banksia speciosa* R. Br.
Growing on deep coastal sands between Hopetoun and Israelite Bay, this spreading shrub grows to 5 m tall with leaves 30–40 cm long and conspicuous flower spikes 10 cm across. The fruiting follicles are large and prominent among the persistent old flowers. Family: Proteaceae

Nodding Banksia † *Banksia nutans* R. Br.
This is a rather dense shrub with leaves 1–2 cm long and pendulous flower spikes 6–7 cm across. The fruit has large wrinkled follicles which squeeze out most of the old flowers. It is common on heaths from the Stirling Range to Esperance. Family: Proteaceae

223 Nodding Banksia (Dec–Feb)

224 Southern Plains Banksia (Mar–Oct)

225 Showy Banksia (any month)

226 Shining Honeypot (Aug–Oct)

228 Blue Smokebush (Aug–Oct)

Blue Smokebush † *Conospermum amoenum* Meisn.
This is an erect or spreading shrub to 70 cm tall with terete leaves 1–2 cm long and tomentose flowers 4–5 mm long. It ranges from Pingelly to Bremer Bay and east to Lake King, while a taller variant occurs in the Darling Range near Perth. Family: Proteaceae

Shining Honeypot † *Dryandra obtusa* R. Br.
This prostrate shrub has underground stems, the leaves being up to 30 cm long and the flower heads 4–5 cm long. It grows in sand on heaths between the Fitzgerald River and Esperance. Family: Proteaceae

Prickly Dryandra † *Dryandra falcata* R. Br.
A shrub of 1–2 m, this species has leaves 3–10 cm long and flower heads 4–5 cm across, surrounded by narrow bracts 1–2 cm long. It grows in sand or gravel on heaths from the Stirling Range to Esperance. Family: Proteaceae

Prickly Honeysuckle † *Lambertia echinata* R. Br.
The typical variant, shown here, is a much-branched shrub less than 1 m tall with leaves 2–4 cm long. The flowers, in heads of 7, have styles 4 cm long, and the fruit is rounded and spiny with a flat beak. It is known only from Esperance. Near Albany, on gravel heaths, occurs a taller variant with bright yellow flowers. Family: Proteaceae

227 Prickly Dryandra (Sept–Nov)

229 Prickly Honeysuckle (Aug–Oct)

Lanoline Bush † *Franklandia fucifolia* R. Br.
Franklandia is a genus of 2 species endemic in south-western WA, a feature being the fine spots on both leaves and flowers. This species is a shrub to 1 m tall with divided leaves up to 10 cm long. The scented flowers are 2–3 cm across with a tube 2.5–3 cm long, and the fruit is a narrow nut with a flat silky crown. It occurs on heaths from Albany to Esperance.
Family: Proteaceae

Coastal Hakea † *Hakea clavata* Labill.
This species has the thickest leaves of any *Hakea*. It is a spreading shrub of 1–2 m with leaves 3–7 cm long and flowers with a sickly-sweet perfume. The ovoid fruit has 2 apical horns and sheds the seed when mature. It grows on granite hills on the coast between Esperance and Israelite Bay.
Family: Proteaceae

230 Coastal Hakea (Aug–Sept)

232 Lanoline Bush (any month)

231 Frog Hakea (July–Sept)

233 Pincushion Hakea (April–July)

Frog Hakea † *Hakea nitida* R. Br.
A rigid, much-branched shrub 1–3 m tall, the Frog Hakea has stiff leaves 6–10 cm long, while the swollen fruit is 2.5 cm long with two short apical horns and is roughly spotted. It extends from Gnowangerup to Israelite Bay, growing on sandheaths, among mallees or on granite hills.
Family: Proteaceae

Pincushion Hakea † *Hakea laurina* R. Br.
The flowers of this shrub or small tree are cream at first and later turn pink or red. The oblanceolate leaves are 10–15 cm long, the flower heads 4–6 cm across, and the thick fruit 2.5 cm long. It grows in clay, sand or gravel between Narrogin, Albany and Israelite Bay.
Family: Proteaceae

White Goodenia † *Goodenia scapigera* R. Br.
This perennial herb, less than 1 m tall, has rather woody stems with narrow leaves 3–8 cm long, and flowers 10–15 mm long. It grows in sand or gravel in mallee or on heaths from the Stirling Range to Israelite Bay and inland to Pingelly and Hyden. It regenerates freely after bushfires.
Family: Goodeniaceae

235 Heath Lechenaultia (Sept–Jan)

Heath Lechenaultia † *Lechenaultia tubiflora* R. Br.
Either cushion-like or erect, this perennial herb has acute linear leaves 2–10 mm long and flowers 12–15 mm long, the lobes scarcely spreading. The flowers may be red, white or various combinations of both. It grows on sandheaths from Albany to Israelite Bay and inland to Tammin, with an outlier near Moora.
Family: Goodeniaceae

234 White Goodenia (Sept–Dec)

236 Pouched Dampiera (Sept–Oct)

Pouched Dampiera † *Dampiera sacculata* F. Muell. ex Benth.
A perennial herb to 30 cm tall with many wiry, angular stems, the Pouched Dampiera has scattered linear leaves 1–3 cm long, and flowers 1 cm long on slender pedicels. The ovary is pouched, due to the curved solitary ovule. The species prefers low-lying heaths or swamps, ranging from the Stirling Range to Esperance and inland to Bruce Rock, occurring also between Bunbury and Augusta.
Family: Goodeniaceae

Black Kennedia † *Kennedia nigricans* Lindl.
This vigorous climber has leaves of 1 or 3 ovate leaflets 5–10 cm long and flowers 3 cm long. The flat pods are 4–7 cm long with many oblique seeds. It is common in deep sand on the coast between Cape Riche and Hopetoun. Family: Papilionaceae

238 Black Kennedia (July–Oct)

Silky Triggerplant † *Stylidium pilosum* Labill.
One of the tallest triggerplants, this has smooth linear leaves 10–30 cm long and hirsute flowering stems up to 70 cm tall. The flowers are about 2 cm long. It grows in deep sand on heaths from Bremer Bay to Israelite Bay. Family: Stylidiaceae

239 Silky Triggerplant (Sept–Nov)

Ravensthorpe Bottlebrush † *Beaufortia orbifolia* F. Muell.
Growing on lateritic hills between Ravensthorpe and Merredin, this bottlebrush is a shrub up to 3 m tall with leaves 5–7 mm long. The flower spikes are 4 cm across, bicoloured at first but later deep red throughout. The small woody fruit are in crowded spikes along the old stems. Family: Myrtaceae

237 Ravensthorpe Bottlebrush (Aug–Jan)

240 Crab Claws (Sept–Nov)

Crab Claws † *Stylidium macranthum* Carlquist
A recently-described species known only from sandheaths near swamps around Esperance, this species has smooth linear leaves 10–20 cm long and hirsute flowering stems 20–30 cm tall. The flowers are 20–25 mm long, and the outer surface is pale yellow with violet spots. Family: Stylidiaceae

241 Pink Starflower (Sept–Dec)

Pink Starflower † *Calytrix decandra* (R. Br.) DC.
One of several pink-flowered *Calytrixes*, this is a slender shrub less than 70 cm tall with crowded linear leaves 1 cm long. The calyx-tube is 15 mm long, with 2 pointed basal bracts, and the petals are 1 cm long. It extends from Ravensthorpe to Israelite Bay, growing on sandheaths.
Family: Myrtaceae

243 Stilted Paper-lily (Aug–Oct)

Stilted Paper-lily † *Laxmannia brachyphylla* F. Muell.
This perennial herb, less than 10 cm high, grows on sandheaths between the Stirling Range and Esperance. The finely pointed leaves are 4–6 mm long with fringed stipules, and the flower 'heads' are 1 cm across. *Laxmannia* is an Australian genus of 8 species, 7 of them in WA. Family: Liliaceae

Coastal Pigface † *Carpobrotus virescens* (Haw.) Schwantes
Carpobrotus is a genus of 20–25 species, mostly South African, with four native to Australia and one to Chile. They are prostrate shrubs with succulent opposite leaves and short, erect flowering branches. This species has white older stems, usually 4 sepals, and the stamens crowded in 4–5 rows. It occurs mainly on coastal dunes and rocks between the Murchison River and Israelite Bay. Family: Aizoaceae

242 Coastal Pigface (Aug–Oct)

Cushion Fan-flower † *Scaevola pulvinaris* (E.Pritzel) Krause
A prostrate and often compact perennial herb, this little plant has linear leaves 1–3 cm long and white to pale blue flowers 5–7 mm long. It grows in deep sand, usually on low-lying heaths, between the Stirling Range and Ravensthorpe. Family: Goodeniaceae

244 Cushion Fanflower (Aug–Sept)

Chittick † *Lambertia inermis* R. Br.
A characteristic plant of deep sands on heaths from Albany to Israelite Bay, Chittick is a shrub to 6 m tall with elliptic to obovate leaves 1–2 cm long. The cream or orange flowers are in heads of 7, with styles 4 cm long. Family: Proteaceae

245 Chittick (any month)

247 A Pink Boronia (Aug–Oct)

A Pink Boronia *Boronia inornata* Turcz.
This is a spreading shrub to 50 cm tall with tripartite leaves less than 1 cm long. The terminal, solitary flowers are 7–8 mm across. It is frequent in clay, loam or gravel in heath, mallee or woodlands from South Stirling to Esperance and inland to Lake King. Also in SA. Family: Rutaceae

Barrel Coneflower † *Isopogon trilobus* R. Br.
A shrub about 1 m tall, this species has fan-shaped leaves 4–7 cm long and silky, cream flowers in heads 3 cm across. The fruiting cone, shown here, is 2.5 cm across. The plant grows on sand-heaths between Ongerup and Israelite Bay. Family: Proteaceae

248 Barrel Coneflower (Fls: Sept–Nov)

246 Tallerack (Jan–Feb)

Tallerack † *Eucalyptus tetragona* (R. Br.) F. Muell.
Another typical plant of southern heaths, this mallee grows from 1–6 m tall and has 4-winged stems. Usually glaucous, it is almost green east of Esperance. The flowers have rounded caps and cream stamens in 4 clusters, and the fruit is 1.5 cm across. It ranges from the Stirling Range to Israelite Bay, and occurs also near the Hill River. Family: Myrtaceae

249 Rough Boronia (Aug–Oct)

Rough Boronia † *Boronia scabra* Lindl.
Another of the many pink *Boronias,* this erect, hirsute shrub, less than 50 cm tall, has linear leaves 5–15 mm long, often clustered. The flowers, in terminal umbels, are 1 cm across. It grows in gravel or clay on heaths from Cape Riche to Mt. Ragged and also to the north of Perth. Family: Rutaceae

Horned Sheoak † *Casuarina thuyoides* Miq.
A spreading shrub of 1–2 m with jointed, leafless stems, this sheoak has cones 2–3 cm across, the spiny bracts enclosing small winged seeds. It grows on heaths from the Stirling Range to Esperance and in scattered areas north to Geraldton. Family: Casuarinaceae

250 Sheath Conostylis (Aug–Oct)

252 Horned Sheoak (Fls: Aug–Sept)

251 Large Waxflower (Sept–Oct)

Sheath Conostylis † *Conostylis vaginata* Endl.
This tough herb forms clumps up to 10 cm tall and 30 cm wide, often supported on wiry prop-roots. The pungent leaves are 4–8 cm long and the flowers 1 cm long, being surrounded by brown ciliate bracts. It grows on sandheaths between Albany and Esperance. Family: Haemodoraceae

Large Waxflower † *Chamelaucium megalopetalum* F. Muell. ex Benth.
Chamelaucium is a genus of over 20 species endemic in south-western WA, including the well-known Geraldton Wax. The Large Waxflower is a slender shrub to 1 m tall with linear leaves 5–10 mm long. The flowers are 1–1.5 cm across, white at first but later turning red. It grows on sandheaths from Ongerup to Israelite Bay and north to Southern Cross. Family: Myrtaceae

Corky Honeymyrtle † *Melaleuca suberosa* (Schau.) C. A. Gardn.
This curious shrub, 30–70 cm tall, has obtuse linear leaves 3–7 mm long and thick corky bark. The flowers 'erupt' through the bark and are 5 mm long, while the woody capsules are 4 mm across. It grows on sandheaths from Albany to Israelite Bay. Family: Myrtaceae

Little Bottlebrush † *Beaufortia micrantha* Schau.
The smallest of the *Beaufortias*, this shrub, less than 70 cm tall, has leaves 1–2 mm long and flower spikes 7–10 mm across. It ranges from Lake Grace to Esperance on heaths. Variants occur with longer, hirsute leaves. Family: Myrtaceae

253 Little Beaufortia (Oct–Dec)

255 Corky Honeymyrtle (Aug–Sept)

254 Silver Teatree (Aug–Sept)

256 Pink Bottlebrush (Sept–Dec)

Silver Teatree † *Leptospermum sericeum* Labill.
Recently rediscovered after more than 100 years, this is a silky-pubescent spreading shrub 1–2 m tall with leaves 1–2 cm long. The flowers are 2–5 cm across and vary from pale to deep pink. It grows on coastal granite hills east of Esperance and on the Recherche Archipelago. Family: Myrtaceae

Pink Bottlebrush † *Beaufortia schaueri* Preiss ex Schau.
A shrub to 1 m tall, this bottlebrush has narrow-linear leaves 2–6 mm long and dense flower-heads 2 cm across. It grows in sand or gravel on heaths and rocky hills from the Stirling Range to Israelite Bay. Family: Myrtaceae

257 Middle Mt. Barren, with Royal Hakeas amid rich heath.

THE BARRENS

Named by Matthew Flinders on 6 January 1802, on his voyage of discovery along the south coast, the Barrens are a system of isolated peaks and small ranges extending over 60 kilometres. Rising to a maximum of 530 metres, they consist of hard quartzites of Proterozoic age, and were islands in the sea when the Tertiary spongolites of the Fitzgerald and Hamersley River valleys were deposited. The vegetation is a mosaic of heath and mallee interspersed with swamp and riverine formations, all of great variety Over 600 species occur here, of which 60 are endemic in the area. Many of the latter are restricted to the peaks themselves. Like most of the south coast, spring is the best flowering season, but there are some flowers to be seen at any time.

Royal Hakea † *Hakea victoria* Drummond
Named after Queen Victoria, this is the only native plant in WA with variegated leaves. These are the floral leaves, each having an axillary cluster of cream and pink flowers with styles 2.5 cm long. The leaves persist for up to 5 years, and the colour becomes deeper each year. At the base of the plant are all-green vegetative leaves, up to 20 cm long, undulate-oblong with prickly margins. The fruit is a rough, woody follicle 2.5 cm long. The plant grows in sandy or quartzite soil on heaths between the Gairdner River and Hopetoun. Family: Proteaceae

258 Royal Hakea

260 Barrens Clawflower (July–Oct)

259 Royal Hakea (June–July)

261 Oak-leaved Dryandra (Aug–Nov)

Barrens Clawflower † *Calothamnus validus* S. Moore
A spreading shrub less than 1 m tall, this species has terete leaves 2–3 cm long and glabrous flowers with staminal bundles 3–4 cm long. The smooth, woody fruit is 1.5 cm long, with 2 prominent lobes. It grows only on the quartzite hills of the Barrens. Family: Myrtaceae

Oak-leaved Dryandra † *Dryandra quercifolia* Meisn.
This prickly shrub up to 2 m tall is one of the largest-flowered *Dryandras*, with flower heads up to 6 cm across. The dentate leaves are 5–9 cm long. It grows on hills of quartzite, shale or laterite between the Fitzgerald River and Ravensthorpe. Family: Proteaceae

262 Barrens Lechenaultia (all year)

264 A Grevillea (Sept–Dec)

A Grevillea † *Grevillea tripartita* Meisn.
This is an erect shrub to 1.3 m tall with pungent, tripartite leaves 2–3 cm long and large flowers with styles 4–5 cm long. The fruit is an ovoid follicle 2 cm long. The species grows on sandheaths between the Gairdner River and Ravensthorpe. Family: Proteaceae

Mountain Banksia † *Banksia quercifolia* R. Br. var. *integrifolia* F. Muell.
Confined to the peaks of the Barrens and the Stirling Range, this is a rigid shrub of 1–3 m with entire or toothed leaves 3–8 cm long and flower spikes 4 cm across. The fruiting spike has smooth, rounded follicles with the old flowers persistent. The typical variety has thinner, dentate leaves, rusty-brown flowers and thinner follicles, and inhabits swamps near Albany. Family: Proteaceae

Barrens Lechenaultia † *Lechenaultia superba* F. Muell.
A rather slender erect shrub to 70 cm tall with soft leaves 1–2 cm long and flowers 18–25 mm long, this *Lechenaultia* grows in thick scrub on a few quartzite hills at the eastern end of the Barrens. Family: Goodeniaceae

Bell-fruited Mallee † *Eucalyptus preissiana* Schau.
Common on rocky hills and heaths from the Stirling Range almost to Esperance, this spreading mallee 1–2 m tall has distinctive elliptic obtuse leaves 5–12 cm long, and flowers in 3's on stout peduncles. The smooth bud-caps are 13–18 mm wide, while the bell-shaped fruit is 2–3 cm long. It is named after Ludwig Preiss, a German collector who visited WA in 1838–41. Family: Myrtaceae

265 Mountain Banksia (May–Aug)

263 Bell-fruited Mallee (Oct–Nov)

Ouch Bush † *Daviesia pachyphylla* F. Muell.
An open, arching shrub to 1 m tall, this has very thick, pungent leaves 1–2 cm long. The flowers, in the upper axils, are followed by triangular pods 15 mm long. It is frequent on sandheaths between Ongerup and Ravensthorpe. Family: Papilionaceae

266 Ouch Bush (July–Sept)

268 Qualup Bell (July–Sept)

267 Queen of Sheba (July–Sept)

Qualup Bell † *Pimelea physodes* Hook.
This is the only *Pimelea* with a large bell-like inflorescence. The bracts are 3–5 cm long, enclosing many greenish-yellow flowers, and turn a deeper colour with age. The plant, is a slender shrub to 70 cm, rarely larger, with leaves 15–25 mm long. It extends from the Gairdner River to Ravensthorpe, growing on sandheath or rocky hills. Family: Thymeleaceae

A Grevillea † *Grevillea macrostylis* F. Muell.
Similar to *G. tripartita* (Pl. 264) in habit, this shrub, to 2 m tall, has flat, pungently-lobed leaves 2–3 cm long and flowers 12 mm long with styles 4 cm long. It grows on sandy or rocky heaths between Ravensthorpe and the coast. Family: Proteaceae

269 A Grevillea (Sept–Nov)

Queen of Sheba † *Thelymitra variegata* (Lindl.) F. Muell.
Widespread but infrequent between the Hill River and Ravensthorpe, this sun orchid has flowers 2.5-3.5 cm across. Although the same colours are always present, their proportions vary, those of the Barrens area having more red and brown than elsewhere. The leaf is narrow and usually spirally twisted. It occurs on open sandheath or, in districts to the west, in woodland. Family: Orchidaceae

270 Dense Clawflower (Aug–Oct)

Dense Clawflower † *Calothamnus pinifolius* F. Muell.
Often almost concealing its flowers among the foliage, this shrub, to 1.5 m tall, has pungent leaves 2–3 cm long and flowers 2 cm long. The hirsute fruit is 8 mm long. It grows in laterite or quartzite among dense scrub between the Gairdner River and Ravensthorpe. Family: Myrtaceae

Bushy Yate † *Eucalyptus lehmanni* (Preiss ex Shau.) Benth.
This is the only Eucalypt with the flowers united into a head. The slender bud-caps are 4–5 cm long. From the Stirling Range to Esperance it is a mallee to 3 m tall, but occasionally, as on Bald Island near Albany, it is a smooth-barked tree to 5 m tall. Family: Myrtaceae

271 Bushy Yate (Nov–Jan)

273 Barrens Regelia (Sept–Nov)

Barrens Regelia † *Regelia velutina* (Turcz.) C. A. Gardn.
Regelia is a genus of 5 species endemic in the South-West and differing from *Beaufortia* and *Eremaea* in floral details. This is the largest species, a shrub to 3 m tall with leaves 10–15 mm long and flower spikes 3–4 cm across. It grows among quartzite rocks on the Barrens. Family: Myrtaceae

272 Flat Wattle (Aug–Sept)

Flat Wattle † *Acacia glaucoptera* Benth.
One of several wattles with flat stems and decurrent phyllodes, this spreading shrub, up to 1 m tall, has glaucous stems 2–4 cm wide and flower heads 5–7 mm across. The pods are narrow and coiled, 1–2 cm long. It is common from the south Stirling to Esperance, growing in sand, clay or gravel on heath and in mallee. Family: Mimosaceae

274 Weeping Gum (Nov–Mar)

Weeping Gum † *Eucalyptus sepulcralis* F. Muell.
One of the most slender Eucalypts, this is a tree or mallee with few stems to 8 m tall and long pendulous branches. The buds, 12 mm long, are in groups of 7 on slender peduncles, and the urn-shaped fruit is 3–4 cm long. It grows on quartzite slopes of a few ranges at the eastern end of the Barrens.
Family: Myrtaceae

Lizard Triggerplant † *Stylidium preissii* (Sond.) F. Muell.
This is one of two triggerplants with small (1–2 mm) leaves closely pressed to the stem. It is a small perennial herb with flowers 4–5 mm across, and grows on sandplain between the Pallinup River and Esperance. A disjunct population occurs near Perth. Family: Stylidiaceae

276 Lizard Triggerplant (Sept–Nov)

275 Thorny Hovea (July–Aug)

Thorny Hovea † *Hovea acanthoclada* (Turcz.) F. Muell.
A rigid, spreading shrub to 1.5 m with spinescent branchlets, this *Hovea* has oblong leaves 2–4 mm long, flowers 8 mm across, and ovoid pods 8–10 mm long with 1–2 seeds. It grows on breakaway cliffs along the Fitzgerald River, on lateritic hills near Ravensthorpe, and in gravelly soil near Kalgoorlie. Family: Papilionaceae

Prickly Hibbertia † *Hibbertia mucronata* (Turcz.) Benth.
Growing on plains and hills from the Gairdner River to Esperance, this shrub, up to 50 cm tall, has pungent leaves 1–2 cm long and flowers 1 cm across. The 5 stamens are on one side of the carpels. The leaves vary in thickness, and the sepals may be glabrous or hirsute. Family: Dilleniaceae

277 Prickly Hibbertia (July–Oct)

278 Late spring on heaths near the Moore River, with Black Kangaroo Paws, Woolly Bottlebrush and Common Smokebush.

NORTHERN SANDPLAINS AND HEATH

Between the Moore River and Shark Bay and extending inland for up to 100 kilometres, sandplains and heaths are the predominant ecological feature. Large sandy or lateritic tracts support a scrub vegetation which is often less than 1 m high. There are also large areas of tall scrub and mallee, some scattered patches of woodland, and a number of fresh or salt lakes. The rivers are mostly small and of intermittent flow, the exception being the Murchison which in its lower reaches has carved a magnificent gorge through sandstone. The flat-topped hills of the Geraldton district are another feature of interest. As in most of the South-West, the banksia, legume and myrtle families are especially prominent in this region, and include many species unique to it. Spring is the main flowering season, but winter and early summer also produce colourful flowers.

Staghorn Bush † *Daviesia epiphylla* Meisn.
This is a curious, leafless shrub to 70 cm tall. The flowers, 2 cm long, are the largest of the genus and are followed by triangular pods 2.5–3 cm long. It grows in shallow sand over laterite on heaths between the Hill River and Eneabba.
Family: Papilionaceae

280 Staghorn Bush (April–July)

Yellow Kangaroo Paw † *Anigozanthos pulcherrimus* Hook.
This strong, rhizomatous perennial herb has flat, tomentose leaves which die off in summer. The flowering stems are up to 1.5 m tall and the flowers 2.5–3 cm long. It is common in deep sand, especially in depressions, between the Moore River and Eneabba. Family: Haemodoraceae

279 Yellow Kangaroo Paw (Nov–Jan)

281 Black Kangaroo Paw (Oct–Nov)

282 Hooker's Banksia (Aug–Oct)

Black Kangaroo Paw † *Macropidia fuliginosa* (Hook.) Druce
Differing from *Anigozanthos* in the one-seeded cells of the ovary which fall as small 'fruit', this monotypic genus is restricted to gravelly heaths and woodlands between Perth and Geraldton. Perennial, strap-like leaves arise from a strong rhizome, and the branched flowering stems grow to 1.3 m, with flowers 5–6 cm long. Family: Haemodoraceae

Hooker's Banksia † *Banksia hookerana* Meisn.
A spreading shrub of 1–2 m, Hooker's Banksia has leaves 10–25 cm long and 7–10 mm wide, while the flower spikes are 6–10 cm long. The persistent old flowers conceal the hirsute follicles of the fruiting spike. It extends from Eneabba to Mingenew, growing in deep sand. Family: Proteaceae

283 Hairy Lechenaultia (Sept–Nov)

284 Velvet Fanflower (Sept–Nov)

285 Lesueur Southern Cross (Sept–Oct)

Hairy Lechenaultia † *Lechenaultia hirsuta* F. Muell.
A sprawling, hirsute, perennial herb, this has linear leaves 1–3 cm long and flowers 2.5–3 cm long. It grows on sandheaths between the Hill River and Shark Bay. Family: Goodeniaceae

Common Verreauxia † *Verreauxia reinwardtii* (De Vr.) Benth.
This is an erect grey-woolly perennial herb with elliptic-obovate leaves 3–8 cm long. The flowers, 7–8 mm long, are in long leafless panicles. Growing in deep sand, it ranges from Geraldton to Gnowangerup and east to Southern Cross. *Verreauxia* is a genus of 3 species endemic in south-western Australia. The two other species are rare. Family: Goodeniaceae

286 Common Verreauxia (Sept–Dec)

Velvet Fanflower † *Scaevola phlebopetala* F. Muell.
This prostrate, hirsute, perennial herb has linear-lanceolate leaves 1–6 cm long, sometimes toothed. The flowers, solitary or in small pedunculate cymes, are 2 cm long with linear calyx-lobes 1 cm long. It grows in deep sand on heaths between Perth and Shark Bay. Family: Goodeniaceae

Lesueur Southern Cross † *Xanthosia tomentosa* A. S. George
On lateritic hills among low heath in the Mt. Lesueur district occurs this spreading perennial herb. The leaves are 1–3 cm long and the inflorescences, on long leafless stems, are subtended by 3-lobed bracts 1.5–2 cm long. Family: Apiaceae

White Plume Grevillea † *Grevillea leucopteris* Meisn.
This showy shrub grows to 3 m tall, much-branched, with pinnate leaves and the flowers on long arching canes. The young buds are covered with sticky pink bracts, while the flowers have a strong unpleasant scent. It is common in deep sand on heaths between Moora and the Murchison River.
Family: Proteaceae

Posy Triggerplant † *Stylidium crossocephalum* F. Muell.
This is a tufted perennial herb with rough, linear leaves 5–10 cm long and flower scapes to 20 cm tall. The flowers, 2 cm long, are surrounded by pointed red bracts with papery lacerated margins. It grows on sandheaths between Perth and Geraldton.
Family: Stylidiaceae

288 White Plume Grevillea (Sept–Nov)

287 Posy Triggerplant (Sept–Oct)

289 Sandplain Cranberry (June–Sept)

Sandplain Cranberry † *Astroloma microdonta* F. Muell. ex Benth.
A small, much-branched shrub to 40 cm tall, this cranberry has flat, linear leaves 5–15 mm long. The flowers have stiff sepals 6–7 mm long and corollas 12–14 mm long, the small lobes being woolly inside. It extends from Perth to Geraldton, growing on sandy and lateritic heaths. Family: Epacridaceae

290 Button Creeper (Fr: Oct–Jan)

Button Creeper † *Tersonia brevipes* Moq.
Tersonia is a monotypic genus endemic in south-western Australia. A dioecious, prostrate, perennial herb, it has axillary female flowers which develop into fruit 1.5 cm across (shown here), and small male flowers in terminal racemes. It grows in sand on heaths between Bunbury and the Murchison River.
Family: Gyrostemonaceae

291 Violet Eremaea (Oct–Dec)

292 Summer Coppercups (Nov–Jan)

293 Yellow Honeypot (Sept–Oct)

Violet Eremaea † *Eremaea violacea* F. Muell.
Eremaea is a genus of about 10 species endemic in south-western WA and characterised by the inflorescence, anthers and seeds. This species is a spreading hirsute shrub to 70 cm tall with linear leaves 5–10 cm long and flowers 10–14 mm long. It grows on sandheaths between the Hill River and Mingenew.
Family: Myrtaceae

Champion Bay Poison † *Gastrolobium oxylobioides* Benth.
Less than 1 m tall, this spreading shrub has leaves in 3's, lanceolate, pungent, 2–5 cm long, with bristly stipules. The flowers, in open terminal racemes, are 1 cm across. It grows in sandy, gravelly or rocky soil on heaths and on hills between Perth and the Murchison River and is toxic.
Family: Papilionaceae

294 Champion Bay Poison (Sept–Nov)

Summer Coppercups † *Pileanthus filifolius* Meisn.
Restricted to WA, the genus *Pileanthus* has 5 species distinguished by the flowers which have 10 calyx-lobes, 5 dentate petals and 20 stamens. This species grows on sandheaths between Perth and Mingenew. It is a slender shrub to 1 m tall with terete leaves 1 cm long and flowers 2 cm across.
Family: Myrtaceae

Yellow Honeypot † *Dryandra tridentata* Meisn.
This plant has many stems to 40 cm tall arising from a lignotuber. The broad-linear leaves 2–3 cm long are often 3-toothed, while the flower heads are mostly near the base and are 4–5 cm across. It grows on sandheaths between the Hill River and Eneabba.
Family: Proteaceae

295 Lesueur Hakea (April–May)

Lesueur Hakea † *Hakea megalosperma* Meisn.
This is a shrub less than 1 m tall with leaves 6–10 cm long. The tiny flowers, 5 mm long, are followed by large fruit 6–7 cm long with 2 apical beaks. It grows on lateritic hills in the Mt. Lesueur district. Family: Proteaceae

296 Awled Honeypot (Sept–Oct)

Awled Honeypot † *Dryandra subulata* C. A. Gardn.
A recently-discovered species, this tufted shrub has linear leaves 20–30 cm long, and flower-heads 2 cm long surrounded by many stiff, pungent, linear bracts. It grows in sand over laterite on heaths between the Hill River and Eneabba. Family: Proteaceae

Murchison Clawflower † *Calothamnus homalophyllus* F. Muell.
This spreading shrub grows to 2 m tall, with linear-obovate leaves 3–5 cm long and flowers 3 cm long. The round, woody fruit is often wrinkled. It grows in sandy or rocky soil among scrub, ranging from Geraldton to the Murchison River. Family: Myrtaceae

297 Murchison Clawflower (Aug–Oct)

Coppercups † *Pileanthus peduncularis* Endl.
A spreading shrub to 70 cm tall, this has thick, linear leaves 2–4 mm long and flowers 10–15 mm across. The bracts enclosing the buds are viscid. It grows in sand over laterite on heaths from Mogumber to the Murchison and eastwards to Merredin, with outliers on sand-dunes north of Carnarvon and in the Kennedy Range. Family: Myrtaceae

298 Coppercups (Sept–Nov)

299 Scarlet Featherflower (Sept–Dec)

300 Claw Featherflower (Sept–Oct)

301 Leafless Hibbertia (Sept–Oct)

Leafless Hibbertia † *Hibbertia conspicua* (Drumm. et Harv.) Gilg.
This wiry, leafless shrub, less than 70 cm tall, has flowers 15–18 mm across with the stamens closely surrounding the carpels. It occurs on sandheaths between the Murchison River and Mingenew, and between Southern Cross and Salmon Gums. Family: Dilleniaceae

Scarlet Featherflower † *Verticordia grandis* Drumm. et Harv.
This straggling shrub 1–2 m tall has rounded opposite leaves 8–15 mm across and axillary flowers 25 mm across with styles 25 mm long. Two united, pointed bracts enclose each bud and persist as a collar when the flower opens. It extends from the Hill River to Mingenew, growing on sandheaths. Family: Myrtaceae

Claw Featherflower † *Verticordia grandiflora* Endl.
With flowers 15 mm across, this has the largest flowers of the yellow *Verticordias*. It is a shrub to 70 cm with linear leaves 5–15 mm long. The flowers turn red-brown with age, and the anthers have claw-like appendages. It is widespread on heaths from the Murchison River to Ravensthorpe. Family: Myrtaceae

Spreading Coneflower † *Isopogon divergens* R. Br.
A spreading shrub to 1.5 m tall, this has leaves 6–10 cm long divided into terete lobes. The flower spikes are 4–5 cm across, with silky flowers. It grows in gravelly or granitic soil from the Murchison River to Perth and SE to Lake Grace. Family: Proteaceae

302 Spreading Coneflower (Sept–Oct)

303 Rusty Eremaea (Sept–Oct)

Rusty Eremaea † *Eremaea acutifolia* F. Muell.
One of several *Eremaeas* with bright orange flowers, this small shrub has linear leaves 4–8 mm long and solitary, terminal flowers 1 cm long with hirsute calyxes. The woody, hirsute, cup-shaped fruit is 9–10 mm wide. It grows on sandheath between the Irwin and Greenough Rivers. Family: Myrtaceae

304 Woolly Bottlebrush (Sept–Nov)

Woolly Bottlebrush † *Beaufortia eriocephala* W. V. Fitzg.
A small spreading shrub to 70 cm tall, this bottlebrush has obtuse, lanceolate leaves 5–10 mm long and spikes of flowers 15–20 mm across, the stamens being woolly in the lower half. It grows in gravel or sand on heaths from the Moore River to Eneabba. Family: Myrtaceae

Oldfield's Foxglove † *Pityrodia oldfieldii* (F. Muell.) F. Muell. ex Benth.
This densely tomentose shrub to 1.5 m tall has ovate-obovate, crenulate leaves 2–4 cm long, and flowers 2 cm long in leafy panicles. The stems and leaves are often red. It is common on sandheaths of the lower Murchison, extending south to Mullewa. Family: Verbenaceae

305 Oldfield's Foxglove (Sept–Dec)

Lesser Diplolaena † *Diplolaena microcephala* Bartl.
This is an aromatic, tomentose shrub to 1.5 m tall with linear, elliptic or obovate leaves 1–4 cm long. The flower heads are 2.5 cm across and are often reddish. It grows in various habitats from the Murchison River to the south coast.
Family: Rutaceae

306 Lesser Diplolaena (July–Sept)

307 Yellow Stackhousia (Sept–Nov)

Yellow Stackhousia † *Stackhousia dielsii* Pampanini
Named after the German botanist Ludwig Diels, who visited WA in 1900-01, this perennial herb has erect, wiry stems to 50 cm with a few linear leaves and dense racemes of flowers, each 7–9 mm long. It grows on sandheaths between the Irwin and Murchison Rivers. Family: Stackhousiaceae

Chapman Creeper † *Billardiera ringens* (Drumm. et Harv.) Bennett
A strong, hirsute climber with leaves 5–9 cm long, this has racemes of crowded flowers each 2 cm long, the corolla lobes spreading to 1.5 cm. It grows in rocky loam over sandstone or limestone, usually near streams, between Mingenew and Kalbarri. Family: Pittosporaceae

309 Chapman Creeper (Aug–Oct)

Common Blackboy † *Xanthorrhoea preissii* Endl.
This familiar plant of the SW extends from the Murchison River to the south coast, growing in diverse habitats. The caudex is up to 5 m tall, often branched, and the flower spikes are up to 3 m long. The north-facing flowers of the spike always open first. Family: Xanthorrhoeaceae

310 Common Blackboy (Sept–Nov)

308 Ribbon Pea (Aug–Oct)

Ribbon Pea † *Brachysema aphyllum* Hook.
An unusual legume with flat, leafless stems either prostrate or ascending, this has flowers 3.5–4.5 cm long. The terete, narrow pod is 4–5 cm long with many seeds. It ranges from Shark Bay to Bonnie Rock, growing on heaths and granite outcrops. Family: Papilionaceae

Wiry Honeymyrtle † *Melaleuca nematophylla* F. Muell.
A shrub to 2 m tall, this has terete leaves 6–10 cm long with flower heads 2.5–3 cm across, the axis growing out after flowering. It grows in sand or loam among tall scrub from the Murchison River to Lake Brown. Family: Myrtaceae

311 Wiry Honeymyrtle (Aug–Oct)

313 Prickly Plume Grevillea (Sept–Oct)

Prickly Plume Grevillea † *Grevillea annulifera* F. Muell.
This much-branched shrub, up to 4 m tall, has divaricately divided prickly leaves 3–5 cm long. The flowers change from cream to pink with age and have an unpleasant scent. A spherical fruit 3–4 cm across contains 2 large seeds. The plant grows on sandheaths of the lower Murchison River. Family: Proteaceae

Rogerson's Grevillea † *Grevillea rogersoniana* C. A. Gardn.
Discovered by amateur botanists in 1961, this erect shrub up to 3 m tall has leaves 5–10 cm long. The styles of the flowers are 13–14 mm long, while the fruit is ovoid and tuberculate, 13–18 mm long. It grows in red sand amid tall scrub to the S of Shark Bay. Family: Proteaceae

314 Rogersons' Grevillea (Aug–Sept)

312 A Button Daisy (Sept–Oct)

A Button Daisy † *Calocephalus francisii* (F. Muell.) Benth.
An ephemeral with narrow leaves 10–15 mm long and compound flower heads 1 cm across, this daisy grows in sand or loam in shrublands or mulga from Dongara to Shark Bay and NE to Meekatharra. Family: Asteraceae

315 Woolly Orange Banksia (Jan–Mar)

Woolly Orange Banksia † *Banksia victoriae* Meisn.
Restricted to a few areas of sandplain N of Northampton, this much-branched shrub grows to 4 m tall with hirsute leaves 30 cm long and 3 cm wide. The woolly flower spikes are 8–9 cm across, and the old flowers persist on the fruit. Family: Proteaceae

316 Ashby's Banksia (Aug–Jan)

Ashby's Banksia † *Banksia ashbyi* E. G. Baker
This showy, spreading shrub grows to 5 m tall, with leaves 25 cm long and 2–3 cm wide. The slightly silky flowers are in spikes 7–8 cm wide, while the fruiting follicles are small, surrounded by the persistent old styles. It grows on sandheaths from Coorow to Shark Bay, and from Carnarvon to North West Cape, this being the only *Banksia* in the North-West.
Family: Proteaceae

Spiked Dampiera † *Dampiera spicigera* Benth.
This tomentose perennial herb, up to 50 cm tall, has oblong-cuneate leaves 2–4 cm long (often dentate) and flowers 12–14 mm long on leafless scapes. It extends from Perth to the Murchison River, and E to Southern Cross. Family: Goodeniaceae

317 Spiked Dampiera (Sept–Dec)

Plume Smokebush † *Conospermum incurvum* Lindl.
A slender shrub less than 1 m high, this has linear, incurved leaves 2–4 cm long crowded on the lower branches, while the flowers, 7–8 mm long, are in long, leafless panicles. It grows in deep sand in woodlands and on heaths between Perth and Geraldton. Family: Proteaceae

318 Plume Smokebush (Sept–Oct)

Irwin Lechenaultia † *Lechenaultia longiloba* F. Muell.
This perennial herb has many stems 5–10 cm tall arising from underground stems. The linear leaves are 1–2 cm long and the flowers, on ovaries 15 mm long, are 3 cm long with narrowly-winged lobes 15–20 mm long. It grows in sand on open heaths between the Irwin and Greenough Rivers.
Family: Goodeniaceae

319 Irwin Lechenaultia (Sept–Dec)

320 Superb Starflower (Dec–Jan)

Superb Starflower † *Calytrix superba* Gardn. & George
A many-stemmed or slender shrub 20–40 cm tall, this has the largest flowers of any *Calytrix*, the petals being 15–20 mm long. The calyx-tube is 11–14 mm long and the lobes 11–15 mm, with 2 bracteoles 10–12 mm. The oblong leaves are 4–8 mm long. It grows on open sandheath near Eneabba. Family: Myrtaceae

321 Murchison Darwinia (Sept–Dec)

Murchison Darwinia † *Darwinia virescens* (Meisn.) Benth.
This shrub has erect leafy stems and arching or prostrate flowering stems, the heads being 2.5–4 cm across and the styles 2 cm long. The linear-terete leaves are 5–10 mm long. The inflorescence bracts are lanceolate and not enlarged. It grows on sandheaths along the lower Murchison River.
Family: Myrtaceae

322 Hill River Lambstail (Oct–Jan)

323 Red Pokers (July–Oct)

324 Woolly Featherflower (Nov–Dec)

Hill River Lambstail † *Physopsis spicata* Turcz.
Physopsis is a genus of 2 species in south-western Australia. This species is an open, woolly shrub to 70 cm with obtuse lanceolate leaves 10–15 mm long and flower spikes 2 cm across. It grows on sandheaths between the Moore River and Eneabba, with outliers near York. Family: Verbenaceae

Shirt Orchid † *Thelymitra campanulata* Lindl.
A smooth, slender plant to 30 cm tall with a narrow leaf, this sun orchid has flowers 1 cm long. Growing in sand on open heaths in near-coastal areas, it extends from the Murchison River to Israelite Bay. Family: Orchidaceae

325 Shirt Orchid (Aug–Sept)

Red Pokers † *Hakea bucculenta* C. A. Gardn.
Allied to *Hakea multilineata* Meisn., this erect shrub to 7 m tall has linear, 1-nerved leaves 10–20 cm long and flower racemes 6–10 cm long. The woody fruit is 2 cm long, swollen at the base, with a thick beak. It grows in sand among tall scrub between Mingenew and Shark Bay. Family: Proteaceae

Woolly Featherflower † *Verticordia monadelpha* Turcz.
This dense, rounded shrub grows to 1 m tall with linear-triquetrous leaves 10–15 mm long and woolly flowers 10–15 mm across. It is common in deep sand on heaths from Wickepin to the Murchison River. Family: Myrtaceae

326 Freckled Sun Orchid (Oct–Nov)

328 Parakeelya (Aug–Oct)

Parakeelya † *Calandrinia polyandra* (Hook.) Benth.
An ephemeral with 1 to many ascending stems and succulent linear-oblong leaves to 4 cm long, this herb has racemes of flowers each 15–20 mm across which open for 1 day only. It is widespread in WA from the north-west coast southwards, and east to the Nullarbor Plain and SA.
Family: Portulacaceae

Freckled Sun Orchid † *Thelymitra sargentii* Rogers
This slender or robust sun orchid to 80 cm tall has a lanceolate leaf, and sweetly-scented flowers 2–3.5 cm across. The column has 2 rounded apical lobes. It occurs on sandheaths and near granite outcrops from the Murchison River to Hyden.

Arrowsmith Spider Orchid † *Caladenia crebra* A. S. George
Only recently discovered, this hirsute orchid has a linear leaf 20 cm long and a single flower on a stem to 45 cm tall. The sepals and petals are 25–45 mm long, and the lip, 10–12 mm wide, has a dense band of narrow calli. It grows in sand on limestone hills S of Dongara.
Family: Orchidaceae

Summer Dampiera † *Dampiera carinata* Benth.
This perennial herb has several leafless stems to 20 cm tall with a basal rosette of thick, linear leaves 3–5 cm long. The corolla is 7–10 mm long, and the ovary has a broad wing on one side. It grows in deep sand on heaths between the Moore River and Eneabba.
Family: Goodeniaceae

327 Arrowsmith Spider Orchid (Aug–Sept)

329 Summer Dampiera (Dec–Mar)

330 Wheatbelt near Brookton with featherflowers and Orange Grevillea on heath, and Salmon Gum woodland beyond.

WHEATBELT

The wheatbelt, comprising the major farming districts of the South-West is now largely cleared. Only in a few reserves, rocky hilltops, road verges and uncleared areas on farms can the original vegetation be seen. The whole area is a mosaic of plant habitats ranging from dense thickets on hilltops, savannah woodland and sandplain to extensive salt lakes. The dominant woodland trees are Wandoo, York Gum and Salmon Gum. Scattered areas of gravelly or sandy heath occur throughout the region. It is these areas, very rich in species, which produce spectacular spring wildflower displays.

Broom Honeymyrtle *Melaleuca uncinata* R. Br.

This is one of the most common shrubs among tall scrub and woodlands of the wheatbelt and heaths of the South-West. Easily recognised by the hooked tips of the terete leaves, it has flower heads 1.5 cm across, followed by small clustered woody fruit. It is also in SA, NSW and Vic.
Family: Myrtaceae

332 Broom Honeymyrtle (Sept–Nov)

Painted Featherflower † *Verticordia picta* Endl.

Verticordia is an Australian genus of over 50 species, one widespread in the north, one in SA and the others endemic in the South-West and southern Eremean Provinces of WA. The flowers have an intricate floral beauty due largely to the calyx-lobes which are elaborately divided and give the flowers their fluffy appearance. In most species they are brightly coloured and produced in masses, providing great splashes of colour especially on sand plains in spring and early summer. One of the few featherflowers in which the petals are more prominent than the much-divided calyx-lobes, this species is widespread on sandheaths from the Murchison River to Lake King. It is a shrub 50–100 cm tall with leaves 4–9 mm long and flowers 1 cm across.
Family: Myrtaceae

331 Painted Featherflower (Sept–Oct)

333 Pink Spike Hakea (July–Sept)

Pink Spike Hakea † *Hakea coriacea* Maconochie

Closely allied to *Hakea multilineata,* this species is distinguished by the longer flower spikes (8–12 cm) and the fruit which has no dorsal groove. A shrub or tree to 7 m, it is common in gravelly soils between Mullewa and Southern Cross. The flowers vary from deep red with cream styles to deep pink throughout.
Family: Proteaceae

334 Glowing Wattle (July–Aug)

Glowing Wattle † *Acacia celastrifolia* Benth.
This wattle has heads of few flowers which have many stamens and so have the typical wattle aspect. A quick-growing glaucous shrub to 3 m, it has phyllodes 4–6 cm long and is common, especially on roadsides and burnt areas, between Mogumber and Katanning. Family: Mimosaceae

Cricket Ball Hakea † *Hakea platysperma* Hook.
The fruits of this species, 4–6 cm across, are the largest of any *Hakea*. It is a shrub to 4 m tall with thick, needle-like leaves and sweetly-scented flowers, and grows on sandy-gravelly heaths between Coorow and Hyden. Family: Proteaceae

336 Cricket Ball Hakea (Aug–Sept)

Shaggy Dryandra † *Dryandra speciosa* Meisn.
One of the few species with linear, entire leaves, this *Dryandra* is a shrub to 1.5 m with pendulous flower heads 4–5 cm long. It grows in gravelly heaths near Tammin and on lateritic hills between Badgingarra and Eneabba. Family: Proteaceae

337 Shaggy Dryandra (Aug–Sept)

335 Common Cauliflower (Nov–Dec)

Common Cauliflower † *Verticordia brownii* (Desf.) DC.
Although the flowers are small (3–4 mm across), their massed production over the shrubs makes this a prominent species on sandheaths in late spring. Annual growth is even over the bush, giving it a layered aspect inside. It ranges from Mingenew to Lake King, and a pink-flowered variant occurs near the coast east of Esperance. Family: Myrtaceae

338 Common Firebush (Sept–Nov)

Common Firebush † *Keraudrenia integrifolia* Steud.
This tomentose shrub of 1–2 m is common after fires and in disturbed areas in the wheatbelt and northern heaths. It also occurs in the pastoral districts and the desert. The flat, oblong leaves are 1–3 cm long, and the flowers 1 cm across, without petals. Family: Sterculiaceae

339 Yellow Dampiera (Oct–Nov)

Yellow Dampiera † *Dampiera luteiflora* F. Muell.
Few *Dampieras* are yellow-flowered. This tomentose perennial herb to 50 cm tall has elliptic leaves 2–4 cm long and terminal panicles of flowers, each 10–15 mm long. It grows in gravelly sand on heaths from Wongan Hills to Coolgardie. Family: Goodeniaceae

Bottlebrush Grevillea † *Grevillea paradoxa* F. Muell.
A prickly shrub to 2 m with spreading branches, this species has flower racemes 4–6 cm long, the axis being very woolly. The exserted styles are 15–18 mm long. It grows on heaths between Mullewa and Hyden. Family: Proteaceae

340 Bottlebrush Grevillea (Aug–Oct)

Crinkle-leaved Firebush † *Keraudrenia hermanniaefolia* J. Gay
Of lower and more spreading habit than Common Firebush, this species has oblong, undulate leaves 5–10 mm long, or longer in northern plants. It ranges from Shark Bay to Wongan Hills, growing on sandy or gravelly heaths. *Keraudrenia* is a genus with 7 species in WA and across northern Australia, as well as 1 species in Malagasy. Family: Sterculiaceae

341 Crinkle-leaved Firebush (Sept–Oct)

342 Native Foxglove (Sept–Nov)

344 Sandplain Woody Pear (Dec–Jan)

Sandplain Woody Pear † *Xylomelum angustifolium* Kippist.
Common on deep sands of heaths between the Murchison River and Corrigin, this is a small tree to 7 m tall with broadly linear leaves 8–15 cm long. The cream flowers, in panicles of dense racemes, appear in summer, while the fruit are 5–7 cm long and persist unopened until a fire occurs. Family: Proteaceae

Native Foxglove † *Pityrodia terminalis* (Endl.) A. S. George
This attractive, grey-felted perennial herb 1 m tall has opposite, obovate-elliptic leaves 2–3 cm long and racemes of flowers, each 15–20 mm long. It grows on heaths between Mullewa and Lake King, the southern populations mostly having white flowers. Family: Verbenaceae

Dwarf Blackboy † *Xanthorrhoea nana* Herbert
One of 7 *Xanthorrhoea* species in WA, this uncommon plant is found between Northam and Bruce Rock. The caudex is very short and the scapes less than 1 m tall, always bent to one side. Family: Xanthorrhoeaceae

Red Billardiera † *Billardiera erubescens* (Putterl.) Bennett
Relatively few climbers occur in WA. This species has broadly-lanceolate leaves 2–7 cm long and flowers 2–2.5 cm long. It extends from Mingenew to the Stirling Range and E to Southern Cross. Family: Pittosporaceae

343 Dwarf Blackboy (Sept)

345 Red Billardiera (Aug–Nov)

King Dryandra † *Dryandra proteoides* Lindl.
This has the largest heads of any *Dryandra*, 8–9 cm long. They are borne on the older stems within a shrub 1–2 m tall, the prickly-lobed leaves being 10–20 cm long. It grows on lateritic ridges between Northam and Narrogin. Family: Proteaceae

347 King Dryandra (Aug–Sept)

Rusty Lambstail † *Lachnostachys ferruginea* Hook.
Densely woolly on all parts, the lambstails have panicles or dense spikes of flowers, each mauve or black flower almost hidden in the wool. There are 8 species, all endemic in southern WA. This species, a shrub to 1 m, extends from the Murchison River to Lake Grace. The hairs are usually rust-coloured. Family: Verbenaceae

346 Rusty Lambstail (Sept–Oct)

348 Mop Bushpea (Sept–Nov)

Mop Bushpea † *Phyllota dasyphylla* Turcz.
A sprawling shrub to 30 cm tall, this pea has lanceolate leaves 6–10 mm long and condensed flower racemes 4 cm across. It grows on sandheaths from the Murchison River to Hyden, northern plants being more erect and very hirsute. Family: Papilionaceae

349 A Wehlia (Oct–Nov)

A Wehlia † *Wehlia coarctata* F. Muell.
A genus of 7 species, all endemic in WA, *Wehlia* is characterised by a 1-celled ovary, a broad calyx with obtuse lobes, and numerous stamens. This species, a small shrub with leaves 3–4 mm long and flowers 1 cm across, inhabits sandheaths between Morawa and Bencubbin. Family: Myrtaceae

350 Large-flowered Baeckea (Sept–Oct)

Large-flowered Baeckea † *Baeckea grandiflora* Benth.
Baeckea is a genus of over 70 species extending from China to Australia, with about 50 species in the South-West. They are difficult to identify, most having small ericoid leaves and small pink flowers. This species has flowers 10–15 mm across, and over 20 stamens with incurved anthers. It is common on heaths from the Murchison River to Hyden. Family: Myrtaceae

Broom Milkwort *Comesperma scoparium* Steetz.
This leafless perennial herb to 70 cm tall has flowers 7–8 mm across. It is widespread from the Murchison River to Gnowangerup and E to Kalgoorlie, and is also in SA, Vic and NSW. Family: Polygalaceae

351 Yellow Star-bush (Aug–Oct)

352 Broom Milkwort (June–Aug)

Yellow Starbush † *Urocarpus squamuligerus* (Hook.) Wilson
Urocarpus is a WA genus of 5 species with white, pink or yellow flowers. This species is a stellate-tomentose shrub to 50 cm with elliptic-obovate leaves 1–3 cm long and flowers 10–14 mm across. It grows in gravelly clay of woodlands between Brookton and Lake Grace, and in jarrah forest of the extreme South-West. Family: Rutaceae

353 Large Myrtle (Nov–Mar)

Large Myrtle † *Hypocalymma puniceum* C. A. Gardn.
A much-branched, spreading shrub to 80 cm tall with leaves 10–15 mm long, this has the largest flowers of the genus, 15–20 mm across. It grows on sandy or gravelly heaths between Wongan Hills and Lake Grace. Family: Myrtaceae

Slender Phebalium † *Phebalium filifolium* Turcz.
Phebalium is an Australian genus of 44 species, of which 11 are endemic in WA. Many species are covered with small silvery scales, including Slender Phebalium. This shrub up to 1.3 m tall has leaves 10–15 mm long, channelled above, and flowers 7–10 mm across. It ranges from Wongan Hills to Lake King and E to Kalgoorlie. Family: Rutaceae

Prickly Poison † *Gastrolobium spinosum* Benth.
Widespread from the Murchison River to Esperance, especially on gravelly soils and sandheaths, this variable species is a shrub to 3 m tall. The typical variety, shown here, has leaves 2–4 cm long and flowers 1 cm across. Other varieties have the leaves narrower or without spiny lobes. Family: Papilionaceae

355 Slender Phebalium (Aug–Sept)

354 Prickly Poison (Sept–Oct)

356 Blue-eyed Smokebush (Sept–Nov)

357 Phalanx Grevillea (Sept–Nov)

Blue-eyed Smokebush † *Conospermum brownii* Meisn.
One of the smokebushes with glabrous flowers, this small shrub has leafy stems 10–30 cm tall and panicles of flowers on leafless scapes 20–30 cm tall. The buds are blue and the flowers white. The oblanceolate leaves are 3–6 cm long. It grows on sandy or gravelly heaths between Wubin and Lake King and E beyond Southern Cross. Family: Proteaceae

Phalanx Grevillea † *Grevillea dryandroides* C. A. Gardn.
An uncommon species found on sandheaths near Wongan Hills, this prostrate shrub has pinnate leaves 10–15 cm long with linear lobes 10–15 mm long. The flowers are 8–10 mm long with styles 18–20 mm. Family: Proteaceae

358 Mottlecah (Sept–Nov)

Mottlecah † *Eucalyptus macrocarpa* Hook.
Largest-flowered of the Eucalypts, this glaucous, often straggling mallee has broad sessile leaves, and solitary flowers 6–8 cm across, usually bright red. The fruits are 5–7 cm across. It grows on sandheaths between the Hill River, Wongan Hills and Corrigin. Family: Myrtaceae

Flame Grevillea † *Grevillea eriostachya* Lindl.
Common on heaths in the E and SE wheatbelt, this is a pine-like shrub to 6 m tall. The branches are usually leafy up to the flowers which are somewhat sticky. The leaves, 15–20 cm long, are divided into linear lobes. Family: Proteaceae

359 Wreath Lechenaultia (Sept–Nov)

361 Flame Grevillea (Sept–Nov)

360 Rose Darwinia (Oct–Dec)

Wreath Lechenaultia † *Lechenaultia macrantha* Krause
Growing annually from a perennial stock to a diameter of 50 cm, this spectacular plant is found between Wubin and Mullewa. The linear leaves are up to 3.5 cm long and the corollas 3–4 cm long with broad wings, larger than any other species. Family: Goodeniaceae

Rose Darwinia † *Darwinia purpurea* (Endl.) Benth.
One of the *Darwinias* with broad flower heads surrounded by short bracts, this is a much-branched shrub to 70 cm with oblong leaves 2–4 mm long and heads 1.5 cm across. It grows on sandheaths and near granite outcrops between Mullewa and Merredin. Family: Myrtaceae

Drummond's Gum † *Eucalyptus drummondii* Benth.
Usually a mallee but sometimes a white-barked tree to 8 m, this gum has smooth buds 10–14 mm long and top-shaped fruit with a wide rim. It grows in lateritic soil on heath or in woodland, between Eneabba and Narrogin.
Family: Myrtaceae

363 Drummond's Gum (Oct–Dec)

A Petrophile † *Petrophile trifida* R. Br.
This is a shrub to 50 cm tall, often rather tangled due to the much-divided leaves which are 10–20 cm long including the long petioles. The flowers are 10–12 mm long. It grows on sandheaths between Wagin and Lake King.
Family: Proteaceae

362 A Petrophile (Sept–Oct)

364 Red Bonnets (Sept–Oct)

365 Yellow Logania (Sept–Nov)

Red Bonnets † *Burtonia hendersoni* (Paxt.) Benth.
The only red-flowered *Burtonia*, this shrub of 70–100 cm has leaves divided into 3 leaflets 2–5 mm long, linear with hooked apices. The flowers are 13–16 mm wide. It grows on sandy or gravelly heaths from Merredin to Southern Cross and SE beyond Hyden.
Family: Papilionaceae

Yellow Logania † *Logania flaviflora* F. Muell.
Logania is a southern Australian genus of about 22 species, 14 of them in WA. This species is a small perennial herb with acute, linear leaves 5–10 mm long and flowers 1 cm across, sometimes pale yellow. It grows on sandheaths from the Murchison River to Lake King.
Family: Loganiaceae

366 Star-leaf Grevillea (June–Sept)

Star-leaf Grevillea † *Grevillea asteriscosa* Diels
This is a shrub to 3 m tall found near granite outcrops or in gravelly soil on heath. The pungently-lobed leaves are 6–10 mm across and the flowers 8–10 mm long with styles 18–22 mm long. It occurs between Kulin and Bruce Rock.
Family: Proteaceae

Tinsel Flower † *Cyanostegia corifolia* Munir.
Cyanostegia is a genus of 5 species, 4 endemic to WA. They are viscid shrubs up to 1.5 m tall, and the purple calyx is the most conspicuous part of the flower. This species has leaves 2–4 cm long and flowers 1–2 cm across. It inhabits sandy or gravelly heaths between Eneabba and Lake King.
Family: Verbenaceae

367 A Petrophile. (Aug–Oct)

369 Tinsel Flower (Sept–Nov)

368 Cluster Boronia (Aug–Nov)

A Petrophile † *Petrophile divaricata* R. Br.
Very prickly from the much-divided leaves 4–8 cm long, this shrub of 1.5 m has flowers 13–18 mm long. It prefers gravelly soil of woodlands and heath from Moora to the Stirling Range and E to Bruce Rock and Esperance. Family: Proteaceae

Cluster Boronia † *Boronia capitata* Benth.
This variable species is typically a pubescent shrub (shown here) to 70 cm with flowers 10–12 mm across, known only from sandheath near Pingelly. Between Corrigin and Nyabing occurs the subsp. *clavata* which is almost glabrous with thicker, clavate leaves, while the subsp. *gracilis* is a slender, glabrous variant from Busselton. Family: Rutaceae

370 Rapier Featherflower (Oct–Dec)

Rapier Featherflower † *Verticordia mitchelliana* C. A. Gardn.
Almost hiding its vivid flowers under the spreading branches, this shrub up to 1 m tall has linear leaves 10–15 mm long and pendulous woolly flowers with remarkable styles 3 cm long. It grows on sandheaths between Dowerin and the Johnston Lakes. Family: Myrtaceae

372 Pink Pokers (Aug–Nov)

Pink Pokers † *Grevillea petrophiloides* Meisn.
This is a shrub to 3 m tall, the lower stems with leaves 8–12 cm long divided into terete, pungent, erect segments, and the flowers on long leafless branches. The small fruit is viscid, with pit-like glands. It grows in gravel or sand among tall scrub between the Murchison River and Merredin. Family: Proteaceae

371 Golden Dryandra (July–Oct)

Golden Dryandra † *Dryandra nobilis* Lindl.
Occurring in gravelly soils of woodlands between Moora and Katanning, this is a much-branched shrub to 4 m tall. The flowers, in heads 5–7 cm across with styles 5 cm long, are borne on densely leafy branches. Family: Proteaceae

373 A Honeymyrtle (Sept–Nov)

A Honeymyrtle † *Melaleuca conothamnoides* C. A. Gardn.
A rather open shrub 1–2 m tall, this has narrow-elliptic leaves 2–4 cm long and flower heads 2 cm across. It is found on sand-heath from Mullewa to Southern Cross. Family: Myrtaceae

374 Yellow Salt-star (Sept–Oct)

Yellow Salt Star † *Gunniopsis intermedia* Diels
This spreading herb has succulent leaves 1–3 cm long and flowers 10–14 mm across, without petals. It grows around salt lakes from Northam east to the goldfields.
Family: Aizoaceae

Dragon Orchid † *Caladenia barbarossa* Reichb. f.
Found in jam, wandoo and granitic country, this unusual spider orchid has a recurved, densely hairy lip with a single large basal callus. The sepals are 18–22 mm long, and the ovate-oblong leaf 2–8 cm. Family: Orchidaceae

375 Coorup (Sept-Nov)

376 Pritzel's Featherflower (Nov–Dec)

377 Dragon Orchid (Sept–Oct)

Coorup † *Billardiera lehmanniana* F. Muell.
A much-branched twiner which may form a shrub, this has linear to narrow-lanceolate leaves 1–3 cm long and flowers 1 cm across. It grows in sand, often near streams or salt lakes, from Kellerberrin to Cranbrook and E to Esperance.
Family: Pittosporaceae

Pritzel's Featherflower † *Verticordia pritzelii* Diels
Named after a German botanist who visited WA in 1900–01, this is a small shrub with linear-terete leaves 1 cm long and flowers 7–10 cm across. It grows on sandheaths between Wongan Hills and Hyden. Family: Myrtaceae

Scarlet Honeymyrtle † *Melaleuca fulgens* R. Br.
A shrub of 1–2 m, this variable species has linear to lanceolate leaves 1–2 cm long and flowers with staminal clusters 15–20 mm long. The round woody fruits are 8–11 mm across. Ranging from Mullewa to Esperance, it grows in gravelly or granitic soil among scrub. Family: Myrtaceae

379 Scarlet Honeymyrtle (Sept–Nov)

Ant Orchid † *Caladenia roei* Benth.
The common name refers to the shiny black calli on the lip which is unfringed and unveined, 11–13 mm wide. It grows in jam and wandoo country from the Murchison River to Esperance and inland almost to Coolgardie. Northern specimens have few calli on the lip. Family: Orchidaceae

378 Ant Orchid (Aug–Sept)

380 Sandalwood (Fls. Mar–May)

381 Purple Mirbelia (Aug–Sept)

Sandalwood *Santalum spicatum* (R. Br.) DC.
Once extensively cut and exported to Asia for its aromatic timber, this tall, semi-parasitic shrub is widespread in inland regions. The scented flowers, 3 mm across, are followed by spherical fruit, the smooth nuts being 15–20 mm wide. Also in SA. Family: Santalaceae

Purple Mirbelia † *Mirbelia floribunda* Benth.
The only purple-flowered species of an Australian genus of 25 species, this is a much branched shrub to 30 cm with linear, uncinate leaves 3–7 mm long in whorls of 3. The flowers, 1 cm across, turn blue with age. It grows on heaths and in woodlands between Eneabba, Perth and Lake King.
Family: Papilionaceae

382 Winter Spider Orchid (June–July)

Winter Spider Orchid † *Caladenia drummondii* Benth.
First collected in the 1840s and not seen again for over 100 years, this is now known to range from Morawa to Kondinin, growing under shrubs in woodlands. The leaf is 1–4 cm long, dark red below, and the sepals are 20–25 mm long.
Family: Orchidaceae

Pimpernel Sundew † *Drosera glanduligera* Lehm.
The bright leaves of this sundew form loose rosettes up to 3 cm across. The inflorescence, up to 10 cm high, has 15–20 flowers, bright orange at first, fading to pink. It is widespread in southern mainland Australia.
Family: Droseraceae

384 Pimpernel Sundew (Sept–Oct)

Bee Orchid † *Diuris laxiflora* Lindl.
Smallest-flowered of the Donkey Orchids in WA, this slender species has narrow, straight leaves, and flowers 15–20 mm across. It inhabits winter-wet areas of swamps and granite outcrops from the Murchison River to Esperance.
Family: Orchidaceae

385 Bee Orchid (Aug–Oct)

383 Hidden Honeymyrtle (Sept–Nov)

Hidden Honeymyrtle † *Melaleuca undulata* Benth.
This spreading shrub of 1–2 m has narrow-cordate, pungent leaves 7–10 mm long, and flowers 1 cm long mostly on older stems within the shrub. It grows on rocky hills between Mingenew, Ongerup and Salmon Gums.
Family: Myrtaceae

A Petrophile † *Petrophile phylicoides* R. Br.
This species is unusual in having glabrous flowers which are 10–12 mm long and have pointed appendages on the perianth lobes. The fruiting bracts are hard and woody. It grows on sandheaths from Wickepin to the Stirling Range and E to Israelite Bay. Family: Proteaceae

387 A Petrophile (Oct–Nov)

A Pigmy Sundew † *Drosera leucoblasta* Benth.
The leaves of this sundew are only 2 mm diameter, the petioles being enveloped by elaborate white stipules which form a protective tuft around the young leaves. The flowers may be white, pink or orange, the last being the largest with petals up to 12 mm long. It grows on heaths in the central and southern wheatbelt. Family: Droseraceae

386 A Pygmy Sundew (Sept–Oct)

388 Upside-down Pea-bush (July–Sept)

389 Curved Mulla Mulla (Sept–Nov)

Upside-down Peabush † *Brachysema daviesioides* (Turcz.) Benth.
This curious little shrub has leafless, pungently-divided stems 10–20 cm tall with flowers, each 2–3 cm long, in basal racemes. It grows on sandheaths from Northampton to Lake Grace and E to the goldfields. Family: Papilionaceae

Curved Mulla Mulla † *Ptilotus declinatus* Nees
Inconspicuous until it flowers, this herb has a perennial stock from which short, prostrate, ephemeral stems arise. The leaves are linear, 1–2 cm long, and the curved flowers 15–25 mm long. It grows in clay, loam or sand of woodlands between Northampton and Katanning. Family: Amaranthaceae

390 Curly Grevillea (Sept–Nov)

392 Smooth Goodenia (Nov)

Smooth Goodenia † *Goodenia brevisepala* Carolin
This is a glabrous perennial herb with linear leaves 1–4 cm long and flowers 12–15 mm long in loose racemes. It is uncommon, being found between Wubin and Merredin. The widespread, related *G. caerulea* has glandular flowers with long calyx-lobes. Family: Goodeniaceae

Curly Grevillea † *Grevillea eryngioides* Benth.
This shrub of 1–2 m has deeply-lobed, glaucous leaves mostly on the lower stems, while the small flowers are on leafless stems. The fruit is flat and sticky. It grows on heaths from Wubin to Lake King. Family: Proteaceae

Downy Stackhousia † *Stackhousia pubescens* A. Rich.
Easily distinguished from other species by its pubescent stems, this perennial herb is widespread in the South-West. The linear leaves are 1–3 cm long and the flowers 7–10 mm, followed by small, nut-like pubescent fruit. Family: Stackhousiaceae

Black Toothbrushes † *Grevillea apiciloba* F. Muell.
Several *Grevilleas* have 'toothbrush' inflorescences with black styles. This is a shrub to 2 m with 3–5-lobed leaves 2–7 cm long, found on sandheaths between Merredin and Southern Cross. Family: Proteaceae

391 Downy Stackhousia (Aug–Oct)

393 Black Toothbrushes (Aug–Oct)

Prickly Toothbrushes † *Grevillea armigera* Meisn.
A much-branched shrub to 3 m, very prickly with the divided pungent leaves, this has dense racemes of flowers with styles 15–18 mm long. The fruit is a pubescent capsule. It inhabits sandheath between Wubin and Dowerin.
Family: Proteaceae

395 Prickly Toothbrushes (All year)

Dark Pea-bush † *Brachysema lanceolatum* Meisn.
A shrub or semi-climber to 1.3 m, often with several stems, this legume has leaves 3–7 cm long and flowers 2.5 cm long. It is common in sandy or gravelly soil in woodlands and in mallee, especially along creeks, extending from Wagin to Bremer Bay with a few localities farther north. Family: Papilionaceae

394 Dark Pea-bush (Aug–Oct)

396 Woolly-headed Dampiera (Oct–Nov)

397 Woolly-headed Dampiera

Woolly-headed Dampiera † *Dampiera eriocephala* De Vr.
Several *Dampieras* have dense racemes of flowers in leafless panicles. They are perennial herbs with ephemeral leaves and scapes. This species is distinguished by the felted undersurface of the obovate leaves which are up to 15 cm long. It grows in various habitats, especially burnt or disturbed areas, ranging from Morawa to the Stirling Range and E beyond Hyden.
Family: Goodeniaceae

398 Guinea-flower (Sept–Oct)

Guinea-flower † *Hibbertia glomerosa* (Benth.) F. Muell.
This is a shrub to 40 cm tall with broadly linear leaves 1–2 cm long, expanded at the bases. The flowers are 2 cm across with many stamens united into bundles, while the sepals are very hirsute. It extends from the Murchison River to Tammin on sandheaths. Family: Dilleniaceae

Mantis Orchid † *Caladenia integra* Coleman
This handsome spider orchid grows to 80 cm tall, with 1 or 2 flowers. The unfringed, delicately-balanced lip is 15–20 mm long. It is known from isolated localities between the Murchison River and Esperance. Family: Orchidaceae

399 Tangled Grevillea (Nov–Jan)

401 Mantis Orchid (Sept–Oct)

400 Native Pomegranate (Sept–Nov)

Tangled Grevillea † *Grevillea flexuosa* Lindl.
Long, much-divided leaves make this a tangled shrub to 30 cm tall x 70 cm broad. The racemose flowers are 3 mm long. It grows in gravelly woodlands between Brookton and Kojonup. Family: Proteaceae

Native Pomegranate † *Balaustion pulcherrimum* Hook.
The 2 species of *Balaustion* are endemic in the South-West. This is a small prostrate or ascending shrub with leaves 2–5 mm long and flowers 17–25 mm long. The ovary is at the base of the prominent tubular calyx. It grows on sandheaths between Perenjori and Hyden. Family: Myrtaceae

Long-leaved Wattle † *Acacia longiphyllodinea* Maiden
A rather open shrub of 2–4 m with glaucous branches and terete phyllodes up to 40 cm long, this has flower spikes 3–4 cm long. The pods are linear, up to 15 cm long, slightly constricted between the seeds. It grows in gravelly loam among shrubs between Wubin and Mullewa. The genus *Acacia* has over 800 species and occurs in most tropical and subtropical countries. There are over 600 species in Australia (300 in WA) where most species have phyllodes which are petioles modified to function as leaves. Wattles are found in all parts of the continent and often dominate the vegetation. Besides the aesthetic qualities, many species are useful for timber, bark and gum extracts, fodder, and pollen for honey production.
Family: Mimosaceae

403 Fringed Mantis Orchid (Aug–Oct)

402 Long-leaved Wattle (Aug–Sept)

Fringed Mantis Orchid † *Caladenia dilatata* R. Br. var. *falcata* Nicholls
Smaller than the Mantis Orchid (Pl. 401), this species has a fringed lip which is delicately balanced and trembles in the breeze. It is widespread in woodlands from Mullewa to Ravensthorpe. The typical variety has spreading, not upturned, lateral sepals and occurs only in eastern Australia. *Caladenia* is one of the largest orchid genera in Australia with over 70 species, 40 of them in the South-West. There are also a few species in Malaysia, New Zealand and the south-west Pacific islands. The name, from Greek words meaning beautiful glands, refers to the calli on the lip of all species. Family: Orchidaceae

404 Pear-fruited Mallee (Sept–Nov)

Pear-fruited Mallee † *Eucalyptus pyriformis* Turcz.
One of the largest-flowered Eucalypts, this spreading mallee of 2–4 m has pendulous, strongly-ribbed buds 4–5 cm long in threes on long peduncles. The flowers are red or yellow. It grows on sandheaths between Mingenew and Dowerin. The name *Eucalyptus*, from Greek words meaning well-covered, refers to the operculum which covers the stamens in the bud. The genus contains over 500 species in Australia, with a few species on islands to the north as far as the Philippines. In WA there are over 170 species found in most areas but chiefly in the South-West, goldfields and Kimberleys. Many are important for timber and honey production while others are aesthetically attractive. They are widely cultivated both in Australia and overseas. Family: Myrtaceae

405 Granite outcrop near Brookton with Gungurru (*Eucalyptus caesia* Benth.).

GRANITE OUTCROPS

Extensive areas of granitic or gneissic rocks, some reaching up to 30 m or more above the surrounding plain, are common in the South-West. Some are flat expanses, others are large dome-like masses. The outcrops are very weathered and plants can grow where soil has accumulated in shallow depressions, crevices and under ledges. Where the soil is deep, especially around the apron of large rocks, dense thickets of sheoak or wattle may occur. Numerous species of shrubs grow in the rock crevices and deeper soil pockets. Shallow, soil-filled depressions are covered by swards of many minute herbs, ferns, mosses and lichens. A few aquatic species occur in seasonal pools. Very wet in winter due to run-off from large rock surfaces, these outcrops become very dry and dormant in summer.

Eight Nancy † *Wurmbea tenella* (Endl.) Benth.
Wurmbea is a small genus of bulbous lilies in South Africa and WA. This species, only a few cm tall, is notable for the flowers, 10–15 mm across, having 8–10 perianth segments. It is found on granite outcrops and woodlands in the wheatbelt, and in sand near the west coast. Family: Liliaceae

407 Eight Nancy (July–Aug)

Large Blind Grass † *Stypandra grandiflora* Lindl.
Stypandra is an Australian genus of 6 species, 2 of them in the South-West. They are grass-like perennials with blue flowers. This species has broadly linear leaves and open panicles of flowers, each 15–18 mm across. It occurs on granitic or lateritic hills between Moora, Cape Leeuwin and Albany.
Family: Liliaceae

406 Large Blind Grass (Sept–Nov)

408 Mudmat (Aug–Oct)

409 Flannel Cudweed & Pygmy Daisy (Sept–Oct)

Mudmat *Glossostigma drummondii* Benth.
There are 5 species of *Glossostigma*, in Australia, India and New Zealand. They are small ephemerals in pools or on mud, with rosetted leaves and tiny flowers on long pedicels. This species is widespread, especially in pools on granite outcrops, and is also in SA, Vic and NSW. Family: Scrophulariaceae

Flannel Cudweed and Pygmy Daisy
Actinobole uliginosum (Gray) Eichler, &
Helipterum australe (Gray) Druce
Many small ephemeral herbs occur on granite outcrops. These two daisies are found in drier areas, between the Murchison River and Norseman. The grey-leaved plants are *Actinobole*. Both species occur also in SA, Vic and NSW.
Family: Asteraceae

410 Granite Kunzea (Sept–Nov)

Granite Kunzea † *Kunzea pulchella* (Lindl.) George
A long-lived, often gnarled shrub to 3 m, this has grey-green, silky, obovate leaves 1 cm long and flowers 2–2.5 cm long in short dense spikes. It grows only on granite outcrops, ranging from Paynes Find to Pingelly and E to Coolgardie. To the E and NE of Southern Cross the flowers are usually white.
Family: Myrtaceae

Granite slopes
Most granite outcrops are partly covered by moss beds which are very wet and green in winter but quite dry and dormant in summer. Besides mosses there are many species of lichens, small ephemeral and bulbous herbs and orchids, making a fascinating miniature flora. In this view, in the Porongurup Range, the trees on the skyline are Bullich, *Eucalyptus megacarpa,* and the white flowered shrubs are *Thryptomene saxicola.*

411 Pincushions (Aug–Oct)

412 Pincushions (Summer)

413 Granite slopes

Pincushions *Borya nitida* Labill.
This tough perennial herb grows in clumps on granite outcrops throughout the South-West, occasionally also on heaths. The crowded, linear, pungent leaves 2–3 cm long turn orange in late spring as the soil dries out and remain dormant until the autumn rains begin. The flowers are in heads 1 cm across, subtended by pungent bracts. It occurs also in the Grampians in Victoria. There are only 2 other species of *Borya*, one in the Kimberleys of WA and one in NE Qld. Family: Xanthorrhoeaceae

Flannelflower † *Actinotus leucocephalus* Benth.

There are 16 species of *Actinotus* in Australia (5 in the South-West) and 1 in New Zealand. This soft, woolly ephemeral species has deeply divided leaves 2–5 cm long and inflorescences 3–5 cm across with many small flowers surrounded by large bracts. Appearing prolifically after fires, it grows near granite outcrops and on heath from the Murchison River to the Stirling Range.

Family: Apiaceae

414 Flannelflower (Oct–Dec)

416 Butterfly Flowers (Sept–Oct)

Butterfly Flowers † *Philydrella pygmaea* (F. Muell.) Caruel

A genus of 1 species endemic in the South-West, this slender herb to 15 cm high has a few linear leaves and flowers of 2 petals 15–18 mm wide. There is 1 stamen and 2 staminodia. It grows on granite outcrops and in winter-wet swamps, especially near the coast, ranging from Mingenew to Esperance.

Family: Philydraceae

Sea Urchin Hakea † *Hakea petiolaris* Meisn.

This robust shrub to 6 m tall has broadly lanceolate-ovate pointed leaves 6–12 cm long and flowers in dense racemes 3.5–5 cm across on the older stems. The fruit is 2.5–3 cm long. It grows on granite outcrops between Wongan Hills, Perth and Hyden.

Family: Proteaceae

415 Wongan Featherflower (Aug)

417 Sea Urchin Hakea (May–July)

Wongan Featherflower † *Verticordia staminosa* Gardn. & George

One of the few winter-flowering species, this spreading shrub has setose branches, and flowers 1 cm across, the brown bracts persistent. It is known from granite outcrops near Wongan Hills and Hyden.

Family: Myrtaceae

418 Mouse Ears (Aug–Oct)

Mouse Ears † *Calothamnus rupestris* Schau.
Restricted to granite outcrops on the Darling Scarp E of Perth, this spreading shrub of 1–2 m has pungent leaves 15–25 mm long and flowers 3–4 cm long with 4 bundles of stamens. The fruit, 15–20 mm long, has persistent, woody, apical lobes.
Family: Myrtaceae

Elbow Orchid † *Spiculaea ciliata* Lindl.
Having stored nutrients in its stem, this orchid dies at the base as flowering begins but completes its development right through to seed maturity. The flowers, 15–18 mm across, have a club-like lip which is hinged but not sensitive. It grows on open soil pockets of granite outcrops from the Darling Scarp E to Coolgardie and Ravensthorpe.

419 A Featherflower (Sept–Dec)

420 Granite Bottlebrush (Sept–Oct)

421 Elbow Orchid (Nov–Dec)

Featherflower † *Verticordia plumosa* (Desf.) Druce
The first *Verticordia* to be described, this variable species is a small shrub with shortly fringed calyx-lobes. This variant, found on granite outcrops from Perth to the south coast, has crowded linear leaves 1 cm long and flowers 5–7 mm across.
Family: Myrtaceae

Granite Bottlebrush † *Melaleuca elliptica* Labill.
This is a much-branched shrub 1–4 m high and wide with opposite elliptic leaves 5–15 mm long, and flowers 2–3 cm long in dense spikes on the older stems. It is common on granite outcrops from Ongerup to Israelite Bay and inland to Coolgardie.
Family: Myrtaceae

Variegated Featherflower † *Verticordia huegelii* Endl.
This very spreading shrub to 50 cm tall has linear-terete leaves 3–6 mm long and flowers 12–15 mm across which open white or cream and turn red. It occurs in granitic soil between Badgingarra and Kojonup, being common in the hills E of Perth.
Family: Myrtaceae

Circus Triggerplant † *Stylidium bulbiferum* Benth.
The stems of this small perennial are held aloft by thin prop-roots. There are tufts of short linear leaves at the nodes from which glandular scapes arise bearing a few pink, red or white flowers 8–10 mm across. It grows on granite outcrops, on heath and in woodlands from Geraldton to Hopetoun.
Family: Stylidiaceae

423 Variegated Featherflower (Oct–Nov)

422 Circus Triggerplant (Sept–Nov)

424 Graceful Honeymyrtle (Sept–Nov)

425 Baxter's Kunzea (Sept–Oct)

Graceful Honeymyrtle † *Melaleuca radula* Lindl.
An erect shrub to 1.5 m, this has opposite leaves 2–4 cm long and flowers also in opposite pairs, each 1 cm long with persistent petals and a broad stigma. It grows on granite outcrops and gravelly heath, extending from the Murchison River to Perth and E to Southern Cross. Family: Myrtaceae

Baxter's Kunzea † *Kunzea baxteri* (Klotzsch) Schau.
Named after William Baxter who collected along the south coast in the 1820s, this bushy shrub of 1–2 m has white-edged oblong leaves 10–15 mm long and flowers 2.5 cm long in dense spikes. It inhabits granite outcrops from Esperance to Israelite Bay. Family: Myrtaceae

426 Salmon Gum woodland (*Eucalyptus salmonophloia* F. Muell.) with an understorey of mixed shrubs.

TRANSITIONAL WOODLAND

A low and unreliable rainfall delimits the eastern edge of the wheatbelt. Beyond this is an extensive area of different soil types which support varied types of vegetation. In the region there is a marked transition from the plant families typical of the South-West to those characteristic of the arid interior. Large areas of loamy soils support a woodland of trees with an undergrowth of shrubs, especially in the eastern part of the region including the goldfields. In northern areas there are tall thickets in which wattles and sheoaks are prominent. Extensive areas, particularly in the southern part are covered by mallees.

Slender Fuchsia *Eremophila decipiens* (R. Br.) Ostf.
This much-branched, often viscid, shrub to 1 m tall has linear to lanceolate leaves 2–3.5 cm long, and flowers 2–2.5 cm long on slender curved pedicels. It extends from the Murchison River SE to Ravensthorpe and E to Laverton and the Nullarbor Plain, and is also in SA. Family: Myoporaceae

Ninghan Grevillea † *Grevillea ninghanensis* C. A. Gardn.
Named after a pastoral property south of Mt. Magnet, this open shrub to 1 m tall has pungent leaves 15–25 mm long and flowers 10–12 mm long with styles 20 mm. It grows in red loam among wattle scrub, ranging from Mt. Magnet to Laverton and south towards Southern Cross. Family: Proteaceae

427 Ninghan Grevillea (July–Sept)

Tan Wattle † *Acacia hemiteles* Benth.
Very common in loamy woodlands between Wubin and Norseman, this grey-green shrub 1–2 m tall has angular stems with phyllodes 3–10 cm long. The flowers, in racemose heads, are followed by flat, curved pods 3–5 cm long. Family: Mimosaceae

Fuchsia Gum † *Eucalyptus forrestiana* Diels subsp. *dolichorrhyncha* Brooker
A slender tree to 6 m tall, this attractive gum has solitary flowers with buds 5 cm long, the beaked cap being 2 cm long. It grows in dense mallee country between Salmon Gums and Gibson, N of Esperance. The typical form has a short, blunt operculum and occurs farther west and east. Family: Myrtaceae

428 Slender Fuchsia (Aug–Oct)

429 Tan Wattle (Sept)

430 Fuchsia Gum (Dec–Mar)

431 Red Velvet (Sept–Oct)

Red Velvet † *Hemiphora elderi* F. Muell.
Hemiphora is a monotypic genus differing from *Pityrodia* in having unappendaged anthers, and from *Chloanthes* in having only 2 fertile stamens. It is a woolly shrub to 70 cm tall with crinkly leaves 1–2 cm long and flowers 2 cm long. Rarely, yellow forms occur. It grows in sand in shrublands between Bonnie Rock and Kalgoorlie and N to Sandstone.
Family: Verbenaceae

Knobby Hibiscus *Hibiscus farragei* F. Muell.
This velvety shrub grows to 3 m tall, with long-stalked leaves 5–10 cm across. The flowers, in panicles, are 5 cm across, the calyx-lobes and bracteoles having thickened apices. It grows in granite or loamy soil, especially in open areas, extending from Morawa to Southern Cross and E to the Nullarbor, and is also in NT.
Family: Malvaceae

432 Yilgarn Dryandra (May–Sept)

433 Crinkly Mintbush (Sept–Oct)

434 Knobby Hibiscus (Oct–Nov)

Yilgarn Dryandra † *Dryandra arborea* C. A. Gardn.
The most inland species of the genus, this is a small tree to 6 m tall with a thick, rough trunk. The rigid leaves are 3–5 cm long and the flower heads 4–5 cm across. It grows on ironstone hills N of Southern Cross.
Family: Proteaceae

Crinkly Mintbush † *Prostanthera eckersleyana* F. Muell.
Widespread in Australia outside the tropics, *Prostanthera* is a genus of over 60 species, about 15 of them in WA. This hirsute shrub, to 70 cm tall, has opposite, crinkly leaves 1 cm long and flowers 15–20 mm long with 2-lipped calyxes. It grows in loamy shrublands between Paynes Find, Wubin and Bonnie Rock.
Family: Lamiaceae

Bead Hopbush † *Dodonaea lobulata* F. Muell.
Dodoaea is a genus of over 60 species of tropical and subtropical countries, over 30 species being in WA. They are dioecious, the male flowers being small with exserted anthers and the females having a long style exserted from the small calyx. The fruit is more conspicuous; in this species it is 3-winged and 1–1.5 cm wide. The shrub grows to 2 m and has viscid leaves 2–3 cm long. It is common in loam and on rocky hills in the Kalgoorlie area.
Family: Sapindaceae

435 Bead Hopbush (Fr: Aug–Oct)

Wheel Grevillea † *Grevillea sarissa* S. Moore
This erect shrub up to 3 m tall has linear, pungent leaves 5–15 cm long. The flowers, sometimes tomentose, are 15–20 mm long with styles 20–25 mm, bent at the ovary. It occurs near salt lakes and on rocky hills between Wiluna and Kalgoorlie.
Family: Proteaceae

436 Wheel Grevillea (Sept–Oct)

437 Swordfish Banksia (Jan–Mar)

Swordfish Banksia † *Banksia elderana* F. Muell & Tate
Rigid leaves up to 35 cm long and 1.5 cm wide give this much-branched shrub (to 3 m tall) a harsh aspect. The pendulous flower spikes are 6 cm wide and the old flowers conceal the rounded, hirsute fruiting follicles. It grows on sandheaths between Lake King, Southern Cross and Coolgardie, with an outlier north of Zanthus. Family: Proteaceae

438 Spongefruit (Sept–Oct)

Spongefruit *Trachymene ornata* (Endl.) Druce
This is a small herb usually less than 20 cm tall with deeply-lobed leaves and umbels of small white flowers. The more conspicuous fruits are covered in dense wool, forming balls 5 mm across. It is found in various habitats between the Murchison River, Laverton and the south coast, and is also in SA.
Family: Apiaceae

Native Senna † *Cassia pleurocarpa* F. Muell. var. *angustifolia* Symon

This smooth shrub to 3 m tall has pinnate leaves with 8–9 pairs of leaflets 5–7 cm long. The flowers, covered in bud by broad bracts, are about 15 cm across, followed by flat oblong pods 6–8 cm long. It extends from Mullewa to Kalgoorlie and differs from the typical variety in the larger habit and longer, narrow leaflets. Family: Caesalpiniaceae

439 Native Senna (Sept–Nov)

441 Open Hemigenia (Aug–Oct)

Open Hemigenia † *Hemigenia westringioides* Benth.

Hemigenia is an Australian genus of about 40 species, mostly endemic in the SW. This species is an open shrub to 1 m tall with linear leaves 1–3 cm long and flowers 15 mm wide on slender pedicels. It grows in sand, loam or gravel in heaths and woodlands between Mullewa, Kalgoorlie and Hyden. Family: Lamiaceae

A Wattle † *Acacia resinomarginea* W. V. Fitzg.

This erect shrub to 4 m tall has phyllodes up to 15 cm long which are quadrangular in section with resinous margins. The flower spikes, 1 cm long, are followed by narrow pods 3–4 cm long. It grows in wattle thickets between Wubin, Laverton and Southern Cross. Family: Mimosaceae

442 A Wattle (Sept–Oct)

Goldfields Bottlebrush † *Melaleuca coccinea* A. S. George

Known from a few granite outcrops between Kalgoorlie and Zanthus, this recently-discovered species is a shrub to 2 m tall with opposite leaves 4–10 mm long and flower spikes 35–45 mm wide, the buds being covered by large bracts. Family: Myrtaceae

440 Goldfield's Bottlebrush (Oct–Nov)

443 Red Rod (Sept–Dec)

445 Bush Pomegranate (Aug–Sept)

Bush Pomegranate † *Balaustion microphyllum* C. A. Gardn.
This is a much-branched shrub up to 70 cm tall with crowded leaves 1–2 mm long and flowers 8–10 mm long. The calyces are densely glandular. It grows in sand among tall scrub E of Mullewa.
Family: Myrtaceae

Red Rod † *Eremophila calorhabdos* Diels
A slender, little-branched shrub to 2 m tall, this species has crowded ovate leaves 15–20 mm long and flowers 20–25 mm long. It grows in sand or loam in woodlands and near salt lakes between Norseman and Salmon Gums.
Family: Myoporaceae

Tangled Fanflower † *Scaevola oxyclona* F. Muell.
Growing on rocky hills between Norseman and the Fraser Range, this tangled shrub, up to 1.3 m tall, has pubescent, spinescent branches with sparse linear-obovate leaves 5–12 mm long and flowers 15–20 mm long.
Family: Goodeniaceae

444 Tangled Fanflower (Sept–Oct)

446 Coral Gum (Sept–Nov)

Coral Gum † *Eucalyptus torquata* Luehm.
Now widely cultivated, the Coral Gum is uncommon in the wild, growing in rocky loam on low hills between Kalgoorlie and Norseman. It is a much-branched tree to 15 m tall with rough dark bark on the trunk. The buds are 2–2.5 cm long, the cap being 1.5 cm, while the fruit are 12–15 mm long.
Family: Myrtaceae

447 Bladder Vetch (Sept–Oct)

Bladder Vetch *Swainsona colutoides* F. Muell.
The Australian genus *Swainsona* contains over 50 species, occurring mostly in the drier regions. They are herbs and are usually procumbent, but Bladder Vetch grows erect to 1 m tall. It is a glabrous ephemeral with pinnate leaves, the leaflets being 1–2 cm long. The flowers are 1.5–2 cm across, followed by inflated pods 3–5 cm long. It grows in sand or loam in mallee and woodland between Merredin and the Nullarbor Plain and is also in SA. Family: Papilionaceae

448 Parakeelya at Queen Victoria Spring (Sept)

Parakeelya at Queen Victoria Spring
Queen Victoria Spring is a unique claypan on the edge of the desert about 80 km N of Zanthus. A small soak lies to one side of the claypan which is dry except after heavy rain. When this occurs, ephemerals abound on its banks, including the common parakeelya, *Calandrinia polyandra* (see also Pl. 328). Surrounding vegetation includes *Acacia, Callitris, Eucalyptus* and *Triodia*.

449 Cundeelee Blackboy (Fl: Oct)

Cundeelee Blackboy † *Xanthorrhoea* sp.
This robust blackboy is known only from the sandy areas around Queen Victoria Spring on the Cundeelee Aboriginal Reserve. Apparently different from the Desert Blackboy (*X. thorntoni* Tate), it has a single straight caudex to 4 m tall and a thick flower spike up to 3 m long (shown here in bud). The spinifex, here in full flower, is *Triodia scariosa* N. T. Burbidge. Family: Xanthorrhoeaceae

450 A Nullarbor Donga (Oct)

A Nullarbor Donga

Slight depressions on the vast Nullarbor Plain are called dongas and often contain a few small shrubs such as Weeping Pittosporum, *P. phylliraeoides* DC. and Miljee, *Acacia oswaldii* F. Muell. After good rains, ephemerals carpet the ground: shown here are Sturt Pea, *Cliarthus formosus,* White Everlastings, *Helipterum floribundum* and Spear Grass, *Stipa* sp.

Nullarbor Frankenia *Frankenia densa* Summerhayes

Frankenia is a genus of subtropical and temperate regions, with about 50 Australian species, mostly of the dry interior. This species is a mat-like perennial with linear, revolute leaves 2–3 mm long and flowers 4–5 mm across. It occurs on open steppe on the Nullarbor Plain in both WA and SA.

Family: Frankeniaceae

451 Nullarbor Frankenia (Sept–Oct)

452 Bluebush and Myall

Bluebush and Myall *Maireana sedifolia* (F. Muell.) P. G. Wilson

A common association, especially around the margins of the Nullarbor Plain, is Bluebush-Myall. Bluebush is widespread on the Plain and is a useful fodder. Myall, *Acacia papyrocarpa* Benth., is a tree to 5 m with a relatively dense crown, narrow phyllodes and small heads of flowers arranged in racemes. It flowers in October.

453 Open mulga plain, carpeted with ephemeral everlastings.

MULGA, WATTLE SCRUB AND SPINIFEX

Inland, beyond the South-West Province, there are seemingly endless plains covered with mulga and wattle scrub with occasional areas of spinifex, low rocky hills and salt lakes. This is a dry land where rain falls irregularly in either summer or winter. After heavy rains the red soil is carpeted with ephemerals, predominantly of the daisy family, while the shrubs produce flowers of all colours. Mulga is the dominant small tree of the region, but in the north west areas it is replaced by other wattles, though of similar aspect.

454 Sticky Everlasting (July–Oct)

455 Splendid Everlasting (July–Sept)

456 Bright Podolepis (July–Oct)

Bright Podolepis *Podolepis canescens* A. Cunn. ex DC.
In contrast to the papery everlastings, this ephemeral daisy has soft female ray-flowers forming the corona to the head, the disc florets being bisexual. The terminal flower heads are solitary and up to 2.5 cm across. The basal leaves are elliptic or lanceolate and white-woolly on the lower surface, with narrower widely-spaced leaves on the wiry, branched stems. The species ranges from Shark Bay through the southern pastoral districts into the desert and southwards through the South-West Province except in coastal areas. It is also in NT, SA, NSW and Vic.
Family: Asteraceae

Sticky Everlasting *Helichrysum davenportii* S. Moore
One of the larger-flowered everlastings, this species is an ephemeral with rather thick, glandular, aromatic leaves up to 5 cm long. The flower heads, up to 3 cm across, are borne singly on leafless stems up to 25 cm tall. The species is frequent in loamy soils in the pastoral areas from the Gascoyne River to Kalgoorlie and east into the NT. Family: Asteraceae

Splendid Everlasting † *Helipterum splendidum* Hemsl.
This species forms carpets, often mingled with *Cephalipterum drummondii* and other ephemerals, in the wattle and mulga scrub, ranging from the Minilya River to Geraldton, south-east to Kalgoorlie and eastwards to the desert fringe. The solitary flower heads, up to 6 cm across, are the largest of the ephemeral everlastings. Family: Asteraceae

Schoenia *Schoenia cassiniana* (Gaud.) Steetz.
This everlasting is common through the pastoral districts from the Gascoyne River south to the agricultural areas and Kalgoorlie and eastwards into the deserts of NT and SA. As with most ephemerals the size of the plant varies, being up to 40 cm tall in a good year. The foliage is glandular-aromatic, and the flower heads are 2–3 cm across. *Schoenia* is a monotypic genus closely allied to *Helichrysum* and included therein by some botanists; it differs chiefly in the outer achenes of the head being flattened instead of terete or angular. Family: Asteraceae

457 Schoenia (July–Oct)

Hairy Mulla Mulla *Ptilotus helipteroides* (F. Muell.) F. Muell.

In late winter and early spring this ephemeral herb in a good season forms swards in open scrub and mulga country, preferring rocky or loamy soil. It grows to 40 cm tall with several branching stems and is loosely hirsute throughout. The narrow leaves are up to 5 cm long on the lower stems, shorter above, while the flower spikes are 1.5–3 cm long and 2 cm wide. It ranges through the North-West, south to Leonora and east into the desert and NT. Family: Amaranthaceae

460 Hairy Mulla Mulla (July–Sept)

458 Bowgada Bush

461 Tall Mulla Mulla (July–Sept)

459 Bowgada Bush (mainly June–Sept)

Tall Mulla Mulla *Ptilotus exaltatus* (Nees) Benth.

One of the largest mulla mullas, this ephemeral in a good season grows to 1.5 m tall, though in poor years it may be only a few cm tall. There is a basal rosette of spathulate-oblanceolate smooth leaves up to 10 cm long, the stem leaves being shorter. The flower spikes are up to 10 cm long and 4 cm across with loosely-hairy flowers. The species is widespread from the North-West coast east into the NT, NSW and Qld and south-east to the eastern agricultural districts, Norseman and into SA. Family: Amaranthaceae

Bowgada Bush *Acacia linophylla* W. V. Fitzg.

This erect or spreading shrub grows to 4 m tall and has linear, terete or flat phyllodes 5–12 cm long. The flower spikes are up to 2 cm long while the pods grow to 12 cm long, and are thick and rounded, grey with brown longitudinal lines. The species ranges from the North-West coast east and south-eastwards through the pastoral districts and the desert. It is also in NT, SA and NSW, and may flower at any season depending on the rainfall. Family: Mimosaceae

Pincushion Mistletoe *Amyema fitzgeraldii* (Blakely) Danser

There are 62 mistletoes in Australia, 55 of them endemic. *Amyema* with 32 species is the largest genus and 16 of these occur in WA. This species has ovate-obovate hoary leaves 1.5–4 cm long. The flowers are in heads of 3–4 flowers, the perianth (2–2.5 cm long) splitting to the base while the red stamens and style remain erect. The succulent fruit, 6 mm long, is hoary outside. It occurs only on *Acacia* species and is found from the Gascoyne River south to Kalgoorlie and eastwards into northern SA. Family: Loranthaceae

462 Pincushion Mistletoe (May–Oct)

464 Kurara (May–Sept)

Kurara *Acacia tetragonophylla* F. Muell.

This common species is a stiff, spreading shrub to 4 m tall, usually glabrous, with clustered phyllodes 2–3 cm long. The flower heads, on peduncles almost as long as the phyllodes, are succeeded by flat, curved pods up to 8 cm long, somewhat constricted between the seeds. Kurara grows in various habitats, extending from the North-West coast south to the northern agricultural districts and east into the desert. It is also in NT, SA and NSW. Family: Mimosaceae

Ranji Bush *Acacia pyrifolia* DC.

Ranji Bush typically is a straggling glaucous shrub to 4 m tall with hard, spinescent stipules. The pods are curved, wavy-margined, flat but swollen over the seeds, up to 7 cm long and 1 cm broad. Variants occur which are scarcely glaucous, and the phyllodes vary greatly in size. It is common on plains and hills from North West Cape to the southern Kimberleys and south-eastwards to Meekatharra and into the desert. It is also in NT. Family: Mimosaceae

463 Ranji Bush (May–Oct)

465 Kingsmill's Mallee (July–Sept)

Kingsmill's Mallee † *Eucalyptus kingsmillii* Maiden

This striking mallee has a wide but interrupted distribution. It grows on the higher rocky hills of the Hamersley Range and extends south to Sandstone and east to the desert where it prefers sandy soils, often associated with spinifex. The buds are cream or reddish-pink and the stamens pale yellow or pink. The fruit is not much enlarged, being 2–3 cm across. The species is named after W. Kingsmill, a former member of the Legislative Council of WA.

Family: Myrtaceae

466 Sturt Pea (June–Sept)

Sturt Pea *Clianthus formosus* (G. Don) Ford & Vickery
Although the vernacular name honours the explorer Charles Sturt, this legume was first collected by William Dampier on a North-West island in 1699. The plant is a softly-hirsute ephemeral with prostrate or ascending stems. The leaves are pinnate with up to 7 pairs of elliptic leaflets, and the flowers, 7–9 cm long, are in condensed racemes on stout erect peduncles. The pod is 5–6 cm long, hard and hirsute, with many seeds. Sturt Pea occurs widely from the NW coast east into the desert and south to Kalgoorlie and the Nullarbor Plain and is also in NT, Qld, NSW and SA. In the Cape Range the 'boss' on the standard is usually red, while albino or semi-albino forms occur near Kalgoorlie. Family: Papilionaceae

Felty Bellflower *Bonamia rosea* (F. Muell.) Hall. f.
This herbaceous perennial herb or shrub is up to 50 cm tall with a very hirsute and often rusty appearance. The leaves are ovate or orbicular, about 1 cm long. The calyx is 5–10 mm long, deeply divided into linear woolly lobes while the corolla is appressed-pubescent outside along the midribs. Pink flowers are rare. The species favours sandy soils in the North-West and desert and is often found with spinifex. It also occurs on sand-heaths along the lower Murchison River and farther south, and is also in NT. Family: Convolvulaceae

468 Felty Bellflower (July–Sept)

467 Poison Morning Glory (May–Sept)

Poison Morning Glory *Ipomoea muelleri* Benth.
Reputedly toxic to stock, this sprawling creeper occurs in alluvial loam or gravelly soil in shrub and steppe country as well as along river courses. It is common from Carnarvon east to the desert and NT and north-east to the Kimberleys. The plant is glabrous or hirsute, with angular-cordate leaves 2–4 cm long on slender petioles. The axillary flowers are solitary or in small panicles, with a calyx about 1 cm long and a corolla 2–4 cm long. The capsule is 1–1.5 cm long, shedding several pubescent seeds. Family: Convolvulaceae

469 A Caltrop (any month)

470 Pied Piper Bush (any month)

471 Yellow Hibiscus (any month)

A Caltrop *Tribulus occidentalis* R. Br.
Named after the caltrop, a 4-pointed military weapon used to lame cavalry horses, the pantropical genus *Tribulus* has about 20 species, of which 9 occur in Australia. This trailing, hirsute species may be ephemeral or perennial. The pinnate leaves are 2–5 cm long with up to 10 pairs of leaflets. The axillary pedunculate flowers have 5 sepals 5–10 mm long and petals 10–20 mm. The fruit is of 5 nutlets ± 1 cm high, rounded and hard with several spines up to 5 mm long and numerous smaller ones. The species is common in the North-West from Carnarvon to the Kimberleys, and across the desert to SA and NSW.
Family: Zygophyllaceae

Lesser Bottlebrush † *Callistemon phoeniceus* Lindl.
This is a large shrub to 4 m tall with linear-lanceolate leaves 3–7 cm long. It grows along watercourses and in depressions, extending from the Gascoyne River almost to the south coast with its eastern limits in the Leonora-Norseman area.
Family: Myrtaceae

472 Lesser Bottlebrush (Aug–Dec)

Pied Piper Bush *Dichrostachys spicata* (F. Muell.) Domin
This is a genus of 20 species in tropical Africa and Australia, 2 species being in Australia. Allied to *Acacia*, it differs in the definite number of stamens (10) which have gland-tipped anthers, and in the curious dimorphic flowers. The lower pink flowers are neuter while the upper yellow ones are bisexual. This species is a spreading shrub to 4 m with rough bark, the branchlets sometimes spinescent. The flower spikes are 2–3 cm long, and the pod is linear but curved, flat, 3–5 cm long, indehiscent or breaking irregularly, with 5–10 seeds. It occurs along rivers and on alluvial flats from Roebourne to the De Grey, and is also in the Kimberleys and NT.
Family: Mimosaceae

Yellow Hibiscus *Hibiscus panduriformis* Burm. f.
A softly-tomentose shrub of 1–2.5 m, this species has rounded leaves 3–9 cm across on long petioles, usually 3-lobed with crenate margins. It is found along river banks from the Ashburton River eastwards to the desert fringe and occurs also across northern Australia and in tropical Asia and Africa.
Family: Malvaceae

473 Burra (July–Oct)

Pinyuru † *Eremophila cuneifolia* Kraenzlin

This colourful species is a viscid shrub about 1 m tall with obovate-cuneate leaves 1–2 cm long. The old stems are rough with persistent leaf bases. The purple calyx lobes 1–1.5 cm long in flower, persist and enlarge around the fruit. The corolla varies from pale purple to blue and is about 2 cm long. The shrub extends from the Lyndon and Ashburton Rivers east and south-east to the desert fringe, growing in loam or rocky soil. Family: Myoporaceae

474 Pinyuru (July–Sept)

Burra † *Eremophila fraseri* F. Muell.

Eremophila is an Australian genus of well over 100 species with over 90 in WA. They are mostly shrubs of inland regions but occur also in tropical and southern regions. Burra is a very viscid shrub up to 3.5 m tall, much-branched and densely-foliaged, the leaf bases persisting to give the branches a very rough aspect. The flowers are on slender, erect pedicels and the calyx enlarges and persists after flowering. The corolla may be white, pink or brownish and is finely spotted inside. The shrub occurs in various soils among mulga, on open flats or rocky hills, extending from the Ashburton River and Hamersley Range south to Paynes Find and Laverton.

Family: Myoporaceae

Spotted Poverty Bush † *Eremophila abietina* Kraenzlin

This viscid shrub 1–2 m tall is much-branched and often fir-like in habit. The thick branches remain very rough with the persistent petioles. The flowers are on long curving pedicels which are upturned below the calyx which persists and enlarges around the fruit. The corolla, 2–2.5 cm long, varies from white to pale mauve with purple spots. The plant is known only from the Laverton district where it occurs on rocky outcrops in open situations.

Family: Myoporaceae

475 Spotted Poverty Bush (Aug–Sept)

476 Native Fuchsia (July–Oct)

Native Fuchsia † *Eremophila maculata* F. Muell. var. *brevifolia* Benth.
Native Fuchsia is a spreading shrub to 1 m tall with stiff, usually white-tomentose, branches. The variable leaves are elliptic, obovate or lanceolate, shortly petiolate, 5–20 mm long, and usually glabrous. The flowers are on S-shaped pedicels 7–20 mm long, red or deep pink, usually spotted within. The species is common through the pastoral districts from Exmouth and Wittenoom south to Kalgoorlie and east across the Nullarbor Plain. It prefers alluvial loam, sometimes saline, in open areas or under mulga. It is strongly cyanogenetic and is reputed to be toxic. The typical variety of *E. maculata* occurs across northern Australia and in the eastern States. Family: Myoporaceae

477 Kopi Poverty Bush (July–Oct)

478 Kopi Poverty Bush (July–Oct)

Kopi Poverty Bush † *Eremophila miniata* C. A. Gardn.
This shrub or small tree to 4 m tall is much-branched with stout densely-leaved branches. The lanceolate leaves are slightly viscid and are 2–3 cm long, while the flowers are on long S-shaped pedicels. Both calyx and corolla vary from cream to pink or reddish-brown. The broad calyx-lobes, about 1.5 cm long, enlarge somewhat around the fruit. The corolla is 1.5–2 cm long and is often spotted inside. The shrub grows in alkaline soils, usually on low rises around salt lakes, ranging from Carnegie south to Mt. Magnet and Kalgoorlie and into the north-eastern wheatbelt. Family: Myoporaceae

479 Turpentine Bush (July–Oct)

Turpentine Bush † *Eremophila clarkei* F. Muell.
This species has several forms. Between Carnarvon, the Murchison River and Paynes Find it is a shrub to 4 m tall with linear, shortly dentate leaves 2–4 cm long, pubescent but resinous. Farther east and south-east it is a smaller shrub with shorter, broader leaves and broader calyx-lobes. The flowers, on long slender pedicels, may be white, pale blue or pink. The species grows in a number of soil types, especially loam and rocky loam, in shrublands and in mulga or on hillsides.
Family: Myoporaceae

Shark Bay Poverty Bush † *Eremophila maitlandii* F. Muell ex Benth.
This shrub, up to 3 m tall and covered with small branched hairs, has leaves 2–4 cm long. The calyx, about 1 cm long, enlarges slightly around the fruit, while the corolla is about 2 cm long and is woolly in the throat. The flowers vary from pale blue to mauve. The species grows in loam or sand in open shrublands, being common between Minilya and Shark Bay and extending some distance inland. Family: Myoporaceae

480 A Poverty Bush (July–Aug)

482 Shark Bay Poverty Bush (Sept–Oct)

481 A Poverty Bush (Aug–Oct)

A Poverty Bush † *Eremophila foliosissima* Kraenzlin
This is a much-branched shrub of 50–120 cm, grey-velvety with short, spreading hairs. The corolla is about 3 cm long, the calyx-lobes being narrow and not enlarging. The species is found typically in mulga country but occurs also on rocky rises. It extends from Meekatharra and Mt. Magnet eastwards to Carnegie and Laverton. Family: Myoporaceae

A Poverty Bush † *Eremophila strongylophylla* F. Muell.
This species is apparently restricted to a small area near the upper Murchison River where it occurs in mulga country. It is a shrub to 1 m tall, densely tomentose with branched hairs which are at first yellow and later white. The rounded leaves are about 1 cm across, on short petioles, while the flowers are 2–2.5 cm long. Family: Myoporaceae

Star Pigweed *Trianthema oxycalyptra* F. Muell.
This prostrate ephemeral with succulent leaves has flowers 10–15 mm across in which the sepals are coloured and the petals are absent. It appears after summer or winter rain in sand or rocky loam in steppe country, extending from Shark Bay to the Kimberleys and NT. Family: Aizoaceae

484 Star Pigweed (mainly winter)

Gee *Dissocarpus paradoxus* (R. Br.) Ulbrich
The most interesting feature of this tough hairy herb is the aggregation of up to 16 flowers into a head. In fruit these are hard, woolly and spiny, forming a head 1–2 cm across. The plant is widespread from Exmouth south to the drier agricultural areas and east into the desert, growing on salt flats, stony plains or among mulga. It occurs in all mainland States. Family: Chenopodiaceae

483 Gee (July–Sept)

485 Little Lobelia (Sept–Nov)

Little Lobelia † *Lobelia winfridae* Diels
Usually under 10 cm tall, this ephemeral has 1 to many stems each bearing one blue or mauve flower about 2 cm long. The leaves are linear, sparsely dentate, 5–15 mm long. The plant grows in rocky or sandy loam among tall shrubs between the upper Murchison River, Ajana and Merredin. Family: Lobeliaceae

486 Cut-leaf Goodenia (July–Sept)

Cut-leaf Goodenia *Goodenia pinnatifida* Schlecht.
This ephemeral has a basal rosette of pinnatifid leaves 3–10 cm long, with spreading, branched floral scapes bearing flowers 15–25 mm long. It occurs in loam in shrublands and woodlands between Shark Bay and Kalgoorlie and east to the Nullarbor Plain. It is also in NT, SA, NSW, and Vic. Family: Goodeniaceae

487 Dunna Dunna (Aug)

Dunna Dunna † *Selenothamnus helmsii* (F. Muell. et Tate) Melville

This curious member of the *Hibiscus* family is a dioecious shrub up to 1 m tall covered with tiny scales. The leaves, only 1–4 mm long, are crowded on short lateral branchlets and almost conceal the flowers: in the males only the stamens and scale-like petals appear, and in the females only the styles. It grows on gypsum flats near salt lakes between Meekatharra and Kalgoorlie, with a disjunct occurrence near Coorow.

Family: Malvaceae

Bronze Bluebush † *Maireana atkinsiana* (W. V. Fitzg.) P. G. Wilson

This bluebush is a woody perennial up to 50 cm tall with succulent leaves about 1 cm long. The axillary flowers are inconspicuous and plate-like, but in fruit the wing expands to 1.5 cm and becomes richly coloured, with several erect processes in the centre. It grows on saline flats among other chenopods, ranging from Carnarvon to Meekatharra and south to Laverton.

Family: Chenopodiaceae

488 Spongy Saltbush (any month)

489 Creeping Monkey flower (May, Aug, Jan)

490 Bronze Bluebush (June–Sept)

Spongy Saltbush *Atriplex spongiosa* F. Muell.

A monoecious ephemeral of 10–30 cm, this saltbush is covered with white scales. The cuneate, angular leaves are 1–3 cm long and the insignificant flowers are in the upper axils. More conspicuous are the spherical, spongy fruit 4–10 mm across, each containing one hard seed. The plant occurs on salt flats and claypans and is widespread in arid parts of Australia.

Family: Chenopodiaceae

Creeping Monkeyflower *Mimulus repens* R. Br.

The stems of this rare ephemeral are prostrate, with small opposite leaves and erect flower-stalks 1–3 cm tall. The corolla is about 1 cm across. The species has been recorded from saline areas in the Meekatharra district, from the Murchison River, and at Wagin in the South-West. It is also in eastern Australia and New Zealand. Family: Scrophulariaceae

491 Bulli Bulli (April–July)

Bulli Bulli † *Tecticornia arborea* P. G. Wilson
This strange samphire is known from only two localities, one north of Carnarvon, the other NW of Cue. It is an erect, openly-branched shrub to 2 m tall with succulent stems, the terminal flower spikes being less than 1 cm long but enlarging to 3 cm in fruit. The anthers are the only visible parts of the flower. The species dominates the claypans in which it grows, and the seed was gathered for food by the aborigines.
Family: Chenopodiaceae

492 Pink Velleia (Aug–Sept)

Pink Velleia † *Velleia rosea* S. Moore
Velleia is a genus of 20 species confined to Australia and New Guinea, 13 species occurring in WA. This is one of the 3 pink-flowered species, the others being yellow. It is ephemeral, with a rosette of spathulate toothed leaves 3–5 cm long and spreading peduncles bearing several flowers 1.5 cm across. It is frequent, often forming carpets, in red loam under mulga scrub or Eucalyptus woodlands, extending from Cue to Laverton, west to Mullewa and south to Kalgoorlie.
Family: Goodeniaceae

493 Marsh Stemodia (June–Oct)

Marsh Stemodia † *Stemodia grossa* Benth.
A sticky, hirsute aromatic ephemeral, this plant is common especially in low-lying areas and on river banks between Shark Bay and Port Hedland, with outliers in the Hamersley gorges. It grows to 1 m tall with opposite dentate leaves 2–5 cm long and flowers 2 cm long. *Stemodia* is a tropical genus of about 30 species of which 6 or 7 occur in Australia.
Family: Scrophulariaceae

494 A canyon in the Cape Range, with Rock Figs (*Ficus platypoda* A. Cunn.); Exmouth Gulf beyond.

RANGES AND TABLELANDS OF THE NORTH-WEST

THE CAPE RANGE

Forming the backbone of the Peninsula along the western side of Exmouth Gulf, the extremely rugged Cape Range consists of Tertiary limestone, very much younger than the Archean rocks of the inland ranges. Many streams, flowing only after heavy rain, have dissected the Range into deep canyons typical of dry country—narrow floors, with steep scree slopes and cliffs. The vegetation is mostly a mixed shrub and spinifex steppe which includes species representative of the Kimberleys and south-west as well as the north-west. About a dozen species are endemic in the Range. Provided that adequate rain falls, the best wildflower times are winter and early spring.

Rock Fig *Ficus platypoda* A. Cunn.
This is a large, much-branched shrub, often sprawling over rocky ledges in the gorges of the Cape and Hamersley Ranges and other hills of the North-West and desert. The leaves are 4–12 cm long while the receptacles, up to 12 mm across, are yellow-green but often are red-brown when ripe. The species is also in NT, SA and Qld, and a hirsute variety, var. *lachnocaulon* (Miq.) Benth, occurs in parts of the North-West.
Family: Moraceae

Cape Range Grevillea † *Grevillea variifolia* C. A. Gardner & A. S. George
Restricted to limestone soils between Lake Macleod and North West Cape, this is a spreading shrub to 70 cm tall with silvery foliage. The variable leaves, mostly cuneate and lobed, are 15–40 cm long, while the flowers are 7–8 cm long with styles 25–27 cm.
Family: Proteaceae

496 Rock Fig (any month)

495 Cape Range Grevillea (June–Aug)

497 Rock Morning Glory (May–Aug)

498 Yardie Morning Glory (May–July)

Rock Morning Glory *Ipomoea costata* F. Muell. ex Benth.
At first a climber, this plant eventually becomes woody, forming a shrub to 3 m tall. The leaves are 4–7 cm long on slender petioles, and the flowers are 4–5 cm across. It is common in the Cape Range and occurs also in the Kimberleys and NT.
Family: Convolvulaceae

Yardie Morning Glory † *Ipomoea yardiensis* A. S. George
Confined to the rocky western slopes of the Cape Range and a few areas on top of the Range, this morning glory is unusual in being a true shrub. It grows to 1 m tall and is covered with dense white woolly hairs. The flowers, about 7 cm across, are, like many *Ipomoeas*, at their best in the early morning. The seeds are covered with dense silky hairs.
Family: Convolvulaceae

499 Yulbah (any month)

Yulbah *Erythrina vespertilio* Benth.
This spreading tree, up to 10 m tall, is common in the canyons of the Cape Range and extends to the Kimberleys, the desert and NT, usually along watercourses. The branches are often thorny, an unusual character in our flora. The leaves, on long petioles, have 3 leaflets, usually wider than long and 2–3-lobed. The flowers are 2.5–3 cm long, followed by terete pods containing red seeds. Family: Papilionaceae

Cork Tree *Hakea suberea* S. Moore
The Cork Tree is widespread in northern and inland Australia. Up to 6 m tall, it has a stout trunk with thick, fissured bark and needle-like leaves up to 40 cm long. The flower is densely pubescent, about 10 mm long with a style up to 22 mm, and abundant nectar is produced. The woody fruit is 3–4 cm long and sheds the seed when mature instead of retaining them as in most hakeas. Family: Proteaceae

500 Toucan Flower (May–Aug)

502 Cork Tree (June–Sept)

501 A Morning Glory (July–Sept)

Toucan Flower † *Brachysema macrocarpum* Benth.
This is a leafless perennial herb with many flattened stems up to 40 cm tall. The flowers are 2.5–3 cm long and are succeeded by terete pods up to 6 cm long, tapering at each end and containing many seeds. It grows in sand or limestone from North West Cape to Lake Macleod, and is on Dorre Island, west of Carnarvon. Family: Papilionaceae

A Morning Glory *Polymeria ambigua* R. Br.
This trailing hirsute ephemeral has leaves 2–4 cm long and flowers in small axillary racemes, the corollas being 1.5 cm across. The seeds are densely pubescent. It is common in the canyons of the Cape Range, and occurs also in the Kimberleys, NT, and Qld. Family: Convolvulaceae

Native Plumbago *Plumbago zeylanica* L.
The only *Plumbago* native to Australia, this species is widespread across the North. In the Cape and Hamersley Ranges it grows in shaded parts of the rocky gorges. It is a straggling shrub with broad leaves up to 8 cm long. The calyx is covered with stiff glandular hairs, while the corolla is 2 cm long and 1 cm across. Family: Plumbaginaceae

504 Native Plumbago (May–Aug)

White Cassia *Cassia pruinosa* F. Muell.
More than 50 species of this world-wide genus occur in Australia. White Cassia is easily recognised by the white bloom on the stems and leaves. It is a shrub to 2 m, often thin and straggling. The pinnate leaves are 5–10 cm long and the long-stalked flowers about 2 cm across. The pod is 3–6 cm long, flat and smooth, with up to 16 seeds. The species occurs on open rocky hillsides, extending from North West Cape through the Pilbara and into the desert. Also in NT, SA, Qld, and NSW. Family: Caesalpiniaceae

503 White Cassia (June–Oct)

505 Mat Mulla Mulla (July–Oct)

506 Wild Cotton (July–Oct)

Mat Mulla Mulla † *Ptilotus axillaris* (F. Muell ex Benth.) F. Muell.
This ephemeral species has broad-lanceolate smooth leaves 2–5 cm long and flower spikes 1–3 cm across. It grows in open spaces on loamy or rocky plains, extending from North West Cape to the Minilya River and east through the Pilbara to the desert. Family: Amaranthaceae

Wild Cotton † *Gossypium robinsonii* F. Muell.
This is a shrub to 3 m tall with deeply-lobed leaves up to 5 cm long and flowers 5–10 cm across. It grows in rocky soil, often along creek-lines, extending from the Cape Range to the Hamersleys and south to the Barlee Range. Family: Malvaceae

507 In the Hamersley Range, with wattle-spinifex steppe.

RANGES AND TABLELANDS OF THE NORTH-WEST

THE INLAND RANGES

Between the upper watersheds of the Gascoyne and Fortescue Rivers are many colourful ranges, dominated by the Hamersley Range which, with two peaks over 1,200 metres, includes the highest mountains in WA. These ranges consist of ancient rocks of Precambrian age, mostly sedimentary but intensely metamorphosed, the lower series highly folded but the upper ones less so, and all intruded by igneous rocks. Erosion has dissected them into rugged and scenic ranges surrounded by level tablelands. The vegetation varies from spinifex steppe to mulga while the rivers, often with permanent pools, are lined with River Gums and Coolibahs. Some deep gorges with permanent water are havens for tropical ferns and other delicate plants. Normally a dry region, good summer or winter rains induce a profusion of flowers of all colours.

508 Slender Petalostylis (June–Oct)

Slender Petalostylis *Petalostylis labicheoides* R. Br.
This species is a slender shrub to 4 m tall, slightly glaucous, with pinnate leaves 4–8 cm long. The flowers are 1.5–2 cm across while the pod is obliquely oblong, 2–3 cm long, with 2–4 seeds. It is widespread in the North-West, mainly along watercourses or on open plains, and is also in the Kimberleys, central Australia, Qld, and SA. Family: Caesalpiniaceae

Smooth Laceflower *Trachymene hemicarpa* (F. Muell.) Benth.
This ephemeral grows to 1 m tall and has smooth, hollow stems. The dentate, reniform leaves, 1.5–4 cm across on long petioles, are mostly at the base of the stems. The umbels are 1–2 cm across and surrounded by many narrow bracts. Only 1 of the 2 carpels develops into a semi-circular, finely papillose fruit, 4–5 mm across. It grows mainly on rocky hillsides and gullies of the North-West ranges and is also in NT. Family: Apiaceae

509 Desert Pepperflower (July–Sept)

510 Woolly Corchorus (April–Sept)

511 Smooth Laceflower (May–Sept)

Desert Pepperflower *Diplopeltis stuartii* F. Muell. var. *stuartii*
This trailing perennial herb is pubescent with both simple and glandular hairs. The leaves are narrow-cuneate, bluntly toothed, 1–2 cm long. The flowers have 4 petals in dissimilar pairs, the broad upper ones being 5–7 mm long, while the fruit is inflated, about 1 cm long, and dehiscent. The species occurs in sandy or gravelly soil, usually on steppe, extending from Wittenoom to Wiluna and east into the desert and NT. Family: Sápindaceae

Woolly Corchorus † *Corchorus walcottii* F. Muell.
A tropical genus of some 100 species (including the commercial jute), *Corchorus* has about 25 species in Australia. This densely stellate-tomentose shrub is frequent on the plains and hills of the North-West from Hamelin Pool to Port Hedland. It grows to 1 m tall, with leaves 3–8 cm long; the sepals are 6–10 mm long and the petals rather shorter. The fruit is a dehiscent capsule ± 1.5 cm long, densely hirsute. Family: Tiliaceae

512 A Cassia (June–Sept)

Cockroach Bush *Cassia notabilis* F. Muell.
This is a short-lived herb, much-branched and up to 70 cm tall. The pinnate leaves are hirsute, 10–15 cm long, with up to 13 pairs of acute leaflets. The flowers are about 1 cm across and bright yellow, and the pods are up to 3.5 cm long. The species occurs widely from North West Cape to the desert and is also in NT and Qld. Family: Caesalpiniaceae

514 Cockroach Bush (Fl: June–Aug)

A Cassia *Cassia venusta* F. Muell.
This is a perennial herb or shrub up to 2 m tall with pubescent stems and pinnate leaves 10–25 cm long. The buds are covered by large deciduous bracts, the open flowers being about 2 cm across. The pod is oblong with transverse ridges over the seeds. The species grows along river courses and on rocky hills in the Pilbara and Kimberleys, as well as a few desert localities. It is also in NT and Qld. Family: Caesalpiniaceae

513 A wild Tomato (May–Sept)

A Wild Tomato *Solanum phlomoides* A. Cunn. ex Benth.
Solanum is a large worldwide genus, with about 80 species in Australia. This woolly shrub grows to 1–2 m tall and is spiny on the stems, petioles, pedicels and calyces. The leaves are 5–10 cm long and the flowers 2–4 cm across. The calyx enlarges to 2.5 cm long around the large berry-like fruit. It grows on rocky hillsides or loamy flats, extending from Carnarvon to Port Hedland, being common in the inland ranges. It is also in the Kimberleys and NT.
Family: Solanaceae

515 Millstream Fan-palm

Millstream Fan-palm † *Livistona alfredii* F. Muell.
Restricted to the Fortescue River at Millstream and possibly a few nearby localities, this tropical relic grows to 6 m tall. The leaves have thick petioles with spiny margins, and the flowers are in drooping panicles. There are 30 species of Fan-palm in SE Asia and Australia; 2 species occur in the Kimberleys. Family: Palmae

Caustic Bush *Sarcostemma australe* R. Br.
This shrub, with copious milky sap in its thick, leafless stems, grows to 2 m high and may be erect or straggling. The cream flowers are about 1 cm across, succeeded by slender fruit 4–7 cm long which split open to release many seeds each with a tuft of silky hairs. Widespread in gorges, on hills or on plains, it extends from Geraldton to the Kimberleys and east to NT, SA, Qld and NSW. Family: Asclepiadaceae

Cork Hopbush † *Kallstroemia platyptera* (Benth.) Engl.
A genus of the Australian and American tropics and subtropics, *Kallstroemia* has 8 endemic species in Australia. This is the only shrubby species here, being 70–100 cm tall with thick corky bark on the stems. The pinnate leaves have 2–5 pairs of leaflets, each 5–12 mm long. The flowers are about 2 cm across, sometimes larger. The fruit is a conspicuous orange 5-winged sphere 1.5–2 cm across which splits into 5 segments. It grows mostly on rocky hills in all the North-West ranges and eastwards into the desert. Family: Zygophyllaceae

517 Caustic Bush (May–Nov)

516 Cork Hopbush (April–Aug)

518 Weeping Mulla Mulla (June–Oct)

519 A Mistletoe (May–Sept)

Weeping Mulla Mulla *Ptilotus calostachyus* (F. Muell.) F. Muell.
An ephemeral or short-lived perennial up to 2 m tall, this species has smooth stems and sparse linear leaves 2–6 cm long. The flowers, each 4–5 mm long, are in spikes about 2 cm long but lengthening to 5–10 cm. It occurs on open plains among spinifex, from the Ashburton River east to the desert and NT, as well as the southern Kimberleys. Family: Amaranthaceae

A Mistletoe † *Lysiana casuarinae* (Miq.) Tiegh.
This striking mistletoe has leaves up to 10 cm long and flowers, solitary or paired, 3–5 cm long. The fruit is ovoid, succulent, and 8–10 mm long. The species occurs on a wide range of hosts and ranges from Wittenoom south to the agricultural fringes and east to the desert. Family: Loranthaceae

Cadjeput *Melaleuca leucadendron* (L.) L.
A graceful paperbark tree up to 20 m tall, this species has lanceolate 5-nerved leaves 10–19 cm long and terminal 'bottlebrush' white flowers in spikes 6–15 cm long. It occurs in some gorges in and near the Hamersley Range and is widespread across northern Australia, in New Guinea and in the Moluccas. Family: Myrtaceae

Wickham's Grevillea *Grevillea wickhamii* Meisn.
This shrub is common in the inland ranges of the North-West and extends to the Kimberleys and NT. Up to 5 m tall, it has leaves 3–8 cm long and flowers 4–5 mm long with recurved yellow tips, while the fruit is a dry capsule 15 mm long containing 2 flat seeds.
Family: Proteaceae

520 Wickham's Grevillea (May–Oct)

522 Cadjeput (May–Sept)

521 Venus-hair Fern (all year)

523 Chinese Brake (all year)

Venus-hair Fern *Adiantum capillus—veneris* L.
Although widespread in other tropical and temperate countries, this fern in WA has been recorded from only a few gorges of the Hamersley Range. Here it favours sheltered rock crevices where there is a permanent trickle of water. The fronds are 15–40 cm long.
Family: Adiantaceae

Chinese Brake *Pteris vittata* L.
Deep in the gorges of the Hamersley Range, this fern spreads its graceful fronds (up to 1 m long) beside pools or from rock crevices. It is known from only two other localities in WA, both in the South-West, but occurs widely in tropical and sub-tropical countries of the Old World. It is in Qld, NSW and Vic. Family: Pteridaceae

524 A North-West Beach

THE NORTH-WEST COAST

From Shark Bay to Port Hedland the coast is a series of sweeping sandy beaches, rugged cliffs and mangrove mudflats. Behind are sandy plains, salt marshes and low rocky hills, crossed by a few rivers. The low, open vegetation contains both cosmopolitan and endemic plants. Among the first parts of Australia to be seen by European mariners, the country to them appeared desolate. Flowers may indeed be few in long dry spells but appear in colourful array after the erratic but heavy rains.

Native Crinum *Crinum flaccidum* Herbert
Looking somewhat incongruous in the WA flora, this amaryllid occurs on alluvial flats near the Minilya and Lyndon Rivers, on the plain west of the Cape Range, and in the Kimberleys. It is also in NT, SA, NSW and Vic. The flowers, 10–15 cm across, and the dark green, strap-like leaves appear after summer or autumn rains. Family: Amaryllidaceae

Hairy Pepperflower † *Diplopeltis eriocarpa* (Benth.) Hemsley
This is a hirsute shrub to 70 cm tall with pinnately-lobed leaves about 2 cm long. Male flowers are shown here, the females appearing on the same plant at a different time, having a style and ovary instead of stamens. The fruit are 7 mm long. The species occurs on the coastal plain, in loam or limestone, between North West Cape and the De Grey River. Family: Sapindaceae

525 Native Crinum (Jan–April)

526 Hairy Pepperflower (July–Aug)

Beach Morning Glory *Ipomoea brasiliensis* (L.) Sw.
Common on tropical seacoasts around the world, this plant grows on or near the beach. In WA it extends south to Carnarvon, usually on sandy shores but occasionally on rocks. The trailing stems bear thick leaves 5–10 cm long, while the flowers are 5 cm across. Family: Convolvulaceae

Green Birdflower *Crotalaria cunninghamii* R. Br.
This is an erect shrub to 2 m tall, softly tomentose, with ovate petiolate leaves 3–10 cm long. The flowers, 2.5–3 cm long, are in terminal racemes, and the pods are sausage-shaped, tomentose, 2–4 cm long and many-seeded. It is widespread in arid and tropical Australia, ranging from the coastal dunes of the North-West through the Pilbara to the Kimberleys and into the desert. Family: Papilionaceae

527 Green Birdflower (May–Sept)

528 Beach Morning Glory (any month)

529 Gregory's Wattle (June–Aug)

530 Rough Bluebell (May–Sept)

Gregory's Wattle † *Acacia gregorii* F. Muell.
A sprawling shrub to 80 cm tall and 1 m or more across, this species is shortly hirsute, with phyllodes 1–2 cm long. The pods are also hirsute, ovate, about 1 cm long and 1-seeded. It grows in sand or on limestone between North West Cape and Lake Macleod, with outliers in the Kennedy Range and on offshore islands. Family: Mimosaceae

Rough Bluebell *Trichodesma zeylanicum* (Burm. f.) R. Br.
Often growing vigorously on roadsides, this perennial herb, up to 2 m tall, is clothed with short stiff hairs. The leaves are lanceolate, up to 10 cm long, and the pale to bright blue flowers are 1.5–2 cm across. It is a widespread plant, growing on coastal dunes, along rivers, in gorges and on desert dunes. It also occurs in NT, SA, Qld, NSW, on the islands to the north, in SE Asia and in tropical Africa. Family: Boraginaceae

Sand Hibiscus *Alyogyne pinonianus* (Gaud.) Fryxell
Alyogyne is an Australian genus of about 5 species, all occurring in WA, differing from the true *Hibiscus* in the undivided style and other less obvious characters. This species is a stellate-tomentose shrub of 1–3 m with 3-lobed leaves mostly 4–6 cm long. The flower is 4–6 cm long with a red centre, while the fruit is a hirsute capsule 1 cm long containing silky-hirsute seeds. It occurs frequently on sandy plains and dunes in the North-West as far south as the Murchison River, as well as in the desert, NT, and SA. Family: Malvaceae

Forrest's Featherflower † *Verticordia forrestii* F. Muell.
There are two featherflowers in the North-West and this species, named after John Forrest, is the more common. It is a spreading shrub of 1–2 m with small rounded leaves and flowers 1 cm across. It grows on sand dunes between Carnarvon and Onslow, and in the Kennedy Range. Family: Myrtaceae

531 Forrest's Featherflower (July–Oct)

Fraser's Lantern Bush *Abutilon fraseri* Hook.
The worldwide tropical genus *Abutilon* has about 30 species in Australia. This species is an open, tomentose shrub of 2–4 m with long-petiolate cordate leaves 1–3 cm long. The flowers are 3–4 cm across, followed by fruit with numerous rounded carpels. It is frequent between Carnarvon and Port Hedland along rivers, on rocky hills or open plains and is also in NT. Family: Malvaceae

Urchins † *Triumfetta chaetocarpa* F. Muell.
Triumfetta is a worldwide tropical genus of about 150 species, 18 of them in Australia. It is characterised by the bristly fruit, the bristles often being hooked. This species, a spreading shrub to 1 m, has small yellow flowers, while the fruit are 2–3 cm across. It grows on sand dunes between Carnarvon and Onslow. Family: Tiliaceae

532 Sand Hibiscus (Aug–Dec)

533 Fraser's Lantern Bush (May–Oct)

534 Urchins (May–July)

535 White Dragon Tree (May–Sept)

536 Coastal Caper (any month)

537 Coastal Coppercups (Aug–Nov)

Coastal Coppercups † *Pileanthus limacis* Labill.
Found on sand dunes on the coast or a little inland between Shark Bay and Exmouth, this is a spreading shrub to 1 m tall by 2 m broad. The thick, linear leaves are 4–7 mm long and the flowers 15–20 mm across. The 20 stamens are forked below the anthers. Family: Myrtaceae

White Dragon Tree *Sesbania formosa* F. Muell.
The handsome flowers of this tree, with petals about 9 cm long, are the largest of any native legume in WA. The many-seeded pods are up to 60 cm long, narrow and slender. The tree, up to 10 m tall, has thick corky bark and pinnate leaves up to 40 cm long. It grows along rivers on the plains of the upper North-West, extending to the Kimberleys and NT.
Family: Papilionaceae

Coastal Caper *Capparis spinosa* L., var *nummularia* (DC) F. M. Bailey
A worldwide genus of warm regions, *Capparis* has about 18 species in Australia. Coastal Caper is a shrub about 1 m tall with rounded leaves 2–4 cm across and spinescent stipules. The flowers have 4 concave sepals and 3 petals about 3 cm long. In the North-West it occurs on rocky coasts, along river banks and around inland depressions. It is also in the Kimberleys and NT.
Family: Capparidaceae

Climbing Daisy † *Brachycome latisquamea* F. Muell.
The largest species of the genus, this daisy scrambles over other shrubs to a height of 2 m. The flower heads, 3–4 cm across, are occasionally white. It grows in sand from Shark Bay to North West Cape. Family: Asteraceae

538 Climbing Daisy (July–Sept)

539 Lennard Gorge, King Leopold Range

THE KIMBERLEY

Water, rugged sandstone, dry grassy woodland: three characteristic aspects of the Kimberley are shown here. An aquatic *Myriophyllum* emerges from the pool, while a mixed low open-woodland with grasses covers the hillside beyond.

540 A fan-palm (August)

A fan-palm *Livistona loriphylla* Beccari
This fan-palm has a slender trunk up to 3 m tall with an open crown of leaves. The small flowers in large panicles are sweetly scented. Restricted to low, rugged, sandstone hills, the species is common near the lower Drysdale River and is also in NT.
Family: Arecaceae

Little Wheel Bush *Stenocarpus cunninghamii* R. Br.
Two species of *Stenocarpus* occur in the Kimberley. The flowers are similar to those of *Grevillea* but the fruit is a long follicle containing many flat seeds. Both species have much-divided juvenile leaves and entire adult leaves. This species is a shrub to 5 m tall with leaves 5-13 cm long and scentless flowers. The fruit is 5-12 cm long. It grows among sandstone rocks in gorges and in vine thicket, in the north-west and north Kimberley, and is also in NT and Qld. Family: Proteaceae

541 Scarlet Gum (June-Aug)

543 Little Wheel Bush (May-Aug)

542 Mangaloo (July-Nov)

Scarlet Gum *Eucalyptus phoenicea* F. Muell.
This is a spreading tree to 12 m tall with flaky, golden-brown bark. The umbels contain 12-20 flowers, slightly ribbed with bud caps 4-5 mm long, and the fruit is narrowly urn-shaped with a rather thin wall. The species is locally common on sandstone plateaus of the north-east Kimberley and extends to the NT and Qld. Family: Myrtaceae

Mangaloo *Planchonia careya* (F. Muell.) R. Knuth
An erect shrub to 6 m tall with a rough, corky grey bark, this deciduous tree can be recognised when in leaf by its reddish tinged mature leaves. The scented flowers have 1 cm long green calyx lobes and white or yellow petals 3-4 cm long. The staminal filaments, which may have a reddish base, are up to 3 cm long. The edible fruits are ovoid, ripening in the wet season to a length of 3 cm. It is widespread in the cental and north Kimberley, as well as in NT, Qld and New Guinea Family: Barringtoniaceae

544 A tree orchid (Sept-Nov)

A tree orchid *Cymbidium canaliculatum* R. Br.
Most common of the 9 known Kimberley orchids, this species is to be seen throughout the region in a number of trees but usually Eucalypts. It has stout pseudobulbs and leathery, channelled leaves 10-30 cm long. The scentless flowers have sepals and petals 12-18 mm long which vary in the proportions of brown and cream. The species is widespread across northern Australia and in northern NSW. Family: Orchidaceae

Quinine Tree *Petalostigma pubescens* F. Muell.
Growing up to 6 m tall, this erect shrub or small tree is widespread in the Kimberley and NT. The leaves vary from almost orbicular to lanceolate and are 2-3 cm long. Young leaves are often densely hairy underneath. The fruits which may be yellow or orange are up to 2.5 cm in diameter, and break into segments on maturity. The unisexual flowers are inconspicuous.
Family: Euphorbiaceae

546 Quinine Tree (fruit, June-Aug)

Tree Featherflower *Verticordia cunninghamii* Schau.
Unlike southern featherflowers, this species is a tall shrub or small tree to 6 m tall with fibrous bark. The leaves are almost terete and 10-15 mm long, while the flowers are 12-15 mm across. It grows in sand among sandstone rocks, in open shrublands or woodlands. It extends from the Packhorse Range north and east, and is also in NT. Family: Myrtaceae

545 Xanthostemon (April-June)

Xanthostemon *Xanthostemon paradoxus* F. Muell.
A bushy shrub or tree to 10 m, this has smooth or flaky pale bark and elliptic leaves 5-13 cm long that are pubescent underneath. The flowers, in cymes, have small petals, and prominent stamens 2-3 cm long. The fruit is a dry, spherical capsule. Found on rocky sandstone hills, Xanthostemon occurs throughout the Kimberley except in southern areas and extends to the NT.
Family: Myrtaceae

547 Tree Featherflower (June-Aug)

548 Crab Eyes (flower, Jan-June, fruit, May-Aug)

Crab Eyes *Abrus precatorius* L.
This annual or perennial creeper or scrambler ranges from Africa to most of tropical Australia. The alternate, compound leaves have up to 15 pairs of bright green leaflets. The pea-shaped flowers are usually less than 1 cm long and vary from pink to violet. The pods usually contain up to 8 seeds which are extremely toxic. One seed is reputed to contain sufficient toxin to kill a man. In the Kimberley this species is frequently found in sandy soils particularly near the beach.
Family: Papilionaceae

551 A screwpine (fruit, Aug)

549 Bauhinia (April-Aug)

550 A fern (fertile any month)

A screwpine *Pandanus darwinensis* St John
Five species of *Pandanus* are known from the Kimberley. They are common along river and creek banks, and in swamps. The spirally-arranged leaves are bordered by sharp spines. Male and female flowers appear on separate plants, the males in crowded panicles shedding their pollen in April and May. The female flowers develop into the prominent fruit shown here, usually green but sometimes turning red when ripe, when they fall in sections. The species is also in NT. Family: Pandanaceae

Bauhinia *Lysiphyllum cunninghamii* (Benth.) de Wit
Bauhinia is very common on the plains of the west Kimberley but extends south to Port Hedland and east into the NT. It is a tree to 12 m with rough bark and hard timber. Each leaf is of two leaflets 2-3 cm long. The flowers have velvety sepals and petals, and exserted stamens 3-4 cm long. The pods are up to 15 cm long and 4-5 cm broad, red at first but turning brown.
Family: Caesalpiniaceae

A fern *Dicranopteris linearis* (Burm. f.) Underwood
This is the only *Dicranopteris* recorded in Australia and is a widespread species in SE Asia and northern Australia. The dichotomously divided fronds may be on a 2 m long rhachis arising from the rhizome. The undersides of the pinnules which are up to 3 cm long bear scattered, rounded sori on a glaucous surface. It grows in damp, sheltered gullies.
Family: Gleicheniaceae

A Grevillea *Grevillea mimosoides* R. Br.
This species grows in basaltic loam, usually rocky in grassy open woodlands. It is normally an erect, little-branched shrub to 4 m tall but sometimes reaches 10 m with a small crown. The falcate leaves are 10-20 cm long and bluish green. The flowers are always on top of the plant. Each flower is 4-5 mm long with a style 9-10 mm long; the similar *G. dimidiata* has flowers 10-12 mm long and styles 18-20 mm. The species extend from Derby to the border and beyond into the NT. Family: Proteaceae

Sticky Kurrajong *Sterculia viscidula* W.V. Fitzg.
Several deciduous Kurrajongs are common in the Kimberley. During the 'wet' they have large, felted leaves but these fall in the dry season and the flowers then appear. This species has the largest flowers, 4-6 cm long. The fruit are 8-10 cm long. The species grows in sand among sandstone or basalt rocks on hills, ranging from near Derby north-eastwards to the western NT. Family: Sterculiaceae

Kapok Bush *Cochlospermum fraseri* Planch.
This also is usually winter-deciduous, a small tree to 5 m tall with grey, lightly fissured bark and soft wood. The flat, lobed leaves, 7-12 cm across, are felted below and may persist during flowering. The scented flowers have 5 petals, each 3-4 cm long and bilobed, often orange-streaked. They are followed by swollen green pods which burst to release many silky seeds. Usually found on rocky hillsides, the species is common throughout the Kimberley and extends to the NT. It is the only species of its genus in WA. Family: Cochlospermaceae

553 A Grevillea (July-Aug)

552 Baobab (Boab) and grassland (winter)

554 Sticky Kurrajong (May-Aug)

555 Kapok Bush (April-Nov)

Baobab (Boab) *Adansonia gregorii* F. Muell.
The Baobab or Boab is a characterisitic tree of the Kimberley. It is especially common on the loamy plains of the Fitzroy and Ord valleys, and on the limestone hills of the Oscar and Napier Ranges. Here it is shown on a basalt slope near Mt. Waterloo, in its leafless, winter state. The large, white flowers appear in late summer and the felted fruit in early winter. The Baobab occurs also in NT and has a close relative in South Africa. Family: Bombacaceae

556 New Holland Rattlepod (Jan-Aug)

558 A triggerplant (June-Aug)

New Holland Rattlepod *Crotalaria novae-hollandiae* DC.
Rattlepods are common herbs of the Kimberley. This species is a stout herb to 70 cm tall with leaves each of a single leaflet 5-12 cm long on a jointed petiole. The flowers are 10-15 mm across with wings covering the pointed keel that is typical of the genus. The pods are sausage-like and inflated, about 2 cm long. The species is common in the Kimberley in rocky or alluvial soil, extending south to the Pilbara and east to the NT and Qld. Family: Papilionaceae

Northern Byblis *Byblis liniflora* Salisb.
Unlike *Byblis gigantea* (Pl. 62) this species is widespread, occurring from the upper Murchison River to Queensland. A tangled plant up to 35 cm tall, the leaves are viscid and function as insect 'flypaper traps'. The flowers which are up to 2 cm across, are borne on slender pedicels arising singly from upper axils. The petals range from lilac-coloured to pale pink or pink-centred with a cream outer part. The species commonly occurs in damp sand or loam near water courses or swamps. Family: Byblidaceae

557 Northern Byblis (Mar-Sept)

559 Justago (Jan-July)

Justago *Justago cleomoides* (F. Muell.) Kuntze
Justago is a genus of 1 species confined to northern Australia. It is an aromatic herb to 1 m tall covered with glandular hairs. The leaves are of 3-5 narrow leaflets each 1-5 cm long. The flowers, on long pedicels in the upper axils, have petals 7-10 cm long; each opens for only a day. A narrow pod contains many small seeds. The plant is found on rocky hillsides in the central and north Kimberley, extending east to the NT and Qld. Family: Capparidaceae

Ribbed Mangrove *Bruguiera exaristata* Ding Hou

This is one of the common species of mangrove on the Kimberley coast and extends south to Cossack. It is found mainly towards the landward edge of the mangal. The tree grows to 7 m, has a buttressed trunk and knee-roots. The elliptic leaves, 5-8 cm long, are smooth and shining. The tubular, ribbed calyx is 2.5 cm long and divided into 8-10 narrow lobes, while there are also 8-10 petals, early deciduous. The species is also in NT, Qld and islands north of Australia.

Family: Rhizophoraceae

560 Ribbed Mangrove (May-Nov)

562 A bladderwort and Braid Fern (May-Aug)

Argyle Cycad † *Cycas pruinosa* Maconochie

This cycad is restricted to sandstone hillsides of the ranges west of Kununurra and Lake Argyle. It grows to 2 m and has fronds up to 1 m long with narrow, revolute pinnae. The male cone is 40-50 cm long with sharp-pointed bracts, and the female, shown here, has many felted bracts with usually 4 seeds per bract. Fruiting is mostly in the dry season. Family: Cycadaceae

561 Argyle Cycad (June-Aug)

A bladderwort and Braid Fern *Utricularia chrysantha* R. Br. *Platyzoma microphyllum* R. Br.

These two species sometimes grow together around freshwater creeks and swamps. The bladderwort (Family: Lentibulariaceae) is an insectivorous annual, usually leafless herb up to 50 cm tall. The two-lipped flowers are up to 1.5 cm across the upper lip having a spur up to 1 cm long. *Platyzoma* (Family: Gymnogrammaceae), a monotypic genus of fern, has erect fronds arising from a rhizome clothed by long, brown hairs. The tiny, rounded pinnae are one of the drought-tolerant features of this plant enabling it to live in relatively dry, open woodlands as well as moist places. Both species are widespread across northern Australia.

563 A native Hoya (May-June)

A native Hoya *Hoya australis* R. Br. ex Traill

Closely related to the commonly cultivated Hoya, this species of the north-west Kimberley was only recently identified when flowers became available. A perennial scrambler of sandstone cliffs, it occurs usually in damp, shady places but sometimes in places more exposed. The thick, pale green leaves are 4-6 cm long and like other members of its family have a milky latex. The waxy flowers, 1 cm across, are sweetly scented. Family: Asclepiadaceae

564 Monochoria (Mar-June)

566 A climbing fern (fertile any month)

A Monochoria *Monochoria cyanea* (F. Muell.) F. Muell.
In the same family as the troublesome, introduced Water Hyacinth, this species is the only *Monochoria* recorded for the Kimberley. It is a perennial aquatic herb with a creeping rootstock submerged in the wet season and erect leafy shoots up to 50 cm long. The six petals which range from purple to intense blue are often striped with a single, central, green vein. The flower is up to 2.5 cm across.
Family: Pontederiaceae

Water Pincushions *Eriocaulon setaceum* L.
Like many aquatic plants this species is widespread, also occurring in tropical Africa and Asia. Rooted at the base, the stems are suspended in the water and are covered by filamentous leaves up to 12 cm long. The rigid flower stalks arise from the stem apex in the dry season and emerge from the water bearing numerous flowers in compact heads held up to 10 cm above water level.
Family: Eriocaulaceae

Climbing Maidenhair *Lygodium microphyllum* (Cav.) R. Br.
The most common fern of the region, it is a perennial climber which may reach up to 5 m above ground in favourable stituations. The frond consists of a wiry rhachis and small pinnae. The fertile pinnae depicted here are deeply lobed with the spores borne on the underside of each lobe. The sterile pinnae are usually longer than broad, with one or sometimes two large lobes near the base. This fern occurs in wet sandy situations across northern Australia.
Family: Schizaeaceae

A Melastoma *Melastoma malabathricum* L.
An attractive shrub of moist, shady places, this plant is in the same family as the widely cultivated *Lasiandra*. It extends over most of tropical Australia, northern NSW and throughout SE Asia as far north as southern China. The correct name of the Kimberley species is in doubt. It has also been called *M. denticulata* or *M. polyanthum*. The elliptical leaves are up to 15 cm long and are covered by rough hairs. The flowers, which have 5 short and 5 long stamens, are 4-6 cm across.
Family: Melastomataceae

565 Water Pincushions (May-Aug)

567 A Melastoma (Aug-Mar)

of the coastal plain occur throughout the forest. These patches have a varied flora including the Banksias mentioned above. The most common shrub, which is always an indicator of deep sand, is the Blueboy, *Stirlingia latifolia* (Pl. 39).

The first farmers of the Swan River Colony settled on the coastal plain. The Darling Ranges and the Jarrah forest presented a barrier to development because of the rough terrain and toxic native plants. James Drummond, the Colonial Naturalist and Agriculturalist, in 1839 suspected the plant now known as Woodbridge Poison, *Isotoma hypocrateriformis* (Pl. 112), of being responsible for stock losses. The next year there was much discussion in the Colony over the cause of death of so many sheep and cattle particularly in the foothills and hills of the Darling Range. After an experiment using a goat, the culprit was identified as *Gastrolobium calycinum,* now known as York Road Poison.

Many poison plants occur throughout the forest. Most of these belong to the genera *Gastrolobium* and *Oxylobium*. The toxic members of these genera have paired or whorled leaves with prominent stipules and racemes of yellow or orange and red flowers. One of the common Darling Range species is Crinkle-leaf Poison, *Gastrolobium villosum,* (Pl. 94).

The Zamia, *Macrozamia riedlei* (Pl. 27, 28) is possibly the earliest recorded local toxic species. The crew of Wilhelm de Vlaming's ship who visited the Swan River in 1697 are reported to have become ill after eating the seeds of the Zamia. The young leaves and seeds are recorded as causing toxic effects in farm animals. The Zamia is not a true palm. It is a Cycad, a small group of dioecious plants distantly related to the Conifers. Common throughout the South-West, the Zamia occurs widely in the Jarrah forest as well as on the coastal plain. The cones appear on some plants during April or May. Male plants develop three to seven cones (Pl. 27). These measure up to 30 cm long and bear numerous cone scales with pollen sacs underneath. Female cones (Pl. 28) occur singly or in pairs and at maturity can reach 50 cm long and 25 cm across, weighing about 14 kg. Pollen is shed from September to November and fertilisation takes place some months later. The seeds are liberated in the following autumn by the rotting of the female cones, the seeds falling onto the ground around the parent plant. Normally the seeds, which are bright red when first shed, lie dormant for a whole year and then germinate readily after the winter rains. Growth of the seedling is very slow for many years during which only a few leaves are produced at any one time.

The Jarrah forest south of the Collie district is wetter than the northern part. The associated species reflect this difference as species which are common in the south occur only in wetter valleys of the northern part of the forest. Shrubs such as the Water Bush, *Bossiaea aquifolia*, and the Native Willow, *Oxylobium linearifolium*, are common in the southern forests and rare in the north. The only native WA member of the *Podocarpaceae* occurs in the southern Jarrah as well as the neighbouring Karri forest: the Koolah, *Podocarpus drouyniana*, is a low shrub with narrow pale-green leaves 5–10 cm long. After a bushfire it produces small male and female cones. Following pollination a single seed develops inside fleshy scales and the cone stalk becomes very fleshy and rounded, up to 3 cm across. At maturity this structure is plum-coloured with a light waxy bloom. It is our largest edible 'fruit' though unfortunately it is quite flavourless.

The Woody Pear, *Xylomelum occidentale*, is also a common tree in the southern Jarrah forest. It has pale-green, flat leaves which have a toothed, undulating margin. The fruits, like those of the Sandplain Woody Pear, *X. angustifolium* (Pl. 344), are composed completely of hard wood. Two other members of the *Proteaceae*, common as understorey trees in the forest, are the Snottygobbles, so called because of their succulent fruits. These are *Persoonia longifolia* and *P. elliptica,* which as the scientific names suggest, are differentiated by their leaf shape.

Lianes, or creepers, occur frequently in the Jarrah forest. The Wild Sarsparilla, *Hardenbergia comptoniana,* is common in the forest as well as on the coastal plain. Probably the most common liane is the Coral Vine, *Kennedia coccinea* (Pls. 115, 116). This species is one of the first to colonise the bare gravel pits especially in the southern forest. Also widespread is *Clematis pubescens*, a creeper with large, 4-petalled white flowers and leaves of 3 broad leaflets on tendril-like petioles. The other lianes belong mainly to the family *Pittosporaceae.* The genus *Billardiera* is represented in the forest by its most attractive species *B. floribunda*. This is common near Albany, but extends far northwards. The loose heads of white flowers appear in summer and the handsome leaves are up to 5 cm long.

The Monocots include the Grasses, Sedges, Lilies and Orchids, and are mostly ground-dwelling species without thick aerial stems. However, three genera of arborescent monocots are common in the Jarrah. The Blackboys are represented by two common species. The Common Blackboy, *Xanthorrhoea preissii* (Pl. 310), usually develops a stem or caudex. This caudex, which may be up to 3 m high, is frequently branched and consists of closely packed leaf bases and vascular tissue. The leaf bases are always burnt and blackened by fire. The rate of growth of the Blackboy is dependent on the frequency of fires because a leafy crown is destroyed easily by fire and a new, vigorous crown soon appears, pushing the burnt leaf bases aside. Without fire, the growth rate is slow, perhaps only a few centimetres per year. The Slender Blackboy, *Xanthorrhoea gracilis* (Pl 103), develops only a small underground stem from which arise a few leaves and a long, slender scape topped by a short flowering spike.

The Black Gin, *Kingia australis* (Pl. 194), a monotypic genus endemic in WA, also develops a tall caudex. The caudex of this species is rarely branched and may reach 8 m. Instead of the familiar long, spear-like flowering spike of the Blackboy, the Black Gin produces numerous, scaly, drumstick-like flowering and fruiting heads on stems up to 30 or 40 cm long. When not flowering or fruiting the Black Gin can readily be recognised by its broad, silky-hairy leaf bases.

The third arborescent monocot of the forest is the Pineapple Bush, *Dasypogon hookeri* (Pl. 130). *Dasypogon* is also a WA endemic with two species in the South-West. *Dasypogon bromeliaefolius* is a low, tufted shrub, common on the sandy soils of the coastal plain and sandy pockets of the forest. The Pineapple Bush is restricted to the Jarrah forest of the sandy soils between Busselton and Nannup, extending west to Yallingup. The caudex of this plant is only about 5–8 cm diameter and consists mostly of vascular tissue and overlapping leaf bases. Stems may reach 1 m though some specimens 3 m long have been recorded.

One of the most interesting plants of the forest is *Pilostyles hamiltonii*. This is the only Australian representative of the family *Rafflesiaceae*, a family of parasitic plants to which belongs *Rafflesia arnoldi*, the world's largest flower. *Pilostyles* has only small flowers, a few millimetres across and, like its larger relative, lives within the tissues of the host as a complete parasite. The hosts of the local *Pilostyles* are the Prickly Bitter-pea, *Daviesia pectinata* (Pl. 22), or *D. incrassata* or less commonly *D. rhombifolia*. The plant body of *Pilostyles* consists of a branching chain of cells living within the cortex of the host. The flowers burst through the stem tissue of the host and can be recognised by their red calyx lobes and small white petals which are about 1 mm across. The biology of this plant is not known, and the pollination and seed dispersal mechanisms remain a mystery.

Apart from the *Proteaceae* there are many small shrubs in the Jarrah. Three species of Banjine are common. The Rose Banjine, *Pimelea rosea* (Pl. 117), is white in Jarrah forest forms. The Silky Yellow Banjine, *Pimelea suaveolens* (Pl. 83), is a very variable species, the largest-flowered variants being found in the Darling Range. However the species with the largest flowers of all is *Pimelea spectabilis* which has white flowers in heads 5 cm across, often tinged with pink.

Most of the species of *Hibbertia*, which characteristically have yellow flowers, are native to the South-West, and a number occur in the forest. The Orange Hibbertia, *H. miniata* (Pl. 126), is the only species which is consistently orange-flowered. *Hibbertia stellaris* (Pl. 123), called Orange Stars, in some areas has yellow flowers.

Some of the most attractive flowers of the forest belong to the *Lechenaultia* family, *Goodeniaceae*. The most popularly known is the Blue Lechenaultia, *L. biloba* (Pl. 109), with flowers of various sky-blue shades. Species of *Dampiera* such as the Common Dampiera, *D. linearis* (Pl. 133), have a more intense royal blue flower colour. The generic name honours William Dampier who was the first person to remark on the prevalence of blue-coloured flowers in the flora of 'New Holland'. Other blue-coloured members of the family are the Royal Robe, *Scaevola striata* (Pl. 101), and the Broad-leaved Fanflower, *S. platyphylla* (Pl. 107). In all of these blue-flowered species, white-flowered variants are sometimes found.

Fire is an extremely important ecological factor in the Jarrah forest. There is no doubt that fires were frequent in the forest long before Europeans appeared in this country. Evidence from fossil peat deposits and the prevalence of old blackened stumps in the forest shows that many fires occurred in the recent past. The vegetation of the forest can be described as a fire climax, the species being adapted to regular fires. The cyclic changes brought about by burning are discussed in the Karri Forest section.

After the disastrous forest fires in the period 1948 to 1961, the consequences of excluding fire from the forest were realised. The build-up of litter and dead or dying trees over a period of ten or fifteen years results in a severe fire hazard. The large amount of combustible material means that many normally resistant trees are killed or damaged. Now the forests are carefully managed by controlled burns over the forest floor which, if not done too frequently, also benefit the native flora.

Karri Forest

Credited with being one of the three tallest hardwoods in the world, the Karri, *Eucalyptus diversicolor*, occurs in magnificent forests in the South-West corner of the State. The tallest Karri, measured in 1939, was 90 metres with a circumference at the base of 7.3 m. The specific name *diversicolor* refers to the colour difference between the upper and lower surfaces of the leaf. The deeper green of the upper surface contrasts with the paler green of the lower, the Karri being one of the relatively few West Australian eucalypts which have spreading leaves instead of pendulous ones.

The Karri forest occurs on sandy loams and loams over gneissic or granitic country rock. The forest areas receive an annual rainall of over 1,000 mm, with a less well-marked dry season than is typical of most of the Jarrah forest. The rainfall during the six driest months, November to April, is over 200 mm.

The main area of forest is south of a line drawn from Nannup, south-east of Busselton, through Manjimup to the Frankland River, near Nornalup and in a narrow coastal belt to Denmark and Torbay near Albany. The western limit of the main forest is the line marking the limit of gneissic rocks from Nannup to the coast near the mouth of the Warren River.

A number of small areas occur outside the larger area. The largest of these is a narrow coastal belt of some 30,000 ha in the extreme South-West corner of the State, between the Margaret River caves and Augusta. The trees of this area grow on the same type of acid, sandy loam as the trees of the main forest though in some cases they are growing on limestone which caps the gneissic rocks. In some of the famous Augusta caves, the roots of Karri can be seen in limestone, many metres below the surface.

Another outlier of only a few hundred hectares occurs on the Porongurup Range, north of Albany. Again, this occurrence is on sandy loams over gneissic rocks. Smaller outliers, some of only a few hundred trees, occur at the mouth of the Scott River, east of Augusta and on the coastal plain south of Northcliffe. The eastermost occurrence of Karri is found on the foothills of the northern slopes of Mt. Manypeaks, east of Albany. The outliers south of Northcliffe are small patches of Karri forest on subsurface gneissic rocks, in some cases the surface of the soil being only a few metres above the surrounding plain of winter-wet peaty sands. From a distance the groves of trees look like island hills until they are approached when they are found to be dense stands of Karri or, in some cases, of Bullich, *Eucalyptus megacarpa* (Pl. 405). The two trees look remarkably similar from a distance though apart from the very different buds and fruits, the Bullich has white bark which matures to a blue-grey colour. Usually Bullich grows in more exposed situations in the lower South-West, either on hilltops or near the coast where it is wind-pruned. In some river valleys in the Jarrah forests, Bullich may occur as a blue-grey tree up to 20 metres tall.

Pure forests of Karri have a very definite structure, consisting of two or three distinct stories. The tall Karri trees dominate and comprise the entire upper storey. Each tree has relatively few leafy branches so that the shade from the crown is light. The amount of wood in the trunk of a mature tree is very great and it is this which provides much of the shade. In the main area of Karri forest, near Pemberton, there is a definite layer of smaller trees far below the crowns of the Karri trees but above the very dense layer of shrubs which is characteristic of the Karri forest. The trees include the Karri Oak, *Casuarina decussata,* which also occurs on granite rocks in the lower South-West; the Peppermint, *Agonis flexuosa* (Pl. 8), which is a widespread coastal species, and the well-known Bull Banksia, *Banksia grandis*, which is common near Perth and in the Jarrah forest.

The dense shrub layer which is always present in the Karri forest often consists of large-leaved shrubs such as *Trymalium spathulatum*. This shrub which is called Karri Hazel, may form impenetrable thickets up to 10 m high though usually only a few metres high. It can be recognised by its leaves which are blue-green above and hoary below. The creamy-white flowers are small and are borne in open panicles. As with nearly all other species of the Karri forest this species is widely distributed in the South-West. Another member of the shrub layer which is almost always present is *Chorilaena quercifolia* (Pl. 152).

Other shrubs include species of *Acacia*, especially the Karri Wattle, *Acacia pentadenia* (Pl. 147). This species also occurs in swampy situations near the south coast. *Acacia urophylla, Acacia myrtifolia* and another member of the Mimosaceae, *Albizia lophantha,* are also important members of the shrub layer. The Karri Wattle is one of the dozen or so WA species of *Acacia* with true leaves rather than the drought-resistant flattened leaf stalks and leaf axes which function as leaves in most species. The other wattles of the Karri have the modified leaves or phyllodes but in these species they are fairly soft structures, not like the sclerophyllous ones characteristic of drier habitats.

The *Acacias* and the *Albizia* are fire-opportunist species. The seeds of these species have a thick testa and are able to remain viable for many years. Seeds over one hundred years old have given quite high germination figures. If a fire destroys the ground vegetation of a Karri forest the first seedlings to appear are usually those of the families Papilionaceae and Mimosaceae. The various species of Acacia or *Albizia lophantha* may, within a very short period, dominate the shrub layer. Other species of the forest including seedling Karri are soon smothered by the faster-growing species, only a few surviving. By the second year following a fire the wattles may bloom and another crop of seed becomes mixed with the leaf litter. After a few years, the fire-opportunist shrubs begin to die and are replaced by the other understorey species. In some cases, disease appears to be responsible for the population decline, particularly in the case of *Albizia* which is readily attacked by the gall rust fungus *Uromycladium*.

Fire in the Karri forest is an important environmental factor to which the flora has adapted, just as it has in other Australian forests. The establishment of Karri tree seedlings cannot occur in the dense, unburnt undergrowth. Not only is it too dark but there would be a tremendous amount of root competition for the few nutrients left in the surface soil.

A bushfire after a long dry summer would destroy much of the ground vegetation and would consume the fallen logs and stumps of dead trees. Stumps and logs burn for days or weeks after a fire has passed through and destroy organic matter, including seeds of the understorey species. Seed of Karri, held in capsules high on the tree, ripens rapidly after a fire and is shed onto the ashbeds. With the winter rains the seeds soon germinate and grow rapidly without heavy shade and without the competition for soil space that occurs between fire-opportunist species away from the ashbeds. It is on the deep ashbeds left by burnt logs and stumps that natural regeneration of Karri occurs. After two years, seedlings may reach 3 or 4 metres high, and a single vigorous Karri may reach up to 25 metres within twenty years.

The buds of Karri take 4–5 years to produce mature seed. Flowering usually takes place half way through this cycle so that there are usually two stages of maturation present on the branches. The older developing fruits are found on the older stems. The flowers are creamy white and are prolific nectar-yielders, the honey produced from Karri being of high quality.

Eucalypts other than Jarrah occur either mixed with Karri or surrounding the Karri forests. Two of these are the Tingles, a name which is apparently an abbreviation of a native name Tingle Tingle. There are three species, restricted to a small area near Walpole. The Red Tingle, (*Eucalyptus jacksonii*), is one of the State's biggest trees. In height it reaches only 70 metres but near the base of the tree may be up to 5 metres in diameter. The circumference of one tree has been measured as 20 metres. In appearance, the trees are similar to Jarrah but can be recognised by the browner bark and denser crown of leaves. The rainfall of the area in which the Red Tingle occurs is over 1,200 mm per annum; this includes a summer rainfall of over 300 mm, a figure which is higher than for any other part of the South-West. The forests of Red Tingle which grow between the Bow and Frankland Rivers near Walpole are familiar to tourists as the 'Valley of the Giants'.

The Yellow Tingle, *Eucalyptus guilfoylei*, is also found in the Walpole area. Generally it is a smaller tree and does not develop the great trunk, being up to 40 metres high with a diameter of just over 1 metre. Apart from the yellowish colour of the wood, Yellow Tingle is distinguished from Red Tingle and from Jarrah by its bud and fruit characters.

The Wattie, *Agonis juniperina*, is another tree of the family Myrtaceae which occurs in the Karri forest area. Mostly occurring as a tall shrub in very moist habitats such as along water courses, this species may attain a trunk diameter of 1 metre and a height of 25 metres. Like the other species of *Agonis* the flowers are white and are borne in axillary clusters towards the ends of the branches.

In the Karri forest and neighbouring Tingle and Jarrah forest there are a number of attractive shrubs and ferns as well as many mosses and liverworts. The best known of the shrubs is undoubtedly the Crowea, *Crowea angustifolia* (Pl. 148). Related to the Crowea is the Karri Boronia, *Boronia gracilipes* (Pl. 153).

The Pea-flowered family is represented by the extremely attractive Tree Hovea, *Hovea elliptica* (Pl. 154) and the Holly Flame-pea, *Chorizema ilicifolium* (Pl. 150). The water bushes, *Bossiaea aquifolia* and *Bossiaea webbii*, are also characteristic of the wetter parts of the Karri and neighbouring forests. The fan-shaped leaves of these species are generally fringed by soft spines which hold drops of water during the frequent light rains of the forest.

One of the few members of the heath family, Epacridaceae, in the forest is the Tassel Flower, *Leucopogon verticillatus* (Pl. 151). The leafy stems of this large-leaved species resemble small bamboo plants though the tassels of flowers give this species its common name.

Three creepers add to the tangled undergrowth of the Karri forest and in spring make great splashes of colour. They are Coral Vine, *Kennedia coccinea* (Pls. 115, 116), Sarsaparilla, *Hardenbergia comptoniana*, and Clematis, *Clematis pubescens*. Sarsaparilla has racemes of purple pea flowers borne in profusion among the trifoliate leaves, while Clematis makes a contrast with its masses of large, white, 4-petalled flowers.

Underneath the shrubs collect the litter, bark and leaves of the Karri and other trees as well as the fallen leaves of the other storeys. In this litter, particularly on the edge of clearings in the forest, grow other flowering species such as the Karri Dampiera, *Dampiera hederacea* (Pl. 149), as well as about five species of ferns and more lowly plants. The mosses and liverworts of this habitat are very poorly known, a number of species growing on fallen logs and around the base of large trees as well as in the litter layer.

The Bracken, *Pteridium esculentum*, is the most common and the largest native fern in the South-West; the fronds may reach 2 metres above the ground when the shrubs are dense. The Maiden Hair, *Adiantum aethiopicum*, frequently grows on moist slopes along with the Screw Fern *Lindsaea linearis* (Pl. 146). Two other species of fern are the soft Necklace Fern, *Asplenium flabellifolium*, which is a common rock fern, and one of the Spleenworts, *Asplenium adiantoides*. This latter species frequently occurs as an epiphyte on the mossy base of large Karri trees.

In late winter, when the forest is very wet and humidity is high, the Helmet Orchid, *Corybas dilatatus*, flowers among the litter and on fallen logs. The hooded, dark red, translucent flowers, about 1 cm across, are borne close to the heart-shaped leaf, but if fertilized their pedicels elongate for up to 15 cm, to assist in seed dispersal.

Albany District

THIS REGION IS A coastal strip between the Donnelly and Pallinup Rivers and includes also the Porongurup Range and south Stirlings area. There is great variety of landform here—rocky headlands and sandy beaches, inlets, lateritic and granitic hills, rolling heaths, rivers, and lakes and swamps, both fresh and saline. The climate is a cool wet winter and a warm to hot summer during which light rains may fall. The rainfall ranges from 600–1200 mm.

King George Sound, at the centre of the region, was discovered on 28 September 1791 by the English navigator Vancouver. Archibald Menzies, surgeon and botanist to the expedition, made a collection of plants, many of which were later described by Robert Brown. Brown himself spent 4 weeks there in 1801–2, on Matthew Flinders' expedition in the *Investigator*. The French botanist Leschenault de la Tour, on the Baudin expedition in search of la Pérouse, also spent almost 4 weeks there early in 1803.

From the beginning it was realised that here was a rich flora strikingly different from that of Europe and in many respects from that of eastern Australia. It has excited the interest of botanists and naturalists ever since.

The vegetation ranges from low heath to tall forest. Coastal dunes and hills carry scrub, often dense and usually windpruned, while inlets are bordered with salt-tolerant samphires, sedges and paperbark trees. Farther inland, especially from Albany westwards, are jarrah and karri forests. Karri forest occurs also on the Porongurup Range, with an isolated pocket on Mt. Manypeaks (see section on karri forest). To the north and east of the Porongurups are stretches of shrublands and heath, often dominated by stunted jarrah. The lakes and swamps vary according to the water level and salinity. Dry swamps have dense scrub while wet ones often are bordered with tall sedges and paperbarks. In the north-eastern parts, clay depressions may be dominated by Flat-topped Yates, while salt lakes support samphires and low paperbarks. Dense belts of trees and shrubs occur along rivers and streams.

As in most of the South-West, Eucalypts are usually the dominant plants of the region, ranging from tall karri to low mallees. A tall smooth-barked tree similar in appearance to karri but with larger buds and fruit is Bullich, *Eucalyptus megacarpa*. It is seen in near-coastal areas, along creeks, and in stunted form on some granitic hills (Pl. 413).

Red-flowering Gum, *E. ficifolia* (Pl. 173), is well-known in cultivation but rare in the wild, being known from a few populations between Denmark and Walpole. Here it is a stunted, rough-barked tree, though old stumps indicate that large trees existed previously.

North and east of the Porongurups, low-lying flats are often dominated by Flat-topped Yates, *E. occidentalis*. This tree grows to 25 m, has rough, dark bark on the lower trunk, and a wide, spreading crown.

Mallee Eucalypts are common on the heaths in the eastern areas. Bell-fruited Mallee, *E. preissiana* (Pl. 263), is common, especially in gravelly soils. Also frequent is the Apple Mallee *E. buprestium* (so named because jewel beetles (buprestids) were seen on the first specimens collected) which has very small flowers, and spherical fruit ± 2 cm across.

At the height of its flowering in March, many summer-dry swamps are ablaze with the brilliant red spikes of Swamp Bottlebrush, *Beaufortia sparsa* (Pl. 179). This is the most spectacular of several prominent bottlebrushes here. Gravel Bottlebrush, *B. decussata*, grows in jarrah forests near Albany and is distinguished by its opposite leaves and dark red flowers with larger petals. Albany Bottlebrush, *Callistemon speciosus* (Pl. 172), one of the two endemic WA species of this Australian genus, grows on the margins of wet swamps.

An unusual bottlebrush is *Melaleuca diosmifolia* which grows on granite rocks along the coast from Albany to C. Riche and flowers in spring. It is a spreading shrub to 3 m with crowded, oblong-elliptic leaves 1–2 cm long and large, greenish-yellow spikes.

Many *Melaleucas* occur here, and a common species on sandy soils of the heaths is *M. thymoides*. This small shrub has lanceolate, 3-nerved leaves ± 1 cm long and small heads of yellow flowers.

Melaleuca cuticularis, the common paperbark of estuaries and salt lakes, has oblong, dark green leaves to 1 cm long and small terminal heads of white flowers surrounded by small brown bracts. Along rivers and fresh lakes the paperbark is *M. rhaphiophylla*, with slender, terete pale green leaves 2 cm long and loose spikes of white flowers.

Another widespread swamp myrtle is *Leptospermum firmum*. This teatree grows to 3 m, with oblanceolate leaves 1–2 cm long, and large white flowers in the upper axils. Peppermints, *Agonis* species, are frequent, best known being *A. flexuosa* (Pl. 8), now widely cultivated. *A. linearifolia*, a shrub with linear-lanceolate leaves 1–3 cm long, frequents the swamps while Wattie, *A. juniperina*, is a tall tree with crowded, short narrow leaves, growing along creeks and in swamps. *A. marginata*, inhabiting granitic hills, is a spreading shrub with obovate-elliptic, hairy-margined leaves. On the eastern heaths, *A. spathulata* occurs, being a small shrub with spathulate leaves to 5 mm long. The 10 species of *Agonis* are endemic in South-Western Australia.

Hypocalymma cordifolium, a white-flowered shrub to 1 m tall, has curious winged stems, sessile cordate leaves to 1 cm long and axillary, pedunculate flowers which appear in spring. It favours swamps while *H. strictum,* grows on coastal sands and is a shrub to 70 cm with linear leaves and axillary sessile pink flowers, appearing in summer. A most unusual myrtle is the Swamp Daisy, *Actinodium cunninghamii* (Pl. 162). Featherflowers, *Verticordia*, are relatively few. Plume Featherflower, *V. plumosa* (Pl. 419), occurs on granitic slopes and Hidden Featherflower, *V. habrantha* (Pl. 163), on the south Stirling heaths. Here, too, is seen *V. multiflora*, a low shrub with bright yellow, woolly flowers. Other myrtles include species of *Astartea*, *Baeckea* and *Thryptomene*.

The Banksia family, Proteaceae, adds many varied and fascinating plants to the vegetation. Among them are 17 species of *Banksia*, ranging from tall trees to prostrate shrubs. The most spectacular is Scarlet Banksia, *B. coccinea* (Pl. 157), while Red Swamp Banksia, *B. occidentalis* (Pl. 168), is the only other red-flowered species here. *B. brownii* has large brownish-red spikes with hooked styles, and finely-divided leaves which are relatively soft; this tall shrub grows in woodlands N of Albany. Oak-leaved Banksia, *B. quercifolia* var. *quercifolia*, is a swamp-dweller with rusty-brown flowers.

The only WA Banksia to be restricted to coastal habitats is *B. praemorsa*. This stiff shrub to 3 m tall has cuneate, toothed leaves 2–3 cm long and large spikes of brown and gold flowers. It grows near the beach between Albany and C. Riche.

Another species confined to the region is the Albany Banksia, *B. verticillata*. This small tree has elliptic-lanceolate entire leaves, closely white-felted beneath, and spikes of golden yellow flowers with hooked styles, appearing in March-April. It grows on granite outcrops near Albany.

About 12 species of *Dryandra* occur here, the most spectacular being Showy Dryandra, *D. formosa*. This shrub of 1–3 m has relatively soft leaves divided into many triangular lobes, and large heads of golden-orange flowers. It is common on the hills and on some gravelly plains. In the eastern part of the region the shrubby *D. cuneata* (Pl. 195) and *D. falcata* (Pl. 227) are common, while prostrate species include *D. nivea* (Pl. 82) and *D. pteridifolia* (Pl. 204). *D. tenuifolia* is a sprawling shrub with erect, linear, sparsely-toothed leaves and heads of dark brown flowers surrounded by bracts 3–4 cm long.

A shrub of similar habit to Scarlet Banksia is Scallops, *Hakea cucullata* (Pl. 196), which is frequent on heaths NE of Albany. *H. ferruginea* is also common, being a much-branched shrub to 5 m with cordate leaves 2–3 cm long and axillary clusters of white flowers followed by thick, beaked fruit. The new growth, like that of many Proteaceae, is protected by dense, rusty hairs which wear off as the leaves mature.

Also on the heaths is *H. baxteri*, with thick, fan-shaped leaves, small brown flowers and large fruit. *H. trifurcata*, widespread in the South-West, is unusual in having both flat and terete leaves, the latter usually divided. The flowers are white with red styles.

In summer *H. ruscifolia* is in flower. The hairy, arching stems have crowded, elliptic-lanceolate, pungent leaves 2 cm long and many clusters of small white honey-scented flowers. It grows in sand on open heaths and extends N beyond Perth.

On granite hills near the coast is *H. suaveolens*, a spreading-erect shrub to 3 m with stiff, terete, often divided, leaves and axillary clusters of white flowers followed by swollen, 2-beaked fruit. This species has become naturalised in the Cape Province of South Africa and is a serious bushland weed there.

In early spring, two *Isopogons* are conspicuous on heaths and in woodlands near Albany—Rose Coneflower, *I. formosus* (Pl. 158), and *I. cuneatus*. The latter is a much-branched shrub to 2.5 m with lanceolate, obtuse leaves 5–10 cm long and large terminal pink flower heads. Another floriferous species is *I. axillaris* which grows to 1.5 m, with linear-oblanceolate leaves 2–4 cm long and axillary clusters of silky pink flowers. It grows only near Albany.

Two distinctive smokebushes are *Conospermum caeruleum* and Tangled Smokebush, *C. flexuosum,* neither having the familiar woolly flowers of most species. Both are perennial herbs, *C. caeruleum* having long basal leaves and open panicles of smooth, deep blue flowers, and *C. flexuosum* having divaricately-branched panicles of silky white or pale blue flowers with spreading lobes. They grow in the woodlands.

Other Proteaceous genera in the region are *Grevillea, Adenanthos, Franklandia* (Pl. 232), *Persoonia, Synaphea* (Pls. 171, 174), *Lambertia* and *Petrophile* (Pl. 159).

This region is the home of Scented Boronia, *B. megastigma*, which is still common in some swamps, though picking has depleted it. It is a small slender shrub with leaves of 3 linear leaflets 1 cm long, and bell-like pedicillate flowers 5–6 mm long, brown outside and golden inside. It is apparently short-lived but regenerates freely from seed after bushfires.

Red Boronia, *B. heterophylla* (Pl. 176), is also scented though rather unpleasantly, while Tall Boronia, *B. molloyae* (Pl. 175), has very aromatic foliage. On the coast, Winged Boronia, *B. alata*, is a common shrub. It has aromatic pinnate leaves (the rhachis being narrowly winged) and umbels of pink flowers with pointed petals. It extends along the coast from Albany to Perth and flowers in October-November.

In jarrah and karri forest and on some peaks, between Pemberton and Mt. Manypeaks, is found Crowea, *C. angustifolia* (Pl. 148). This is a glabrous shrub to 3 m tall with linear to elliptic, denticulate leaves 2–3 cm long and axillary, 5-petalled flowers which are usually white but may be red-tinged.

Also in this family is Blister Bush, *Phebalium anceps* which grows in swamps and along creeks. A shrub to 3 m, often covered with small silvery scales, it has angular branchlets, elliptic leaves 7–12 cm long and cymes of white 5-petalled flowers. The sap causes blisters on the skin of some people.

There are many legumes in most habitats of the region ranging from prostrate creepers to small trees. Representatives are shown in Pls. 169 *(Daviesia oppositifolia)* and 182 *(Chorizema reticulatum)*. *Oxylobium lanceolatum*, a tall shrub often seen along creeks and rivers, is a tall shrub with lanceolate leaves 5–8 cm long and terminal racemes of orange flowers.

In woodlands and forests occurs *Mirbelia dilatata*, a glabrous shrub to 2 m with cuneate, pungently-lobed leaves 2 cm long and short axillary racemes of bright pink flowers. It extends N to Perth and E to Esperance.

Among the numerous wattles are Drummond's Wattle, *Acacia drummondii* (Pl. 198), and Prickly Moses, *A. pulchella* (Pl. 14). An attractive species is *A. myrtifolia*, a glabrous shrub to 3 m tall with angular stems, lanceolate-elliptic phyllodes 3–10 cm long and racemes of cream flowers. Each head has only a few flowers but the dense stamens give them the usual round appearance. The linear, curved pods have prominent undulate margins. It is common in woodlands, flowering in late winter and early spring.

The heath family, Epacridaceae, is highly developed with 12 genera and many species here. While most have white flowers, Spindle Heath, *Cosmelia rubra* (Pl. 166), has deep red flowers, and the *Andersonias* are also colourful; three common species have pink calyxes and blue corollas. Foxtails, *Andersonia caerulea*, is a shrub to 40 cm with crowded linear-lanceolate leaves 5–10 mm long and small flowers on dense leafy shoots. It occurs in woodlands and swamps, flowering mainly in winter. *A. sprengelioides* is a cushion-like shrub on coastal granite slopes: it has many stems with dense, stiffly-spreading leaves, and flowers 7 mm long crowded in the upper axils. Spiked Andersonia, *A. simplex* (Pl. 208), may have blue or pink corollas.

In this region are 4 of the 5 species of Curry Flower, *Lysinema*, a genus endemic in the South-West. *L. ciliatum* (Pl. 48), is common. *L. fimbriatum* is a slender shrub to 70 cm with appressed lanceolate leaves 4–5 mm long and a few large terminal flowers nearly 2 cm across, each with prominently-lacerated brown bracts. It grows on open heaths between Albany and the Stirlings, flowering in winter and spring. On swamp margins at the same seasons is seen *L. lasianthum*, a slender shrub to 50 cm with sparse, linear, obtuse leaves 5 mm long and loose racemes of flowers with small corollas. *L. conspicuum* also grows on swamp margins, between Albany and Augusta; it grows to 70 cm tall and has slightly spreading acute leaves to 1 cm long with dense terminal leafy racemes of flowers, the corolla lobes being acute.

There are six species of the genus *Sphenotoma*, all endemic in the South-West. The pure white corollas have broad spreading lobes which dry out and have given rise to the common name paper-heaths. *S. capitatum* is a stiff erect shrub to 70 cm with straight, lanceolate, acute leaves 2 cm long and large flowers in terminal spikes 2–3 cm long. It grows in woodlands and on heaths from Augusta to Hopetoun. *S. dracophylloides* is a similar shrub with very spreading leaves and flower spikes up to 6 cm long. *S. gracilis* is a swamp dweller and is more slender, with narrow leaves less than 1 cm long, the lower ones spreading or recurved, the upper ones appressed; the flower spikes are 2–4 cm long.

Although there are many species of Goodeniaceae here, few are prominent plants. Two widespread *Lechenaultia* species are Heath Lechenaultia, *L. tubiflora* (Pl. 235), which here is a small erect perennial with cream flowers, and *L. expansa*, a shrub to 50 cm with small pale blue flowers. Both grow in open, sandy areas and flower in late spring to early summer. Red Lechenaultia, *L. formosa*, becomes common in the eastern part of the region. A number of *Goodenia, Dampiera* and *Scaevola* species occur on swamp margins. On the coast, the shrubby *Scaevola crassifolia* and *S. nitida* are frequent, both having large, obovate, crenulate leaves and terminal panicles of blue flowers. Between Augusta and Albany in swamps is found *Diaspasis filifolia*, an endemic monotypic genus distinguished partly by the corolla tube being entire at the base. It is a slender perennial herb with linear-terete leaves 1–4 cm long and pedunculate white or pink flowers 1.5–2 cm across.

If any one habitat of this region could be mentioned for its outstanding interest it is the swamplands. In and around these are many fascinating plants, often endemic to the region. Orchids abound here (e.g. Pls. 181, 183–188) and are especially prevalent after bushfires. There are many insectivorous plants such as the Albany Pitcher Plant, *Cephalotus* (Pls. 164–5), sundews, *Drosera* species, and bladderworts, *Utricularia* and *Polypompholyx*. Sedges and rushes of many genera make up a large proportion of the swamp flora, and there are several unusual ferns such as *Schizaea* and *Lycopodium*.

Stirling Range

NAMED AFTER THE FIRST Governor of Western Australia, Captain James Stirling, the Stirling Range contains the highest peaks in the southern part of the State, rising to over 1100 metres. They are impressive from any direction, and were noted by Flinders as he sailed along the south coast in January 1802. The earliest botanical collections there were made by William Baxter in 1829 and James Drummond in 1844 and 1846.

The Range consists of hard, metasedimentary rocks of Proterozoic age. Outcrops are many and rugged, often forming faces which provide the best climbing in WA. The strata are clearly seen and ripple-marked rocks are frequent—evidence of the deposition of sediments in water millions of years ago.

The green mantle which clothes the peaks is mostly scrub which is often dense and harsh. It extends down across the plains where it is often broken by woodlands. Over 550 species of plants occur in the Range, many being restricted to it. Almost half this number belong to 3 families—Myrtaceae, Proteaceae and Papilionaceae.

The Myrtaceae is the largest family with over 100 species. There are 24 *Eucalyptus* species and they are often the dominant trees and mallees, most common being jarrah, marri and wandoo, with some yate and bullich in sheltered valleys. Of the mallees, the most conspicuous with its pale green foliage is Tallerack, *E. tetragona* (Pl. 246). More striking florally are Bell-fruited mallee, *E. preissiana* (Pl. 263), and Four-winged mallee, *E. tetraptera* (Pl. 216), which has large thick leaves and solitary, square red flowers.

The mountain bells, *Darwinia* species, are perhaps the most famous flowers of the Range and are mostly restricted in their occurrence. On Bluff Knoll are *D. collina*, with quaint little lemon-yellow bells, and *D. squarrosa* (Pl. 202) with pink bells. The largest and most handsome is Mondurup Bell, *D. macrostegia*, with red and white bells 3–4 cm long, found on the western peaks. *D. hypericifolia* occurs on most of the central peaks: it is a slender shrub to 70 cm with oblong leaves 1–2 cm long and narrow red bells 2–3 cm long. Also widespread is *D. leiostyla*, with pink and white bells, but Cranbrook Bell, *D. meeboldii* (Pl. 190), with bells banded with green, white and red, is restricted to Hamilla Hill.

Conspicuous among the scrub are several bottlebrushes, *Beaufortia* species. The largest is *B. decussata*, with deep red flowers, the leaves being arranged in opposite rows up the stem. *B. anisandra* is a small shrub with ovate, spreading leaves and heads of maroon flowers, while Stirling Range Bottlebrush, *B. heterophylla* (Pl. 206), has narrow leaves and deep red flowers. There are also several one-sided bottlebrushes, *Calothamnus*. In sandy soils is *C. gracilis*, a low shrub with terete leaves and deep red flowers which emerge through the bark of the stems.

Of several *Kunzea* species, the most distinctive is Mountain Kunzea, *K. recurva* var. *montana* (Pl. 193). The other species have pink flowers. *Kunzea* is an Australian genus of about 30 species of which 12 are endemic in the South-West.

Two attractive myrtles endemic in the Range are *Hypocalymma myrtifolium* and *H. speciosum*. The former is a shrub of 1–2 m with elliptic leaves 2 cm long, the margins often shortly fringed; the flowers are creamy-white and sessile in the leaf axils. It grows on the higher slopes. More widespread, *H. speciosum* is a tufted or spreading shrub to 70 cm with angular stems and round leaves less than 1 cm across. The deep pink flowers are pedicillate and axillary.

Featherflowers, *Verticordia*, are not prominent here, but several attractive species occur, including Hidden Featherflower, *V. habrantha* (Pl. 163). Waxflowers are represented by *Chamelaucium confertiflorum* which is common in sandy woodlands in Red Gum Pass. It is a slender shrub to 1 m with narrow acute leaves, and flowers crowded towards the ends of the branches, white turning pink. The Swamp Daisy, *Actinodium cunninghamii* (Pl. 162), occurs in some low-lying areas.

The Proteaceae, well-named after the Greek god Proteus who could change his form at will, are represented by over 85 species of great diversity. The Banksias range from Bull Banksia, *B. grandis*, a tree with large leaves and pale yellow spikes, down to the prostrate *B. repens* and *B. prostrata*. The flower cones of the two latter species, of a pinkish-cream and rusty-brown respectively, rest on the surface of the soil. Scarlet Banksia, *B. coccinea* (Pl. 157), is common in sandy soils. In sheltered gullies and on some peaks is *B. brownii*, with soft, feathery foliage and large red-brown flower spikes. Stirling Range Banksia, *B. solandri* (Pl. 203) is frequent, especially on the slopes of the eastern peaks, while Mountain Banksia, *B. quercifolia* var. *integrifolia* (Pl. 265), is confined to the summits. Five other Banksias are present in the Range.

The related *Dryandras* have heads of flowers and the foliage is usually prickly. However the Showy Dryandra, *D. formosa*, is a tall shrub with relatively soft leaves and golden-orange flowers. Two other common species on the plains and slopes are Wedge-leaved Dryandra, *D. cuneata* (Pl. 195), and Prickly Dryandra, *D. falcata* (Pl. 227). Similar in habit to Tangled Honeypot (Pl. 204) is *D. drummondii* which has large, triangular-lobed leaves and golden flowers surrounded by red-brown bracts. Two species are restricted to the Range,

D. concinna and *D. foliolata*, both of which have small yellow heads hidden among the prickly leaves.

Smokebushes, *Conospermum* are generally inconspicuous plants unless flowering. The individual flowers are small, as with most of our wildflowers, but are usually produced in large numbers, often obscuring the branches and leaves. Typical of these is *C. distichum,* a small shrub with slender terete leaves and masses of white woolly flowers: it inhabits deep sandy areas. Also in these areas is *C. teretifolium*, a shrub with long terete leaves and large panicles of long, cream flowers without any wool at all. On the higher slopes is the blue-flowered Stirling Range Smokebush, *C. dorrienii* (Pl. 192).

The coneflowers, *Isopogon* and *Petrophile,* are present in varied forms and colours. Best known is the magnificent *Isopogon latifolius* of the peaks. This large-leaved shrub has heads of bright pink flowers up to 8 cm across, appearing in late spring. Other pink-flowered species are Stirling Range Coneflower, *I. baxteri* (Pl. 199), and Rose Coneflower, *I. formosus* (Pl. 158). On gravelly soils of the plains is *Petrophile serruriae* which has finely-divided prickly leaves and many small heads of cream or pink flowers on arching stems. Long-leaved Petrophile, *P. longifolia* (Pl. 159), occurs in sandy soils.

Sixteen species of *Hakea* in the Range illustrate the wide variety of fruit forms of this genus. The woody follicles persist on the plant and split open when dried, as in a bushfire, to release two winged seeds. Some are large, as in *H. baxteri* which has a thick fruit 3–4 cm long; this tall stiff shrub has attractive fan-shaped leaves. In Blue Hakea, *H. lehmanniana* (Pl. 201), the fruit is smaller and covered with prickly bristles. Scallops, *H. cucullata* (Pl. 196), is a tall slender shrub widespread on the plains; the smooth, swollen fruit has a thick beak.

Wild Honeysuckles, *Lambertia*, are represented by two common species—Chittick, *L. inermis* (Pl. 245), and *L. ericifolia*, a tall open shrub with linear leaves and flowers similar to Chittick.

The pea flowers of the family *Papilionaceae* are often prominent in the spring. A beautiful shrub of the higher slopes is Mountain Pea, *Oxylobium atropurpureum* (Pl. 209), in which the red flowers hang rather like bells. Various species of Flame Pea, *Chorizema,* have bright red, pink, orange and yellow flowers.

A strange pea flower in Chester Pass is *Cupulanthus bracteolosus.* A straggling, prostrate shrub with linear leaves and solitary reddish flowers borne in cup-like bracts and calyxes, it is the only species of its genus.

Several Bitter Peas, *Daviesia*, are present, including Rattle Pea, *D. oppositifolia* (Pl. 169), in which the bracts enlarge around the pods. It is common in the woodlands. Known only from the Range is *D. trigonophylla,* a shrub with curious winged stems and clusters of orange and maroon flowers.

An unusual colour combination is seen in *Gompholobium venustum,* a low, spreading shrub with pinnate leaves and terminal small blue and red flowers.

Stirling Range Poison, *Gastrolobium velutinum,* is the commonest of three toxic species in the Range. It is a shrub to 1.3 m tall with oblong leaves 1–2 cm long, opposite or in 3s, and terminal racemes of small orange and red flowers. Prickly and Heart-leaf Poison are also here.

About ten species of the *Boronia* family occur here. Most are pink-flowered Boronias, but a curious species is *Muiriantha hassellii* which is confined to the Range and is quite rare. It is a slender shrub to 40 cm with lanceolate leaves 1–2 cm long and solitary, pendulous, cream, bell-like flowers 2 cm long.

The heath family, Epacridaceae, is well represented but its species are often inconspicuous as the flowers are small, especially in the many species of *Leucopogon.* However, on the upper slopes of some mountains, Giant Andersonia, *A. axilliflora* (Pl. 211), is often prominent, as well as the related *A. echinocephala* which has smaller, twisted leaves. Their cream flowers and bracts stand out against the pungent, dark green leaves. At the other extreme is the tiny Red Andersonia, *A. grandiflora* (Pl. 210). On the plains the Foxtail Andersonia, *A. caerulea,* displays its dense spikes of blue and pink flowers in winter, while Spiked Andersonia, *A. simplex* (Pl. 208) is also common.

Two species of Paper-heath, *Sphenotoma,* are in flower in late spring, *S. drummondii* (Pl. 212) being restricted to rock crevices near the summits. *S. dracophylloides* is a taller, erect shrub, to 70 cm high, with crowded acute leaves 2–3 cm long and dense flower spikes up to 6 cm long. It also occurs on the slopes.

Numerous species of triggerplants, *Stylidium,* are to be seen, especially in spring. Their usual lowly form is offset by brightly coloured flowers which have the added attraction of the sensitive column. The latter, bearing both anthers and stigma which mature at different times, is sensitive and flicks over at a slight touch, resetting itself within a short time. The climbing *S. scandens* (Pl. 161) with whorled, hooked leaves and bright pink flowers is common, while a rare species is *S. verticillatum* which also has whorled leaves and pink flowers and is known only from Mondurup. In winter the Tile-leaved Triggerplant, *S. imbricatum,* bears racemes of purple or pink flowers on wiry stems which are covered with tiny scale leaves.

In the *Lechenaultia* family, Goodeniaceae, a prominent species on the higher slopes in late spring is the golden-flowered *Velleia foliosa.* Red Lechenaultia, *L. formosa,* is common, and many *Dampieras* are present.

The Southern Cross, *Xanthosia rotundifolia* (Pl. 180), is common in the Stirlings, and a variant restricted to the Range is the var. *hypoleuca* which has a white-felted undersurface to the leaves.

Kangaroo Paws, *Anigozanthos*, are represented by the Red Kangaroo Paw, *A. rufus,* which has tall branching stems and grows in sandy areas, and the Dwarf Kangaroo Paw, *A. gabrielae* (Pl. 191), which occurs in winter-wet areas.

Nearly 50 species of orchids have been recorded for

the Range, representing many genera. The outstanding species is the Butterfly Orchid, *Caladenia lobata,* which grows in sheltered gullies of the foothills. It grows to 35 cm tall and has a single large red and green flower with upturned lateral sepals and an elegantly fringed labellum 2–3 cm across which trembles in the slightest breeze. At the other extreme is the Dwarf Spider Orchid, *C. bryceana*, which is only a few cm tall and has a flower less than 1 cm across, the smallest of the genus. It occurs in Chester Pass but is rare. Others such as the Cowslip Orchid, *C. flava* (Pl. 10), and White Spider Orchid, *C. patersonii* var. *longicauda* (Pl. 122), are common.

An interesting plant is the Slipper Orchid, *Cryptostylis ovata*, which is pollinated by male ichneumon wasps attempting to mate with the flower. The brown labellum 2–3 cm long is the most conspicuous feature of the inverted flowers which appear well into the summer months. The species extends to the summits and is the only south-western orchid with perennial leaves.

Southern Sandplains and Heath

THIS REGION INCLUDES THE undulating plains along the south coast from the Pallinup River to Israelite Bay and extending inland to Lake Grace. (The area known as the Barrens, between Bremer Bay and Hopetoun, contains many endemic plants and is treated separately in the next section.) The land here is relatively flat, rising gradually as one goes inland, and the few hills are remnants of granite or laterite or quartzite. The highest peak is Mt. Ragged, a quartzite ridge near Israelite Bay which reaches 583 metres. There are few rivers, all of intermittent flow and mostly saline, while there are a few salt lakes in the NW part of the region.

The soils are mostly sand, clay and loam overlying laterite which in turn overlies a granite basement. The vegetation is generally low or tall heath, often with emergent mallee Eucalypts which are sometimes dense. Low woodlands or thickets of taller Eucalypts occur in places, and between Lake Grace and Ravensthorpe are pockets of Salmon Gum woodland.

Historically and botanically an important district in the region is Esperance, for here some of the earliest plant collections in Australia were made. The French botanist Labillardière, on the d'Entrecasteaux expedition in search of la Pérouse, spent seven days there in December 1792. Among the many plants collected were specimens of a kangaroo paw, *Anigozanthos rufus*, the first species of this intriguing genus to be seen by Europeans. Later, in January 1802, Robert Brown, on Flinders' voyage in the *Investigator*, spent three days at Lucky Bay and collected about 100 plants.

By far the major families in this region are the Proteaceae and Myrtaceae. However, many genera and species of many families occur on sandplains where the diversity is always a striking feature, and dominant species can rarely be singled out.

Banksias again are a feature here. On dunes near the coast, between Hopetoun and Israelite Bay, Showy Banksia, *B. speciosa* (Pl. 225), and Teasel Banksia, *B. pulchella* (Pl. 222), are common. Nodding Banksia, *B. nutans* (Pl. 223), also grows here and extends west to the Stirling Range. Scarlet Banksia, *B. coccinea* (Pl. 157), and Baxter's Banksia, *B. baxteri* (Pl. 167), extend from Hopetoun westwards.

Farther inland, Southern Plains Banksia, *B. media* (Pl. 224), is often a prominent shrub, especially in deep sand. Usually a rounded shrub to 5 m tall, if left unburnt it becomes an untidy tree to 8 m with a thick trunk, while on the coast it is kept almost prostrate by onshore winds.

Four of the true prostrate Banksias are present here, two of them localised and as yet unnamed. The most common is Creeping Banksia, *B. repens*, which has underground stems, erect leaves with large coarsely-toothed lobes and spikes of creamy-pink flowers opening in October-November. East of Esperance is *B. petiolaris* which has stems on the surface, erect, shortly toothed leaves which are white on the undersurface, and cream-pink flowers appearing in November-December.

Woolly Banksia, *B. baueri*, is a rounded shrub of 1–2 m inhabiting deep sands as far east as the Oldfield River. It has very large spikes, the flowers being hairy and tipped by long awns, and usually pale mauve or brown. It flowers in May and June.

Two species with pendulous spikes occur between Ongerup and Ravensthorpe: *B. lemanniana* has pale yellow flowers, and *B. caleyi* has red flowers. Both flower in late spring and have very large fruit.

A widespread species with short, linear, entire leaves is *B. violacea*. This small shrub has flower spikes 5–6 cm across, purplish-brown and green, with exserted hooked styles, appearing mainly in late summer.

Many *Dryandras* are present, their leaves usually more pungently lobed than those of *Banksias*. Four representative species are shown in Pls. 82, 195, 226 and 227. The fruit of *Dryandras* are small follicles hidden among the floral bracts of the old heads. They are woody, but thinner than those of *Banksias*, though usually still requiring a bushfire to make them open and shed their seeds. While some species are killed by fire and regenerate from seed, others have lignotubers from which they regenerate after fire.

Grevillea and *Hakea* species are many and varied. A common *Grevillea* of the heaths is *G. hookerana* (Pl. 218) which has a pine-like or spreading habit and is one of several species in WA with 'toothbrush' inflorescences. Red Combs, *G. concinna* (Pl. 220), is another of the group but is a sprawling shrub with shorter racemes.

Between Lake Grace and Lake King, Flame Grevillea, *G. eriostachya*, is often prominent. This also is a pine-like shrub to 6 m tall, with long leaves divided into linear segments, and large racemes of orange, somewhat sticky flowers. Another species here is *G. integrifolia*, a shrub to 2 m with obovate-spathulate leaves 2–3 cm long and terminal racemes of small yellow flowers.

There are a number of red-flowered *Grevilleas*. *G. nudiflora* is a prostrate shrub with erect, linear leaves and long, trailing, leafless flowering branches which bear small racemes of bright red flowers. *G. pauciflora* is an erect shrub to 1 m with narrow-obovate entire leaves 3–4 cm long and a few axillary flowers. *G. pectinata* has pinnately-divided leaves 2–3 cm long and loose racemes of deep pink flowers.

Of the *Hakeas*, Pincushion Hakea, *H. laurina* (Pl. 233) is the best known, being often cultivated. It is an attractive winter-flowering shrub of 2–5 m and is especially common around Ravensthorpe. In this district also is an allied species, *H. obtusa*, which is a much-branched shrub to 3 m with elliptic, 3-nerved leaves 3–7 cm long and round clusters of flowers mainly on the old branches. The flowers, appearing in July-August, open cream and turn bright pink, and are followed by rough, beaked fruit 2–3 cm long, often crowded in clusters.

A common species throughout the southern heaths is *H. crassifolia*. This shrub to 5 m tall has thick, smooth, oblanceolate leaves 5–10 cm long, axillary clusters of brown and cream flowers, and large fruit 4–5 cm long often with speckled bark. It flowers in spring.

In the north-west areas *H. multilineata* occurs on gravelly heaths. A shrub to 5 m tall, it has broad-linear, many-nerved leaves 10–14 cm long, dense axillary spikes of bright pink flowers, and swollen fruit 2 cm long with a dorsal groove. It flowers in August-September.

Ashy Hakea, *H. cinerea* (Pl. 219), occurs in deep sand between Hopetoun and Esperance. A similar, more widespread species is *H. corymbosa*. It has a cauliflower-like habit, with narrow, pungent, glabrous leaves and greenish-cream flowers which cover the top of the shrub. The fruit is 1.5–2 cm long, swollen but tapering into a sharp beak. It extends from the Stirling Range to Esperance, flowering in late winter. Like *H. cinerea*, it has disjunct populations in the Hill River heaths north of Perth.

A prominent shrub of deep sands between the Stirling Range and Israelite Bay is Chittick, *Lambertia inermis* (Pl. 245). On the other hand Prickly Honeysuckle, *L. echinata* (Pl. 229), in its typical form is known only from near Esperance. An erect, yellow-flowered form occurs near Albany. The genus *Lambertia* contains 11 species, all except one endemic in the South-West, the other occurring in NSW. Besides the characteristic flowers, they also have distinctive fruit which are follicles 1–2 cm long, usually beaked and spiny, and containing two flat round seeds.

Species of *Isopogon* and *Petrophile* are numerous. Nodding Coneflower, *Isopogon teretifolius* (Pl. 221), is widespread and is unusual in the nodding flower heads. The terete leaves vary from entire to divaricately divided. *I. villosus* is an attractive little shrub of more inland areas, having short stems with long, much divided terete leaves forming a tangled network, while the woolly yellow flowers are in heads near the base of the plant. Barrel Coneflower, *I. trilobus* (Pl. 248), is common on heaths near the coast, and a similar species is *I. tripartitus* in which the leaves are deeply divided into flat lobes. It extends from the Stirling Range to Israelite Bay.

Petrophile ericifolia is a shrub to 1 m with linear-terete leaves 1–2 cm long and terminal heads of hirsute yellow flowers, the surrounding bracts being often viscid. It grows on inland heaths. *P. phylicoides* is a similar species with glabrous flowers, leaves 1 cm long and fruiting heads with grey, woody bracts. On sandy soil near the coast is *P. teretifolia*, a small shrub with terete, incurved leaves 3–8 cm long and heads of woolly, pale pink flowers with prominent orange-red styles.

There are several varied, showy smokebushes. Typical of the woolly-flowered species is *Conospermum distichum*, which is common in deep sands. It is a shrub to 70 cm with slender, terete, incurved leaves and dense panicles of white flowers which appear in September-October. Blue Smokebush, *C. amoenum* (Pl. 228), is a pale blue-flowered species of heaths in the western part of the region, especially between Lake Grace and Lake King. Quite different from these species are *C. teretifolium* and *C. leianthum* which have glabrous cream flowers. The former is a broad, many-stemmed shrub to 1 m with terete leaves up to 30 cm long and large panicles of flowers, each nearly 2 cm long with long lobes. It grows in sand in near-coastal areas from the Stirling Range to Israelite Bay, flowering in November-December. *C. leianthum* grows on heaths east from Hopetoun and is an erect shrub to 1 m with slender terete leaves to 12 cm long, often crowded, and panicles of small spikes of flowers, each 8 mm long.

An unusual member of the Proteaceae is Lanoline Bush, *Franklandia fucifolia* (Pl. 232), which is widespread on the southern heaths. This genus of two species is endemic in the South-West. The other species, *F. triaristata*, occurs near Busselton and has large, white and brown, vanilla-scented flowers and a fruit with three long awns.

In the family Myrtaceae, the Eucalypts are again prominent, with over 40 species in the region. Tallerack, *E. tetragona* (Pl. 246), is the most conspicuous of the mallee species with its blue-green leaves and glaucous stems and flowers. East of Esperance the white bloom almost disappears and the leaves are often stalked, giving the plants a different aspect. Red-flowered Moort, *E. nutans* (Pl. 215), Four-winged Mallee, *E. tetraptera* (Pl. 216), Warted Yate, *E. megacornuta* (Pl. 217), and Bell-fruited Mallee, *E. preissiana* (Pl. 263), further illustrate the varied forms of Eucalypt in the region.

Between Ongerup and Ravensthorpe, on clay soils which become waterlogged in winter, the Moort, *E. platypus*, is often dominant, sometimes forming pure stands. It is a small tree with orbicular-lanceolate leaves and umbels of 4–9 sessile flowers on flat, recurved peduncles.

Salmon Gums, *E. salmonophloia* (Pl. 426), form woodland pockets on loamy soils between Lake Grace and Ravensthorpe.

Melaleucas are very frequent in most habitats of the region, ranging from low shrubs to paperbark trees, with flowers of white, yellow or pink. Some are summer or autumn-flowering and add colour to the bush at these relatively drab seasons. A common species, especially in clay heaths or mallee associations, is Broom Honeymyrtle, *M. uncinata* (Pl. 332). In deep sands, often near rivers and lakes, *M. pentagona* is found. This is a shrub to 3 m with needle-like leaves 1–2 cm long and heads of pink flowers. *M. pungens*, found mainly between Dumbleyung and Ravensthorpe on heaths, also has needle-like leaves, 1–3 cm long, and pale yellow heads of flowers. Near the coast in deep sands is *M. striata*, a shrub to 1 m with linear, pungent, striate leaves 1–2 cm long and oblong spikes of pink flowers.

Corky Honeymyrtle, *M. suberosa* (Pl. 255), is an unusual shrub in which the flowers emerge through the thick bark of the stems. Another distinctive species is *M. pulchella* which is a small shrub with obtuse, elliptic leaves 3–4 mm long and scattered glabrous pink flowers with prominent petals; the stamens are on broad claws which arch into the centre of the flower. It grows near the coast between Hopetoun and Israelite Bay.

Bottlebrushes—*Beaufortia* and *Calothamnus*—are widespread though with relatively few species. Ravensthorpe Bottlebrush, *B. orbifolia* (Pl. 237), is an attractive, rather open shrub of lateritic soils from Ravensthorpe northwards. The flowers are red and yellow-green at first, later becoming red throughout. Pink Bottlebrush, *B. schaueri* (Pl. 256), and Little Bottlebrush, *B. micrantha* (Pl. 253), are common, the latter showing much variation.

Calothamnus gracilis is frequent in sandy soils from Bremer Bay to Israelite Bay. It is a spreading or erect shrub to 70 cm with slightly corky bark, terete leaves mainly on the upper branches, and deep red flowers along the older stems. Dense Clawflower, *Calothamnus pinifolius* (Pl. 270), occurs on lateritic and quartzite hills of the Ravensthorpe district.

Of several *Leptospermum* species here, Silver Teatree, *L. sericeum* (Pl. 254), is the most spectacular and has the largest flowers of the ten WA species of the genus. It is restricted to granitic slopes of the Esperance district, including the islands of the Recherche Archipelago. Much more widespread in the South-West is *L. spinescens*, a rigid shrub to 1 m with short, spreading, spinescent branches, and cream flowers 10–15 mm wide closely set on the main stems. The capsular fruit are broad, woody and persistent. There are over 40 species of *Leptospermum* which extends from Malaysia to New Zealand but is chiefly Australian.

Featherflowers are often spectacular on the sandheaths. Between Lake Grace and Lake King, late spring sees the flowering of Roe's Featherflower, *Verticordia roei*, and Yellow Featherflower, *V. chrysantha*, often in massed displays (Pl. 213). Painted Featherflower, *V. picta* (Pl. 331), is also common, while in early summer the Common Cauliflower, *V. brownii* (Pl. 335), dots the landscape. A variant of the latter, smaller in habit and with pink flowers, grows on near-coastal heaths east of Esperance. From Ravensthorpe north-westwards, the Claw Featherflower, *V. grandiflora* (Pl. 300), is seen in September-October.

In late summer and early autumn several featherflowers add colour to the sandheaths in the Esperance area. *V. sieberi* is a slender shrub with linear leaves and small pale pink flowers. The featherflower with the smallest flowers of all is *V. minutiflora*, a shrub to 70 cm with linear leaves crowded on short branchlets and dense corymbs of tiny white or pale pink flowers with exserted styles.

There are several waxflowers of which the Large Waxflower, *Chamelaucium megalopetalum* (Pl. 251) is common in sandy habitats east to Israelite Bay. Esperance Waxflower, *C. axillare*, is a taller shrub, growing to 2 m, with linear leaves 1–2 cm long, and flowers 1 cm across in the upper axils; as in most waxflowers, they are white at first, turning red later. This species grows only around Esperance. Several small-flowered species are common. There are about 15 species of *Chamelaucium*, endemic in the South-West.

Members of the *Boronia* family Rutaceae are recognisable, as are the myrtles, by the oil glands in the leaves which give them a distinctive perfume when crushed. There are about 12 *Boronia* species in the region, mostly pink-flowered shrubs such as *B. inornata* (Pl. 247) and Rough Boronia, *B. scabra* (Pl. 249). However, the smallest-flowered species of the genus is widespread here, especially in clay or rocky soil in tall mallee associations. This is *B. inconspicua*, a straggling shrub to 30 cm with pinnate leaves 1–2 cm long, of 3–7 thick, linear leaflets, and axillary white flowers only 2–3 mm long.

Species of *Phebalium* and *Microcybe* are common, mainly in clay or rocky soils of mallee thickets. They are small shrubs usually covered with small silvery scales, and have cream or white 5-petalled flowers with 10 prominent stamens. In *Phebalium* the flowers are usually in umbels or cymes, or sometimes axillary, while in *Microcybe* they are sessile in small heads.

A distinctive monotypic genus of the Rutaceae is *Nematolepis phebalioides*. This is a shrub to 1 m tall with oblong-elliptic leaves 1–3 cm long and axillary, pendulous flowers with tubular corollas 15 mm long, bright red with green tips and shortly exserted stamens.

It grows in clay, loam or laterite in mallee thickets between Lake Grace and Israelite Bay.

There are many species of the *Lechenaultia* family, Goodeniaceae. Blue Lechenaultia, *L. biloba* (Pl. 109), is common between Lake Grace and Lake King, and Red Lechenaultia, *L. formosa* is widespread. The latter near the coast is usually an erect perennial, while inland it is mat-like and is often covered with the scarlet flowers. Heath Lechenaultia, *L. tubiflora* (Pl. 235), is also common; east of Esperance it shows great variety in the proportion of red and cream in individual flowers.

White Goodenia, *G. scapigera* (Pl. 234), is often seen on roadsides and in burnt areas but becomes less common as the bush matures. An attractive yellow-flowered species is Silver Goodenia, *G. affinis* (Vic. 134), a mat-like plant with grey-felted leaves. Examples of *Scaevola* and *Dampiera* are seen in Pls. 244 and 236.

Belonging also to the Goodeniaceae, the genus *Anthotium* is endemic in the South-West and has three species, two of them occurring on the southern heaths. Both are small herbs with perennial rootstocks, rosetted linear leaves and short scapes with the flowers crowded towards the apices, appearing in late spring. *A. rubriflorum* has deep red flowers less than 1 cm long, and grows in sandy soil between Ravensthorpe and Merredin. *A. humile* has white flowers 5 mm long and inhabits clay or sandy heaths from Gnowangerup to Israelite Bay.

Other families which are well-represented in this region are the pea flowers, Papilionaceae, wattles, Mimosaceae, sheoaks, Casuarinaceae, heaths, Epacridaceae, triggerplants, Stylidiaceae, and Rhamnaceae.

Among the monocots, orchids are many but on the true sandheaths are relatively infrequent. Mallee thickets, woodlands and rocky hills provide more suitable habitats and shelter a number of species, especially of greenhoods, *Pterostylis*, spider orchids, *Caladenia* and sun orchids, *Thelymitra*.

Red Kangaroo Paws, *Anigozanthos rufus*, occur on deep sands, mainly near the coast. There are several attractive *Conostylis* species, including Sheath Conostylis, *C. vaginata* (Pl. 250). *C. petrophiloides* is a widespread tufted perennial herb with dense heads of woolly white flowers. *C. bealiana* is unusual, being one of two species in the genus with tubular corollas 2–3 cm long. It grows along the coast east from Hopetoun and has deep yellow flowers among the tufted, linear leaves. A subspecies of the other long-flowered species, *C. androstemma* (Pl. 141), grows on heaths west and north from Ravensthorpe—subsp. *argentea* which has narrow, cottony leaves and cream flowers 4 cm long.

The Barrens

BETWEEN BREMER BAY AND HOPETOUN on the south coast rises a series of hills and small ranges known as the Barrens. Three of these, West, Middle and East Mt. Barren, were named by Flinders in January 1802. The first land explorer here was the botanical collector William Baxter in 1828. Edward John Eyre passed through the region on his journey from Adelaide to Albany in 1841 but collected no plants. However James Drummond (1847–48), John Roe (1848) and George Maxwell (1863) all made collections and botanists immediately recognised the richness of the flora. The number of species recorded for the region totals over 600 of which over 60 do not occur elsewhere, even within WA.

The hills themselves consist of hard quartzite rock of Proterozoic age which have resisted erosion more than the surrounding plains. Although not high—Thumb Peak at 530 m is the highest—they rise on or near the coast and scenically gain the full advantage of their height. The coast has rugged cliffs and sandy beaches, while the plains consist mostly of laterite and sand. In recent geological time (Tertiary), while the Barrens were islands in the sea, soft spongolite beds were deposited nearby and following uplift were cut into by rivers such as the Fitzgerald and Hamersley to form colourful cliffs.

The area has a warm to hot dry summer and cool wet winter, with an annual rainfall of about 400 mm.

The vegetation is predominantly heath but there are also tall shrublands, mallee and riverine formations, with scattered swamps. The hills carry a dense heath among the outcropping quartzite and many of the endemic plants are found here.

As usual, the myrtle and Banksia families are predominant on the hills. The most striking of the myrtles is the Barrens Regelia, *R. velutina* (Pl. 273), which is common on the eastern peaks and on some coastal headlands. It is attractive for its silvery foliage alone, but in spring holds its brilliant red flowers like torches.

Four Eucalypts are confined to the hills. Weeping Gum, *E. sepulcralis* (Pl. 274), grows in wispy stands on the lower slopes of the eastern hills, its large urn-like fruit 2–3 cm long looking too large for the slender stems. The Crowned Mallee, *E. coronata*, occurs on the upper slopes of East Mt. Barren and the Whoogarup Range. It has large, strongly ribbed buds and fruit, the latter having 4 or 5 swollen appendages on top. Also on East Mt. Barren is *E. burdettiana*, allied to the Warted Yate (Pl. 217) but of mallee habit and with smaller buds and fruit. On Thumb Peak and Middle Mt. Barren is *E. acies*, a newly-found species which is a spreading mallee with very angular stems, large leaves, and rather small, slightly ribbed buds with blunt caps. The Bushy Yate, *E. lehmanni* (Pl. 271), is common on most of the hills.

Among a number of *Melaleuca* species is one endemic, the yellow-flowered *M. citrina.* This is a shrub of 1–2 m with linear, dark green leaves and the flowers in short spikes below the ends of the branches. It grows among quartzite rocks on all the hills.

Two unusual *Baeckea* species are *B. ovalifolia* and *B. oxycoccoides.* The former, restricted to the hills, is an erect, rather stout shrub to 70 cm tall with crowded, narrow-elliptic leaves 4–8 mm long and white or pale pink flowers 10–15 mm across. The latter is slender and procumbent with spreading, elliptic leaves 3–5 mm long and bright pink flowers 1 cm across on very long pedicels; it occurs also in the Stirling Range.

The Barrens Clawflower, *Calothamnus validus* (Pl. 260), is endemic, being more common on the western hills, while the Dense Clawflower, *C. pinifolius* (Pl. 270), is also common. Another myrtle restricted to the peaks is a form of *Agonis linearifolia* which here is a shrub to 1.5 m with grey-green obovate leaves, not linear as in the widespread typical form.

Although there are many species of Proteaceae on the peaks few are endemic there. In the gullies is *Hakea hookerana*, a robust shrub to 5 m tall with oblanceolate, blunt leaves 10–12 cm long and small rusty-brown flowers in axillary clusters. The fruit is large and thick, about 4.5 cm long, with a short beak, and two ridges along a depression on one side. It flowers in late spring. Two unnamed red-flowered *Grevilleas* are restricted to the central hills, while an unnamed *Adenanthos* is known only from one hill.

There are 15 *Banksias* and 12 *Dryandras* in the region, and several are common on the hills. *B. lemanniana* is a stout shrub with short toothed leaves and pendulous, pale yellow flower spikes. Mountain Banksia, *B. quercifolia* var. *integrifolia* (Pl. 265), occurs only on the peaks but is also on the Stirling Range.

Oak-leaved Dryandra, *D. quercifolia* (Pl. 261), is frequent, and has very pungently-toothed leaves, while other species include Wedge-leaved Dryandra, *D. cuneata* (Pl. 195), and Prickly Dryandra, *D. falcata* (Pl. 227).

Several interesting species of Goodeniaceae are confined to the hills. On the eastern ones is the Barrens Lechenaultia, *L. superba* (Pl. 262), which is an upright shrub to 70 cm with crowded, soft, linear leaves and red flowers. In sheltered gullies on the central hills is *Coopernookia georgei*, a slender shrub to 1.5 m, slightly viscid, with elliptic, dentate leaves 2–5 cm long and mauve flowers 1.5–2 cm long. This recently-named genus of 5 species is distinguished from *Goodenia* chiefly by the swollen, not flat, strophiolate seeds and the stellate hairs on the flowers. Three species occur in WA, one extending to SA, and the other two are in SE Australia.

On some peaks is an endemic shrubby *Goodenia*, *G. stenophylla*, which grows to 50 cm and has crowded narrow leaves and terminal racemes of small white flowers. *Dampiera loranthifolia* is also confined to the hills; this perennial herb has angular stems, cuneate toothed leaves, and hairy deep blue flowers.

Of many legumes, *Jacksonia compressa* is endemic, being a shrub of 1 m with flattened, pale green stems and orange and yellow pea flowers. An unusual wattle is known only from these hills—*Acacia cedroides* which is a small shrub with whorled, linear, pungent phyllodes 2–3 cm long and heads of cream flowers.

There are twelve triggerplants in the region, two endemic on the hills. Yellow Mountain Triggerplant, *Stylidium galioides,* is a trailing perennial with whorled, lanceolate leaves 2–3 cm long and cream flowers 1 cm across. It occurs only on East Mt. Barren and the Eyre Range. On East Mt. Barren also is *S. albomontis* which has a tuft of long, linear leaves and a tall panicle of large white flowers.

An endemic variety of the native foxglove, *Pityrodia uncinata*, occurs on most hills. It is a perennial herb with opposite, wrinkled, linear leaves and dull red tubular flowers, differing from the typical variant in being almost glabrous.

On the plains around the hills, the Proteaceae are again prominent. Some common species of *Hakea, Conospermum, Isopogon, Petrophile,* etc. have been described in the section on Southern Sandplains and Heath.

The most striking plant in this family is the Royal Hakea, *H. victoria* (Pls. 258, 259) which holds its stiff, colourful stems above the scrub like totem poles. The coloured leaves are the floral ones, each having a cluster of cream flowers in the axil during the first year. The colour deepens with age from cream through orange to red. Near the base of the plant are oblong, undulate-denticulate juvenile leaves which remain all-green. The variegated leaves are unique among the native flora of WA.

Among the Barrens, the Woolly Banksia, *B. baueri*, often has flowers of a rich rusty-brown colour. It is unfortunate that this species hides its large flower spikes within the bush. Scarlet Banksia, *B. coccinea* (Pl. 157), and Baxter's Banksia, *B. baxteri* (Pl. 167) are very common in deep sandy areas on the plains. Above the valley of the Fitzgerald River in rocky soil is found the typical form of *B. laevigata.* This shrub to 3 m tall has broad-linear leaves 5–10 cm long, shortly dentate towards the apices and spherical, pale yellow flower spikes 6 cm across with very fine styles, opening in October-November. It is restricted to this small area, but two varieties occur near Ravensthorpe and farther north.

Of more than 12 *Grevillea* species in this region, *G. tripartita* (Pl. 264) and *G. macrostylis* (Pl. 269) are the most conspicuous. All but one of the *Grevilleas* here have flowers of various shades of red; the other is white-flowered (*G. teretifolia).*

Apart from deep sandy areas where Proteaceae are dominant, mallee Eucalypts are again the prominent plants of the sandheaths. Tallerack, *E. tetragona* (Pl. 246), is common, and Bell-fruited Mallee, *E. preissiana* (Pl. 263), is frequent in rocky ground. Red-flowered Moort, *E. nutans* (Pl. 215), is widespread but less conspicuous except when in flower.

An endemic Eucalypt, growing around the foot of some of the eastern hills, is *E. chrysantha*. This mallee has the habit of *E. preissiana*, but the flowers and fruit appear intermediate between this species and *E. sepulcralis*. No viable seed is set, and the plants may be natural hybrids.

In swampy depressions on the plains, and along the rivers, the Flat-topped Yate, *E. occidentalis*, is the dominant tree, growing to 25 m with a rough-barked trunk.

Along the spongolite cliffs of the Fitzgerald River is a variant of the Warted Yate, *E. megacornuta* (Pl. 217), in which the bud-caps are narrower and quite smooth.

There are many species of other myrtles such as *Melaleuca, Beaufortia, Baeckea, Calytrix, Agonis*, and *Chamelaucium*. Featherflowers, *Verticordia*, are rarely as prominent as on heaths farther north, but several intriguing species are present. Only the Autumn Featherflower, *V. harveyi*, forms colourful patches but these are evident at a season when few wildflowers are in bloom. It is a slender shrub to 70 cm with linear leaves and corymbs of pink flowers, and grows in deep sand on the open heaths.

Two species are natural bonzai subjects. Bonzai Featherflower, *V. oxylepis*, grows to only a few cm tall but then has horizontal branches spreading to 20 cm across. The leaves are linear and short, and the star-like creamy-pink flowers are arranged on top of the plant with the styles pointing vertically upwards. It flowers in October and November. Mouse Featherflower, *V. fastigiata*, has an erect habit but in the form of a miniature tree, up to 15 cm tall, with crowded linear leaves and tiny red or gold flowers which glisten with nectar. The flowers smell like mice and appear in autumn. Three unnamed featherflowers are endemic to the region.

One of the most striking plants of the area is Qualup Bell, *Pimelea physodes* (Pl. 268). The vernacular name is derived from the old Qualup homestead on the Gairdner River. The plant is a slender shrub of 50–70 cm, rarely taller and more branching. The bell is a head of many flowers surrounded by large bracts 3–5 cm long which are red and green and become deep red-brown with age. It grows mainly on sandy heaths or rocky slopes and flowers from July to September. Seven other *Pimeleas* occur in the region, with pink, white or yellow flowers.

Many genera of pea flowers, Papilionaceae, occur here. The largest genus is *Daviesia* with about 12 species, of diverse form, but all having the characteristic triangular pod. A conspicuous species is Ouch Bush, *D. pachyphylla* (Pl. 266), a formidable 'needle-bush'. It is a glaucous shrub of open heaths, with spreading branches, thick, short, terete pungent leaves and orange and dark red flowers. Black Kennedia, *K. nigricans* (Pl. 238), is a strong creeper of coastal sands with an unusual colour combination of black and yellow. In early days the tough, wiry stems were often used as rope by travelling horsemen.

Along the spongolite cliffs of the Fitzgerald River grows Thorny Hovea, *H. acanthoclada* (Pl. 275). This rigid, spinescent shrub with deep purple flowers grows also in the Ravensthorpe Range and near Kalgoorlie. It typifies several species of the area which have ranges extending far inland.

Several toxic species of *Oxylobium* and *Gastrolobium* occur in the region. One is endemic, being known only from the Fitzgerald River valley. This is Narrow-leaved Poison, *Gastrolobium stenophyllum*, a shrub to 2 m tall with very narrow leaves 2–3 cm long arranged in 3s, and short terminal racemes of yellow and red flowers which appear in September-October.

Over 40 wattles are recorded for this region, a number of them as yet being unnamed. Ranging from prostrate to tall shrubs, they are mostly phyllodinous but several have bipinnate leaves. An unusual species is Flat Wattle, *Acacia glaucoptera* (Pl. 272), which is common especially in clay soils among mallee or moort associations. The flat stems with broad decurrent wings have heads of flowers arising from the midribs. The young growth of this species is an attractive red colour.

Three *Lechenaultia* species are widespread here, the most conspicuous being Red Lechenaultia, *L. formosa*. Here it is the typical erect form, growing to 20 cm tall, and the flowers vary from pink to bright red. It appears prolifically after bushfires on the sandheaths. Heath Lechenaultia, *L. tubiflora* (Pl. 235), occurs in deeper sands, usually with cream flowers. In the eastern half of the region, usually in deep sand where Chittick and Banksias are dominant, Claw Lechenaultia, *L. heteromera*, occurs as a small straggling shrub. It has stiff short leaves and sparse, terminal pale blue flowers. The upper corolla lobes are unwinged and claw-like.

The heath family, Epacridaceae, is represented by thirteen genera and more than 30 species. The Beard Heaths, *Leucopogon*, are most numerous and are mainly winter-flowering. Nearly all are white-flowered, but *L. rubicundus* has deep pink to red tubular flowers 7–8 mm long. This stiffly-branched shrub to 1 m tall has narrow, pungent leaves 7–9 mm long with revolute margins and grows mainly in gravelly clay in mallee scrub, flowering from June to August.

An attractive little heath common on deep sandy soils from the Stirling Range to Israelite Bay is *Oligarrhena micrantha*. This is a small shrub to 20 cm tall with acute, linear leaves 2 mm long and spikes of cream flowers, each 2 mm long, crowded in the upper axils.

Northern Sandplains and Heath

NORTH OF PERTH, BETWEEN the Moore River and Shark Bay and within 120 km of the coast, large tracts of sandy or lateritic plain support a scrubby vegetation known as sandplain or sandheath. The country is undulating, mostly below 300 m in altitude, with only a few rivers, all of intermittent flow. The major river is the Murchison which drains a large area extending inland almost to Meekatharra. In its lower reaches it has carved a deep, winding gorge into colourful sandstone rock. The soils of the sandplains are mostly poor sands and gravels lacking trace elements such as nitrogen, and phosphorus. Yet it is on these plains that some of the richest development of the flora has occurred. Many species are endemic on the northern plains.

The vegetation is typically a low scrub, but is tall in places and often includes mallee eucalypts. The scrub is mostly tall and dense north of the Murchison River. There are some areas of low woodland, and, especially to the north of Moora, some large salt lakes.

The most prominent plant families are the Proteaceae, Myrtaceae and the legumes, all with a wealth of species far too numerous to enumerate in detail. There are, for example, 20 species of *Banksia*, some widespread, such as Menzies' (Pl. 20), and the yellow Slender Banksia, others more localised. Bright orange flowers are a feature of 5 species, including Hooker's (Pl. 282), Woolly (Pl. 315) and Ashby's (Pl. 316) Banksias. Acorn Banksia, *B. prionotes*, and *B. burdettii* have white woolly buds and orange flowers appearing in late summer. The former is a tall shrub or tree with short, triangular lobes on the leaves, the latter a dense spreading shrub with shortly-toothed leaves. *B. prionotes* is common on deep sands from Perth to Shark Bay, and *B. burdettii* is confined to the Mogumber-Badgingarra area.

On the Murchison plains, two yellow-flowered species are found. *B. sceptrum* is a spreading shrub to 4 m tall with short, blunt leaves and large spikes, the flowers having prominent curved styles. The spikes are on the ends of the branches and make a spectacular sight in mid-summer. Later in the season, *B. lindleyana* flowers. This is a smaller shrub with narrow, toothed leaves and broad flower spikes, the styles being straight and rigid. The flowers are mostly within the shrub, on the older stems.

South of Dongara, the Propellor Banksia, *B. candolleana*, is a common shrub, less than 1 m tall but up to 2 m broad. The long, narrow leaves have acute, triangular lobes, and the golden flower spikes are relatively small, appearing in autumn and winter. The fruiting follicles are few but very large and somewhat curved, with a small lateral beak.

A strange species is *B. elegans*, found near Eneabba. It is a stiff straggling shrub to 3 m tall, the long leaves pale green with short triangular lobes, while the pale yellow flowers are in rounded spikes. Fruit are rarely set, and the small follicles usually contain abortive seeds. The plants are able to sucker, this being the only *Banksia* in WA known to have this capability.

Six species of the *Banksia sphaerocarpa* group occur in the region, and there is one prostrate species, as yet unnamed, which flowers in late spring.

There are many *Dryandra* species, ranging from prostrate to tall erect shrubs. The two shown in Pls. 293 and 296 have erect leaves and short stems, but the flowers are usually at ground level. Most *Dryandras* and *Banksias* produce abundant nectar and although birds and insects are attracted by this, it is thought that small marsupials are the true pollinators of the flowers. Many of the low and prostrate species hide the flowers among the foliage where they are largely obscured from above. Couch Honeypot, *Dryandra nivea* (Pl. 82), is a widespread example. Restricted to the sandplains near the Hill River is the extraordinary *D. nana* which has a habit similar to that of *D. nivea* but the leaves are shorter and more deeply lobed. The striking feature of this plant is the style of the flower—6–8 cm long, much exceeding the perianth and the longest style of any *Dryandra*. It would be interesting to study the pollination of such a flower.

The inefficiency of the Proteaceae (and many other families in WA) in seed production is also an intriguing subject. For example, a *Banksia* flower spike may contain 1,000 flowers but perhaps only 15 will set fruit, or often none at all. In many species this does not affect survival in the wild, since they regenerate from perennial underground stocks after bushfires and hence do not require seeds. However others are killed by fire and depend on seeds to perpetuate themselves. Under natural conditions sufficient seeds are produced, usually over a number of years between fires, but the inefficiency is still present.

Other *Dryandras* on the northern sandplains include Shaggy Dryandra, *D. speciosa* (Pl. 337), which grows on lateritic hills north of the Hill River; it is one of the few species in the genus with linear, entire leaves. *D. shuttleworthiana* has similar, shaggy flower heads, the old ones persisting down the stem, but the leaves are finely toothed. Two species with the flower heads more prominently displayed are *D. carlinoides* and *D. kippistiana*. Both are small, erect short-leaved shrubs, the former having few-toothed lanceolate leaves and cream flowers and the latter rigid, many-toothed leaves and yellow flowers.

The most spectacular of the *Grevilleas* is White Plume

Grevillea, *G. leucopteris* (Pl. 288), whose large clusters of cream flowers on long arching stems are prominent in mid and late spring. Easy to cultivate, its only disadvantage is the strong unpleasant odour of the flowers.

Prickly Plume Grevillea, *G. annulifera* (Pl. 313), is also showy but is a more straggling shrub with divaricately-lobed prickly leaves. The flowers are often tinged with pink and green and are also unpleasantly scented. The fruit is unusual both in being large and spherical, and in the irregular dehiscence; most *Grevillea* fruit split open into two similar halves.

Grevillea candicans also has a large spherical fruit which however does not open to shed the seeds. It is a tall shrub with long leaves divided into linear lobes and clustered, erect racemes of viscid cream flowers appearing in November-December. It grows between Mullewa and the Murchison River. A similar species is *G. candelabroides* which has smooth, non-viscid flowers and an ovoid, viscid fruit.

Another white-flowered species is *G. polybotrya* which is prominent in November-December on sandplains between Eneabba and Geraldton. It is a shrub to 4 m with short, obovate leaves and dense panicles of small flowers with a sickly-sweet perfume.

On the Murchison plains, the red-flowered *G. dielsiana* is showy in winter and early spring. A shrub to 2 m tall, it has divaricately-divided prickly leaves and rather loose racemes with pendulous flowers.

Discovered quite recently, Rogerson's Grevillea, *G. rogersoniana* (Pl. 314), is a tall shrub with reddish-pink flowers; it is found in red sand near Shark Bay. *G. petrophiloides* has similar flowers but on long, leafless stems, while the leaves, lower on the shrub, are deeply and finely divided. It has small viscid fruit with curious pits on the surface, and is widespread from the Murchison River to Wongan Hills, usually in gravelly soils.

An unusual species which grows near the Hill River is *G. thyrsoides*, a sprawling shrub with pinnate leaves and terminal racemes of pink, hirsute flowers.

The genus *Hakea* also shows great variety in this region, in habit, form and flower colour, the latter ranging through white, pink, red, yellow and brown. One of the brightest is Red Pokers, *H. bucculenta* (Pl. 323), which is common in the tall scrub north of the Murchison River. Another red-flowered species is the Bird Hakea, *H. orthorrhyncha*, a tall shrub with long terete leaves, and clusters of flowers along the older stems. In late afternoon sunlight the flowers glow as if lit within. The fruit is large and swollen, with a long apical beak. The species grows in red loam in the Murchison district.

Hakea stenophylla is also a tall shrub found north of the Murchison River, It has linear leaves and clusters of small cream flowers followed by large fruit 2–3 cm long.

In the Hill River district there are two *Hakeas* with fan-shaped leaves. *H. baxteri* has many acute teeth across the apex of the leaf, while *H. flabellifolia* has a few rather coarse teeth. Both are low shrubs and have small brown flowers with large woody fruit. The latter are swollen, with coarse grey bark, in *H. baxteri*, compressed and mottled with brown and purple in *H. flabellifolia*. *H. baxteri* also grows on southern sandheaths.

Another species which grows on both southern and northern heaths is *H. obliqua*. This is a straggling shrub to 3 m with short, needle-like leaves and clusters of white flowers. The swollen fruit are covered with thick corky bark. This occurs on areas of deep sand.

In early spring, the candle-like spikes of *Hakea costata* may be conspicuous on heaths near the Hill River and farther south. This rigid shrub has short, crowded, linear, pungent leaves and small flowers densely packed in the upper axils. The fruit are very small.

The native pear genus, *Xylomelum*, has 4 species, all endemic in Australia. Two species occur in WA, the other 2 in NSW and Qld. Sandplain Pear, *X. angustifolium* (Pl. 344), is common on the northern plains. Its large clusters of cream flowers appear in mid-summer and attract many insects. The large woody fruit usually will open only after a bushfire. The other species here, *X. occidentale*, inhabits forest areas farther south and has rather oak-like leaves. The fruit open when removed from the tree, releasing two large winged seeds which spin like a propellor when dropped.

Smokebushes are a conspicuous group of the Proteaceae in spring and early summer, favouring deep sandy soils. Common Smokebush, *Conospermum stoechadis* (Pl. 34), is widespread through the region. Between the Moore River and Eneabba, Plume Smokebush, *C. incurvum* (Pl. 318), is frequent and very attractive with its woolly flowers, in larger, more dense panicles than those of *C. stoechadis*.

In December the Summer Smokebush, *C. crassinervium* begins to flower. It has short, woody stems with long, thick, linear leaves, and tall leafless flowering stems with dense corymbs of white woolly flowers at the top. It is found in open sandy woodlands between Gingin and Eneabba.

A different type of smokebush is the blue-flowered *C. nervosum* which inhabits gravelly hills between the Hill River and Eneabba. It is a small shrub with elliptic, 3-nerved leaves and small clusters of flowers which lack the dense hairs typical of many species.

Among the numerous and varied Myrtaceae there are many Eucalypts, both tree and mallee forms. River Gums, *E. camaldulensis*, occur along river courses, showing an interesting gradation from typical white-barked trees along the Murchison to rough, grey-barked trees south of the Hill River—the Flooded Gum (*E. rudis*) of the South-West. Scattered groves of York Gum, *E. loxophleba*, occur in the Hill River and Murchison districts; they are tall trees with spreading crowns and dark rough bark on the lower trunk. Pockets of Marri, *E. calophylla*, are also found northwards to beyond the Hill River.

The near-coastal hills south of Dongara and north of the Murchison are the natural home of the Illyarrie, *E. erythrocorys,* now well-known in cultivation. This white-barked tree grows to 10 m and has large, red-capped buds which open to reveal bright yellow stamens in four clusters.

Flowers with the stamens in four clusters are also to be seen in two white-flowered mallees which as well usually have the leaves in opposite pairs. One is the Tallerack, *E. tetragona* (Pl. 246), a glaucous species common on southern sandheaths but also found near the Hill River. The other is *E. eudesmoides* which is typically green and, like Tallerack, has a somewhat 4-angled fruit. It is widespread and variable between the Hill River and Shark Bay.

The Mottlecah, *E. macrocarpa* (Pl. 358), is also a spreading glaucous mallee, found between the Moore and Hill Rivers, as well as in the wheatbelt. Its solitary flowers, usually deep red, are the largest of the genus, and in fact are the largest of any Australian Myrtaceae.

Another large-flowered species is the Pear-fruited Mallee, *E. pyriformis.* It has typical green leaves and long-stalked, pendulous, ribbed buds, the flowers being either red or yellow. It is common to the east of Eneabba.

Some of the most brilliant shrubs of the region are the featherflowers, *Verticordia,* which make colourful displays from October to December. The three species in Plates 299, 300 and 324 illustrate some of the intricate beauty of the flowers. In southern areas the yellow *V. chrysantha* is common, it being similar to Claw Featherflower but with smaller flowers and the anthers lacking claw-like appendages.

In late spring the Northern Cauliflower, *V. polytricha,* dots the sandheaths between Mingenew and the Murchison River. Like the Common Cauliflower, *V. brownii* (Pl. 335), these shrubs grow evenly and so maintain their regular, dome-shaped habit from year to year. This species is distinguished from *V. brownii* by the longer leaves and smaller flowers with pubescent petals.

One of the tallest featherflowers in the South-West is *V. chrysostachys* of the Murchison sandheaths. An openly-branched shrub to 2 m or more, it has rounded leaves 5 mm across and spikes of deep yellow flowers which appear in late spring and turn red as they age. *V. muellerana* is a similar species with maroon flowers; it extends southwards to Wongan Hills and flowers from November to January.

A species with large flowers (2 cm across) is *V. oculata,* found on the sandheaths near the Murchison. It is a branching shrub with glaucous, rounded leaves 5 mm across and flowers of a delicate silvery-white and purple, appearing in November-December. A similar species but with smaller, all-white flowers is *V. ovalifolia* which occurs farther south.

Bright red flowers are a feature of *V. etheliana,* a shrub with small rounded leaves and relatively large flowers, occurring near the Murchison. It was named in 1941 after the wife of Dr W. E. Blackall, an eminent amateur botanist who produced illustrated keys to the flora of South-Western Australia.

Brilliant flowers also occur in the small genus *Pileanthus,* the coppercups, which are endemic in WA. There are three named species, illustrated in Pls. 292, 298 and 537, the last being a north-west coastal species. The flowers are unusual in having 10 calyx-lobes which persist after flowering to form the 'copper cups'. The 20 stamens each bear 2 adnate anthers and in 2 species—*P. filifolius* (Pl. 292) and *P. limacis* (Pl. 537)—the filaments are forked below the anthers. There are 2 unnamed species on the Murchison sandplains, one a tall, spindly shrub with pale pink flowers, the other smaller with intensely red flowers.

Darwinia is an intriguing genus of about 40 species endemic in Australia (30 in the South-West) with much diversity in the form of the inflorescence. Some have rounded or flattened heads, often compound, with small involucral bracts, while others have heads enclosed by large, colourful bracts. The latter include the mountain bells of the Stirling Range. Two of this type are common on the northern plains, flowering in spring. *D. speciosa* is a small sprawling shrub with oblong leaves 5 mm long and narrow, ovoid heads enclosed by dark reddish-brown bracts 3 cm long which scarcely open to reveal the green flowers within. It extends from the Hill River to Mingenew. From Eneabba southwards one finds *D. nieldiana,* a small shrub with crowded linear leaves up to 1 cm long and often ciliate, the flower heads nodding and surrounded by many narrow, hirsute, reddish bracts 2 cm long.

Two species of *Darwinia* having small bracts around the flowers are to be seen on the Murchison sandplains. Murchison Darwinia, *D. virescens* (Pl. 321), is a small sprawling shrub flowering in late spring and summer. *D. oldfieldii* is a much-branched shrub to 50 cm tall with small, rounded, ciliate leaves and deep red flowers with long, exserted styles.

Like the *Verticordias,* the genus *Calytrix* is notable for its masses of brilliant flowers which often completely cover the bush. Typical of this habit are *C. brevifolia,* a bright pink-flowered species of the Murchison-Shark Bay area, and *C. brachyphylla* with deep purple flowers, common on heaths farther south. Less floriferous but with the largest flowers of any *Calytrix* is the Superb Starflower, *C. superba* (Pl. 320).

A widespread species is *C. strigosa* which has hirsute bracts and calyxes and purple flowers; it is a spreading shrub with many stems and short, linear leaves.

Many species of Honeymyrtles, *Melaleuca,* are to be seen, having flowers coloured red, pink, yellow, cream or mauve. Wiry Honeymyrtle, *M. nematophylla* (Pl. 311), is a showy species. Another large-flowered species is *M. megacephala* of the Murchison River, with flat, ovate leaves and pale yellow flower heads 2–3 cm across. A bottlebrush type in the same area is *M. calothamnoides,* a much-branched shrub with linear leaves and pale red flowers.

This region is the home of the genus *Eremaea* which

differs from *Melaleuca* in having basifixed, not versatile, anthers, flowers solitary or in heads of 2–3, and angular seeds with fringed margins. They are small shrubs with bright orange, pink or purple flowers. The genus has about 10 species, all endemic in the South-West. Two species are shown in Plates 291 and 303.

There are about 10 species of *Calothamnus* in the region. This genus of about 25 species is endemic in southern WA. Murchison Clawflower, *C. homalophyllus* (Pl. 297), is closely allied to the common One-sided Bottlebrush, *C. quadrifidus,* but has flat, narrow-obovate leaves. Flowering in mid-summer is *C. blepharospermus,* a many-stemmed shrub to 1.5 m with stiff, rough, lanceolate leaves and large bright orange-red flowers.

In the southern areas, two unusual species have short stems which are thickened and corky, the deep red flowers 'erupting' through the bark. They are *C. longissimus* with long, terete leaves, and *C. pachystachyus* with long, narrow-lanceolate leaves.

The Geraldton Wax, *Chamelaucium uncinatum,* long popular in gardens, has its natural home along the coast between Perth and Dongara. It grows in sandy hollows between limestone hills, and in the wild has pale pink flowers.

There are many species of the genera *Baeckea, Micromyrtus, Scholtzia* and *Thryptomene* but they are notoriously difficult to identify. Other myrtaceous genera include *Beaufortia, Calythropsis, Conothamnus, Hypocalymma Lamarchea, Leptospermum, Lhotzkya, Phymatocarpus,* and *Regelia.*

Of the legumes, wattles are again ubiquitous. A common species forming thickets in deep sand between the Moore River and Geraldton is *A. blakelyi.* This tall shrub has broad-linear phyllodes to 10 cm long distinguished by a small gland on the midrib towards the base, not on the margin as in most wattles. The bright yellow flowers are in axillary racemes.

Another bright species is *A. multispicata,* a many-stemmed shrub less than 1 m tall with terete, finely striate phyllodes 2–3 cm long and dense spikes of flowers.

Wattles are prominent in the tall scrub north of the Murchison River, two frequent species being Bowgada Bush, *A. linophylla* (Pls. 458–9), and Kurara, *A. tetragonophylla* (Pl. 464). The Jam Tree, *A. acuminata,* which is common in the wheatbelt, is also to be seen here.

An unusual pea flower is Staghorn Bush, *Daviesia epiphylla* (Pl. 280), which is the only species of the genus with such a broad-stemmed habit and such large red flowers. Most other species have small yellow, orange and red flowers.

Another curious species is Ribbon Pea, *Brachysema aphyllum* (Pl. 308). It is often seen on roadsides where its flattened stems form sprawling mats. A similar species in the Murchison is *B. tomentosum* which has a more erect habit, flat silky stems, and pale yellow-green flowers mostly at the base of the plant. As in most *Brachysemas,* the upper petal (standard) is small and the keel with its wings is the most prominent part of the flower. The genus contains about 15 species, endemic in the South-West except for a few in the desert and northern Australia.

Poisonous plants of the genus *Gastrolobium* occur throughout the region. These shrubs, containing monofluoroacetic acid, have caused pastoralists trouble since the early days of settlement. Champion Bay Poison, *G. oxylobioides* (Pl. 294), is a widespread example. All such toxic plants have the leaves opposite or whorled and the flowers in terminal racemes.

Other genera of pea flowers are numerous but difficult to describe briefly since so many are of similar aspect. The species of *Jacksonia* are mostly leafless shrubs, either low or of broombush habit, often with angular, spinescent branchlets, and orange and yellow flowers. Globe Peas, *Sphaerolobium,* are also leafless shrubs, small in stature with dense racemes of orange and red flowers (rarely pink). Their common name refers to the small spherical pod which contains 1 or 2 seeds.

A striking *Hovea* occurs between the Moore River and Eneabba. *H. stricta* is similar to Devil's Pins (Pl. 95) but is a many-stemmed shrub to 50 cm with stiff, pungent leaves and large purple flowers. Another purple-flowered pea is Purple Mirbelia, *M. floribunda* (Pl. 381), a small, much-branched shrub with linear leaves less than 1 cm long and numerous axillary flowers. It extends north almost to Geraldton, and south-east to Lake King, growing usually in clay or gravel.

Some attractive shrubs are those of the family Verbenaceae. They are mostly covered with dense branched hairs which are often red or yellow, especially on young growth. Some appear rapidly after bushfires but are uncommon in unburnt areas. They include the Native Foxglove, *Pityrodia oldfieldii* (Pl. 305). *P. atriplicina* is a similar shrub of the Murchison area but has a close grey indumentum and leafy panicles of pink flowers. In the same area is *P. verbascina* var. *aurea,* an erect shrub to 1 m covered with bright yellow or red hairs, the leaves being linear and the flowers white, pale pink and orange. The typical *P. verbascina* occurs between the Hill River and Eneabba and has a pale indumentum and broader leaves. The 24 species of *Pityrodia* are endemic in southern WA except for one species in the Kimberleys.

To this family belongs the Lambstail group, in which the tiny flowers are concealed in dense wool. The petals and sepals are much reduced and the purple or black stamens are the only obvious part of the flower, and then for a short time only. The Hill River Lambstail, *Physopsis spicata* (Pl. 322), occurs between that river and Eneabba. Lambswool, *Lachnostachys eriobotrya,* is widespread. It is a grey shrub with linear leaves and open panicles of white flowers. The other species of *Lachnostachys,* mostly found to the east and southeast, have dense spikes of flowers.

The genus *Newcastelia,* with about 12 species all endemic in Australia, also has dense flower spikes, either white or yellow. The largest species of the genus occurs in red sand among tall scrub between the Murchison River and Shark Bay: *N. chrysophylla* grows to 5 m tall and has broadly obovate leaves which are dark green above but covered with yellow hairs on the lower surface, while the flowers also are bright yellow, in branched spikes. The other species occur in dry inland regions.

Flowers of many colours are to be seen in the family Goodeniaceae. Even in *Lechenaultia* with about 25 species, the flowers may be blue, white, yellow, red, orange or green. The well-known blue Lechenaultia, *L. biloba* (Pl. 109), is common as far north as Mingenew. The brilliant red Hairy Lechenaultia, *L. hirsuta* (Pl. 283), is unusual in being the only hirsute species of the genus. Irwin Lechenaultia, *L. longiloba* (Pl. 319), displays the suckering habit which is frequent in this family and accounts for the clumping of plants so often seen. Five other *Lechenaultias* occur in the region.

By contrast, the flowers of *Dampiera* species are usually deep blue, though pale blue, white, pink and yellow also occur. Spiked Dampiera, *D. spicigera* (Pl. 317), is a frequent species while Summer Dampiera, *D. carinata* (Pl. 329), is uncommon but has intensely blue flowers. The flowers of this genus have a small fold near the base of each of the two uppermost corolla lobes between which the top of the style lies in the bud.

The Button Creeper, *Tersonia brevipes* (Pl. 290), belongs to the family Gyrostemonaceae which is endemic in Australia and contains species noted for their rapid growth after bushfires. They are short-lived trees or shrubs which regenerate from seed, grow rapidly, flower and fruit and then die as the more permanent vegetation grows up. They survive as seed in the soil until the next fire occurs. The species are monoecious or dioecious, with relatively inconspicuous flowers. Several species are to be found, in the right conditions, on the northern sandheaths. A prominent species is the Native Poplar, *Codonocarpus cotinifolius* (Vic. 161), which is widespread in arid regions and extends into the area south of Shark Bay.

As in most of the South-West, the monocots are usually not a dominant feature of the bush, apart from the Blackboys which are frequent. However, most families are represented, though the species are often inconspicuous among more spectacular wildflowers. The Common Blackboy, *Xanthorrhoea preissii* (Pl. 310), is widespread, and it is interesting that the north-facing flowers at the base of the spike are always the first to open. Smaller in habit and with a glaucous floral stem is *X. brevistyla* which is also widespread but less common; it extends south to Cranbrook. The allied Black Gin, *Kingia australis* (Pl. 194), is found in a few sandy areas as far north as Mt. Lesueur.

The most spectacular monocots are the kangaroo paws. The Black Kangaroo Paw, *Macropidia fuliginosa* (Pl. 281), is the most unusual, the black indumentum being a rare colour in flowers. The plant prefers laterite hills among heath, and flowers best after a bushfire.

The Yellow Kangaroo Paw, *Anigozanthos pulcherrimus* (Pl. 279), occurs in deep sands between the Moore River and Eneabba. The flowering stems may be deep red or of a pale straw colour. Mangles' Kangaroo Paw, *A. manglesii* (Pl. 12), extends north almost to Shark Bay. In places north of Geraldton the flowering stems have a branching habit similar to that of the Yellow Kangaroo Paw. Cat's Paw, *A. humilis*, also extends to the Murchison River.

In the same family, Haemodoraceae, are the cottonheads, *Conostylis,* of which there are many species here. Bristly Cottonhead, *C. setigera* (Pl. 129), and Mat Cottonhead, *C. prolifera* (Pl. 132), are typical examples. The deep golden-flowered *C. aurea*, whose leaves are often somewhat viscid, grows as far north as the Murchison, while the common Grey Cottonhead, *C. candicans,* with grey-felted leaves, reaches Shark Bay, the northern limit of the genus.

The allied Winter Bell, *Blancoa canescens* (Pl. 19), grows in deep sands on heaths from Mt. Lesueur southwards.

Although a number of orchids occur on the sandheaths they are rarely frequent. Many widespread species extend north to the Murchison River, e.g. Shirt Orchid, *Thelymitra campanulata* (Pl. 325), Cowslip Orchid, *Caladenia flava* (Pl. 10), and Common Donkey Orchid, *Diuris longifolia* (Pl. 92). In the Moore-Hill River area an unusual variant of Queen of Sheba, *Thelymitra variegata* (Pl. 267), is found. The yellow 'ears' of the column are tipped with fine points, and the plants flower in June and July, much earlier than those farther south.

The Arrowsmith Spider Orchid, *Caladenia crebra* (Pl. 327), is a recently-discovered species growing between Eneabba and Dongara.

Several species of native conifers are found on the heaths and associated hills. The Sandplain Cypress, *Actinostrobus arenarius*, is an attractive pine-like shrub to 5 m tall, usually glaucous, the cones being 1 cm across and surrounded by many bracts. It grows in deep sand from Moora to beyond the Murchison.

Between Moora and Eneabba among low heath occurs the Dwarf Cypress, *A. acuminatus.* It has many stems less than 50 cm tall arising from a woody, underground stock.

Wheatbelt

EAST OF THE JARRAH forest lie the woodlands, shrublands and heaths of the wheatbelt. Most of the area has been cleared for farming, especially to the east of Perth where only remnants of the original vegetation still exist.

A widespread tree typical of the western part of the wheatbelt is York Gum, *Eucalyptus loxophleba.* This is a straggling tree usually branched near the base into several trunks covered with rough, dark grey bark. It usually grows in association with the Jam Tree, *Acacia acuminata*, a small tree up to 8 m high. The wood of the latter species is highly prized for cabinet work and has a raspberry-like odour when freshly cut. These trees form an open woodland with low shrubby or herbaceous undergrowth on soils directly above the granitic country rock. They usually indicate good grazing country and occur together from the central western wheatbelt as far north as the Murchison River. These areas were favoured by the first pioneers and for many years were the site of the only established farms.

Beyond the Jarrah forest, woodlands of Wandoo, *Eucalyptus wandoo,* are widespread and are often interspersed with the York Gum woodlands. On the gravelly hills of this belt grow the Powder-bark Wandoo, *Eucalyptus accedens.* As the common name suggests, this tree can be distinguished from ordinary Wandoo by the powder on its bark which will rub off easily onto the palm of the hand. It also has larger fruit and thicker, obtuse buds.

Still further east the countryside is gently undulating with broad valleys and low laterite-capped hills. The valleys, which contain sandy or loamy soils, have been extensively cleared for cereal growing and pasture development. Only the laterite hills, the narrow roadside verges and small pockets of uncleared land remain outside the few reserves of the wheatbelt.

The rainfall of the wheatbelt varies from about 650 mm to 400 mm per annum, most falling in the winter months from May to August. The rainfall and its reliability decrease to the transitional zone east of the Wheatbelt.

The Brown Mallet, *Eucalyptus astringens,* is common on the laterite breakaways of the Wandoo belt. Fine examples of Brown Mallet are found in the plantations of the Dryandra State Forest which is one of the few remaining natural locations of this and associated species in the western wheatbelt. The Mallets are well known for their tannin-producing bark. The Blue Mallet, *Eucalyptus gardneri,* and the White Mallet, *Eucalyptus falcata*, occur in colonies on lateritic hilltops throughout most of the southern wheatbelt. The Swamp Mallet, *Eucalyptus spathulata*, grows on low-lying loams and is common between Katanning and Ongerup. The ground flora beneath Mallets is very poor, containing only a few scattered shrubs and herbs. All of the Mallets are very fire sensitive, the trees being killed by fire. Regeneration is by seed and dense thickets of young trees soon develop. For most native plants, fire is an important factor of the environment because it prunes and re-fertilises. If it is too frequent new seed cannot be produced and some species are wiped out of whole areas.

In the southern districts, the Yates are common. The Flat-topped Yate, *Eucalyptus occidentalis,* is a black-stockinged tree with a remarkably regular funnel-shaped crown of leaves. It prefers the clay soils and is common in poorly drained areas between Wagin and the Stirling Range.

The most widespread tree of the wheatbelt is the Salmon Gum, *Eucalyptus salmonophloia.* Named botanically by the famous Australian botanist Ferdinand Mueller, the early wheatbelt settlers had already given this tree its common name. The bark colour varies from brownish pink at the end of summer to whitish with grey-purple patches in winter. Underneath the bark, the wood is usually salmon pink when fractured.

Since the turn of the century, the Salmon Gum has been regarded as an indicator of good soil in the wheatbelt. Usually land classification was based on the presence of Salmon Gum and Gimlet, *Eucalyptus salubris,* which when growing together indicate a heavy clay which was then favoured for farming. The ground vegetation of a Salmon Gum woodland is usually sparse and thus was of little use to the early pastoralists. Species of *Acacia* and, particularly in the eastern part of the wheatbelt, the white-leaved members of the *Chenopodiaceae*, are very common.

Other Eucalypts are common and widespread in the wheatbelt but most are not tall trees. Many are mallees which is a general term to cover those Eucalypts which develop underground stems or 'mallee roots'. This habit is considered to be an adaptation to fire, the main stem being underground and protected by the soil. Numerous aerial stems arise from each underground structure and if they are destroyed by fire, new shoots soon arise. Several Eucalypt species possess both a mallee and a tree form.

Mallees occur over a wide area of the wheatbelt but more particularly in the south and south-east. These areas and the sandheaths, having infertile soils, were the last to be developed for farming, following the introduction of trace elements. Mallees commonly occur on sandy loam as dense thickets composed of one or several mallee species or as isolated shrubs in heathlands. While many white-flowered species grow in the south, several spectacular species are found in northern areas. The Pear-fruited Mallee, *Eucalyptus pyriformis* (Pl. 414), occurs in poor sandy country over most of the northern wheatbelt. Another shrubby Eucalypt which like the Pear-fruited Mallee has very large flowers is the Mottlecah, *Eucalyptus macrocarpa* (Pl. 358). This is the largest-flowered of all Eucalypts and has the broadest fruit in the genus. This species grows on sandy or gravelly soils dominating low heath and has practically stalkless, solitary flowers and stalkless leaves. The Rose Mallee, *Eucalyptus rhodantha,* is regarded either as a variant of the Mottlecah or as a separate species. It has smaller leaves than the Mottlecah and the smaller, more richly coloured, stalked flowers can be seen more readily. The Rose Mallee occurs naturally only from the Hill River to near New Norcia but has been widely planted.

Other Eucalypts of the wheatbelt are the Gimlets. The smooth bark is reddish brown and the trunk especially in young trees is spirally twisted like a gimlet. The best known species is the common Gimlet, *Eucalyptus salubris,* which was once common throughout the wheatbelt.

On poor sandy clays there is frequently a tall thicket formation known as wodjil. It is dominated by *Acacia* species, especially *A. neurophylla,* but has also a mixture of other shrubs such as *Casuarina, Hakea* and *Grevillea.* Another vegetation type is tamma which is also a shrub formation but is less than 2 m high and is dominated by *Casuarina campestris.* Both wodjil and tamma are widespread in eastern parts of the wheatbelt.

Dense thickets of the Broom Honeymyrtle, *Melaleuca uncinata* (Pl. 332), are also common where the surface soil is sandy clay. The famous Underground Orchid, *Rhizanthella gardneri,* was first described from a plant collected near decayed stems of the Broom Honeymyrtle in 1928. The white stem was 30 cm below ground level and at its summit was found a head of small orchid flowers. Nothing is known of the biology of this plant, and it is probably now extremely rare because so much of the habitat has been destroyed.

Sandalwood, *Santalum spicatum* (Pl. 380), was once very common from the Avon Valley eastwards. Trees up to 8 m high with a trunk diameter of 30 cm were common before the species was exploited for its aromatic wood. Now, small trees remain in a few locations in the wheatbelt, though the species extends further inland. The related species *Santalum acuminatum* or Quandong (Vic. 154) with its characteristic round, pitted fruit is still common in the wheatbelt.

Apart from the Powder-bark Wandoo and the Mallets, lateritic hilltops support a varied shrub cover. Frequently, dense thickets of *Dryandra* clothe the entire hill. Typical species are Golden Dryandra, *D. nobilis* (Pl. 371), and King Dryandra, *Dryandra proteoides* (Pl. 347), which has flowers resembling those of the South African genus *Protea;* their similarity illustrates parallel evolution during similar climatic conditions. Most of the laterite hills of the wheatbelt have been quarried for gravel and only a few species are capable of re-colonising these pits. Apart from species of *Dryandra,* the Tinsel Flower, *Cyanostegia lanceolata* (Pl. 364), is able to colonise gravel pits or even gravel roadsides.

The open heath and the mallee heath of the wheatbelt support a wealth of wildflowers. These heaths are developed on deep, white or yellow sand or on shallow sand over laterite. Such heaths are popularly known as 'Sandplain' in the wheatbelt. The shrubs are usually less than 1 m high and no one species is dominant. Three of the largest Australian families, *Epacridaceae, Myrtaceae* and *Proteaceae,* are well represented. South-Western Australia has a total of over 1,500 species of these three families, nearly one third of their Australian total. It is on the northern and southern sandplains as well as the pockets of sandplain in the wheatbelt that these species mostly occur in this State. The species richness of some small areas of wheatbelt heath is remarkable. Tuttanning Reserve for example has over 400 species in an area of about 2,000 ha, a degree of richness which can not be matched in the forest or woodland formations.

Among the few taller species of the heaths are the Sandplain Pear, *Xylomelum angustifolium* (Pl. 344), and the Acorn Banksia, *Banksia prionotes,* which occur as small trees on deep, yellow sand. On northern and eastern sandplains tall species of *Grevillea* are common, for example the Bottlebrush Grevillea, *G. paradoxa,* and the Flame Grevillea, *G. eriostachya* (Pl. 361).

The sandy or gravelly soil under the heath shrubs is usually bare except for some drought-resistant mosses, a few orchids, some colonial sedges forming small, cushion-like clumps, and Sundews. One of the most common Sundews of this habitat is the Painted Sundew, *Drosera zonaria* (Pl. 44). This species like many other western ones has a round tuber up to 10 cm below the ground level. An upright stem from the tuber has a dense sheath of fibrous roots and at the surface there is a rosette of dark-tipped leaves. Masses of rosettes occur together because the upright stems branch underground to produce two or more tuber-producing stolons. The Painted Sundew flowers only rarely, following both a summer bushfire and summer rains in February or March. As in the related Red Ink Sundew, *Drosera erythrorhiza* (Pl. 42), the flowers are formed underground and are forced through the previous year's root sheath to the surface. Later, the leaves appear at the base of the flower stalk and the flowers wither.

Other species of *Drosera* are the Pygmy Sundews, tiny rosetted species which do not have tubers or bulbous roots. The Cone Sundew, *Drosera androsacea,* and the Pearly Sundew, *D. pycnoblasta,* are common on white sand. Extensive colonies of these plants grow under the heath shrubs as well as on the open ground. They are well adapted to the short growing season and always flower profusely. The flowers are usually less than 1 cm diameter, the same size as the entire leaf rosette. The largest-flowered Pygmy Sundews grow on gravelly soil. The Orange Sundew *Drosera miniata* (Pl. 386), and Drummond's Sundew, *D. drummondii*, prefer this habitat. All of these species are able to withstand the dry summer because the centre of each rosette is protected by a dense mat of tangled leaf bases and stipules.

The featherflowers of the family *Myrtaceae* are examples of elaborated flowers referred to in the discussion of that family in the section on the Swan Coastal Plain. The calyx lobes and sometimes the petals of these plants are deeply divided into finger- or feather-like segments. The wheatbelt featherflowers are frequently found on disturbed soil near roadsides and in gravel pits. One of the most prominent Featherflowers is the Common Cauliflower-bush, *Verticordia brownii* (Pl. 335). Another member of this genus common in the wheatbelt is the Painted Featherflower, *Verticordia picta* (Pl. 331).

The flowers of the *Proteaceae* form varied kinds of inflorescence. Species of *Adenanthos* and some *Grevilleas* for example have scattered solitary flowers each with the same basic structure of a perianth tube with four lobes. In *Dryandra, Petrophile* and *Isopogon* the flowers are aggregated into heads. Those of *Dryandra* are always surrounded by large bracts. Most of the species of *Hakea* and *Grevillea* have their flowers in racemes without prominent bracts. In some species the racemes are one-sided such as the Prickly Toothbrush, *Grevillea armigera* (Pl. 395), and the Phalanx Grevillea, *G. dryandroides* (Pl. 357).

Some species of *Hakea* exhibit a remarkable adaptation to fire in their features of seed liberation. The large woody follicles of the Cricket Ball Hakea, *Hakea platysperma* (Pl. 336), are opened by fire to reveal the two large, winged seeds. Each seed has a number of dry projections into pits of the woody inner fruit wall and cannot be removed easily when it is first opened. After the heat of a fire has opened the follicle to expose the seeds the projections loosen slowly so that the seed will not fall onto hot ash. The large wing around each seed allows wind-dispersal over short distances.

The salt lakes of the wheatbelt are another habitat which is common over many parts of the dry interior. They represent the remnants of once extensive river systems. Only in exceptionally wet years do some of these salt lakes connect and flow towards the existing river systems. The Mortlock River flats for example are remnants of a more extensive Swan-Avon river system which existed in the past. Some wheatbelt species are adapted to the saline soils. A Sheoak, *Casuarina obesa,* and a Paperbark, *Melaleuca cuticularis,* are common in this habitat. Samphires, succulent members of the family *Chenopodiaceae*, are common low shrubs forming dense mats in the moist salt flats.

Granite Outcrops

An impressive feature of the countryside in Western Australia is the granite outcrop rising like an island of rock from the surrounding sea of scrub. Granite outcrops are common throughout most of the South-West. Some occur as sheets of rock with pockets of soil, the total area varying from a few square metres to a few hectares. Other outcrops, particularly in the Wheatbelt and Transitional zones, occur as rounded monadnocks reaching up to 60 metres above the surrounding plain.

These outcrops, which are of gneissic or granitic rocks, are either erosion residuals which now remain above the level of the surrounding plains or they are erosion scars left on hillsides. In the western part of the Great Western Plateau they represent the remains of large masses of granitic country rock which have been eroded to a rounded hill or even a flat sheet. The large granite domes common to the wheatbelt and transitional zone as well as the countryside surrounding the 'greenstones' of the goldfields, are also the result of eons of weathering. In most cases the inland outcrops probably represent the erosion residuals of 'bosses', large granitic invasions into the country rock.

The value of granite outcrops as a source of water in the long dry summer was soon realised by the first explorers who travelled east of York and Toodyay in the early days of the Swan River Colony. Lefroy's expedition in 1863 to the area now called the Goldfields, noted the value of the 'bald hills' of granite for water supplies. Later, these hills were to provide water catchments for the steam engines travelling to Kalgoorlie and Coolgardie. Many towns such as Merredin and Moorine Rock were founded because they were near reliable water supplies long before the Goldfields Water Scheme was completed. It was soon realised by the early engineers and first settlers that most of the water falling on a granite dome runs off and that with the construction of walls and channels, water could be saved. Remains of these rock catchments and associated reservoirs are still very evident on the granite outcrops of the well-settled districts. Some catchments have been maintained and improved to give reliable water supplies in time of need.

The surface of granite outcrops is always very weathered and uneven. Fissures, ridges and depressions are everywhere and represent the differential action of weathering on the harder and softer rocks and minerals. Some fissures are the result of widening of the original jointing planes of the granitic rocks. Ridges may be the result of weathering of veins of silica-rich rock. In some cases these veins are harder than the granitic rock they once intruded and now they stand out as long straight ridges of feldspar crystals and masses of quartz, the ridges being from a few centimetres to many centimetres wide. In cases where the veins are softer or their margins are softer they have been weathered to form straight channels, ideal for water moving off the rock during a downpour. The surface itself is usually very pitted by weathering particularly where the larger crystals of feldspar have broken down to liberate the quartz fragments and micaceous minerals to form soil.

The breakdown of the rock into tiny soil particles has occurred over millions of years so that the crevices and hollows have become soil filled. Around the base of the outcrops, soil aprons have been built up from the breakdown of the rocks into a brown gritty loam. Soil also accumulates under large boulders which have been left standing as tors by the weathering of jointing planes. The large boulders are nearly always well rounded. The angular corners of rocks exposed to the hot sun and cold night air soon shear off to produce a rounded boulder. The same action of weathering on a larger scale is responsible for the roundness of the large granite domes. On such outcrops large sheets of rock exfoliate leaving slabs of all sizes scattered over the surface.

Even a small shower of rain will cause rills and streams of water to cascade off a rock surface. On the top of a granite dome where the surface is relatively flat, pools of water are nearly always found. These pools have arisen by the chemical action both of the rain water and the plants they support so that in some cases pools may be many square metres in area and up to 30 cms deep. Pools are also found where large gnamma holes have been weathered into the rock surface. These may be two or three metres deep and are frequently funnel shaped cavities with the narrow portion near the top, so that evaporation is less. These gnamma holes are usually a permanent source of water.

It is in the rock pools, the soil pockets and the apron soils that one finds the peculiar flora of the granite rocks. The plants of these habitats are adapted to the incredibly changeable environment of a rock surface with its shallow soil and extremes of climate. In winter the soil is waterlogged and the rock is cold and mostly exposed to the cold winds. In summer the soil bakes, especially where it is shallow, and the plants are exposed to searing winds. The rocks surface becomes very hot during the day, often up to 50°C, baking the algae, lichens and small plants and reflecting the light and heat onto the leaves of the shrubs and trees in the deeper soil pockets. The water plants which have become adapted to the rock pools have to complete their annual cycle in a few months, before the summer drought and heat dry them up. So too do the aquatic animals which live in these pools.

The first winter rainstorms flood the granite. The soil soon becomes waterlogged and the roots and perennating organs of plants are activated. The almost-bare rock springs to life. Many species of lichens and algae cling to the tiny depressions in the rock giving a black, grey or pale green colour to its surface. The black colour of some rock surfaces is due to the prolific growth of tiny threads of algae, adapted to the short, wet winters and long dry summers. The vertical streaks of Wave Rock near Hyden are caused by the growth and death of algal colonies. The dark black stains are colonies of living algae attached to the granite. When the water supply to a vertical streak is cut off by the deposition of sediment on the crest of the 'wave' the black streak changes to brown as the algae die. Meanwhile the water is channelled to a neighbouring streak and it becomes black with living algae. Algae which have been dead for a few seasons fall away from the rock leaving fresh bare granite rock. The weathering by these algae could well be partly responsible for many of the strange formations on the granite outcrops.

Where the soil and litter have accumulated to a few millimetres deep, a moss sward is developed. In the wetter parts of the South-West, granite slopes may be almost covered by a thick mat of mosses. In the Porongurups (Pl. 413) these mosses become bright yellow-green in winter and spread wherever they can obtain a foothold. In the moss swards grow tiny flowering plants which have adapted to the habitat by reducing their size and shortening their life cycle. Some plants with bulbous roots or rhizomes also grow in these swards. The Eight Nancy, *Wurmbaea tenella* (Pl. 407), and the Blue Quill, *Chamaescilla corymbosa,* which has bright blue flowers, are two members of the lily family which are common. Another common plant of wetter granite slopes is *Tribonanthes*, a relative of the Kangaroo Paws. The grey-white felted flowers of this plant appear in masses in the late winter on the granite slopes of the Darling Range.

The most common plant of the shallow soil pockets is Pincushions, *Borya nitida* (Pls. 411, 412). During summer the leaves are red and very dry and brittle, and the plants are dormant. After the first rains they absorb moisture and the leaves become green and relatively soft and pliable. Another perennial, also in the Lily family, though without any obvious adaption to the habitat is the Blind Grass, *Stypandra grandiflora* (Pl. 406). This is a close relative of *Stypandra imbricata*, a confirmed toxic species, and both species are treated with caution by farmers. Sheep or other animals after feeding on these species may develop blindness and locomotory disturbances prior to death.

The flora of the shallow soil of the drier inland granite outcrops is as rich as that of wetter areas in the South-West. A few square metres can yield twenty or thirty species of flowering plants as well as a few species each of mosses, liverworts and lichens. Some of the flowering plants are so minute that they can be collected only with a pair of fine forceps, for example some small daisies.

Frequently the flora of shallow soil pockets exhibits an incredible sharing of space and flowering time. For example in the late winter, the tiny sedges mature and set seed. Later, in spring, the daisies mature and flower, and in late spring, moss swards may support masses of Triggerplants such as the Circus Triggerplant, *Stylidium bulbiferum* (Pl. 422). Usually these plants are dried by the oncoming summer, and their seeds are blown away by the drying winds. Some of the daisies are only a few centimetres high with a few leaves and a terminal head of flowers which is large with respect to the size of the plant, for example Flannel Cudweed, *Actinobole uliginosum,* and the Pygmy Daisy, *Helipterum australe* (Pl. 409).

Other small plants adapted to the shallow soils are the Butterfly Flowers, *Philydrella pygmaea* (Pl. 414), and orchids such as the Elbow Orchid, *Spiculaea ciliata* (Pl. 421). This orchid exhibits an unusual adaptation to the short growing season which is similar to that of Woodbridge Poison, *Isotoma hypocrateriformis* (Pl. 47). The flower stem of these species is rather fleshy and is apparently a storage organ for food and water. Flowering may continue long after the basal leaves and lower stem have withered. Granite outcrops are havens for many other orchid species.

The insectivorous plants of the genus *Drosera* (sundews) are further examples of moisture-loving species adapted to the winter-wet loams. The most common South-Western species, *Drosera macrantha*, is present on the granite rocks. It is a robust climber which trails over shrubs in deeper soil pockets. The flowers which are usually white but frequently pink make an attractive display. A *Drosera* which is restricted to granite outcrops is a lime-green-coloured variant of *Drosera stolonifera*. This commonly grows in red loam on outcrops of the central wheatbelt and occurs in masses where the soil is more than 5 or 6 cm deep. The fan-shaped leaves of this variant are exceptionally sticky and are quite capable of catching large insects such as butterflies and blowflies. Rosetted sundews are also very widespread on granite outcrops.

The seasonal rock pools which have a layer of gritty mud support a specialised aquatic flora. Frequently the mud will be covered by a colony of Quillworts, species of *Isoetes*. These fern-allies are perennial, the tufts of narrow fronds arising each winter from a fleshy rootstock buried in the mud. Another aquatic is the Mudmat, *Glossostigma drummondii* (Pl. 408). This species frequently grows with the Quillworts and has tiny spoon-shaped leaves. When the rock pool is almost dry tiny pale mauve flowers appear and set seed before the pool dries. At the same time the Quillworts form drought resistant spores which are also liberated into the drying mud. In deeper ephemeral pools grow aquatic species of *Crassula* with long threadlike stems, small scattered leaves and tiny white flowers which just break the surface of the water. Deeper pools with thick mud have a longer growing season and a chance for larger aquatic plants to aestivate. Such pools are rare on inland granite rocks but more common near the coasts. Species of Water Milfoil, *Myriophyllum* (Vic. 270), and Swamp Lily, *Ottelia ovalifolia* (Vic. 271), commonly occur in this habitat.

Ferns are also adapted to granite outcrops and frequent the loam soil under overhangs and boulders where they are protected from drying. The most common is the Rock Fern, *Cheilanthes tenuifolia*. A related species, *Cheilanthes distans,* has a rusty appearance due to a dense covering of brown hairs.

The shrubs of granite outcrops exhibit various mechanisms to combat the intense heat of the summer. Most have effective root systems which can penetrate small fissures in search of water. The Granite Kunzea, *Kunzea pulchella* (Pl. 410), has hoary leaves to reflect the sun's rays and retain the leaf moisture. Other rock dwellers such as Mouse Ears, *Calothamnus rupestris* (Pl. 418), and the Graceful Honeymyrtle, *Melaleuca radula* (Pl. 424), have small narrow leaves.

Other shrubs which are common are *Hakea petiolaris,* which has tough, leathery leaves, and *Ricinocarpos tuberculatus*. Both of these occur on rocks of the southern wheatbelt. The latter species may grow into a tall shrub up to 3 m with masses of white flowers. The red, hop-like fruits of *Dodonaea attenuata* are prominent in spring. The narrow leaves of this shrub have a sticky covering to reduce water loss. In the apron soils surrounding an outcrop a wattle, *Acacia lasiocalyx*, often forms dense thickets. It has whitish stems with long, narrow, pale green phyllodes and catkin-like inflorescences.

Because of the shallow soil, few tree species can grow on an outcrop. The most common is the Sheoak, *Casuarina huegeliana*, a tree which, where the soil is over a metre deep, can grow up to 6 m high. Pure stands of this tree are frequent in deep soil pockets or on apron soils. A Eucalypt adapted to outcrops is the Gungurru, *Eucalyptus caesia* (Pl. 405). One of the most attractive of our eucalypts and one which is now widely cultivated, this species grows in clefts of granite rocks in the central wheatbelt near Pingelly and Kellerberrin as well as further inland.

Fire rarely destroys the vegetation cover on granite outcrops since the rock surfaces form natural firebreaks. Many plants of these habitats have perennial rootstocks from which regrowth occurs after fire, for example Gungurru and Blind Grass. However even those which are killed by fire and regenerate from seed may reach a great age due to the long intervals between fires. This is evident from the trunks, very thick and gnarled relative to the size of the plants, of shrubs such as Granite Kunzea and Wongan Featherflower.

One of the most interesting features of the granite outcrop flora is that because of the greater effective rainfall on some soil pockets and the reasonable soil quality, many plants have an extended range into drier inland areas. Some of these outliers are no doubt remnants of a once wider distribution. For example Jarrah, *Eucalyptus marginata*, occurs at Jilakin Rock some 80 km east of the main occurrence of this species. The Christmas Tree, *Nuytsia floribunda*, occurs on clefts of granite rocks near Tammin many kilometres east of its normal distribution. In contrast, some species which are more characteristic of drier regions are also found on granite outcrops. An example is the mauve-flowered Rock Isotome, *Isotoma petraea*, which ranges from the wheatbelt to central Australia.

Transitional Woodlands and Nullarbor Plain

Beyond the wheatbelt the rainfall becomes low and unreliable, and marked changes occur in the vegetation. This is the boundary of the South West vegetation Province; plants commonly found in the South-West become infrequent or are absent, while those typical of the inland Eremean Province appear in greater numbers. There are also species confined to this transitional zone.

The boundaries of the region (as indeed of most plant regions) are indefinite. Incursions and outliers of plants from both the South West and Eremean Provinces are common and it is partly the presence of these which make the region a fascinating one. There is always the anticipation of the unexpected, the possibility of finding new populations of plants from either Province, or new species restricted to the region.

The countryside here is flat or gently undulating, its elevation above sea level ranging from 200 metres in the north and south to over 400 metres around Kalgoorlie. Isolated hills and small ranges rise up to 100 metres above the plain, for example Mt. Singleton and the Koolyanobbing Range. Eastwards the land falls gradually to the Nullarbor Plain, this vast expanse sloping gently from an altitude of 200 m along its northern edge to 80–150 m in the south.

Rainfall is about 180–300 mm, coming partly from inland extensions of southern winter depressions and partly from tropical summer cyclones which occasionally move this far south. However the rains are unreliable and in some years are too light for the vegetation to respond. At such times it remains dormant, and flowers are few.

The soils are mostly red loams and loamy sands, yellow sands and gravelly loam. There are many salt lakes, while the hills are mostly laterite or decaying granite. There are also granite outcrops similar to those of the South-West, though the surface is often weathered to an orange-brown colour.

Plant groups which are typical of the South-West but far less common in this region include the sedges, *Restionaceae*, banksias, *Proteaceae*, many pea flowers, *Papilionaceae*, native buttercups, *Hibbertia*, heaths, *Epacridaceae*, and triggerplants, *Stylidium*. Eremean groups which assume greater prominence include grasses, *Poaceae*, mulla mullas, *Ptilotus*, wild tomatoes, *Solanum*, poverty bushes, *Eremophila* and daisies, *Asteraceae*.

Most widespread of the vegetation types are the woodlands. These are extensive in the Kalgoorlie-Norseman area (often referred to as the Goldfields) and occur also along the narrow corridor reaching towards Shark Bay. They are dominated by *Eucalyptus* species, and it is extraordinary that stout-trunked trees up to 30 m high are so common in a region of such low rainfall. The trees are often unbranched for many metres and then branch into spreading, rather open crowns. Unlike the jarrah and karri forests where single species may form pure stands, the transitional woodlands usually have a mixture of species.

Probably the most widespread species is Salmon Gum, *Eucalyptus salmonophloia* (Pl. 426), especially on the Goldfields. It extends north-westwards to Mullewa, south beyond Norseman, and is also common in the Wheatbelt. It is a tall, attractive tree with a single trunk, the bark being smooth and salmon-coloured, often deeper in tone in the autumn. The shining foliage forms a wide, light crown, while the rounded flowers and fruit are very small. Similar in aspect is Dundas Mahogany, *E. brockwayi*, which has the buds and fruit contracted in the middle. It is found in the Norseman district, often on greenstone hills.

Often seen with Salmon Gums on the Goldfields are Common Gimlet, *E. salubris*, and Silver-topped Gimlet, *E. campaspe*. The Gimlets are trees with smooth, often fluted, trunks, the bark thin, reddish-brown or bronze, and shining. Common Gimlet, which also extends to Mullewa and Lake Grace, grows to 25 m and has a dense, shining, dark green crown, while Silver-topped Gimlet reaches only 12 m and has glaucous branchlets and dull green leaves. Both have axillary clusters of buds with smooth, rounded caps and hemispherical fruit with strong exserted valves. The buds and fruit of Silver-topped Gimlet are glaucous.

York Gum, *E. loxophleba*, already described for the Wheatbelt region, is a common species of the woodlands between the Murchison River and Coolgardie. The rough, dark bark on the lower trunk of this tree occurs, with some variation in texture and colour, in a number of species and has given rise to the common name of Blackbutt for some. Such is the Goldfields Blackbutt, *E. lesouefii* which is found between Menzies and Norseman and east towards the Nullarbor. It is a tree to 12 m with a rather dense crown of dull green foliage; the broad buds are 1.5–2 cm long, strongly ribbed, with pointed caps. Farther west, between Southern Cross and Coolgardie, grows the Rough-fruited Blackbutt, *E. corrugata,* which is similar to *E. lesouefii* but the ribbed buds are flat on top; it may also be seen as a mallee, and prefers rocky soil.

Another is Cleland's Blackbutt, *Eucalyptus clelandii*, very widespread on the Goldfields and extending north-westwards to Mt. Gibson. The tree grows to 12 m tall and has glaucous branchlets, buds and fruit, the buds being smooth with ribbed caps and about 1 cm long. Dundas Blackbutt, *E. dundasii*, is found in alluvial loams in the Norseman district and is a tree to 20 m with a wide glossy crown. The sessile buds are cylindrical, about 1 cm long, with short, pointed caps, and the fruit are slightly ribbed.

These and many of the other species making up the Eucalypt flora of the region are white-flowered, but there are also some colourful species, such as the Coral Gum, *E. torquata* (Pl. 446). Strickland's Gum, *E. stricklandii,* has bright yellow flowers opening in summer. It is a spreading tree to 12 m with a short, rough-barked trunk, the smooth upper bark being various shades of pink, brown and grey, and the branchlets are glaucous. The thick, sessile buds, 2 cm long, are slightly constricted in the middle and have conical caps. It occurs in the woodlands between Coolgardie and Norseman, especially on rocky hills. Another yellow-flowered species is *Eucalyptus woodwardii,* the Lemon-flowered Gum. Restricted to a few areas between Karonie and Zanthus on the Trans-Australia railway, this is a tree to 12 m with smooth pale bark, pendulous glaucous branchlets and bell-like flowers and fruit which also are glaucous. Hybrids have been developed between this species and the Coral Gum and make colourful ornamental trees.

In a year of heavy flowering (which usually follows a year of good rains) many of the Eucalypts of this region produce abundant nectar and pollen and are much sought-after by beekeepers. Some of the larger species also provide good timber and have been extensively utilised on the Goldfields, especially in the mines. The aesthetic appeal of many and their ability to grow in dry conditions has resulted in their cultivation for shade and ornament in other inland regions of Australia, as well as overseas.

The woodlands support an understorey containing a mixture of tall and low shrubs and herbs. In a good season these make a colourful showing during spring. Prominent among the shrubs are species of *Eremophila*, the poverty bushes. Several have a broombush-type habit—single-stemmed at the base but with many vertical branches rising to a rounded crown. The tallest is *Eremophila interstans* which grows to 8 m and has slender terete, uncinate leaves 1 cm long. The clustered flowers have calyxes 4–5 mm long with elliptic, ciliate lobes, and white, bell-like corollas 7–8 mm long. It flowers in spring and ranges from Coolgardie to Norseman and east almost to the Nullarbor. A similar species in the same districts is *E. dempsteri* which is shorter and has sparse, recurved, uncinate leaves less than 5 mm long. The flowers are usually solitary, with a densely ciliate calyx 5–6 mm long and a violet, pubescent corolla 1 cm long.

Some species have a viscid covering on the leaves and stems, for example *E. paisleyi* and *E. ionantha.* The former is a broom-bush to 3 m having broad-linear, uncinate leaves 2–4 cm long, and clustered flowers with a pink calyx and a white or mauve, scented corolla. The calyx is 4–5 mm long with obovate lobes and the corolla 1 cm long. It also extends from the Goldfields to the Nullarbor, flowering in September and October. *Eremophila ionantha* reaches 2 m tall and has terete, obtuse incurved leaves 10–15 mm long. The purple flowers are on slender pedicels 5–10 mm long, the calyx having acute lobes 3 mm long, while the corolla is 2 cm long, much inflated above the narrow base. Found through the Goldfields, it flowers from September to November.

Similar to *E. ionantha* but covered with silvery scales and having mauve flowers is Silver Poverty Bush, *E. scoparia* (Vic. 141) while another common species widespread in southern arid Australia is Weeooka, *E. oppositifolia* (Vic. 140). The latter is a tall hoary shrub with linear uncinate leaves often in pairs; the calyx is cream and the tubular corolla is pale pink to red. Turpentine Bush, *E. clarkei* (Pl. 479), is a widespread and variable species throughout the region.

Among the smaller shrubs Daisybushes, *Olearia*, are often prominent when in flower. Mueller's Daisybush, *O. muelleri*, is the most frequent. It is a shrub to 1 m tall, viscid on the leaves and branches, the leaves obovate, crinkly-margined and less than 1 cm long. The flower heads have rays which are white inside and purplish outside. Burrobunga, *O. pimelioides* (Vic. 163), is a hoary-leaved, non-viscid species with the ray flowers white inside and outside. Both these species extend to Victoria.

In the southeastern woodlands, the understorey is often dominated by Greybush, *Cratystylis conocephala.* A much-branched shrub to 1 m tall, this has obovate leaves 5–8 mm long, grey with dense short curled hairs, and terminal white flower heads lacking rays. There are only 3 species of this genus, all endemic in arid Australia.

Of similar appearance and also covered with dense curled hairs is Bluebush, *Maireana sedifolia*. However, this belongs to the chenopod family and has short, terete, succulent leaves which spread horizontally. The flowers are axillary and inconspicuous but in fruit develop a flat circular wing almost 1 cm across, pale green to reddish in colour. Very common on the Nullarbor Plain, Bluebush is also widespread in the woodlands of the southeast, and is an important fodder plant.

There are many wattles in the region, the Tan Wattle, *Acacia hemiteles* (Pl. 429), being widespread. Another tall species is *A. burkittii,* a shrub rather like the Jam Tree *(A. acuminata)* of the Wheatbelt but more bushy; its linear phyllodes have finely hairy margins and the flowers are in spikes. There is much variety in habit among the wattles, some having short, broad phyllodes, others slender and terete, while a few species have spinescent branches.

Besides the Eucalypts, the Myrtaceae are poorly represented in the woodlands but a few *Melaleuca* species are common. Boree, *M. sheathiana*, is a broombush which in flower may look like a huge cauliflower, the creamy-white flowers covering the bush. It grows to 4 m high and has thick, terete, spreading leaves 2–3 mm long. The flowers appear in late spring or early summer. A similar species is *M. pauperiflora* which has longer, acute leaves, erect or slightly recurved.

A shrub which has found a use in medicine is Currant Bush, *Scaevola spinescens*. It is usually about 1 m tall and has linear-oblanceolate leaves 1–2 cm long clustered on the spinescent branches. The sparse flowers are fan-like, about 1 cm long and cream with thin purple lines inside. An infusion from the plant is used to alleviate the pain of cancer. The species is widespread in the transitional region and extends into arid Australia.

Many ephemeral herbs appear during winter and spring, and in good seasons make a magnificent display of colour in some districts. Among them are everlastings and other daisies, Sturt Pea, Mulla Mullas such as *Ptilotus exaltatus* (Pl. 461) and vetches such as *Swainsona colutoides* (Pl. 447).

Other Formations

Thickets of tall scrub are widespread especially in the north-western areas of this region. They contain many species which, although belonging to different families, are often remarkably similar in habit and foliage. This is especially evident in species which have long narrow leaves, phyllodes, or branchlets such as are found in the wattles, sheoaks, *Grevilleas, Hakeas* and *Calothamnus*. Scattered through the thickets are a few species of mallee Eucalypts, while other myrtles such as *Thryptomene, Baeckea* and *Melaleuca* are more common. Some species are restricted to small areas, such as the Bush Pomegranate, *Balaustion microphyllum* (Pl. 445).

Several small trees are widespread but never dominant in the Transitional thickets. There are two Native Cypress species, *Callitris huegelii* (with smooth or slightly wrinkled cones 1.5–2 cm across) and *C. preissii* subspecies *verrucosa* (with wart-covered cones—Vic. 133). They occur especially where the soil is somewhat sandy, sometimes near salt lakes.

The kurrajong, Ngalta, *Brachychiton gregorii*, occurs as scattered individuals, the dense crown of brighter green foliage conspicuous among the other shrubs. The leaves are deeply lobed and the flowers, appearing in summer, are small bells of cream and brown. A boat-shaped follicle 2–4 cm long with several furry seeds forms the fruit. This also extends to the NT and SA.

In sandy areas, two grass-like plants forming tussocks are common. In north-western areas is *Ecdeiocolea monostachya* which has many wiry, leafless stems and terminal spikes 1–2 cm long containing tiny flowers within shining bracts. It is the only species of its family, *Ecdeiocoleaceae*. From Lake Moore to the Nullarbor the spinifex, *Triodia scariosa*, is frequent. Its needle-like leaves protrude in all directions from the large clumps, and the inflorescences are somewhat wheat-like in appearance. This spinifex is also associated with open mallee formations.

Other species of sandy or pebbly-sandy soils include some colourful shrubs and herbs. Some appear briefly for a few years after bushfires and then die down to lie dormant as seeds until the next fire occurs. Such are Red Velvet, *Hemiphora elderi* (Pl. 431), and Upside-down Peabush, *Brachysema daviesioides* (Pl. 388), though the latter may be more persistent.

The Lambstails also prefer burned areas. On the Goldfields, *Lachnostachys coolgardiensis* occurs in sandy areas. It is a much-branched shrub to 70 cm, densely woolly all over, with narrowly-winged stems and short spikes of flowers. In north-western areas is *L. verbascifolia* which is taller and more loosely woolly, the stems terete and the leaves and flower spikes larger.

Sandheaths are extensive in some areas, especially between Southern Cross and Coolgardie and farther south. In general they are similar to those already described for the Wheatbelt. Their plants include many typical of the South-West and represent a large proportion of the outliers previously mentioned.

Throughout this southern part of the region there are also large tracts of mallee, dominated by many species of *Eucalyptus* of either mallee or small tree form. Low and tall shrubs of many genera are associated with these and, as with the sandheaths, usually represent inland extensions of south-western species.

The rocky hills and outcrops provide different habitats where a number of interesting plants occur. On the ironstone hills north of Southern Cross grows Yilgarn Dryandra, *D. arborea* (Pl. 432), which is the most inland species of the genus. Here, too, one may find the rare *Tetratheca harperi*, an almost leafless perennial herb with bristly stems and scattered, deep pink, 5-petalled flowers, the purple anthers forming a column around the style.

Broom Spurge, *Calycopeplus helmsii*, is another leafless shrub often seen on rocky hills between Mullewa and Southern Cross. It is a broombush up to 4 m tall, the dark green stems containing milky sap and bearing small unisexual flowers.

On granite outcrops of the Goldfields occur several distinctive species of *Eucalyptus* such as Bookleaf Mallee, *E. kruseana*, Round-leaved Mallee, *E. orbifolia* and Webster's Mallee, *E. websterana*.

In the Fraser Range east of Norseman the Tangled Fanflower, *Scaevola oxyclona* (Pl. 444), forms spinescent, intricately-branched shrubs on the rocky slopes. Hop-bushes, *Dodonaea* species, also prefer such habitats but are more widespread in their distribution.

Orchids are far less common in this region than in the South-West, but the rocky hills and granite outcrops provide refuges where a number of species survive.

They are mostly widespread species such as the Common Donkey Orchid, *Diuris longifolia* (Pl. 92), the Snail Orchid, *Pterostylis nana* (Vic. 342), and the Elbow Orchid, *Spiculaea ciliata* (Pl. 421). Several ferns and other herbs also find shelter among the rocks.

Several large and many small salt lakes occur in the Transitional zone. They are similar to those in other parts of WA and contain water only after heavy rain. The floors are either bare or covered with a low association of salt-tolerant plants such as samphires *(Arthrocnemum)*, saltbushes *(Atriplex)* and bluebushes *(Maireana)*. On low rises around the margins are often dense thickets of shrubs and small trees such as poverty bushes *(Eremophila)*, wattles *(Acacia)* and sheoaks *(Casuarina)*.

The Nullarbor Plain

East of the Goldfields the woodlands extend to the Nullarbor Plain. The transition to the Plain is often quite sudden and occurs where the soil changes from red loam to limestone. The Eucalypts disappear, Black Oaks *(Casuarina cristata)* are common, and a bluebush-myall association (Pl. 452) often marks the beginning of the Plain. Beyond this are the vast, treeless expanses of the Plain itself. It is almost flat, sloping gently from about 200 m above sea level along its northern edge to 80–150 m in the south. For the most part it is covered with a low, open shrubland dominated by chenopods, most common being the Bluebush, *Maireana sedifolia* (Pl. 452). Other species of *Maireana*, as well as *Atriplex* and *Sclerolaena* are also frequent. The little Nullarbor Frankenia, *F. densa* (Pl. 451), is one of the very few species restricted to the Plain; the others spread into adjacent areas to the west and east.

Slight depressions known as dongas carry the only tall shrubs on the Plain (Pl. 450). These include Myall *(Acacia papyrocarpa)*, Miljee *(Acacia oswaldii)*, Weeping Pittosporum *(P. phylliraeoides)*, Kurara *(Acacia tetragonophylla*, Pl. 464), Berrigan *(Eremophila longifolia*, Vic. 142) and *Grevillea nematophylla*.

After rain, ephemerals appear on the Plain in great numbers. White Everlastings, *Helipterum floribundum*, and Sturt Pea, *Clianthus formosus* (Pl. 450), add colour to the scene, and there are other common daisies and legumes. Spear Grasses, *Stipa* spp., often form dense swards and can be unpleasant when in fruit as the long-awned seeds have a pungent base and can penetrate clothing.

The Nullarbor proper is not seen along the Eyre Highway (1) on the WA side of the State border. Instead, the route passes through an eastward extension of the transitional woodlands. The trees are low and open and are intermixed with other shrubs, especially wattles.

Mulga, Wattle Scrub and Spinifex

BEYOND THE TRANSITIONAL ZONE from the South-West Botanical Province lies the true Eremean Province. Here the level or undulating plains roll on for many miles, broken in places by rocky hills and salt lakes. This is essentially a dry land where rain falls irregularly, coming from either southern movements of tropical cyclones in summer, or northern extensions of mid-latitude depressions in winter. The average rainfall is 170–230 mm but a year may see almost none or over 500 mm. Summer is very hot and winter is mild with cold nights but rarely below freezing. During long dry spells the flora becomes almost completely dormant.

Geologically most of the region is very old, being underlain by the Precambrian Great Plateau of WA. The soils are red loams and sands, with a few remnants of a recent lateritic capping forming scattered hills which are usually flat-topped. Only in the north do the ranges become higher (see Ranges and Tablelands of the North-West). The rivers are usually dry, flowing only after heavy rains, but there are a few permanent pools.

Floristically the region is dominated by the families Mimosaceae (wattles), Poaceae (grasses), Chenopodiaceae (saltbushes, etc.), Asteraceae (daisies) and Myoporaceae (poverty bushes). Many pea flowers are present but they belong mostly to genera different from those of the South-West. The dominant families of the South-West are lacking or are poorly represented, e.g. Myrtaceae, Proteaceae and Epacridaceae. Another contrast is the large number of annual plants which appear after rains in the Eremean Province. It should be noted that the flowering of wildflowers here is dependent on the rainall and is very poor in a dry year.

The principal formation of the region is the mulga scrub (Pl. 453). Several *Acacia* species are known as mulga, by far the most common being *A. aneura*. This itself has several variants, with narrow or broad phyllodes. It forms an open low woodland, the widely-spaced trees growing to 8 m tall. Covering thousands of hectares, the grey-green of the mulga soon becomes familiar to the outback traveller.

Although mulga may often be seen flowering sparsely, it is rarely seen with ripe pods. Apparently it flowers best after good late summer rains, and with follow-up winter rains will then set fruit. The flowers are in short spikes and the pods are relatively thin, irregularly oblong with a network of fine veins.

Young mulga plants are rarely seen except in disturbed areas such as roadsides. Stands usually appear to be of uniform age, and it is thought that regeneration occurs in cycles, a new cycle beginning only after a stand has died of old age, drought or fire.

Mulga extends over much of inland Australia and in WA ranges from Gascoyne Junction south-eastwards to Menzies, north-eastwards to Wittenoom, and eastwards through the desert to NT, Qld, NSW and SA. It often forms pure stands but other wattles of similar habit may be associated with it. Such a species is *Acacia kempeana*, a spreading shrub to 3 m tall with narrow-elliptic or lanceolate phyllodes 3–5 cm long, finely-nerved and sometimes falcate; the flowers are in pedunculate spikes and the pod is broadly oblong, up to 5 cm long, with transverse seeds.

A widespread species is Kurara, *A. tetragonophylla* (Pl. 464), which is a spreading shrub with clustered, pungent phyllodes, and flowers in heads. *A. cuthbertsonii* is also a spreading shrub with pale green, linear to narrow-lanceolate phyllodes 5–10 cm long and flowers in spikes. The pods are cream, thick, flat and curved, up to 15 cm long, smooth when fresh but becoming wrinkled on drying.

Between Wittenoom and Sandstone and eastwards, the WA Gidgee, *A. pruinocarpa*, is a conspicuous tree. It has one or several trunks with rough, dark bark and the phyllodes are oblong, 8–15 cm long and bluish-green. The flower heads are in racemes, appearing in early summer, and the flat pods are oblong and slightly glaucous.

Other wattle species take over from mulga around the margins of the region. Bowgada Bush, *A. linophylla* (Pls. 458–9), is very common. In the north, Ranji Bush, *A. pyrifolia* (Pl. 463), is widespread, while others include *A. translucens*, *A. xiphophylla* and *A. ancistrocarpa*. In the west and south, common species are a shrubby form of *A. acuminata, A. grasbyi* and *A. craspedocarpa*.

In southern areas, *A. quadrimarginea* is frequent. This is a tree to 6 m, very spreading, with curved, lanceolate phyllodes up to 10 cm long, red-margined, and the flowers in spikes followed by thick, 4-angled pods.

Of the undershrubs in the mulga and wattle scrub, the principal genus is *Eremophila*, the poverty bushes, of which over 40 species occur in the region. They are of diverse form in habit, leaves and flowers. The foliage is often aromatic. Flowering is mainly after winter rains, and often the calyx is brightly coloured as well as the corolla, and persists around the fruit. A number of species are shown in Plates 473–482.

Another frequent and variable species is *E. latrobei* which has dark green, linear to oblong leaves, somewhat rugose, with revolute margins; the flowers are dull red with exserted stamens. *E. leucophylla* is a shrub to 1 m with pale, obovate leaves, densely tomentose (yellow when young), and pale red flowers also with exserted stamens. *E. glabra* is similar to *E. decipiens* (Pl. 428) but has almost sessile flowers.

Green flowers, rare among the *Eremophilas*, are a feature of *E. serrulata* which is a sticky shrub of 1–2 m with oblanceolate, toothed leaves 2–3 cm long. The flowers are 2–3 cm long on curved pedicels and have exserted stamens.

The vivid yellow flowers of *Cassias* are often prominent here. They are mostly shrubs though annual species occur in northern areas. *Cassia oligophylla* is widespread, and a similar species is *C. helmsii* which has densely white-felted leaves. White Cassia, *C. pruinosa* (Pl. 503), is frequent especially on rocky hills, and Sticky Cassia, *C. glutinosa*, is similar but is green and sticky. Silver Cassia, *C. artemisioides*, can be recognised by its finely divided silky leaves.

Two semi-parasitic shrubs are widespread though rarely common. Sandalwood, *Santalum spicatum* (Pl. 380), is a rough-barked shrub with pale grey-green leaves, and small greenish-red flowers with an unusual scent. The spherical fruit, 1.5 cm across, has a thin green rind enclosing a hard, smooth nut. These are often eaten by emus, not as food but as 'grindstones' for their stomachs. They are later passed out in the droppings. The aromatic timber of Sandalwood was once extensively cut and exported to India and China.

Like Sandalwood, Quandong, *Santalum acuminatum* (Vic. 154), is a root-parasite. It has a more drooping habit with longer, pointed, yellow-green leaves. The succulent skin of the fruit turns bright red when ripe and is edible, and the nut has a very wrinkled surface.

Mistletoes are parasitic and are often seen on wattles, eucalypts, sheoaks, kurrajongs and Grevilleas. Over 20 species in 5 genera occur in WA, two of them shown in Pls. 462 and 519. Many mistletoes have fruit with a fleshy outer layer. When the fruit are eaten by birds, this layer is removed in the stomach and the hard sticky seed passed out in the droppings.

The Banksia family, Proteaceae, is poorly represented inland, but several *Hakeas* are widespread—e.g. Cork Tree, *H. suberea* (Pl. 502), in the north, and *H. recurva* in the south. The latter is a small tree with stiff, curved, needle-like leaves and cream flowers in dense axillary clusters. As in the Cork Tree, the woody fruit do not persist but open to shed the seed as soon as they are mature.

On rocky hills some different genera occur, often representing groups more common in the South-West, e.g. *Calytrix, Eriostemon* and *Mirbelia*. The Native Cypress, *Callitris columellaris*, grows in this habitat, while in sheltered spots such as breakaways, delicate herbs are found, e.g. wild tobacco, *Nicotiana* species, and Rock Fern, *Cheilanthes tenuifolia*.

Tall trees are seldom seen in this region, but along the rivers the River Gums, *Eucalyptus camaldulensis* (Vic. 226), may grow to 30 m tall. Although widespread in Australia, this species was named from specimens cultivated in an Italian monastery of the Camalduli religious order, near Naples. The Coolabah, *E. microtheca* grows along rivers also but prefers non-saline claypans. It is a smaller tree than the River Gum, with smooth white bark and very small buds and fruit. Paperbarks such as the Cadjeput, *Melaleuca leuca-*

dendron (Pl. 522), occur along some rivers, as does the Yulbah, *Erythrina vespertilio* (Pl. 499).

Shrubby plants of river banks include the Lesser Bottlebrush, *Callistemon phoeniceus* (Pl. 472), as far north as the Gascoyne, and a number of *Abutilon* and *Sida* species. In the north, the Pied Piper Bush, *Dichrostachys* (Pl. 470), is an interesting shrub with male and hermaphrodite flowers in the same spike.

Although shrubs and trees are the perennial and dominant plants of the mulga, the most spectacular colour is provided by countless ephemeral herbs. These appear after rains, especially those of autumn and winter, summer rains bringing up mainly grasses. Within a few days after good rain, the ground becomes green with seedlings. In late winter and spring, profuse flowers of many colours are produced, though often one species dominates an area, producing discrete patches of colour.

Many families are represented among these ephemerals, but by far the dominant one is Asteraceae—the daisy family. *Helichrysum* and *Helipterum* are the main genera with many species of the everlasting type, four common species being shown in Pls. 454–457. Another is *Cephalipterum drummondii*, which has many clusters of flowers, each cluster surrounded by yellow or white bracts, and all combined in a pom-pom-like head. Several species of *Waitzia* are also common (e.g. *W. acuminata*—Vic. 171). The everlasting daisies have floral bracts of a stiff papery texture and retain their form and colour when dried.

Other daisies with soft, petal-like flowers are also widespread. *Brachycome* is a typical genus, having 20 species in WA and over 50 in Australia, with only a few elsewhere. They are mostly small ephemeral herbs with divided or lobed leaves and mauve ray (female) flowers forming a circle around the yellow disc (hermaphrodite) flowers. A number of species occur in the mulga and wattle scrub.

A genus of shrubby daisies is *Olearia* which has over 80 species in Australia, New Guinea and New Zealand. They have usually small leaves, often white-woolly underneath, and heads of flowers 1–2 cm across with white, rarely mauve, ray flowers. Several species are found here.

In northern areas an interesting genus is *Pterocaulon*, so named from the decurrent leaf bases which form wings down the stem. The plants are glandular-hairy, aromatic perennial herbs with oblong or spherical compound heads of small pink-cream flowers.

Many colours are found among the mulla mullas, species of *Ptilotus*. All except one of the 100 species in this genus occur in Australia, mostly in the drier regions. They are ephemeral or perennial herbs, with heads or spikes of flowers which are usually hairy and various shades of pink, yellow, green or white. Two common species are shown in Pls. 460 and 461. One of the few shrubby species is also very common—*P. obovatus*. This grows to 70 cm tall and is covered with dense, branched hairs giving it a whitish appearance. The pink flowers are in ovoid heads 1.5 cm across.

Sturt Pea, *Clianthus formosus* (Pl. 466), is a striking plant of irresistible attraction. It occurs through most of the dry regions of WA, usually in open areas where it often forms large mats. Occasionally white or pink-flowered variants are found.

Among the ephemerals the vetches, *Swainsona* species, are also colourful, with their racemes of purple and maroon flowers. They are prostrate or erect herbs with pinnate leaves. There are more than 50 species, all restricted to Australia. Several are important as fodder plants in pastoral regions.

One of the unusual features of the dry regions of Australia is the scarcity of succulent plants. This contrasts strongly with other countries, for example the cacti of North American deserts and the Euphorbiaceae of South Africa. In Australia only a few shrubs of low stature are succulent, such as the samphires which occur on salt lakes (see below). Otherwise, succulence is confined to the leaves of several groups. Among these the parakeelyas, *Calandrinia*, are often conspicuous. These members of the *Portulaca* family are small, often prostrate, herbs, either ephemeral or with perennial tubers. They have pale to deep pink flowers which open once only and are usually closed by mid-afternoon. In Australia there are some 30 species of this genus which occurs also in North and South America. Several native *Portulaca* species also occur here, having small bright yellow flowers.

A number of plants in this region have spiny or barbed fruit which penetrate or cling to animals and so are dispersed. The bindieye, *Sclerolaena* species, are widespread examples. Among the mulga and wattle scrub caltrops, *Tribulus*, are often found. These are prostrate ephemerals with hairy, pinnate leaves, bright yellow 5-petalled flowers, and spiny fruit which break into 5 sections. *T. occidentalis* (Pl. 469) is a common species.

The *Lechenaultia* family, Goodeniaceae, contributes many species to the herbaceous flora. Although *Lechenaultias* are absent, there are many *Goodenia* and *Velleia* species. These are herbs with yellow, pink or purple flowers, e.g. *G. pinnatifida* (Pl. 486) and *V. rosea* (Pl. 492), and they are often numerous in the mulga. A common shrubby member of the family is Currant Bush, *Scaevola spinescens*. This has spinescent branchlets, linear-oblong leaves and small creamy-white fan-shaped flowers.

Where the soil is sandy, mulga is usually absent and spinifex is the dominant plant, with only scattered trees, shrubs and herbs. The grasses commonly called spinifex belong to the genera *Triodia* and *Plectrachne*, both of which are confined to Australia. They are perennials having a tussock-like habit with needle-like leaves projecting in all directions. The growth is centrifugal, the central part of the tussock later dying so that rings are formed. Spinifex flowers after summer or autumn rains, sending up narrow panicles of flowers which, when dense, produce the aspect of a field of wheat. The seeds were collected by aborigines and ground into flour.

Spinifex is extremely common in the drier regions. There are about 35 species of *Triodia* and 10 species of *Plectrachne*.

Few trees occur among spinifex. In the south-east of the region, Bara Gum, *Eucalyptus gongylocarpa,* sometimes gives the country an attractive park-like aspect. It is a white-barked tree to 10 m tall, rather like the wandoo of the South-West in appearance. A more widespread but scattered species is the bloodwood, *E. terminalis*, also a tree but with prickly, flaky bark and large terminal panicles of cream flowers followed by urn-shaped fruit. Several mallee eucalypts are also found, among them Kingsmill's Mallee, *E. kingsmillii* (Pl. 465).

Two *Grevillea* species are attractive when in flower. In northern areas *G. pyramidalis* is a tall shrub with deeply-divided leaves and panicles of white flowers held aloft above the foliage. In the south, *G. juncifolia* bears racemes of bright orange, sticky flowers in the axils of long, linear leaves. Here, too, is *Hakea francisiana,* also a tall shrub with broadly linear, many-nerved leaves and axillary racemes of crowded pink flowers. In more inland areas is *H. rhombalis,* a shrub with long, needle-like leaves and small clusters of deep red flowers which have an unpleasant scent. The swollen woody fruit are somewhat prickly.

An adaption to prevent excessive water loss in some plants of dry regions is the development of a protective covering of hairs. This is highly developed in the group known as Lambstails—the genera *Newcastelia* and *Dicrastylis* of the family Verbenaceae. In these the stems, leaves and even the flowers are covered with dense, much-branched hairs. They are low shrubs with spikes or panicles of small flowers hidden in white or yellow wool. Often the only visible part of the flower is a ring of stamens which may be purple or white. They can be quite spectacular, especially among the regrowth following a bushfire.

A few myrtles besides the eucalypts occur here, all low to medium-sized shrubs. *Calytrix longiflora* has very short, thick leaves, and bright pink star-like flowers covering the top of the bush. *Micromyrtus flaviflora* also has small leaves, and bright yellow flowers which later turn red. *Calothamnus gilesii* has long terete leaves, and bright red claw-like flowers, mainly on the older stems; it occurs in southern areas.

The only inland *Kennedia* grows among the spinifex—*K. prorepens* which is a prostrate creeper with trifoliate leaves, and small purple flowers on erect peduncles. A curious legume is the Upside-down plant, *Brachysema chambersii:* the stems are leafless, much-branched and pungent, up to 30 cm tall, and the long red flowers are in racemes resting on the soil around the base of the shrub.

Salt lakes

Low-lying areas in this region usually accumulate salt and are vegetated with plants adapted to soils with high salt concentrations. The dominant family on these open flats is the Chenopodiaceae which includes the salt bushes, *Atriplex* (Pl. 488), bluebushes, *Maireana* (Pl. 490), bindieye, *Sclerolaena* (Pl. 483), and samphires, *Arthrocnemum,* etc. The samphires are succulent, leafless plants with jointed stems and inconspicuous flowers in small spikes. They are usually small shrubs but one species, Bulli Bulli, *Tecticornia arborea* (Pl. 491), grows to 2 m. This curious plant is so far known from only two localities.

Species of the other genera are numerous but often difficult to identify. The *Maireanas* have woody or herbaceous stems and small succulent leaves. The flowers are inconspicuous but in fruit develop a prominent appendage which is usually flat and wing-like and may become quite colourful. Several species have woolly fruit.

Another group of herbs with succulent leaves is the Twin-leaves, *Zygophyllum* species. Each leaf has 2 leaflets and the small flowers are yellow or white, while the fruit is usually 4-angled or winged. They are common in the arid regions, with over 15 species in Australia, the genus also occurring in arid lands of other countries.

A strange plant is Dunna Dunna, *Selenothamnus helmsii* (Pl. 487), which grows on gypsum rises around salt lakes. At first glance it bears no resemblance to the familiar members of its family, Malvaceae, e.g. *Hibiscus*.

Also seen in such habitats is the Kopi Poverty Bush, *Eremophila miniata* (Pls. 477, 478), and in southern areas the Cue York Gum, *Eucalyptus striaticalyx*. This tall tree has rough dark bark on the lower trunk, and small flowers and fruit.

Where the soil is less saline, several colourful herbs occur. The purple vetch, *Swainsona pterostylis,* often forms carpets near salt lakes. It is an ephemeral herb with pinnate leaves of small rounded leaflets and erect racemes of pea flowers; the pods are small and wrinkled.

In north-western areas the Marsh Stemodia, *S. grossa* (Pl. 493), also adds splashes of purple with racemes of tubular flowers on glandular, aromatic stems.

Ranges and Tablelands of the North-West

THE CAPE RANGE

THE FLORA OF THE CAPE RANGE peninsula has become well-known only recently. Inhabited by a few pastoralists and the lighthouse keeper at Vlaming Head, and far removed from the North-West Coastal Highway, it was rarely visited until the 1950s. Interest in the area was stimulated by the discovery of oil there in 1953, when exploration roads made it more accessible. Botanical surveys have revealed its intriguing flora which has links with the tropical north and temperate south, as well as the adjacent inland regions.

The Cape Range forms the backbone of the peninsula, with a coastal plain on each side. It is a ridge of Tertiary limestone, rising to a highest point of 315 metres at Mt. Hollister, and tapering gradually at each end. The Rough Range is a lower ridge near the south end of the Cape Range. The latter is extremely rugged and rocky, and has been deeply eroded into canyons up to 120 metres deep. Typical of dry country, they are steep-sided with cliffs and scree slopes falling to narrow creek beds, providing spectacular scenery. The creeks flow only after heavy rain, and there is almost no permanent surface water in the Range.

Although the rainfall is relatively low at 25–30 cm, it is received both as heavy falls from summer cyclones and lighter but more regular falls in winter. It is probably the latter which allows the existence here of representatives of the South-Western flora such as *Banksia, Thryptomene* and *Hibbertia.*

The vegetation is mostly a shrub steppe, dominated by wattles and eucalypts with a lower storey of small shrubs and spinifex. The taller wattles—up to 3 m tall—include Ranji Bush, *Acacia pyrifolia* (Pl. 463), Kurara, *A. tetragonophylla* (Pl. 464), and an interesting variant of *A. victoriae.* The latter is usually a much-branched shrub with phyllodes 2–3 cm long, but here it is rather spindly with phyllodes 4–6 cm long. A frequent smaller species is *A. bivenosa* with short, broad, pale-green phyllodes having two prominent nerves.

The Eucalypts are a mixed group. The bloodwood, *E. terminalis*, is a common tree with rough bark, large panicles of cream flowers and large, urn-shaped fruit. Weeping Box, *E. patellaris*, is a more slender tree with several stems and thinner rough bark, the flowers being small, with top-shaped fruit. It also occurs in the Hamersley Range but is known otherwise only from the Kimberleys and Northern Territory. There is a typically southern species in *E. foecunda*, a mallee with small flowers and fruit. The fourth common species is *E. prominens*; it is also a smooth-barked mallee, with fruit which have prominent valves when open. Occasional patches of Coolabah, *E. microtheca,* are seen.

A striking tree which tends to occur as scattered individuals is the kurrajong, *Brachychiton australe.* This has a thick trunk and branches, with large, bright green, lobed leaves which are deciduous. The small cream flowers are followed by large black boat-shaped fruit.

In the canyons the bright-red-flowered Yulbah, *Erythrina vespertilio* (Pl. 499), is common. Four species of this tropical genus occur in Australia, and this is the only WA species. Also in sheltered parts is an unnamed species of wild fig, *Ficus*, with bright green shining foliage and small speckled fruit. The Rock Fig, *F. platypoda* (Pl. 496), is very common over the range.

Among the smaller shrubs, *Cassias* are prominent with five species. *C. oligophylla* is the most frequent, with pinnate leaves of a few broad leaflets. White Cassia, *C. pruinosa* (Pl. 503), is a slender shrub, attractive for the white bloom on its leaves and stems. Sticky Cassia, *C. glutinosa*, has a similar habit but is viscid and not glaucous.

Genera of the family Malvaceae are well-represented, including *Abutilon, Gossypium, Hibiscus* and *Sida.* Two species of native cotton, *Gossypium*, occur in the Range. The most common is *G. robinsonii* (Pl. 506), which is restricted to the North-West. Sturt's Desert Rose, *G. sturtianum* is a more slender shrub with rounded entire leaves and smaller but more brightly coloured flowers. It has a disjunct distribution, further populations being in the deserts of WA and central Australia. The seeds of native cotton are silky-hairy but very much less so than those of commercial cotton.

Morning Glories are usually creepers, but in this area two shrubby species occur. Rock Morning Glory, *Ipomoea costata* (Pl. 497), has trailing stems which thicken to eventually form a shrub up to 3 m tall. It is frequent on top of the Range. More restricted and found mainly along the western edge of the Range is the Yardie Morning Glory, *I. yardiensis* (Pl. 498). This is a true shrub and is remarkable for the densely woolly hairs covering all parts of the plant. The bright pink flowers with dark throats are often damaged by birds seeking nectar. In contrast, *Polymeria ambigua* (Pl. 501), is a trailing ephemeral morning glory with small white or pale pink flowers, found usually in the canyons.

There are two *Grevilleas* in the Range, both restricted to the area. Cape Range Grevillea, *G. variifolia* (Pl. 495), is a small silvery-grey shrub with pungently-lobed leaves and racemes of bright red flowers. Its closest relatives in the genus all occur in the South-West. *G. calcicola* is a tall shrub with leaves divided into long, linear lobes, and white flowers in terminal panicles. Both species are common. The only other member of the Proteaceae in the Range proper is the Cork Tree,

Hakea suberea (Pl. 502), which can be recognised by its thick, corky bark, long needle-like leaves, and dense racemes of pale yellow flowers. However, towards the southern end of the Range as well as on coastal dunes right up to the Cape, the orange-flowered *Banksia ashbyi* (Pl. 316), occurs as a low, spreading shrub.

There is one species of *Lechenaultia—L. subcymosa*, which is a low perennial herb with short leaves on the lower stems and open panicles of white to mauve flowers. It appears more profusely after bushfires, and is restricted on the mainland to the area between North West Cape and Lake Macleod. It occurs also on Dirk Hartog Island. Another perennial herb of the same family is *Dampiera incana* which is covered with dense whitish hairs and has small dark blue flowers. There are also species of *Goodenia* and *Scaevola*.

The smaller legumes in the Range are mostly ephemerals and include species of *Indigofera*, *Swainsona* and *Tephrosia*. Sturt Pea, *Clianthus formosus* (Pl. 466), is common but in this area almost always has a dark red, not black, centre to the flower. Toucan Flower, *Brachysema macrocarpum* (Pl. 500), is a leafless perennial herb with an unusual pea-flower and long, tapering pods. It is the only North-West species of the genus, the others being South-Western, with a few desert species.

Another link with the South-West is *Hibbertia spicata* which extends south to Geraldton. It is a small shrub with linear leaves and spikes of bright yellow flowers, and is frequent on the Range. Similar examples are two myrtles, *Melaleuca cardiophylla*, a shrub with small cordate leaves and cream flowers on the older stems, and *Thryptomene baeckeacea*, with small pink flowers. Both are common in the Range but occur also south of Shark Bay.

On the other hand, Native Plumbago, *P. zeylanica* (Pl. 504), is typically a tropical Australian Plant. Here it straggles over shrubs in sheltered parts and has white flowers but is otherwise similar to the cultivated *Plumbago*.

THE INLAND RANGES

THE FIRST EXPLORER IN this region was the surveyor Francis Gregory, who made two expeditions, in 1858 and 1861, in search of pastoral country. On the latter he discovered and named the Hamersley Range. The many inland ranges are dominated by the Hamersley Range which rises to 1252 metres at Mt. Meharry, the highest mountain in WA. The ranges are rugged and vividly coloured—blue from a distance, red contrasting with pale yellow and green vegetation at closer quarters. Because of their outstanding natural scenery and the recent iron ore boom, they are better known than other parts of the North-West. However, easy access is limited to the main centres such as Wittenoom and Tom Price.

These ranges unlike the Cape Range, consist of very old (Precambrian) and hard rocks, both sedimentary which have been metamorphosed, and igneous. Many streams and rivers have eroded them into gorges and valleys where red rocks and spinifex make a sharp contrast with the scenery of the South-West. Springs and permanent pools are frequent in the gorges, the largest being at Millstream on the Fortescue River, where a flow of many millions of gallons per day occurs.

The rainfall of this region is variable, averaging 25–35 cm, and comes mostly from summer cyclones, though winter rains sometimes occur. Floristically the northern ranges have strong links with the Kimberleys and are usually included in the Northern Floristic Province of the State. The number of tropical species decreases as one moves south.

Apart from the rivers and gorges, the ranges are covered with spinifex steppe and mulga woodland. The latter occurs on the flat loamy plains and has a similar association of plants to that described in the section on Mulga and Wattle Scrub. The spinifex, comprised of *Triodia* and *Plectrachne* species, is sparse on hillsides and more dense on gravelly plains. It is accompanied by an assortment of small trees, shrubs and herbs both ephemeral and perennial.

The Snappy Gum, *Eucalyptus leucophloia*, is frequent, especially on rocky hills. It is a short, often straggly, tree with pure white bark, small, obtuse leaves and small cream flowers. The bloodwood, *E. terminalis*, with rough, prickly bark and urn-shaped fruit, is widespread but less common. On some of the highest mountains is found Kingsmill's Mallee, *E. kingsmillii* (Pl. 465), also to be found farther south and in the desert. Another mallee is *E. gamophylla*, with blunt, opposite glaucous leaves and small white flowers having the stamens in four clusters; it also is widespread in the desert.

Of the family Proteaceae, only a few species of *Hakea* and *Grevillea* occur in the ranges. Cork Tree, *H. suberea* (Pl. 502), is common, as also are two Grevilleas, Wickham's Grevillea, *G. wickhami* (Pl. 520), and *G. pyramidalis*. The latter is a tall shrub with deeply-divided, narrow-lobed leaves, and paniculate racemes of white flowers.

A native cypress, *Callitris columellaris*, adorns some rocky slopes with its grey-green foliage. It is widespread in arid Australia. In the Fortescue region, a Kurrajong, *Brachychiton australe*, already noted in the Cape Range region, occurs sporadically on hills.

Cassias are abundant. In addition to the five occurring in the Cape Range there are several other notable species including *C. venusta* (Pl. 512), *C. notabilis* (Pl. 514) and *C. helmsii*, a shrub with obovate grey-felted leaflets. Two other interesting species of restricted occurrence are *C. pilocarina*, a small shrub with pinnate leaves of small, close-set, narrow leaflets, known only from the Barlee Range, and *C. ferraria* growing in the iron-rich areas of the Hamersley Range. The latter species is a stout shrub with relatively large pinnate leaves and elliptic leaflets.

Closely related to *Cassia* is the genus *Petalostylis* which has 3 species all endemic in Australia. The dorsal petal of these flowers has a prominent red 'horse-shoe' mark towards the base. The style is boat-shaped and there are three stamens and two staminodia. Slender Petalostylis, *P. labicheoides* (Pl. 508), is common in the Ranges and may be seen growing in thickets along roadside drains.

Other yellow-flowered legumes here especially on the plateaus of the Hamersleys, are the rattlepods, *Crotalaria trifoliastrum*, with small leaves and flowers, and the larger *C. novae-hollandiae*.

Bright orange pea flowers are seen on *Burtonia polyzyga*, a small tomentose shrub with pinnate leaves of round leaflets and terminal racemes. It appears more commonly on recently-burnt areas. *Swainsonas* add splashes of purple and maroon, especially in northern areas. While some species are prostrate, *S. stenodonta* is an erect ephemeral with racemes of deep red flowers, occurring mainly in the northern Hamersleys.

On some ranges is found the only northern species of *Gastrolobium*, a genus with many toxic species in the South-West. This is Wallflower Poison, *G. grandiflorum*, which grows to 1.7 m tall, with large oval-elliptic leaves and racemes of gold and maroon pea flowers.

Besides mulga, many other wattles occur in the ranges. Two unusual species are low, spreading shrubs with very narrow phyllodes arranged in whorls up the stem. Both have flowers in heads on long stalks, and oblong, sticky pods. *Acacia adoxa* has grey-hirsute phyllodes less than 1 cm long, while *A. spondylophylla* has longer, sticky phyllodes.

The *Hibiscus* family, Malvaceae, is well-represented in the ranges. There are several *Hibiscus*, including Yellow Hibiscus, *H. panduriformis* (Pl. 471), found along water courses. *H. goldsworthii* has a pretty red-centred mauve flower but the shrub also has an unpleasant aspect, as it is covered with sharp stellate hairs which became easily detached and 'grip' if the plant is handled. Species of *Abutilon* and *Sida* are both numerous and difficult to identify. They are perennial herbs or shrubs, usually grey-tomentose and yellow-flowered. Two curious *Sidas* are *S. inclusa* and *S. physocalyx*, both spreading perennials with calyxes which enlarge greatly around the fruit, in the former being rounded and many-ribbed, in the latter angular like a Cape Gooseberry (*Physalis*) fruit.

A very common shrub is *Corchorus walcottii* (Pl. 510), in the allied family Tiliaceae.

The dense woolly indumentum which helps prevent excessive water loss in such plants is also seen in many *Solanum* species in this region. These wild tomatoes usually have spines on stems, leaves and calyxes. *S. phlomoides* (Pl. 513), is a widespread species. Even more woolly is *S. gabrielae*, a sprawling shrub of rocky slopes restricted to the Hamersleys and a few hills to the east. Other common species are *S. lasiophyllum, S. ellipticum* and *S. sturtianum*, the latter having lanceolate leaves which are almost glabrous and green on the upper surface.

A number of Poverty or Emu Bush species, *Eremophila*, may be seen, though not as frequently as in the mulga bush. The tallest is *E. longifolia*, a small tree with narrow-lanceolate leaves and dull, pale red flowers. More spectacular is *E. cuneifolia* which is a shrub with small, sticky, rounded leaves (which after shedding leave projecting leaf bases on older stems) and purple flowers with striking maroon-purple calyxes.

A curious leafless shrub on rocky plains and hills is Caustic Bush, *Sarcostemma australe* (Pl. 517). The stems exude copious milky sap when broken. Although considered toxic in the eastern States, it has not been incriminated in WA, and in some areas is even reported as good fodder.

An interesting shrub endemic in the Hamersley Range is the Iron Plant, *Astrotricha hamptoni*. It grows to 2 m tall with thick, corky stems, lanceolate leaves which are tomentose beneath, and large leafless panicles of small yellow flowers. The whole plant is strongly curry-scented and occurs only on steep cliffs in areas of high-grade iron ore; its presence is noted by prospectors. It is the only WA species of the genus, the other ten growing along the Dividing Range in eastern Australia.

Many herbs appear after rains, and provide much of the spectacular colour of a good season. A prominent family is Amaranthaceae with many species of Mulla Mulla, *Ptilotus* (Pls. 460, 461, 505, 518). Two frequent species with large pale green spikes are *P. macrocephalus*, an ephemeral with mostly basal leaves, and *P. clementii*, a perennial with hairy leaves up the stems. Perhaps the most spectacular of all *Ptilotus* is *P. rotundifolius*. This is a shrub to 1 m tall with rounded, wavy margined, grey-felted leaves and large spikes of bright pink flowers. It favours rocky hillsides of the ranges, extending south beyond Wiluna.

The daisy family (*Asteraceae*) and grasses (*Poaceae*) provide many herbaceous species, both ephemeral and perennial. Other prominent families are Aizoaceae, Brassicaceae (crucifers) and Goodeniaceae, the genus *Goodenia* of the latter having a number of both blue and yellow-flowered species.

The Gorges

To enter a gorge of the North-West ranges is often to enter a different world. Deeply cut into the hills, their red rocky walls often shelter permanent fresh streams or pools, a habitat moister and cooler than the dry hills and plateaus above. Besides water-loving trees and shrubs, there are ferns and delicate herbs tucked away in these oases.

Two ferns grow from wet crevices on the shaded

walls—Chinese Brake, *Pteris vittata* (Pl. 523), with long pinnate fronds, and Venus-hair Fern, *Adiantum capillus-veneris* (Pl. 521), with delicate, much-branched fronds.

At Millstream on the Fortescue River is the submerged aquatic fern *Ceratopteris thalictroides* which has much-divided fronds. It occurs across northern Australia and in the tropical Old World.

Other true aquatic plants in the pools include the fern Nardoo, *Marsilea*, with floating leaves like four-leaved clover, and *Potamogeton javanicus* with oval leaves floating on the surface and submerged spikes of small green flowers. Completely submerged is the Water Nymph, *Najas tenuifolia*, which has narrow, finely toothed leaves and minute axillary unisexual flowers. Nardoo, which is more commonly known as Milly Milly in the North-West, was formerly used by natives as a food. The small nut-like fruits were gathered, crushed between stones and made into cakes. This plant sometimes appears in dense mats beside the receding margins of drying pools.

Near or in the water are many sedges such as *Fimbristylis, Cyperus, Baumea* and *Scirpus*, and bulrushes, *Typha domingensis*. The Tropical Reed, *Phragmites karka*, holds its plume-like inflorescences high above the leaves. On mud near the water are delicate creeping herbs. *Lobelia quadrangularis* has small ovate, serrate leaves and mauve flowers on long pedicels, while *Stylidium alsinoides* has narrow leaves and small pink flowers. Both species are widespread across tropical Australia in wet situations.

The principal trees are River Gums, *Eucalyptus camaldulensis* and Cadjeputs, *Melaleuca leucadendron* (Pl. 522). *Melaleuca glomerata*, smaller than Cadjeput in habit and with round heads of cream flowers and dark fibrous bark, is also common. Straggling among rocks near the water as well as on dry slopes is the Rock Fig, *Ficus platypoda* (Pl. 496), while the Rough Fig, *F. orbicularis*, with leaves like sandpaper, is less common. A tall spreading shrub with soft, broadly obovate leaves is *Phyllanthus baccatus*. It is dioecious, and the fruit are small white berries. Common in northern Australia, it is found in the Hamersley Range.

In the more open valley of the Fortescue River at Millstream is a fine stand of the Fan-palm *Livistona alfredi* (Pl. 515), representing a genus known mainly from tropical areas to the north. Although discovered by Francis Gregory in 1861, it was 1892 before it was named by Mueller, in honour of the then Duke of Edinburgh. A similar relic population is that of *Livistona mariae* at Palm Valley in the NT.

North-West Coast

THE NORTH-WEST COAST is a succession of long, sandy beaches, rocky bluffs and tidal mudflats, broken by river estuaries. It has a distinctive flora comprising local species and representatives of the inland flora as well as common plants of seacoasts elsewhere. The plants of these habitats are often adapted in various ways to exposure to strong, salt-laden winds and intense sunlight.

The sandy shores are backed by dunes vegetated with a variety of shrubs and perennial herbs. A conspicuous creeper above high-water mark is the Beach Morning Glory, *Ipomoea brasiliensis* (Pl. 528), whose bright pink flowers with dark centres are displayed among shining leaves. The flowers have brief glory, for they open only once, are closed by mid-afternoon, and are often torn apart by birds seeking nectar. It is widespread on tropical coasts. Another strong, prostrate creeper here is the Jack Bean, *Canavalia maritima*, a strand plant also common on other tropical coasts, with thick leaves and large pink pea-flowers in erect racemes followed by very thick, strong pods.

A recent arrival on these shores is *Launea bellidifolia*, a creeping daisy with heads of bright yellow flowers. It is native to coasts of the western Indian Ocean and was first recorded here in 1947. It now occurs on beaches between Shark Bay and North West Cape, as well as on the Monte Bello Islands.

The sand dunes are often dominated by the grass *Spinifex longifolius* (Pl. 524), whose large, bristly fruiting-heads are a familiar sight on all our beaches. Often mixed with the *Spinifex* is the Gummy Spinifex, *Triodia pungens*. Among the common shrubs are several species of *Acacia*, especially *A. coriacea*, a spreading shrub with long, curved grey-green phyllodes, cream flowers and a pod which is constricted between the seeds. *Acacia bivenosa* is another common species, having short, broad phyllodes distinguished by two prominent nerves.

North of Roebourne the Green Birdflower, *Crotalaria cunninghamii* (Pl. 527), occurs on the coastal dunes. A touch of blue, the flower-colour which so impressed William Dampier on these shores in 1699, is provided by Rough Bluebell, *Trichodesma zeylanicum* (Pl. 530). This is an erect perennial, rough with short stiff hairs, and flowers varying from pale to deep blue. It is also widespread in many habitats inland.

The name Dampier also springs to mind in connection with another common dune shrub, the Coastal Daisybush, *Olearia axillaris*. This variable species occurs on southern coasts also, but in the north has narrow, dark-green leaves and flower-heads with only a few ray-flowers. The plant reminded Dampier of the English rosemary and he named one of the offshore islands after it.

Along the coast from Shark Bay to North West Cape

is another shrubby composite, *Brachycome latisquamea* (Pl. 538). This straggling shrub has large, typical daisy flowers with mauve or rarely white rays. It often scrambles over other shrubs to a height of 2 metres and is unique in its genus, as the other species are small ephemeral or perennial herbs.

A composite with different flowers is *Angianthus cunninghamii*, a low shrub of the dunes from North West Cape to the Murchison River, with a few populations farther south. The leaves are small and closely grey-felted, while the yellow flowers are all of the disc type, arranged in compound, spherical heads.

From Exmouth to Shark Bay on coastal dunes and a little inland is the Coastal Coppercups, *Pileanthus limacis* (Pl. 537). This spreading shrub has cream or pale pink flowers with a yellowish calyx which persists for some time after flowering. It is the type species of this small but interesting genus and was collected by the French botanist Leschenault, on the Baudin expedition which called at Shark Bay in 1801.

Ashby's Banksia, *B. ashbyi* (Pl. 316), occurs as a sprawling shrub on dunes between Carnarvon and North West Cape. It is more common on sandheaths south from Shark Bay, and is the only species of Banksia to extend into the North-West.

On rocky coasts, the vegetation is more sparse, leaving extensive bare areas. There are often cliffs, usually low and undercut, dropping onto reefs which may be exposed at low tide. Only a few shrubs and grasses exist near the sea. The Rock Fig, *Ficus platypoda* (Pl. 496), occurs sporadically, forming tangled clumps. Its fruit are edible but very small and rather dry. Not far from the shore, though not common, occurs the Coastal Hibiscus, *Alyogyne cuneiformis*. This tall shrub has smooth, flat, linear leaves, often divided into several lobes, and large hibiscus-like flowers. On the mainland, between Carnarvon and North West Cape, the flowers are pale mauve, but on Bernier, Dorre and Dirk Hartog Islands they are white, though always red-centred. It is also found on sand dunes.

An attractive shrub is the broad-leaved Coastal Caper, *Capparis spinosa* var. *nummularia* (Pl. 536). The delicate white flowers may open at night or in the day and last only a few hours; they have a sweet perfume. *Scaevola crassifolia* is a shrub which is common farther south but extends as far north as Quobba. It has flat, obovate, dentate leaves and small blue Lechenaultia-like flowers.

Sea-heath, *Frankenia pauciflora*, is a mat-like perennial herb with linear leaves and small pink flowers. It can colonise areas exposed to salt spray while being frequent on saline flats inland as well. The genus can be recognised by the revolute leaves which have the petioles expanded on each side as a fringed sheath which clasps the stem. In similar habitats one finds the grass *Sporobolus virginicus*, a tufted perennial species resembling rank couch grass.

Mangroves occur on the tidal mudflats and estuaries from Shark Bay northwards. In this region there are three species of mangrove, the commonest being the White Mangrove, *Avicennia marina* (Vic. 191). This shrub or small tree grows to 6 m tall and has erect pneumatophores arising from the underground roots. These modified roots are spongy in texture and enable the plant to exchange gases when the root system is otherwise submerged. The opposite, ovate-lanceolate leaves are dull, dark green above, pale and closely felted beneath, while the small golden flowers have an unusual wine-like scent. The seeds germinate after falling from the plant.

The two other mangroves, *Rhizophora mucronata* (with prop roots) and *Ceriops tagal*, occur from the Ashburton River northeastwards. They have shining bright green leaves and are viviparous, the seeds germinating on the plant so that the seedlings can be quickly established after falling. All mangrove seeds float and can be dispersed on the tide.

Behind the coast lie open, flat or undulating plains, broken in places by rivers and sometimes studded with low rocky hills. The plains carry an open or thick scrub, dominated usually by wattles, while some areas are simply grassy plains with scattered shrubs. The wattles include such tall species as Bowgada Bush (Pls. 458, 459), Ranji Bush (Pl. 463) and Kurara (Pl. 464). Two common small wattles are *Acacia translucens*, with short, broad, curved phyllodes and flowers in long-stalked heads, and *A. orthocarpa* with narrow phyllodes and flowers in spikes. Gregory's Wattle, *Acacia gregorii* (Pl. 529), is a more restricted species; it is named after the Gregory brothers, Augustus and Francis, who explored parts of western and northern Australia in the mid-nineteenth century.

In this region there is only one wattle with bipinnate leaves instead of phyllodes—*Acacia farnesiana*, which is common in most tropical countries. It is a spreading shrub to 4 m tall with spinescent stipules, and flowers in heads. It grows along creeks and in depressions from Shark Bay northwards.

Other common shrubs include species of *Cassia, Solanum* (Wild Tomatoes), *Sida, Abutilon, Corchorus* (Pl. 510) and *Scaevola*. Fraser's Lantern Bush, *Abutilon fraseri* (Pl. 533), is one of several species in this region. They are velvety-tomentose shrubs with rounded, sometimes lobed, flat leaves and hibiscus-like flowers, usually bell-like and not opening as widely as in *A. fraseri*. The most common *Scaevola* is Currant Bush, *S. spinescens*, which is widespread and variable. In this region it is a spreading shrub to 2 m tall without spines. The clustered leaves are linear to narrow-obovate, 1–2 cm long, and the cream, fan-like flowers are 1 cm long.

Two species of Pepperflower, *Diplopeltis*, occur here. The name *Diplopeltis*, meaning two shields, refers to a conspicuous gland in the flower. It is yellow at first, later turning red, and glistens with nectar. The plants are monoecious, having male and female flowers on the same plant; these open at different times, to prevent self-pollination. Hairy Pepperflower, *D. eriocarpa* (Pl.

526), is a small attractive shrub which forms colonies in loamy or rocky soil between Exmouth and Port Hedland.

Grey Pepperflower, *Diplopeltis intermedia* var. *incana*, is a low, spreading shrub with broad, lobed, grey-tomentose leaves and small pale pink flowers. It grows on low sandy rises to the south of Exmouth Gulf.

In the northern areas, between Roebourne and Port Hedland, the coastal plains sometimes support a low open savannah with trees such as the Cork Tree, *Hakea lorea* (Pl. 502), Whitewood, *Atalaya hemiglauca* and Native Walnut, *Owenia reticulata*. *Owenia* is a genus of six species occurring across northern Australia, three of them in WA. *O. reticulata* is a tree to 8 m with dark, furrowed bark and large, coarse, pinnate leaves, net-veined, on thick branchlets. The small flowers are in panicles, and the fruits are hard, spherical nuts 2–3 cm across.

In some non-saline depressions the Coolabah, *Eucalyptus microtheca,* is attractive with its white trunks. The flowers are very small, and arranged in panicles. Another white-barked species is the Rough-leaved Range Gum, *E. aspera,* which has short, opposite, rough leaves and thin, cup-shaped fruit.

Throughout the plains, grasses are common. Spinifexes *(Triodia)* are dominant, while other widespread genera are Spear Grasses *(Aristida)*, Love Grasses *(Eragrostis)*, *Eriachne*, and Kangaroo Grass *(Themeda)*. A very common species introduced for pastures is Buffel Grass, *Cenchrus ciliaris*, which grows to 40 cm tall and has spikes of purple bristly flowers.

After rains, many herbs appear and in a good season make a colourful sight. Common genera are *Ptilotus, Crotalaria, Cassia, Tephrosia, Euphorbia, Goodenia, Mollugo, Trianthema* and *Ipomoea,* as well as many daisies. Among the Mulla Mullas, three common species are the Hairy Mulla Mulla, *Ptilotus helipteroides* (Pl. 460), the Mat Mulla Mulla, *P. axillaris* (Pl. 505), and the Tall Mulla Mulla, *P. exaltatus* (Pl. 461). There are also several species of the related genus *Gomphrena* in which the leaves are opposite instead of alternate.

The ephemeral *Cassias* are Cockroach Bush, *C. notabilis* (Pl. 514), and *C. venusta* (Pl. 512), the former growing on the plains and the latter along creek banks. Like these, the ephemeral *Crotalarias* have bright yellow flowers, the pointed keel petal being a distinctive feature in the genus. The *Tephrosias* have typical pea-flowers of pink or orange and can be recognised by the standard which is hairy on the outside.

In the Ashburton-Fortescue area the Ashburton Pea, *Swainsona macullochiana*, is a glorious sight in a good season. The largest of the *Swainsonas,* it grows to 2 m tall with long erect racemes of large purple flowers.

Between Carnarvon and Onslow are several areas of red sand dunes which carry some very colourful shrubs. Forrest's Featherflower, *Verticordia forrestii* (Pl. 531), has large flowers varying from pale to deep pink, forming a dense mass over the bush. Another myrtle, *Calytrix brevifolia,* has bright pink star-like flowers. Coppercups, *Pileanthus peduncularis* (Pl. 298), which is familiar on sandheaths north of Perth, occurs here as isolated populations but grows to 1 m or more tall.

Two species of native foxglove grow here—*Pityrodia petiolaris* with panicles of pink flowers whose calyxes are densely woolly, and *P. paniculata* which has pink or mauve flowers and is greyish with a close indumentum. A touch of pale purple is given by the Sand Hibiscus, *Alyogyne pinonianus* (Pl. 532). A striking ephemeral herb is the Tangled Mulla Mulla, *Ptilotus latifolius*, which is covered with woolly heads of white flowers.

Rising above the shrubs are two Grevilleas, *G. stenobotrya* with panicles of white flowers, and the spreading *G. eriostachya* with dense racemes of sticky, orange-yellow flowers on long leafless branches.

In saline depressions which are common near the coast, the saltbush family, Chenopodiaceae, is dominant. There are various species of Saltbush *(Atriplex)*, Bluebush *(Maireana)*, Bindieye *(Sclerolaena)* and *Rhagodia*, as well as the samphires, *Arthrocnemum*. White Pigface, *Carpobrotus rossii,* is attractive on flats near Carnarvon. More widespread are the purple-flowered Marsh Stemodia, *Stemodia grossa* (Pl. 493), and *S. viscosa*, both of which are aromatic with sticky, glandular hairs. The purple vetch, *Swainsona pterostylis*, is also common; this prostrate or ascending ephemeral has pinnate leaves and short wrinkled pods.

The genus *Crinum* has over 100 species in tropical and subtropical countries, 10 species being in Australia. *Crinum flaccidum* (Pl. 525) is the only WA species, its white, trumpet-like flowers and dark-green leaves appearing after summer or autumn rains. The large seeds germinate as soon as they are ripe. It occurs on open flats near the Lyndon and Minilya Rivers and is common on the plain along the Western side of the Cape Range.

The river courses across the plains are usually dominated by River Gums, *Eucalyptus camaldulensis*, with Coolabah, *E. microtheca*, less common. The sandy or rocky river beds are mostly dry except after rain, but permanent fresh pools occur. Many grasses, rushes and sedges grow on the banks, and the Bulrush, *Typha domingensis,* is found near permanent water. Here, too, is the Nardoo, *Marsilea hirsuta*, a stoloniferous fern with long-stalked leaves like four-leaf clover. The nut-like sporocarps (spore cases) at the base of the leaves, were used by the Aborigines to make flour.

An unusual riverbank tree is the White Dragon Tree, *Sesbania formosa* (Pl. 535), a short-lived legume with thick corky bark, long pinnate leaves and very large cream pea flowers. *Sesbania* is a genus of 35 species in the tropics and subtropics, chiefly of the Old World. There are 10 species in Australia, 7 of them endemic.

The Cadjeputs, *Melaleuca leucadendron* (Pl. 522) and *M. argentea* (with silvery leaves), both grow on river banks, mainly in the northern part of the region.

The Kimberley

NORTH OF THE LONG WHITE STREAK that is the 80 Mile Beach, north of the vast red dunes of the Great Sandy Desert, lies a region that contrasts with the rest of the State. In geology, climate and biology the Kimberley stands apart, linked rather with the top end of Australia and the islands to the north. Rugged ranges of sandstone, limestone and basalt rise from wide plains and river valleys; gorges and waterfalls are frequent; and a dissected coastline of high cliffs and mangrove flats is washed by twice daily tides of up to 11 metres. The hot, wet summer and warm, dry winter sustain a vegetation of grassy plains, savannah woodlands and occasional vine thicket. Lush growth occurs where there is permanent water. Typically Australian genera of plants mingle with tropical elements.

The Kimberley was first explored from the sea. Tasman came first, in 1644, followed by Dampier in 1688, Baudin in 1801 and 1803, and Flinders in 1803. The first detailed mapping and plant collecting came in 1819-22 when the botanist Allan Cunningham accompanied Philip King on a survey of the Australian coast. Exploration by land began with Grey in 1837-8. Following Alexander Forrest's expedition of 1879, the region was named after the Earl of Kimberley, then Secretary of State for the Colonies. Good plant collections, however, were not made until the 20th century. W. V. Fitzgerald in 1905-6 and C. A. Gardner in 1921 and later years travelled extensively in the region; they published the first major contributions to the knowledge of the flora. With the development of the pastoral industry and other activities as well as improved roads and air travel there has been both the stimulus and the opportunity to learn more about the flora which is now reasonably well known. There is still, however, a general lack of collections of the species that flower in the 'wet', for at that season travel is difficult.

The Kimberley is geologically stable, its oldest rocks being Archaean sediments and volcanics. These outcrop in many places but more commonly are covered by Proterozoic sandstones. The latter are usually dissected into a very rugged surface with frequent picturesque gorges. In the southern Kimberley old Devonian limestone reefs form ranges such as the Oscar and Napier. A few areas of Tertiary laterite occur in the north, notably on the Mitchell Plateau. The large valleys of the Fitzroy River and to a lesser extent the Ord contain extensive alluvial deposits.

The rainfall varies from over 1200 mm in the northwest to 350 mm on the desert fringe. Rivers flow strongly in the 'wet' (December to March) but become trickles or pools in the dry season. The main flush of growth and flowering comes also with the 'wet'; but while many species go dormant and may shed their leaves in the winter, at this season there are still species in flower, especially on sandstone hills and in damp areas.

The Kimberley flora as presently known contains over 1500 species of which 1200 do not occur farther south in Western Australia, but only 350 are restricted to the region. Much of the vegetation is woodland of varying composition with a prominent ground layer of grasses. On some plains the trees are few or absent. Dense bands of trees, shrubs and screwpines often line river banks. Rocky screes in the north and north-west often support pockets of vine thicket in which typically Australian species are few.

A distinctive plant community is that of the mangroves which are extensive along the Kimberley coast, especially around the large estuaries such as the Glenelg, Prince Regent, Drysdale and Ord Rivers. They are clearly demarcated along the upper limit of spring tides. Within them, a twice daily tide leaves a film of slippery grey mud over the lower trunks and roots. Some species are buttressed, some have prop roots and others have pneumatophores or knee roots. Seventeen species in 15 genera are known in the Kimberley. The most common are *Avicennia marina* (Vic. 191), *Ceriops tagal, Bruguiera exaristata* (Pl. 560) and *Rhizophora stylosa*. Apart from lichens, no other plants grow in the weird world of the mangroves, except the fern *Acrostichum speciosum* which may occur near the landward edge, and the mangrove mistletoe, *Amyema thalassium*, which grows on *Avicennia.*

The largest family of plants in the Kimberley is the Poaceae (grasses), followed by the Papilionaceae (pea flowers), Mimosaceae (wattles), Myrtaceae and Cyperaceae (sedges). Grasses are usually common in the ground storey throughout the region. Many are perennial, many ephemeral, but most grow and flower in the 'wet'. The spinifexes (*Triodia* and *Plectrachne*) are common on rocky hills and the dry southern plains. Most of the spinifexes here are relatively soft but some are very sticky. Annual sorghum, *Sorghum stipoideum*, is very common in sand and on sandstone such as at Kununurra. It germinates with the first rains, grows rapidly to 2-4 m, then produces large 'ears' of brown, long-awned flowers. It is unpalatable to stock.

A common grass, and one likely to make its presence felt, is Bunch Speargrass, *Heteropogon contortus*. A perennial grass, it has long-awned fruits with sharppointed seeds which become entwined in bundles that cling to and penetrate clothing.

The Tropical Reed, *Phragmites karka*, forms dense stands on some river banks. Resembling a small bamboo, it produces large, feathery, pale brown panicles of flowers.

Other commonly-seen genera are spear grasses (Aristida), love grasses (Eragrostis), wanderrie grasses (*Eriachne*), oilgrasses (*Cymbopogon*) and kangaroo grasses (*Themeda*). Two excellent native pasture genera are Flinders Grass, *Iseilema*, and Mitchell Grass, *Astrebla*.

Visually the Myrtaceae vie with the grasses as the dominant family in the Kimberley. Except in wet places, in the rainforest and on the blacksoil plains, the Eucalypts, as elsewhere in Australia, are the principal trees, though other genera are also often present. The largest group of Eucalypts here is the bloodwoods which are characterised by large panicles of cream (rarely red) flowers and urn-shaped fruit. Unlike many southern species, the buds and fruits of bloodwoods develop quickly and shed their seed when mature. Another species is the Woollybutt, *E. miniata*, which is common throughout the region except on the dry southern fringe. It has rough fibrous bark on the trunk, a spreading crown with cream branchlets, ribbed, usually glaucous buds and brilliant orange flowers.

Another prominent genus is *Melaleuca* of which 4 species occur as cadjeputs or tropical paperbarks, on river banks and in swamps. The most common is *M. viridiflora* with broad, leathery, dark green leaves. *M. leucadendron* (Pl. 522) is a massive tree to 30 m with narrow, bright green pendulous leaves, while Silver Cadjeput, *M. argentea*, has narrow, silvery leaves. Cadjeputs have cream (rarely red) bottlebrush-like flowers.

Species of *Eugenia* also occur along rivers and creeks, usually in the rocky bed, sometimes on the banks. Eucalypt-like in aspect, they have opposite leaves and flowers with usually 4 petals. The fruit is a berry. A common myrtaceous tree of rocky, sandstone hills is *Xanthostemon paradoxus* (Pl. 545). There are several species of fringe myrtle, *Calytrix*, and one of *Verticordia* (Pl. 547), usually found in sand or on sandstone hills. In habit they are much larger than their southern counterparts, some being small trees. The most common *Calytrix* is *C. exstipulata* which has tiny, crowded leaves and bright pink flowers produced in winter.

Pea flowers in the Kimberley are many and varied: over 100 species ranging from small ephemerals to tall trees, some inconspicuous, others forming a prominent part of the vegetation. Among the latter is the White Dragon Tree, *Sesbania formosa* (Pl. 535), which is common on river banks. Other species of *Sesbania* are tall herbs with pale yellow flowers that are brown-spotted outside, and long, narrow, many-seeded pods. They occur in low-lying areas. Another arborescent pea is Yulbah, *Erythrina vespertilio* (Pl. 499), which is seen here in basaltic soil.

A common shrub in woodlands on sandstone of the central and north Kimberley is *Bossiaea bossiaeoides*. This is a leafless plant with broad, flat stems and yellow flowers about 15 mm across. Another genus of leafless peas is *Jacksonia*, in which the stems are either terete or flattened and the flowers, about 5 mm across, are yellow or yellow and red with reflexed calyx lobes. They grow usually in sand, in open woodland.

There are several species of rattlepods, *Crotalaria* (Pl. 556), which are annual or perennial herbs with leaves of one or 3-7 leaflets. They have clusters or racemes of bright yellow flowers followed by sausage-like pods containing up to 30 seeds. One species, *C. verrucosa*, has purple flowers. Rattlepods cause Kimberley Horse Disease.

Two genera of pea flowers easy to recognise are *Psoralea* and *Tephrosia*, both containing annual and perennial herbs. The former usually have glands on the stems and black dots on the leaves, and the flowers, in axillary racemes, are pale purple or pink. *Tephrosia* can be recognised by the pubescent outer surface of the standard; they usually have pink, orange or maroon flowers in racemes. Other herbaceous peas in the region are the genera *Desmodium*, *Indigofera*, *Rhynchosia* and *Zornia*.

The *Cassia* family, *Caesalpiniaceae*, is well represented in the region. *Cassia mimosoides* is a small shrub, less than 1 m high with finely divided leaves. *Cassia venusta* (Pl. 512) is also widespread in the Kimberley and is a frequent roadside plant. The Ironwood, *Erythrophleum chlorostachys*, is a toxic member of the *Cassia* family. It has iron-grey, rough, tessellated bark, leaves of up to 9 large leaflets, dense spikes of green flowers with prominent stamens like a wattle and dark brown, flat pods with large seeds. Quite common in loam over basalt this species also grows over sandstone as a shrub or tree up to 15 m. *Lysiphyllum cunninghamii* (Pl. 549), previously known as Bauhinia, is related to the Ironwood and is common south of the King Leopold Range.

There are over 80 species of wattle, *Acacia*, in the region, most having phyllodes. They occur in most habitats. In the south-western Kimberley, on red loamy plains, they are often dominant in a formation called Pindan. Typical species of the Pindan are *A. eriopoda*, *A. holosericea*, *A. sericata* and *A. tumida*. An unusual species of the north and east Kimberly is *A. dunnii*, which is a glaucous, little-branched shrub with ear-like phyllodes up to 35 cm long.

Many species of the family Euphorbiaceae are known in cultivation. The Bleeding Heart, *Homalanthus populifolius*, is grown in Perth gardens and is native to forests in north Kimberley as well as similar habitats elsewhere in northern Australia. This shrub or small tree has broadly ovate bluish-green leaves which turn bright red before they fall. Species of *Phyllanthus* are also well known in cultivation. About 6 species occur in the region. One, *P. baccatus*, is a scrambling plant in rocky areas. In the same family is the Quinine Tree, *Petalostigma pubescens* (Pl. 546), and the closely related *P. quadriloculare* which is a shrub less than 1 m high. Both are widely distributed especially in sandstone areas in woodlands of *Eucalyptus miniata*. The outer part of the fruit is very bitter.

The family Apocynaceae is characterised by a milky latex, star-shaped, propellor-like flowers and opposite leaves. A number of species occur in northern Australia, some being toxic to stock. *Alstonia actinophylla* is a tree to 15 m with dark brown, rough, curly bark and copious milky sap. The 'water currant', *Carissa ovata*, is a common small shrub with small, ovoid purple fruits which were eaten by Aboriginals. An erect or spreading bush commonly found on sandstone slopes is *Ervatamia orientalis*. This has paired, banana-shaped, orange fruits up to 2 cm long.

The family Rubiaceae, represented in the South-West by only a few herbaceous species, in the Kimberley has many herbaceous, shrubby and arborescent species. The family can be recognised by its leaves arranged in opposite pairs and joined around the stem by stipules in the form of a narrow or broad sheath. The flowers are usually small and often inconspicuous. A number of species of *Gardenia* occur in northern Australia. In the Kimberley, *Gardenia megasperma* occurs as a partially deciduous tree 5-10 m high with very viscid buds, large leaves up to 20 cm x 14 cm and large, green fruits which are 5-6 angled. Another member of the family is the Leichhardt Tree, *Nauclea coadnata*, which is a pyramidal tree up to 22 m with numerous horizontally spreading branches, large, elliptical leaves and fruit in spherical, bristly heads. The tree grows in deep, moist soil of river banks and has a beautiful timber suitable for cabinet wood. Other arborescent members of the family include *Randia* and *Timonius*. The principal herbaceous genera are *Borreria*, with heads of blue, white or red flowers, and *Oldenlandia* with white or blue flowers either solitary or in small clusters.

The Terminalias, variously called Ironwood, Wild Almond, Wild Chestnut or Kabing, range from small shrubs to tall trees. In the family Combretaceae, they are partially or completely deciduous plants with Eucalypt-like leaves. The fruits are variously winged or pear-shaped and are regarded as edible, some species with an acid flavour. They grow especially along rivers, in coastal areas and on blacksoil plains but occur in other areas also. One striking species is the Crocodile Tree, *Terminalia arostrata*, seen in the north-east Kimberley and NT. It has deeply fissured, tessellated bark, pendulous branchlets and globular, succulent fruit. Another common tree of this family is *Buchanania* which has rough, dark grey bark, penninerved leaves and small cream flowers in racemes. The fruit is a dry drupe. *Buchanania* grows in sand among sandstone rocks and occasionally basalt.

In constrast to South-West Australia, species of Proteaceae are relatively few. There are about 20 species of *Grevillea*, some very common, e.g. *G. refracta*, *G. agrifolia*, *G. pyramidalis*, and *G. pteridifolia*. The latter is a tree to 10 m with finely divided leaves and dense racemes of bright orange flowers. It frequents low-lying sandy areas in the north and north east, flowering in the dry season.

There is one tropical *Banksia*, *B. dentata*, which extends from the King Leopold Range north and east to the Northern Territory and Queensland as well as Papua-New Guinea. It is a small tree with large, wavy leaves and yellow flowers produced from January to April.

Other Proteaceae here are several species of *Hakea*, one of *Persoonia* and two of *Stenocarpus*. *Hakea arborescens* is a common small tree, rough-barked with linear, nerveless leaves, clusters of small cream flowers and woody fruit 4-6 cm long.

To southern eyes many Kimberley plants look out of place, and one of these is the White Cedar, *Melia composita*. Very closely related to the Cape Lilac of gardens, it is a small deciduous tree with bright green, soft, pinnate leaves, panicles of small, scented mauve flowers and spherical fruits. It is fairly common on the rugged Oscar and Napier Ranges.

Another widespread tree of the same family (Meliaceae) is the Kimberley Walnut, *Owenia vernicosa*. It has a robust, rough-barked trunk and spreading branches with rather clumped foliage. The deep green pinnate leaves are often pendulous. The flowers are inconspicuous, but the hard, spherical fruits, each 2-3 cm across, hang in loose clusters.

The Stinkwood, *Gyrocarpus americanus*, is another unusual tree. It grows to 6 m, has a short, stout trunk with fairly smooth creamy-green bark and a bushy crown. The large, lobed leaves are deciduous in the dry season when the fruits ripen. These hang in clusters; each fruit is a wrinkled nut about 1 cm long with two broad, curved wings which spin the fruit like a propellor as it falls. The species grows in alluvial soil in several areas of the Kimberley, especially the upper Fitzroy valley.

Kurrajongs are to be seen especially on rocky slopes. Most are deciduous in winter and while leafless produce bright red or pink bell-like flowers. The fruits are large, boat-shaped pods containing many round seeds. A common species is the Sticky Kurrajong, *Sterculia viscidula* (Pl. 554); closely related to it are *Brachychiton paradoxum* and, with smaller pink and green flowers, *B. viridiflora*. *Brachychiton diversifolium* has smaller cream flowers with red-brown markings, in open panicles; they appear in August while the leaves are still present. It is a tall tree with fissured, grey bark and is found in the central and north Kimberley.

There are many Kimberley species in the family Malvaceae, especially in the genera *Abutilon* (lantern bushes), *Gossypium* (cotton), *Hibiscus*, *Sida* and *Thespesia*. The *Hibiscus* may be yellow, mauve or bright pink and often grow in valleys, especially near watercourses. Several, such as *H. setulosus* have vicious branched spines on the stems. The native cottons, like their cultivated relatives, produce bolls of cottony seeds. The mauve *G. australe* occurs along the dry, southern edge of the Kimberley.

One of the most distinctive and well-known plants of the Kimberley is *Adansonia gregorii*. A close relative in Africa, *A. digitata*, is known as the *Baobab*. This common name has been used for the Australian tree but it is frequently called the Boab. These extraordinary plants are thought to live to a great age, probably over 1000 years. It is unfortunate that many have been disfigured with carved names and initials since it takes many years for the letters to be grown over. *Adansonia* belongs to the family Bombacaceae. The only other member of the family in the Kimberley is *Bombax ceiba*, a deciduous, thorny tree of the vine thickets with large red flowers.

Wild figs are often to be seen especially among sandstone rocks and on river banks. A common shrubby species is Rock Fig, *Ficus platypoda* (Pl. 496). Similar but with larger, silky figs and sometimes forming a tree is *F. leucotricha*. *Ficus coronulata* is a tree of river banks, with narrow, pendulous leaves and small figs. There are two cauliflorous species, i.e. having the flowers and fruit borne on the trunk and older branches. These are *F. hispida*, a tree with hollow branchlets, and *F. racemosa*, a massive tree with solid branchlets. Both occur in vine thicket or sometimes on river banks, in the central and north Kimberley. All figs have milky latex. The fruits are edible but often dry.

Many river and creek banks as well as swamps are inhabited by the distinctive screwpines, *Pandanus*, which are in their own family, Pandanaceae. Usually in the form of small trees, they have dense crowns of narrow, tapering leaves arranged in 3 spiral series. The leaves have short spines on the margins and often on the midribs. The leaf-scars make a spiral pattern on the trunk. The plants are dioecious, the males producing inconspicuous dense spikes of small, staminate flowers. More prominent are the fruits of female plants, hanging in large clusters resembling pineapples. They are green but may turn red when ripe and fall in sections. Each section (phalange) contains several one-seeded flowers joined together. Five species occur in the Kimberley, the southern limit of screwpines in WA being the Edgar Range. The most common species is *Pandanus aquaticus*, a slender species with bright green leaves and small, usually one-seeded phalanges 4-5 mm across in clusters 6-8 cm across. It forms dense thickets on the banks of the larger rivers, the fruit ripening in April and May. The other species resemble *P. darwinensis* (Pl. 551).

True palms are represented by 5 species of fan-palm, *Livistona*. They are usually seen as scattered plants on rocky slopes but are common in several areas in the north Kimberley. On the lateritic Mitchell Plateau *L. eastonii* is co-dominant with Eucalypts in an extensive woodland; a smaller area occurs on Doongan Station. On either side of the lower Drysdale River, *L. loriphylla* (Pl. 540) is common on low, sandstone hills.

Resembling palms are the cycads (Pl. 561) but in fact they are gymnosperms, related to the pines. They have an unbranched trunk 1-4 m tall with a dense crown of leaves 1-2 m long and divided into many narrow, parallel lobes. Cycads are dioecious. The males have cones with the pollen borne on the underside of many upturned, pointed bracts. Pollen is wind-blown to the females where the ovules are borne on the margins of erect woolly bracts that form a tuft-like cone in the centre of the crown. Each spherical fruit contains one seed. There are 5 species of *Cycas* in the Kimberley.

A native cypress, *Callitris intratropica*, grows in rocky (usually sandstone) or sandy soil in mixed woodlands through the central and north Kimberley. It is a robust tree to 15 m but is killed by fire and its numbers have fallen with frequent burning in the region.

Lianes and creepers are far more numerous than elsewhere in WA. Some are massive species of the vine thickets, others small and herbaceous. There are several true vines of the family Vitaceae with tendrils, and panicles of small flowers producing grape-like fruit. Wild melons of the Curcurbitaceae also have tendrils but the small yellow flowers are unisexual and solitary. The melons of native species are small. There are many species of the morning glory family, Convolvulaceae, some prostrate, others climbing. The flowers may be white, pink or blue. The principal genera are *Ipomoea* and *Polymeria*. In the wetter areas a tough climber of thickets on rocky hills is *Flagellaria indica*. Somewhat bamboo-like, it clings by means of the rolled leaf-tips, and has panicles of small cream flowers. Common throughout the Kimberley is *Tinospora smilacina* which is usually seen entwined about trees. Its stem becomes thick with corky bark and the leaves are triangular but with rounded corners; the species is deciduous. The family Apocynaceae provides a number of lianes, characterised by milky latex, opposite leaves and fruit forming a follicle which opens to release many silky seeds. Typical Kimberley genera are *Parsonia* and *Wrightia*. Many creepers occur in the Papilionacease, e.g. *Abrus* (Pl. 548), *Canavalia*, *Mucuna*, *Galactia*, *Rhynchosia* and *Vigna*. Mention must also be made of an introduced climber that is now so common as to seem native : the passionflower, *Passiflora foetida*, is a soft-leaved, hirsute creeper with white and purple flowers and small, orange, edible fruit. It grows on river banks, often forming tangled masses.

Over 30 species of fern are recorded in the Kimberley. The most common species is the Climbing Maidenhair, *Lygodium microphyllum* (Pl. 566). This frequents damp rock faces or shady trees. Another common fern of damp rock faces is *Lindsaea ensifolia*. Like *Lygodium* and *Dicranopteris linearis* (Pl. 550), *Lindsaea ensifolia* is widespread in tropical Australia as well as SE Asia. The Braid Fern, *Platyzoma microphylla* (Pl. 562), grows only in Australia and is widespread in the north. This latter species is one of the few drought-adapted ferns of the region. The rhizome is well protected from desiccation by long, brown hairs. The fronds are simple, with small, rigid pinnae which quickly assume a golden-green colour in periods of water stress. During the dry period fronds of the Braid Fern may die and wither, only plants in perpetually moist places remaining green and thriving above ground. With the onset of the wet period the rhizomes send out new fronds some of which are sterile and short, others having the coiled tips characteristic of young fern fronds.

Blechnum orientale is also commonly encountered in the region. It usually frequents the walls of narrow gorges and seepage areas near creeks and has fronds up to 1 m long. An unexpected habitat for a fern is the landward edge of the mangroves. Here, washed by spring tides, grows *Acrostichum speciosum*, which has leathery fronds on rigid stalks.

Aquatic plants are more commonly encountered in the Kimberley than in other parts of WA. Most species found are pantropical although a few are known to occur only in the Kimberley and the neighbouring 'Top End' of the territory. One of the most widespread aquatics in the region is the common aquarium plant *Vallisneria spiralis*. Another widespread water plant is Water Pincushion, *Eriocaulon setaceum* (Pl. 565), which occurs in Indonesia, India and North Africa as well as across northern Australia.

The enormous lake created by the Ord River Dam has provided a haven for many native aquatics which were once subjected to the annual scouring of the Ord floods. Lake Argyle and the older Lake Kununurra now support plagues of the native *Hydrilla verticillata*, *Najas graminea* and *Potamogeton tricarinatus*.

Quiet-water lagoons and sheltered backwaters of large rivers support a wealth of aquatics such as Water Lilies, *Nymphaea gigantea*. Two marshworts, *Nymphoides indica* (white flowers) and *N. hydrocharoides* (yellow), have water lily-like leaves with small fringed flowers arising from the upper part of the leaf stalk. Both *Nymphaea* and *Nymphoides* inhabit Lily Creek on the southern boundary of Kununurra.

Damp alluvial soils bordering water courses or in wet depressions provide a habitat for numerous sedges and related families. Sedges, members of the family Cyperaceae, are well represented by the genera *Cyperus* and *Fimbristylis*. A sedge-like group of plants which have yellow or cream 3-petalled flowers in a densely packed, scaly head also frequent damp places. These are species of *Xyris* in the family Xyridaceae.

Ephemeral herbs occur in all habitats except the mangroves. Their flowers are often brightly coloured. Most flower during or just after the 'wet', but in damp areas may continue through the winter. The widespread Tall Mulla Mulla, *Ptilotus exaltatus* (Pl. 461), is common in the Kimberley as well as in the more arid parts of the State. It is frequently found in woodlands in this region or it may grow close to fringing mangroves.

Pluchea rubelliflora is an attractive herb of the daisy family, Compositae or Asteraceae. This species resembles a mulla mulla at first glance. Other short-lived herbs of this family are various species of *Blumea* which have yellow, pink or purple florets. Many of these have strongly scented flowers and, as with many arid region daisies, the leaves and stems are often very aromatic. One of the most commonly found herbs of this famliy is *Pterocaulon sphacelatum*, a winged-stemmed plant with a dense covering of matted hairs and small purple florets in a compact head.

In the Goodeniaceae are many herbaceous species of *Goodenia* (usually yellow-flowered), several of *Scaevola*, the golden Cabbage Poison, *Velleia panduriformis*, and a *Lechenaultia*, the last having deep blue flowers like southern *Dampieras*. Triggerplants, *Stylidium*, may be seen in swamps, woodlands and sheltered rock crevices. Most tropical species have pink flowers. In the Loganiceae is the genus *Mitrasacme* containing slender herbs with white, cream or yellow 4-petalled flowers that close at night. The buds are angular and often orange outside. The Scrophulariaceae contains mimulus-like flowers of blue, purple, pink, white or yellow. Some intriguing flower shapes occur among the bladderworts, *Utricularia*, in the Lentibulariaceae. The most common is the bright yellow *U. chrysantha* (Pl. 562). Several species are free-floating.

Few orchids are known in the Kimberley. The most common is *Cymbidium canaliculatum* (Pl. 544). Another tree orchid is *Dendrobium dicuphum*, found in vine thicket of the north-west Kimberley; its flower is white with a purple lip, appearing at the end of the wet season. A ground orchid, *Eulophia venosa*, bears a raceme of pale green and deep red flowers on a tall, leafless stem; the strap-like leaf appears later on a separate stem.

GLOSSARY OF BOTANICAL TERMS USED

(some adjectival equivalents in parenthesis)

ACHENE A small, dry, hard, 1-seeded, non-opening fruit, as in daisies and buttercups.

ACUMINATE Tapering to a narrow, acute point.

ANTHER That portion of a stamen which contains the pollen, usually bilocular, and sessile or attached to a filament.

ARISTATE Tapering to a stiff point.

AWN Stiff, bristle-like appendage, as often found in grass flowers.

AXILLARY Arising from the angle of a leaf and branch.

BISEXUAL Having both functional stamens and ovary.

BRACT Small modified leaf at base of flower-stalk or surrounding a cluster of florets, sometimes dry or colourless.

BRACTEOLE A small bract, often paired, on flower-stalk or base of calyx.

CALLI Gland-like hairs or excrescences, as on the labellum of various orchids.

CALYX The outermost ring of floral segments (sepals), usually green and sometimes rudimentary.

CILIATE Having marginal hairs forming an eyelash-like fringe.

COLUMN Combination of stamens and styles in one central body, as in orchid flowers.

CORDATE Heart-shaped.

COROLLA The interior ring of floral segments (petals), often coloured, and sometimes fused or absent.

CORYMB A loose, flat-topped, centripetal floral arrangement, in which each stalked flower reaches a common level.

CRENATE With rounded teeth and alternating scallops around margin.

CULM Flowering stem (often hollow) of a grass or sedge.

CUNEATE Wedge-shaped.

CYME (CYMOSE) A centrifugal floral arrangement in which the oldest flower is central and lowest.

DECURRENT Running down along the stem, often like wings, as when leaf-bases are prolonged below their point of attachment.

DECUSSATE In pairs which are alternately at right angles along the stem (appearing cross-shaped from above).

DEHISCENT Opening spontaneously when ripe, as in capsular fruits.

DENTATE Toothed.

DENTICULATE Finely or minutely toothed.

DIOECIOUS Having the sexes on different plants.

DIVARICATE Spread out widely, as in divergent branches of some shrubs.

DRUPE A stone-fruit, with single, hard-coated seed in fleshy pulp or leathery jacket.

ENDEMIC Confined to a certain country, region or locality.

ENTIRE Without toothing, lobing or division of any kind.

EPHEMERAL Short-lived plant, completing its life-cycle in one season.

EXSERTED Protruding, as valves on a capsule or stamens beyond the floral parts.

FAMILY A group of genera having many features in common, e.g. orchids, pea-flowers, or daisies.

FLORET Small individual flower, usually stalkless, in a head-like cluster.

FOLLICLE Fruit composed of a single carpel, and splitting open along a suture to which the seeds are attached.

GALEA A helmet or cowl-like structure formed of connivent floral segments as in some orchids (e.g. greenhoods).

GENUS (GENERA) A group of closely related species, e.g. wattles, banksias.

GLABROUS Smooth and hairless.

GLAUCOUS Covered with a bluish-green or silvery bloom (powdery-waxy secretion).

HALOPHYTIC Growing under a high concentration of salt, as in coastal saline marshes.

HIRSUTE Clothed with long hairs.

INFLORESCENCE The arrangement of flowers on the floral axis (raceme, spike, head, etc.).

INVOLUCRE (INVOLUCRAL) The collar or cup of bracts surrounding a flower-head, as in daisies and dryandras.

IRRITABLE Easily excited by stimuli, moving at a touch, as with the columns of triggerplants and the lips of some orchids.

LABELLUM The modified third or odd petal of an orchid flower (often called 'lip' or 'tongue').

LANCEOLATE Tapering at each end but broadest towards the base.

LINEAR Several times longer than wide, with parallel edges.

MALLEE A eucalypt with several stems arising from a woody stock; a plant association dominated by eucalypts of this habit.

MONOTYPIC Having one component, e.g. a genus with one species.

NODE Point of stem where a leaf or whorl of leaves arises (often swollen in grasses).

OBLANCEOLATE Tapering at each end but broadest towards the apex.
OBOVOID Shaped like a hen's egg but broadest in upper half.
OPERCULUM A lid; the bud-cap of *Eucalyptus* species.
OPPOSITE Of two organs arising at the same level on opposite sides of a stem.
ORBICULAR With circular outline.
OVARY Central female reproductive organ of a flower, containing the ovules and becoming the fruit.
OVATE Shaped as in the longitudinal section of a hen's egg and narrowed towards the apex.
OVOID Egg-shaped.

PANICLE (PANICULATE) A loose and branching arrangement of flowers.
PAPILLOSE Covered with small nipple-like glands or superficial protruberances.
PAPPUS Tuft of hairs or scales on top of some fruit (e.g. achenes of daisies).
PEDICEL The stalk of a single flower.
PEDUNCLE The main stem of a flower or cluster of flowers.
PERENNIAL Living for at least several years.
PERIANTH The complete floral envelope of calyx and corolla, one or other sometimes being absent.
PETAL Each segment, often coloured and delicate, of the interior ring or series of floral parts.
PETIOLE The stalk of a leaf.
PHYLLODE A leaf-stalk enlarged and usually flattened, resembling and performing the functions of a leaf, as in many wattles.
PINNAE (PINNATE) Primary divisions or leaflets of a compound leaf.
PROSTRATE Lying closely along the ground.
PUBESCENCE Covering of soft hair or down.
PUNGENT Sharply pointed.

RACEME (RACEMOSE) Arrangement of equally stalked flowers along an individual axis.
RECEPTACLE The summit of a pedicel on which the floral parts are arranged; or the expanded summit of a peduncle on which the flowers are inserted, as in daisies and dryandras.
RENIFORM Kidney-shaped.
REVOLUTE With the margins rolled under.
RHACHIS The principal axis, as of a fern frond or inflorescence.
RHIZOME A prostrate stem, often underground, from which roots and leaves grow.

SCABROUS (SCABRID) Rough to the touch, like sandpaper.
SCAPE Leafless floral axis or peduncle arising from the ground.
SEPAL Each segment, usually green or colourless, of the outermost series of floral parts.
SERRATE With sharp, marginal, forward-pointing teeth.
SESSILE Without a stalk and seated directly on the axis, as in many leaves or flowers.
SPATHULATE Oblong with narrowed base, or somewhat spoon-shaped.
SPECIES A group of genetically similar and freely interbreeding individuals—the unit of botanical classification.
SPIKE (SPICATE) Aggregation of stalkless flowers along a common axis.
STAMEN Male reproductive organ of a flower, consisting of the filament or stalk (sometimes absent) and pollen-bearing anther. The stamens are sometimes united into bundles.
STANDARD Large upper or posterior petal, especially in pea-flowers.
STELLATE Star-shaped or star-like, often used of radiately-branched hairs.
STIPULE A scale or leaf-like appendage on each side of a leaf-base.
STYLE The attenuated, often stalk-like apex of the ovary, terminating in the stigma receptive to pollen.

TERETE Cylindrical and usually tapering.
TOMENTUM (TOMENTOSE) A covering of dense hairs.
TRUNCATE Abruptly shortened at the end, as if cut off.
TUBERCULATE With small, blunt projections.

UMBEL Floral arrangement in which several flower-stalks all spring from the same point.
UNDULATE Wavy, especially on the margins.

VERSATILE With the filament (stalk) attached near the middle of an anther so that the latter can move.
VISCID Sticky, from a mucilaginous or varnish-like exudate.

WHORL (WHORLED) A ring of organs, usually leaves, at intervals around a stem.

INDEX

Bold figures indicate colour plates

Abrus 218
precatorius L. **172**
Abutilon 167, 207, 209, 211, 213, 217
fraseri Hook. **167**, 213
Acacia 13, 129, 142, 147, 149, 179, 205, 212, 216
acuminata Benth 195, 197, 203, 206
adoxa Pedley 211
alata R. Br. **50**
ancistrocarpa Maiden & Blakely 206
aneura F. Muell. ex Benth 205
baxteri Benth. **64**
bivenosa DC 209, 212
blakelyi Maiden 195
burkittii F. Muell. ex Benth. 203
cedroides Benth. 190
celastrifolia Benth **112**
coriacea DC 212
craspedocarpa F. Muell. 206
cuthbertsonii Luehm. 206
drummondii Lindl. **73**, 183
dunnii (Maiden) Turrill 216
eriopoda Maiden & Blakely 216
extensa Lindl. **43**
farnesiana Willd. 213
glaucoptera Benth. **94**, 191
grasbyi Maiden 206
gregorii F. Muell. **166**, 213
hemiteles Benth **137**, 203
holosericea A. Cunn. ex G. Don 216
kempeana F. Muell. 206
lasiocalyx C. Andrews 201
lateriticola Maslin **38**, **46**
linophylla W.V. Fitzg. **146**, 206
longiphyllodinea Maiden **129**
multispicata Benth. 129
myrtifolia (Sm.) Willd. 179, 183
neurophylla W. V. Fitzg. 198
orthocarpa F. Muell. 213
oswaldii F. Muell. 143, 205
papyrocarpa Benth. 143, 205
pentadenia Lindl. **57**, 179
pruinocarpa Tindale 206
pulchella R. Br. 13, 15, **21**, 183
pyrifolia DC. **147**, 206, 209
quadrimarginea F. Muell. 206
resinomarginea W. V. Fitzg. **140**
sericata A. Cunn. ex Benth. 216
spondylophylla F. Muell. 211
tetragonophylla F. Muell. **147**, 195, 205, 206, 209
translucens A. Cunn. 206, 213
tumida F. Muell. ex Benth. 216
urophylla Benth. ex Lindl. 179
victoriae Benth 209
xiphophylla E. Pritzel 206
Acanthocarpus preissii Lehm. 13
Acrostichum speciosum Willd. 215, 218
Actinobole uliginosum (A. Gray) Eichler **131**, 201
Actinodium cunninghamii Schau. ex Lindl. **62**, 182, 184
Actinostrobus acuminatus Parl. 196
arenarius Gardn. 196
Actinotus leucocephalus Benth. **133**
Adansonia gregorii F. Muell. **173**, 217
Adenanthos 29, 182, 190, 199
barbigerus Lindl. **46**
cygnorum Diels 15, **31**
obovatus Labill. 15, **29**
Adiantum aethiopicum L 180
capillus-veneris L. **164**, 212
Agonis 180, 181, 182, 191
flexuosa (Spreng.) Schau. 13, **19**, 179, 181
grandiflora Benth. **37**
juniperina Schau. 180, 181
linearifolia (DC.) Schau. 181, 190
marginata (Labill.) Schau. 181
spathulata Schau. 181
Albizia lophantha (Willd.) Benth. 179
Alstonia actinophylla (A. Cunn.) K. Schum. 216
Alyogyne 167
cuneiformis (DC.) Lewton 213
pinonianus (Gaud.) Fryxell **167**, 214
Amyema 147
fitzgeraldii (Blakely) Danser **147**
thalassium Barlow 215
Andersonia 76, 183
axilliflora (Stschegl.) Druce **77**, 185
caerulea R. Br. 183, 185
echinocephala (Stschegl.) Druce 185
grandiflora (Stschegl.) **77**, 185
simplex (Stschegl.) Druce **76**, 183, 185
sprengelioides R. Br. 183
Andersonia, Giant **77**, 185
Red **77**, 185
Spiked **76**, 183, 185
Angianthus cunninghamii (DC.) Benth. 213
Anigozanthos 47, 97, 185
bicolor Endl. **47**
flavidus Red. **66**
gabrielae Domin. **71**, 185
humilis Lindl. 196
manglesii D. Don **20**, 196
preissii Endl. **66**
pulcherrimus Hook. **97**, 196
rufus Labill. 185, 186, 189
viridis Endl. 14, **30**
Anogramma leptophylla (L.) Link 13
Anthocercis 61
viscosa R. Br. **61**
Anthotium humile R. Br. 189
rubriflorum F. Muell. ex Benth. 189
Aristida 214, 216
Arthrocnemum 205, 208, 214
Asplenium adiantoides (L.) Lam. 180
flabellifolium Cav. 180
Astartea 182
Astrebla 216
Astroloma 30
ciliatum (Lindl.) Druce **43**
microdonta F. Muell. ex Benth. **99**
stomarrhena Sond. 14, **30**
Astrotricha hamptoni F. Muell. 211
Atalaya hemiglauca (F. Muell.) F. Muell. ex Benth. 214
Athrixia pulverulenta (Lindl.) Druce **24**
Atriplex 205, 208, 214
spongiosa F. Muell. **154**
Avicennia marina (Forsk.) Vierh. 13, 213, 215

Bacon and Eggs **33**
Baeckea 116, 182, 190, 191, 195, 204
grandiflora Benth. **116**
ovalifolia (F. Muell.) F. Muell. 190
oxycoccoides Benth. 190
Baeckea, Large-flowered **116**
Balaustion microphyllum Gardn. **141**, 204
pulcherrimum Hook **128**
Banjine, A **23**
Rose **27**, **48**, 117
Silky Yellow **39**, 178
Banksia 14, 22, 182, 186, 190, 192, 209, 217
ashbyi Bak. f. **106**, 210, 213
attenuata R. Br. 14
baueri R. Br. 186, 190
baxteri R. Br. **64**, 186, 190
brownii Baxter ex R. Br. 182, 184
burdettii Bak. f. 192
caleyi R. Br. 186
candolleana Meisn. 192
coccinea R. Br. **61**, 182, 184, 186, 190
dentata L. f. 22, 217
elderana F. Muell. et Tate **139**
elegans Meisn. 192
grandis Willd. 14, 16, 179, 184
hookerana Meisn. **97**
ilicifolia R. Br. 14
laevigata Meisn. 190
lemanniana Meisn. 186, 190
lindleyana Meisn. 192
littoralis R. Br. 16
media R. Br **81**, 186
menziesii R. Br. 14, 16, **17**, **22**, 192
nutans R. Br **81**, 186
occidentalis R. Br. **64**, 182
petiolaris F. Muell. 186
praemorsa Andrews 182
prionotes Lindl. 14, 192, 198
prostrata R. Br. 184
pulchella R. Br. **81**, 186
quercifolia R. Br. Var. *quercifolia* 182
var. *integrifolia* F. Muell. **92**, 184, 190
repens Labill. 184, 186
sceptrum Meisn. 192
solandri R. Br. **75**, 184
speciosa R. Br. **81**, 186
sphaerocarpa R. Br. 192
verticillata R. Br. 182
victoriae Meisn. **106**
violacea Gardn. 186
Banksia, Acorn 14, 192, 198
Albany 182
Ashby's **106**, 192, 213
Baxter's **64**, 186, 190
Bull 14, 16, 179, 184
Creeping 186
Holly-leaved 14
Hooker's **97**, 192
Menzies' 14, 16, **17**, **22**, 192
Mountain **92**, 190
Nodding **81**, 186
Oak-leaved 182
Propellor 192
Red Swamp **64**, 182
River 16
Scarlet **61**, 182, 184, 186, 190
Showy **81**, 186
Slender 16, 192
Southern Plains **81**, 186
Stirling Range **75**, 184
Swordfish **139**
Teasel **81**, 186

Woolly 186, 190
Woolly Orange **106**, 192
Baobab **173**, 217
Basket Flower 15, **29**
Bassia, see *Sclerolaena* and *Dissocarpus*
Bauhinia **172**
Baumea 212
articulata R. Br. 13
Bean, Jack 212
Beard-heath **32**
Beaufortia 15, 76, 184, 188, 191, 195
anisandra Schau. 184
decussata R. Br. 181, 184
eriocephala W. V. Fitzg. **103**
heterophylla (Turcz.) Domin **76**, 184
micrantha Schau. **89**, 188
orbifolia F. Muell. **85**, 188
schaueri Preiss. **89**, 188
sparsa R. Br. **67**, 181
squarrosa Schau. 15, **30**
Bell, Cranbrook **71**
Fringed 15, **31**
Mogumber **50**
Mondurup 184
Pink Mountain **74**
Qualup **93**, 191
Winter **22**, 196
Bellflower, Felty **148**
Berrigan 205
Billardiera 52, 177
erubescens (Putterl.) Bennett **114**
Floribunda (Putterl.) F. Muell 177
lehmanniana F. Muell. **122**
ringens (Drumm. ex Harv.) Bennett **104**
variifolia (DC.) **52**
Billardiera, A **52**
Red **114**
Bindieye 207, 208, 214
Birdflower, Green **166**, 212
Bitter-pea 185
Prickly **23**, **38**, 178
Blackboy, Common **104**, 177, 196
Cundeelee **142**
Desert 142
Dwarf **114**
Slender **44**, 177
Blackbutt, Cleland's 203
Dundas 203
Goldfields 202
Rough-fruited 203
W.A. 16
Black Gin **70**, **72**, 177, 196
Bladderwort **175**, 183
Blancoa canescens Lindl. **22**, 196
Blechnum orientale L. 218
Bleeding Heart 216
Blind Grass, Large **131**, 200
Blister Bush 183
Bluebell, Rough **166**, 212
Blueboy 15, **27**, 177
Bluebush **143**, 203, 205, 208, 214
Bronze **154**
Blue Quill 200
Blumea 219
Boab **173**, 217
Bombax ceiba L. 217
Bonamia rosea (F. Muell.) Hall. f. **148**
Bonnets, Red **119**
Bookleaf **41**
Boree 204
Boronia 182, 185, 188
alata Sm. 182
capitata Benth. **120**
subsp. *clavata* Wilson 120
subsp. *gracilis* Wilson 120
fastigiata Bartl. **51**
gracilipes F. Muell. **59**, 180
heterophylla F. Muell. **66**, 182
inconspicua Benth. 188
inornata Turcz **87**
megastigma Nees 59, 182
molloyae Drumm. **66**, 182
scabra Lindl. **88**, 188
Boronia, Bushy **51**
Cluster **120**
Karri **59**, 180
A Pink **87**
Red **66**, 182
Rough **88**, 188
Scented 182
Tall **66**, 182
Winged 182
Borreria 217
Borya nitida Labill. **35**, **132**, 200
Bossiaea aquifolia Benth 177, 180
bossiaeoides (A. Cunn. ex Benth.) Court 216
webbii F. Muell 180
Bottlebrush, Albany **65**, 181
Goldfields **140**
Granite **134**
Gravel 181
Lesser **149**, 207
Little **89**
One-sided 195
Pink **89**, 188
Ravensthorpe **85**, 188
Sand 15, **30**
Stirling Range **76**, 184
Swamp **67**, 181
Woolly **96**, **103**
Bowgada Bush **146**, 195, 206, 213
Box, Weeping 209
Brachychiton australe (Schott). Terr. 209, 210
diversifolium R. Br 217
gregorii F. Muell. 204
paradoxum Schott. 217
viridiflora (W. V. Fitzg.) C. A. Gardn. 217
Brachycome 207
iberidifolia Benth. 13, **18**
latisquamea F. Muell. **168**, 213
Brachyloma preissii Sond. **25**
Brachysema 195
aphyllum Hook. **104**, 195
chambersii (F. Muell.) F. Muell. ex Benth. 208
daviesioides (Turcz.) Benth. **125**, 204
lanceolatum Meisn. **127**
macrocarpum Benth. **158**, 210
tomentosum Benth. 195
Bracken 180
Braid Fern **175**, 218
Bristle-daisy **24**
Bruguiera exaristata Ding Hou **175**, 215
Buchanania 217
Bulli Bulli **155**, 208
Bullich **132**, 179, 181, 184
Bulrush 13, 212, 214
Burra **150**
Burrobunga 203
Burtonia 73
hendersonii (Paxt.) Benth **119**
polyzyga (F. Muell) F. Muell. ex Benth 211
scabra R. Br. 73
villosa Meisn. 73
Bushpea, Mop **115**
Buttercups, Yellow 13, **25**
Butterfly Flowers **133**, 201
Byblis gigantea Lindl. 14, **33**, 174
liniflora Salisb. 33, **174**
Byblis, Northern 33, **174**
Southern 14, **33**

Cadjeput **164**, 206, 212, 214, 216
Silver 216
Cakile maritima Scop. 13
Caladenia 129, 189
barbarossa Reichb. f. **122**
bryceana Rogers 186
cairnsiana F. Muell. **68**
crebra A. S. George **109**, 196
dilatata R. Br. **129**
discoidea Lindl. 14
drummondii Benth. **124**
flava R. Br. **20**, 186, 196
gemmata Lindl. **43**
integra Coleman **128**
lobata R. Fitzg. 186
longiclavata Coleman **68**
macrostylis R. Fitzg. **47**
patersonii R. Br. var. *longicauda* (Lindl.) Rogers **50**, 186
plicata R. Fitzg. **68**
roei Benth. **123**
sericea Lindl. **54**
Calandrinia 207
polyandra (Hook.) Benth. **109**, **142**
Calectasia cyanea R. Br. 13
Callistemon 65
phoeniceus Lindl. **149**, 207
speciosus (Sims) DC. **65**, 181
Callitris 142
columellaris F. Muell. 206, 210
huegelii (Carr) Franco 204
intratropica Baker & Smith 218
preissii Miq. 13, 204
Calocephalus francisii (F. Muell.) Benth. **105**
Calothamnus 15, 184, 188, 195, 204
blepharospermus F. Muell. 195
gilesii F. Muell. 208
gracilis R. Br. 184, 188
homalophyllus F. Muell. **101**, 195
longissimus F. Muell. 195
pachystachyus Benth. 195
pinifolius F. Muell. **94**, 188, 190
quadrifidus R. Br. 195
rupestris Schau. **134**, 201
validus S. Moore **91**, 190
Caltrop **149**, 207
Calycopeplus helmsii F. Muell. & Tate 204
Calythropsis 195
Calytrix 191, 194, 206, 216
asperula Schau. **74**
brachyphylla Turcz. 194
brevifolia Meisn. 194, 214
decandra R. Br. ex DC. **86**
exstipulata DC. 216
flavescens A. Cunn. 15, **23**
glutinosa Lindl. **35**
longiflora F. Muell 208
strigosa A. Cunn. 194
superba Gardn. & George **107**, 194
Canavalia 218
maritima (Aubl.) Urb. 212
Cape Lilac 217
Caper, Coastal **168**, 213
Capparis spinosa L. var. *nummularia* (DC.)

F. M. Bailey **168**, 213
Carissa ovata R. Br. 216
Carpobrotus 86
rossii (Haw.) Schwantes 214
virescens (Haw.) Schwantes **86**
Cassia 159, 206, 209, 210, 211, 213, 21
artemisioides Gaud. 206
ferraria Symon 211
glutinosa DC. 206, 209
helmsii Symon 206, 210
mimosoides L. 216
notabilis F. Muell. **162**, 210, 214
oligophylla F. Muell. 206, 209
pilocarina Symon 210
pleurocarpa F. Muell **140**
pruinosa F. Muell. **159**, 206, 209
venusta F. Muell. **162**, 210, 214, 216
Cassia, Silver 206
Sticky 206
White **159**, 206
Cassytha **32**
Casuarina 21, 198, 205
campestris Diels 198
cristata Miq 205
decussata Benth. 179
fraserana Miq. 14, 16
huegeliana Miq. 201
humilis Otto et Dietr. **21**
obesa Miq. 199
thuyoides Miq. **88**
Cat's Paw 196
Albany **66**
Cauliflower, Common **112**, 188, 194, 199
Northern 194
Caustic Bush **163**, 211
Cedar, White 217
Cenchrus ciliaris L. 214
Cephalipterum drummondii A. Gray 145, 207
Cephalotus follicularis Labill. **63**, 183
Ceratopteris thalictroides (L.) Brongn. 212
Ceriops tagal (Perr.) C. B. Rob. 213, 215
Chamaescilla corymbosa (R. Br.) F. Muell. 200
Chamaexeros serra (Endl.) Benth. **75**
Chamelaucium 88, 188
axillare F. Muell. ex Benth. 188
confertiflorum Domin 184
megalopetalum F. Muell. ex Benth. **88**, 188
uncinatum Schau. 15, 195
Cheilanthes distans (R. Br.) Mett. 201
tenuifolia (Burm. f.) Swartz 201, 206
Chinese Brake **164**, 212
Chittick **87**, 185, 187
Chorilaena quercifolia Endl. **59**, 179
Chorizema 53, 185
dicksonii Grah. **53**
ilicifolium Labill. **58**, 180
reticulatum Meisn. **67**, 183
Christmas Tree 14, **24**, 202
Clawflower, Barrens **91**, 190
Dense **94**, 188, 190
Murchison **101**, 195
Clematis pubescens Hueg. 177, 180
Clianthus formosus (G. Don) Ford et Vickery **143**, **148**, 205, 207, 210
Cochlospermum fraseri Planch. **173**
Cockies' Tongues 13, **20**
Cockroach Bush **162**, 214
Codonocarpus cotinifolius (Desf.) F. Muell. 196
Comesperma scoparium Steetz. **116**
Coneflower, Barrel **87**, 187
Nodding **80**, 187
Pincushion **41**
Rose **61**, 182, 185
Spreading **102**
Stirling Range **73**, 185
Conospermum 185, 190
amoenum Meisn. **82**, 187
brownii Meisn. **117**
caeruleum R. Br. 182
crassinervium Meisn. 193
distichum R. Br. 185, 187
dorrienii Domin **71**, 185
flexuosum R. Br. 182
glumaceum Lindl. **40**
huegelii R. Br. **36**
incurvum Lindl. **106**, 193
leianthum E. Pritzel 187
nervosum Meisn. 193
stoechadis Endl. 15, **26**, 193
teretifolium R. Br. 185, 187
Conostylis 52, 189, 196
androstemma (Lindl.) F. Muell. **55**, 189
subsp. *argentea* Green 189
aurea Lindl. 196
bealiana F. Muell. 189
candicans Endl. 196
petrophiloides F. Muell. ex Benth 189
prolifera Benth. **52**, 196
setigera R. Br. **52**, 196
vaginata Endl. **88**, 189
Conostylis, Sheath **88**, 189
Conothamnus 195
Coolabah 206, 209, 214
Coopernookia georgei Carolin 190
Coorup **122**
Coppercups **101**, 194, 214
Coastal **168**, 213
Summer **100**
Coral Vine **48**, 177, 180
Corchorus walcottii F. Muell. **161**, 211, 213
Cork Tree **158**, 206, 209, 210, 214
Corybas dilatatus (Rupp & Nicholls) Rupp & Nich. ex Rupp 180
Cosmelia rubra **63**, 183
Cotton, Wild **159**, 209
Cottonhead, Bristly **52**, 196
Grey 196
Mat **52**, 196
Crab Claws **85**
Crab Eyes **172**
Cranberry, Candle **43**
Red Swamp 14, **30**
Sandplain **99**
Crassula 201
Cratystylis conocephala (F. Muell.) S. Moore 203
Creeper, Button **99**, 196
Chapman **104**
Crinum flaccidum Herb. **165**, 214
Crocodile Tree 217
Crotalaria 214, 216
cunninghamii R. Br. **166**, 212
novae-hollandiae DC. **174**, 211
trifoliastrum Willd. 211
verrucosa L. 216
Crowea angustifolia Sm. **58**, 180, 182
Cryptandra arbutiflora Fenzl. 16, **36**
Cryptandra, Waxy 16, **36**
Cryptostylis ovata R. Br. 186
Cudweed, Flannel **131**
Cupulanthus bracteolosus (F. Muell.) Hutch. 185
Currant Bush 204, 207, 213
Curry Flower **29**
Cyanostegia corifolia Munir **120**, 198
Cycad, Argyle **175**
Cycas 218
Cycas pruinosa Maconochie **175**
Cymbidium canaliculatum R. Br. **171**, 219
Cymbopogon 216
Cyperus 212, 219
Cypress, Dwarf 196
Native 206, 210, 218
Rottnest 13
Sandplain 196

Daisy, Button **105**
Climbing **168**
Pygmy **131**, 201
Swamp **62**, 182, 184
Swan River 13, **18**
Daisybush, Mueller's 203
Coastal 212
Rough **19**
Dampiera 53, 127, 178, 183, 185, 189, 196
carinata Benth. **109**, 196
eriocephala De Vr. **127**
hederacea R. Br. **58**, 180
incana R. Br. 210
linearis R. Br. **53**, 178
loranthifolia F. Muell. ex Benth. 190
luteiflora F. Muell. **113**
sacculata F. Muell. ex Benth. **84**
spicigera Benth. **106**, 196
Dampiera, Common **53**, 178
Karri **58**, 180
Pouched **84**
Spiked **106**, 196
Summer **109**, 196
Woolly-headed **127**
Yellow **113**
Darwinia 15, 31, 184, 194
carnea Gardn. **50**
collina Gardn. 184
hypericifolia (Turcz.) Domin 184
leiostyla (Turcz.) Domin 184
macrostegia (Turcz.) Benth. 184
meeboldii Gardn. **71**, 184
nieldiana F. Muell. 15, **31**, 194
oldfieldii Benth. 194
purpurea (Endl.) Benth. **118**
speciosa (Meisn.) Benth. 194
squarrosa (Turcz.) Domin **74**, 184
vestita (Endl.) Benth. **79**
virescens (Meisn.) Benth. **107**, 194
Darwinia, Murchison **107**, 194
Pom-pom **79**
Rose **118**
Dasypogon bromeliaefolius R. Br. 178
hookeri Drumm. **52**, 178
Daviesia 185, 191
cordata Sm. **41**
epiphylla Meisn. **97**, 195
incrassata Sm. 178
oppositifolia Endl. **64**, 183, 185
pachyphylla F. Muell. **93**, 191
pectinata Lindl. **23**, **38**, 178
rhombifolia Meisn. 178
trigonophylla Meisn. 185
Dendrobium dicuphum F. Muell. 219
Desmodium 216
Devil's Pins **42**, 195
Diaspasis filifolia R. Br. 183
Dichrostachys spicata (F. Muell.) Gardn. **149**, 207

Dicranopteris linearis (Burm. f.) Underwood **172**
Dicrastylis 208
Dioscorea hastifolia Endl. **37**
Diplolaena 18
  angustifolia Hook **18**
  dampieri Desf. **26**
  microcephala Bartl. **103**
Diplolaena, Lesser **103**
  Southern **26**
Diplopeltis 213
  eriocarpa (Benth.) Hemsl. **165**, 213
  intermedia George var. *incana* George 214
  stuartii F. Muell. var. *stuartii* **161**
Dissocarpus paradoxus (R. Br.) Ulbrich **153**
Diuris 41
  laxiflora Lindl. **124**
  longifolia R. Br. **41**, 196, 205
Dodder **32**
Dodonaea 139, 204
  attenuata A. Cunn. 201
  lobulata F. Muell. **139**
Dragon Tree, White **168**, 214, 216
Drakaea elastica Lindl. **69**
Drosera 14, 28, 183
  androsacea Diels 19
  drummondii Lehm. 199
  erythrorhiza Lindl. **28**, 198
  glanduligera Lehm. 14, **124**
  leucoblasta Benth. **125**
  macrantha Endl. 201
  menziesii R. Br. **28**
  microphylla Endl. **55**
  miniata Diels 199
  platystigma Lehm. **54**
  pycnoblasta Diels 198
  stolonifera Endl. 201
  zonaria Planch. **28**, 198
Dryandra 13, 39, 182, 184, 186, 190, 192, 199
  arborea Gardn. **138**, 204
  carduacea Lindl. **42**
  carlinoides Meisn. 192
  concinna R. Br. 185
  cuneata R. Br. **72**, 182, 184, 190
  drummondii Meisn. 184
  falcata R. Br. **82**, 182, 184, 190
  foliata R. Br. 185
  formosa R. Br. 182, 184
  kippistiana Meisn. 192
  nana Meisn. 192
  nivea R. Br. **39**, 182, 192
  nobilis Lindl. **121**, 198
  obtusa R. Br. **82**
  praemorsa Meisn. **45**
  proteoides Lindl. **115**, 198
  pteridifolia R. Br. **75**, 182
  quercifolia Meisn. **91**, 190
  sessilis (Knight) Domin 15, **46**
  shuttleworthiana Meisn. 192
  speciosa Meisn. **112**, 192
  subulata Gardn. **101**
  tenuifolia R. Br. 182
  tridentata Meisn. **100**
Dryandra, Golden **121**, 198
  King **115**, 198
  Oak-leaved **91**, 190
  Prickly **82**, 184, 190
  Shaggy **112**, 192
  Showy 182, 184
  Urchin **45**
  Wedge-leaved **72**, 181, 190
  Yilgarn **138**, 204
Dunna Dunna **154**, 208

Ecdeiocolea monostachya F. Muell. 204
Elythranthera brunonis (Endl.) George 67
  emarginata (Lindl.) George **67**
Eragrostis 214, 216
Eremaea 100, 194
  acutifolia F. Muell. **103**
  violacea F. Muell. **100**
Eremaea, Rusty **103**
  Violet **100**
Eremophila 150, 202, 203, 205, 206
  abietina Kraenzlin **150**
  calorhabdos Diels **141**
  clarkei F. Muell. **152**, 203
  cuneifolia Kraenzlin **150**, 211
  decipiens Ostf. **137**, 206
  dempsteri F. Muell. 203
  foliosissima Kraenzlin **152**
  fraseri F. Muell. **150**
  glabra (R. Br.) Ostf. 206
  interstans (S. Moore) Diels 203
  ionantha Diels 203
  latrobei F. Muell. 206
  leucophylla Benth. 206
  longifolia F. Muell. 205, 211
  maculata F. Muell. **151**
  maitlandii F. Muell. ex Benth. **152**
  miniata Gardn. **151**, 208
  oppositifolia R. Br. 203
  paisleyi F. Muell. 203
  scoparia (R. Br.) F. Muell. 203
  serrulata (A. Cunn.) Druce 206
  strongylophylla F. Muell. **152**
Eriachne 214, 216
Eriocaulon setaceum L. **176**, 219
Eriochilus dilatatus Lindl. 34
  scaber Lindl. **34**
Eriostemon 206
  spicatus A. Rich. **32**
Ervatamia orientalis (R.Br.) Domin 216
Erythrina vespertilio Benth. **158**, 207, 209, 216
Erythrophleum chlorostachys (F. Muell.) Baill.
Eucalyptus 129, 142, 184, 216
  accedens W. V. Fitzg. 197
  acies Brooker 189
  aspera F. Muell. 214
  astringens Maiden 197
  brockwayi Gardn. 202
  buprestium F. Muell. 181
  burdettiana Blakely & Steedman 189
  caesia Benth. **130**, 201
  calophylla R. Br. ex Lindl. 14, 193
    var. *rosea* Maiden 16
  camaldulensis Dehnh. 193, 206, 212, 214
  chrysantha Blakely & Steedman 191
  clelandii (Maiden) Maiden 203
  coronata Gardn. 189
  corrugata Luehm. 203
  diversicolor F. Muell. **56**, 178
  drummondii Benth. **119**
  dundasii Maiden 203
  erythrocorys F. Muell. 194
  eudesmoides F. Muell. 194
  falcata Turcz. 197
  ficifolia F. Muell. 16, **65**, 181
  foecunda Schau. 209
  forrestiana Diels **137**
  gamophylla F. Muell. 210
  gardneri Maiden 197
  gomphocephala DC. 13
  gongylocarpa Blakely 208
  guilfoylei Maiden 180
  jacksonii Maiden 180
  kingsmillii Maiden & Blakely **147**, 208, 210
  kruseana F. Muell. 204
  lehmannii (Preiss ex Schau.) Benth **94**, 190
  lesouefii F. Muell. 202, 203
  leucophloia Brooker 210
  loxophleba Benth. 193, 197, 202
  macrocarpa Hook. **118**, 194, 198
  marginata Donn ex Sm. 14, 201
  megacarpa F. Muell **132**, 179, 181
  megacornuta Gardn. **79**, 188, 191
  microtheca F. Muell. 206, 209, 214
  miniata A. Cunn. ex Schau. 216
  nutans F. Muell. **79**, 188, 191
  occidentalis Endl. 181, 191, 197
  orbifolia F. Muell. 204
  patellaris F. Muell. 209
  patens Benth. 16
  phoenicea F. Muell. **170**
  platypus Hook. 188
  preissiana Schau. **92**, 181, 184, 188, 191
  prominens Brooker 209
  pyriformis Turcz. **129**, 194, 198
  rhodantha Blakely & Steedman 198
  rudis Endl. 193
  salmonophloia F. Muell. **136**, 188, 197, 202
  salubris F. Muell. 197, 198, 202
  sepulcralis F. Muell. **95**, 189, 191
  spathulata Hook. 197
  striaticalyx W.V. Fitzg. 208
  stricklandii Maiden 203
  terminalis F. Muell. 208, 209, 210
  tetragona (R. Br.) F. Muell. **87**, 184, 187, 191, 194
  tetraptera Turcz. **79**, 184, 188
  todtiana F. Muell. 14
  torquata Luehm. **141**
  wandoo Blakely 16, **35**, 197
  websterana Maiden 204
  woodwardii Maiden 203
Eugenia 216
Eulophia venosa (F. Muell.) Reichb. f. ex Benth. 219
Euphorbia 214
Everlasting, Bushy **45**
  Splendid **145**
  Sticky **145**
  White **143**, 205

Fanflower, Broad-leaved **45**, 178
  Cushion **86**
  Tangled **141**, 204
  Velvet **98**
Fan-palm **170**
Fan-palm, Millstream **162**, 212
Featherflower, Autumn 191
  Bonzai 191
  Claw **102**, 188
  Forrest's **167**, 214
  Hidden **62**, 182, 184
  Mouse 191
  Painted **111**, 188, 199
  Plume 134, 182
  Pritzel's **122**
  Rapier **121**
  Roe's 188
  Scarlet **102**
  Tree **171**
  Variegated **135**
  Wongan **133**, 201
  Woolly **108**

Yellow**78**, 188
Fern, Maiden Hair 180
Necklace 180
Rock 201
Screw **57**, 180
Venus-hair **164**, 212
Ficus coronulata F. Muell. 218
hispida L. f. 218
leucotricha Miq. 218
orbicularis A. Cunn. 212
platypoda A. Cunn. **156**, **157**, 209, 212, 213, 218
racemost L. 218
Fig, Rock **156**, **157**, 209, 212, 213, 218
Rough 212
Fimbristylis 212, 219
Firebush, Common **113**
Crinkle-leaved **113**
Flagellaria indica L. 218
Flag, Hairy **51**
Purple **29**
Yellow **44**
Flame Pea 185
Holly **58**, 180
Showy **67**
Yellow-eyed **53**
Flannelflower **133**
Foxglove, Native **114**, 214
Oldfield's **103**
Foxtails 183, 185
Frankenia 143
densa Summerhayes **143**, 205
pauciflora DC. 13, 213
Frankenia, Nullabour **143**, 205
Franklandia 83, 182
fucifolia R. Br. **83**, 187
triaristata Benth. 187
Fringe-leaf, Little **75**
Fuchsia, Native **151**
Slender **137**

Galactia 218
Gardenia megasperma F. Muell. 217
Gastrolobium 42, 177, 191, 195
calycinum Benth. 177
grandiflorum F. Muell. 42, 211
oxylobioides Benth. **100**, 195
spinosum Benth. **117**
stenophyllum Turcz. 191
velutinum Lindl. 185
villosum Benth. **42**, 177
Gee **153**
Gerbera, Native **54**
Gidgee, W. A. 206
Gimlet, Common 197, 198, 202
Silver-topped 202
Glossostigma drummondii Benth. **131**, 201
Gompholobium capitatum A. Cunn. **25**
venustum R. Br. 185
Gomphrena 214
Goodenia 183, 190, 207, 210, 211, 214, 219
affinis De Vr. 189
brevisepala Carolin **126**
caerulea R. Br. 126
fasciculata (Benth.) Carolin **43**
pinnatifida Schlecht. **153**, 207
scapigera R. Br. **84**, 189
stenophylla F. Muell. 190
Goodenia, Bristly **43**
Cut-leaf **153**
Silver 198
Smooth **126**
White **84**, 189
Gossypium 209, 217
australe F. Muell. 217
robinsonii F. Muell. **159**, 209
sturtianum Willis 209
Grass, Buffel 214
Flinders 216
Kangaroo 214, 216
Love 214, 215
Mitchell 216
Oil 216
Spear 143, 205, 214, 215
Wanderrie 216
Greenhood, Banded **54**
Grevillea 13, 15, 182, 187, 190, 198, 199, 204, 209, 217
agrifolia A. Cunn. ex R. Br. 217
annulifera F. Muell. **105**, 193
apiciloba F. Muell. **126**
armigera Meisn. **127**, 199
asteriscosa Diels **120**
bipinnatifida R. Br. 16, **35**
calcicola Gardn. & George 209
candelabroides Gardn. 193
candicans Gardns. 193
concinna R. Br. **80**, 187
dielsiana Gardn. 193
dimidiata F. Muell. 173
dryandroides Gardn. **117**, 199
endlicherana Meisn. 16, **37**
eriostachya Lindl. **118**, 187, 198, 214
eryngioides Benth. **126**
flexuosa (Lindl.) Meisn. **128**
hookerana Meisn. **80**, 187
integrifolia Meisn. 187
juncifolia Hook. 208
leucopteris Meisn. **99**, 193
macrostylis F. Muell. **93**, 190
mimosoides R. Br. **173**
nematophylla F. Muell. 205
ninghanensis Gardn. **137**
nudiflora Meisn. 187
paradoxa F. Muell. **113**, 198
pauciflora R. Br. 187
pectinata R. Br. 187
petrophiloides Meisn. **121**, 193
polybotrya Meisn. 193
pteridifolia Knight 217
pyramidalis A. Cunn. 208, 210, 217
refracta R. Br 217
rogersoniana Gardn. **105**, 193
sarissa S. Moore **139**
stenobotrya F. Muell. 214
teretifolia Meisn. 190
thyrsoides Meisn. 193
tripartita Meisn. **92**, 190
variifolia Gardn. & George **157**, 209
wickhamii Meisn. **164**, 210
wilsonii A. Cunn. **39**
Grevillea, Bottlebrush **113**, 198
Cape Range **157**, 209
Curly **126**
Flame **118**, 187, 198
Fuchsia 16, **35**
Ninghan **137**
Orange **110**
Phalanx **117**, 199
Prickly Plume **105**, 193
Rogerson's **105**, 193
Spindly 16, **37**
Star-leaf **120**
Tangled **128**
Wheel **139**
White Plume **99**, 192
Wickham's **164**, 210
Wilson's **39**
Greybush 203
Guineaflower **128**
Gum, Bara 208
Coral **141**, 203
Cue York 208
Drummond's **119**
Flooded 193
Fuchsia **137**
Lemon-flowered 203
Red 16
Red-flowering **65**, 181
River 193, 206, 212, 214
Rough-leaved Range 214
Salmon **110**, **136**, 188, 197, 202
Scarlet **170**
Snappy 210
Strickland's 203
Weeping **95**, 189
York 193, 197, 202
Gungurru **130**, 201
Gunniopsis intermedia Diels **122**
Gyrocarpus americanus Jacq. 217

Hakea 13, 15, 49, 185, 187, 190, 193, 198, 199, 204, 210, 217
arborescens R. Br. 217
baxteri R. Br. 182, 185, 193
bucculenta Gardn. **108**, 193
cinerea R. Br. **80**, 187
clavata Labill. **83**
coriacea Maconochie **111**
corymbosa R. Br. 187
costata Meisn. 193
crassifolia R. Br. 187
cucullata R. Br. **72**, 182, 185
ferruginea Sweet 182
flabellifolia Meisn. 193
francisiana F. Muell. 208
hookerana Meisn. 190
laurina R. Br. **83**, 187
lehmanniana Meisn. **74**, 185
lissocarpha R. Br. **49**
megalosperma Meisn. **101**
multilineata Meisn. 108, 111, 187
nitida R. Br. **83**
obliqua R. Br. 193
obtusa Meisn. 187
orthorrhyncha F. Muell. 193
petiolaris Meisn. **133**, 201
platysperma Hook. **112**, 199
prostrata R. Br. 15, **20**
recurva Meisn. 206
rhombalis F. Muell 208
ruscifolia Labill. 182
stenophylla A. Cunn. ex R. Br. 193
suaveolens R. Br. 182
suberea S. Moore **158**, 206, 210
trifurcata (Sm.) R. Br. 182
victoria Drumm. **90**, **91**, 190
Hakea, Ashy **80**
Bird 193
Blue **74**, 185
Coastal **83**
Cricket Ball **112**, 199
Frog **83**
Harsh 15, **20**
Lesueur **101**
Pincushion **83**, 187

Pink Spike **111**
Royal **90**, **91**, 190
Sea Urchin **133**
Hardenbergia comptoniana (Andr.) Benth. 177, 180
Hazel, Karri 179
Heath, Globe **25**
Spindle **63**, 183
Helichrysum 145, 207
bracteatum (Vent.) Andr. **45**
davenportii F. Muell. **145**
Helipterum 207
australe (A. Gray) Druce **131**, 201
floribundum DC. **143**, 205
spendidum Hemsl. **145**
Hemiandra 40
linearis Benth. **40**
pungens R. Br. 13, **18**
Hemigenia 140
sericea Benth. **36**
westringioides Benth. **140**
Hemigenia, Open **140**
Silky **36**
Hemiphora elderi F. Muell. **138**, 204
Heteropogon contortus (L.) Beauv. ex R. & S. 215
Hibbertia 57, 178, 202, 209
conspicua (Drumm. & Harv.) Gilg. **102**
cuneiformis (Labill.) Gilg **57**
glomerosa Benth. **128**
hypericoides (DC.) Benth. 13, **25**
lasiopus Benth. **51**
miniata Gardn. **51**, 178
mucronata (Turcz.) Benth. **95**
spicata (Drumm. & Harv.) F. Muell. 210
stellaris Endl. **50**, 178
Hibbertia, Cutleaf **57**
Large **51**
Leafless **102**
Orange **51**, 178
Prickly **195**
Hibiscus 154, 167, 211, 217
farragei F. Muell. **138**
goldsworthii F. Muell. 211
panduriformis Burm. f. **149**, 211
setulosus F. Muell. 217
Hibiscus, Coastal 213
Knobby **138**
Sand **167**, 214
Yellow **149**, 211
Homalanthus populifolius (Reinw.) Grah. 216
Honeybush **49**
Honeymyrtle, Broom **111**, 188, 198
Chenille 15, **19**
Corky **89**
Graceful **135**, 201
Grey 15, **30**
Hidden **124**
Scarlet **123**
Wiry **105**, 194
Honeypot, Awled **101**
Couch **39**, 192
Shining **82**
Tangled **75**
Yellow **100**
Honeysuckle 185
Prickly **82**, 187
Hopbush, Bead **139**
Cork **163**
Hovea 42
acanthoclada (Turcz.) F. Muell. **95**, 191
elliptica (Sm.) DC. **59**, 180
pungens Benth. **42**
stricta Meisn. 195
trisperma Benth. 15, **25**
Hovea, Common 15, **25**
Thorny **95**, 191
Tree **59**, 180
Hoya australis R. Br. ex Traill **175**
Hoya, a native **175**
Hydrilla verticillata (L. f.) Royle 219
Hypocalymma 25, 195
angustifolium Endl. 14, **31**
cordifolium (Lehm.) Schau 182
myrtifolium Turcz. 184
puniceum Gardn. **116**
robustum Endl. 15, 26
speciosum Turcz. 184
strictum Schau. 182

Illyarrie 194
Indigofera 210, 216
Ipomoea 214, 218
brasiliensis (L.) Sw. **166**, 212
costata F. Muell. ex Benth. **157**, 209
muelleri Benth. **148**
yardiensis A. S. George **157**, 209
Iris, Morning **55**
Iron Plant 211
Ironwood 216
Iseilema 216
Isoetes 201
Isopogon 41, 182, 185, 187, 190, 199
axillaris R. Br. 182
baxteri R. Br. **73**, 185
cuneata R. Br. 182
divergens R. Br. **102**
dubius (R. Br.) Druce **41**
formosus R. Br. **61**, 182, 185
latifolius R. Br. 185
sphaerocephalus Lindl. **41**
teretifolius R. Br. **80**, 187
trilobus R. Br. **87**, 187
tripartitus R. Br. 187
villosus Meisn. 187
Isopogon, Drumstick **41**
Isotoma 47
hypocrateriformis (R. Br.) Druce **47**, 177, 201
petraea F. Muell. 202
Isotome, Rock 202

Jacksonia 195, 216
compressa 190
Jam Tree 195, 197, 203
Jarrah 14, 16, **38**, 180, 184
Johnsonia 23
lupulina R. Br. **62**, **76**
pubescens Lindl. **23**
Jugflower, Hairy **46**
Justago 174
cleomoides (F. Muell.) Kuntze **174**

Kallstroemia 163
platyptera (Benth.) Engl. **163**
Kangaroo Paw, Black **96**, **97**, 196
Dwarf **71**, 185
Green 14, **30**
Little **47**
Mangles' **20**, 196
Red 185, 189
Tall **66**
Yellow **97**, 196
Kapok Bush **173**
Karri **56**, 178, 181
Karri Hazel 179
Karri Oak 179
Kennedia 48
coccinea Vent. **48**, 177, 180
nigricans Lindl. **85**, 191
prorepens F. Muell. 208
stirlingii Lindl. **45**
Kennedia, Black **85**, 191
Bushy **45**
Keraudrenia 113
hermanniaefolia J. Gay **113**
integrifolia Steud. **113**
Kimberley Walnut 217
Kingia australis R. Br. **70**, **72**, 177, 196
Koolah 177
Kunzea 184
baxteri Schau. **135**
pulchella (Lindl.) George **132**, 201
recurva Schau. var. *montana* Diels **71**, 184
Kunzea, Baxter's **135**
Granite **132**, 201
Mountain **71**, 184
Kurara **147**, 195, 205, 206, 209, 213
Kurrajong 209, 210
Sticky **173**, 217

Laceflower, Smooth **161**
Lachnostachys 115, 195
coolgardiensis S. Moore 204
eriobotrya (F. Muell.) Druce 195
ferruginea Hook. **115**
verbascifolia F. Muell. 204
Lamarchea 195
Lambertia 182, 185, 187
echinata R. Br. **82**, 187
ericifolia R. Br. 185
inermis R. Br. **87**, 185, 187
Lambstail, Hill River **108**, 195
Rusty **115**
Lambswool 195
Lanoline Bush **83**, 187
Lantern Bush, Fraser's **167**, 213
Launea bellidifolia Cass. 212
Laxmannia brachyphylla F. Muell. **86**
Lechenaultia 183, 191, 196, 207, 219
biloba Lindl. **46**, 178, 189, 196
expansa R. Br. 183
formosa R. Br. 183, 185, 189, 191
heteromera Benth. 191
hirsuta F. Muell. **98**, 196
longiloba F. Muell. **107**, 196
macrantha Krause **118**
subcymosa Gardn. & George 210
superba F. Muell. **92**, 190
tubiflora R. Br. **84**, 183, 189, 191
Lechenaultia, Barrens **92**, 190
Blue **46**, 178, 189, 196
Claw 191
Hairy **98**, 196
Heath **84**, 183, 189, 191
Irwin **107**, 196
Red 183, 185, 189, 191
Wreath **118**
Leichhardt Tree 217
Leptocarpus 34
canus Nees 13, **34**
Leptospermum 188, 195
ellipticum Endl. 14
firmum (Schau.) Benth. 181
sericeum Labill. **89**, 188
spinescens Endl. 188

Leucopogon 32, 185, 191
pulchellus Sond. **32**
rubicundus (F. Muell.) Benth. 191
verticillatus R. Br. **58**, 180
Lhotzkya 195
Lianes 218
Lily, Blue Tinsel 13
Hooded **62, 76**
Pipe **23**
Swamp 13, 201
Water 219
Lindsaea ensifolia Sw. 218
linearis Swartz. **57**, 180
Little Wheel Bush **170**
Livistona 218
Livistona alfredii F. Muell. **162**, 212
eastonii C.A. Gardn. 218
loriphylla Beccari **170**, 218
mariae F. Muell. 212
Lobelia quadrangularis R.Br. 212
winfridae Diels **153**
Lobelia, Little **153**
Logania 119
flaviflora F. Muell. **119**
Logania, Yellow **119**
Lomandra 22
endlicheri (F. Muell.) Ewart **22**
Lycopodium 183
Lygodium microphyllum (Cav.) R.Br. **176**, 218
Lysiana casuarinae (Miq.) Tiegh. **163**
Lysinema 29, 183
ciliatum R.Br. **29**, 183
conspicuum R. Br. 183
fimbriatum F. Muell. 183
lasianthum R.Br. 183
Lysiphyllum cunninghamii (Benth.) De Wit **172**, 216

Macropidia fuliginosa (Hook.) Druce **97**, 196
Macrozamia riedlei (Gaud.) Gardn. **24**, 177
Mahogany, Dundas 202
Swan River 16
Maireana 197, 205, 208, 214
atkinsiana (W.V. Fitzg.) P.G. Wilson **154**
sedifolia (F. Muell.) P.G. Wilson **143**, 203, 205
Mallee, Apple 181
Bell-fruited **92**, 181, 184, 188, 191
Bookleaf 204
Crowned 189
Four-winged **79**, 184, 188
Kingsmill's **147**, 208, 210
Pear-fruited **129**, 194, 198
Rose 198
Round-leaved 204
Webster's 204
Maidenhair, Climbing **176**, 218
Mallees 181, 191
Mallet, Blue 197
Brown 197
Swamp 197
White 197
Mangaloo **170**
Mangrove, Ribbed **175**
White 13, 213
Marri 14, 16, 184, 193
Marsilea 212
hirsuta R.Br. 214
Mat-rush, Tiered **22**
Melaleuca 13, 15, 181, 188, 190, 191, 194, 195, 204, 216
argentea W.V. Fitzg. 214, 216
calothamnoides F. Muell. 194
cardiophylla F. Muell. 210
citrina Turcz. 190
coccinea George **140**
conothamnoides Gardn. **121**
cuticularis Labill. 13, 181, 199
diosmifolia Andr. 181
elliptica Labill. **134**
fulgens R.Br. **123**
glomerata F. Muell. 212
huegelii Endl. 15, **19**
lanceolata Ott. 13
leucadendron (L.) L. **164**, 206, 212, 214, 216
megacephala F. Muell. 294
nematophylla F. Muell. **105**, 194
pauperiflora F. Muell. 204
pentagona Labill. 188
polygaloides Schau. 15, **30**
preissiana Schau. 13
pulchella R.Br. 188
pungens Schau. 188
radula Lindl. **135**, 201
rhaphiophylla Schau. 13, 181
sheathiana W.V. Fitzg. 204
striata Labill. 188
suberosa (Schau.) Gardn. **89**, 188
thymoides Labill. 181
uncinata R. Br. **111**, 188, 198
undulata Benth. **124**
viridiflora Sol. ex Gaertn. 216
Melastoma malabathricum L. **176**
Melia composita Willd. 217
Mesomelaena tetragona (R.Br.) F. Muell. **31**
Microcybe 188
Micromyrtus 195
flaviflora (F. Muell.) Gardn. 208
Milfoil, Water 201
Miljee **143**, 205
Milkwort, Broom **116**
Milly Milly 212
Mimulus repens R.Br. **154**
Mintbush, Crinkly **138**
Mirbelia 123, 206
dilatata R.Br. 183
floribunda Benth. **123**, 195
Mirbelia, Purple **123**, 195
Mistletoe 14, **163**, 206
Mangrove 215
Pincushion **147**
Mitrasacme 219
Mollugo 214
Monkeyflower, Creeping **154**
Monochoria cyanea (F. Muell.) F. Muell. **176**
Moort 188
Red-flowered **79**, 188, 191
Morning Glory **158**, 209
Beach **166**, 212
Poison **148**
Rock **157**, 209
Yardie **157**, 209
Mottlecah **118**, 194, 198
Mouse Ears **134**, 201
Mucuna 218
Mudmat **131**, 201
Muiriantha hassellii (F. Muell.) Gardn. 185
Mulga **144**, 205, 211
Mulla Mulla, Curved **125**
Hairy **146**, 214
Mat **159**, 214
Stirling's **26**
Tall **146**, 214, 219
Tangled 214
Weeping **163**
Myall **143**, 205
Myriophyllum **169**, 201
Myrtle, Large **116**
Swan River 14, **26**
White 14, **31**

Najas graminea Delile 219
tenuifolia R.Br. 212
Nancy, Eight **131**, 200
Nardoo 212, 214
Native Willow 177
Nauclea coadnata J.E. Sm. 217
Nematolepis phebalioides Turcz. 188
Newcastelia 195, 208
chrysophylla Gardn. 196
Ngalta 204
Nicotiana 206
Nuytsia floribunda (Labill.) R.Br. ex Fenzl. 14, **24**, 202
Nymphaea gigantea Hook. 219
Nymphoides hydrocharoides (F. Muell.) Kuntze 219
indica (L.) Kuntze 219

Oak, Black 205
Oldenlandia 217
Olearia 207
axillaris (DC.) F. Muell. 212
muelleri (Sond.) Benth. 203
pimelioides (DC.) Benth. 203
rudis F. Muell. ex Benth. **19**
Oligarrhena micrantha R.Br. 191
Orange Stars **50**, 178
Orchid, Ant **123**
Arrowsmith Spider **109**, 196
Banded Greenhood **54**
Bee 14, **124**
Bird **49**
Blue China **43**
Blue Lady **49**
Bronze Shell **18**
Butterfly 186
Clubbed Spider **68**
Common Donkey **41**, 196, 205
Cowslip **20**, 186, 196
Crablipped **68**
Dragon **122**
Dwarf Spider 186
Elbow **134**, 201, 205
Flying Duck **55**
Freckled Sun **109**
Fringed Leek **39**
Fringed Mantis **129**
Hammer **69**
Helmet 180
Jug **53**
King Leek **69**
Leaping Spider **47**
Mantis **128**
Pink Bunny **34**
Pink Enamel **67**
Pouched Leek **69**
Shirt **108**, 196
Silky Blue **54**
Slipper 186
Snail 205
a tree **171**
Underground 198
White Spider **50**, 186
Winter Spider **124**
Zebra **68**

Orthrosanthus 55
laxus (Endl.) Benth. **55**
Ottelia ovalifolia (R.Br.) L.C. Rich 13, 201
Ouch Bush **93**, 191
Owenia reticulata F. Muell. 214
vernicosa F. Muell. 217
Oxylobium 177, 191
atropurpureum Turcz. **77**, 185
capitatum Benth. **33**
lanceolatum (Vent.) Druce 183
linearifolium (Don) Druce 177

Painted Lady **73**
Pandanus 172, 218
aquaticus F. Muell. 218
darwinensis St. John **172**
Parsonsia 218
Paperbark 13, 15, 181
Salt-water 13
Paperheaths 183, 185
Mountain **77**
Paper-lily, Stilted **86**
Paracaleana 55
nigrita (Lindl.) D. Blaxell **55**
Parakeelya **109, 142**, 207
Parrot Bush 14, 15, **46**
Passiflora foetida L. 218
Patersonia occidentalis R.Br. **29**
rudis Endl. **51**
xanthina F. Muell. **44**
Pea, Ashburton 214
Globe 195
Mountain **77**, 185
Rattle **64**, 185
Ribbon **104**, 195
Yellow **25**
Pea-bush, Dark **127**
Upside-down **125**, 204
Pepper and Salt **32**
Pepperflower, Desert **161**
Hairy **165**, 213
Grey 214
Peppermint, Strange **37**
W.A. 13, **19**, 179
Persoonia 182, 217
elliptica R.Br. 177
longifolia R.Br. 177
saccata R.Br. **27**
Petalostigma pubescens F. Muell. **171**, 216
quadriloculare F. Muell. 216
Petalostylis 211
labicheoides R.Br. **161**, 211
Petalostylis, Slender **161**, 211
Petrophile 35, 182, 185, 187, 190, 199
biloba R.Br.**35**
divaricata R.Br. **120**
ericifolia R.Br. 187
linearis R.Br. **29**
longifolia R.Br. **61**, 185
phylicoides R.Br. **125**, 187
serruriae R.Br. 185
teretifolia R.Br. 187
trifida R.Br. **119**
Petrophile, Granite **35**
Long-leaved **61**, 185
Phebalium 117, 188
anceps DC. 183
filifolium Turcz. **117**
Phebalium, Slender **117**
Philydrella pygmaea (F. Muell.) Caruel **133**, 201
Phragmites karka (Retz.) Trin. ex Steud. 212, 215
Phyllanthus baccatus F. Muell. ex Benth. 212, 216
Phyllota dasyphylla Turcz. **115**
Phymatocarpus 195
Physopsis spicata Turcz. **108**, 195
Pied Piper Bush **149**
Pigface, Coastal **86**
White 214
Pigweed, Star **153**
Pileanthus 100, 194
filifolius Meisn. **100**, 194
limacis Labill. **168**, 194, 213
peduncularis Endl. **101**, 214
Pilostyles hamiltonii Gardn. 178
Pimelea 191
floribunda Meisn. **23**
physodes Hook. **93**, 191
rosea R.Br. **27, 48,** 178
spectabilis (Fisch. & Mey.) Lindl. 178
suaveolens (Endl.) Meisn. **39**, 178
Pincushions **132**, 200
Pineapple Bush **52**, 178
Pingle **42**
Pin-heath, Common **21**
Pinyuru **150**
Pitcher Plant, Albany **63**, 183
Pittosporum phylliraeoides DC. 143, 205
Pittosporum, Weeping 143, 205
Pityrodia 195
atriplicina (F. Muell.) F. Muell. ex Benth. 195
oldfieldii (F. Muell.) F. Muell. ex Benth. **103**, 195
paniculata (F. Muell.) F. Muell. ex Benth. 214
petiolaris E. Pritzel 214
terminalis (Endl.) George **114**
uncinata (Turcz.) Benth. 190
verbascina (F. Muell.) F. Muell. ex Benth. 195
var. *aurea* E. Pritzel 195
Pixie Mops **29**
Planchonia careya (F. Muell.) R. Knuth **170**
Platytheca juniperina Domin 32
verticillata (Hueg.) Baill. **32**
Platyzoma microphyllum R.Br. **175**, 218
Plectrachne 207, 208, 210, 215
Pluchea rubelliflora (F. Muell.) Robinson 219
Plumbago zeylanica L. **159**, 210
Plumbago, Native **159**, 210
Podocarpus drouyniana F. Muell. 177
Podolepis canescens A. Cunn. ex DC. **145**
Podolepis, Bright **145**
Poison, Cabbage 219
Champion Bay **100**, 195
Crinkle-leaf **42**, 177
Heart-leaf 185
Narrow-leaf 191
Prickly **117**, 185
Stirling Range 185
Wallflower 211
Woodbridge **47**, 177
York Road 177
Pokers, Pink **121**
Red **108**, 193
Polymeria 218
Polymeria ambigua R.Br. **158**, 209
Polypompholyx 14, 183
Pomegranate, Bush **141**, 204
Native **128**
Pom Poms **44**
Poplar, Native 196
Portulaca 207
Potamogeton javanicus Hassk. 212
tricarinatus F. Muell. & Benn. ex Benn. 219
Poverty Bush **152**, 211
Kopi **151**, 208
Shark Bay **152**
Silver 203
Spotted **150**
Prasophyllum 39
fimbria Reichb.f. **39**
gibbosum R.Br. **69**
regium Rogers **69**
Prickly Moses 13, 15, **21**, 183
Pricklybark 14
Prostanthera 138
eckersleyana F. Muell. **138**
Protea 198
Psoralea 216
Pteridium esculenteum (Forst.F.) Nakai 180
Pteris vittata L. 164, 212
Pterocaulon 207
sphacelatum (Labill.) F. Muell. 219
Pterostylis 53, 189
barbata Lindl. **49**
nana R.Br. 205
plumosa Cady 49
recurva Benth. **53**
scabra Lindl. **18**
vittata Lindl. var. *vittata* **54**
var. *subdifformis* Nicholls **54**
Ptilotus 44, 202, 207, 211, 214
axillaris (F. Muell.) F. Muell. **159**, 214
calostachyus (F. Muell.) F. Muell. **163**
clementii (Farmer) Benl 211
declinatus Nees **125**
exaltatus Nees **146**, 204, 214, 219
helipteroides (F. Muell.) F. Muell. **146**, 214
latifolius R.Br. 214
macrocephalus (R.Br.) Poir. 211
manglesii (Lindl.) F. Muell. **44**
obovatus (Gaud.) F. Muell. 207
rotundifolius (F. Muell.) F. Muell. 211
stirlingii (Lindl.) F. Muell. **26**
Purple Tassels **27**

Qualup Bell **93**
Quandong 198, 206
Queen of Sheba **93**, 196
Quillwort 201
Quinine Tree **171**

Rainbow, Golden **55**
Pink **28**
Randia 217
Ranji Bush **147**, 206, 209, 213
Rattlepod
New Holland **174**
Rattlepods 211, 216
Redcoats 14, **33**
Red Combs **80**, 187
Red Pokers **108**, 193
Red Rod **141**
Red Toothbrushes **80**
Red Velvet **138**, 204
Red, Tropical 212, 215
Regelia 94, 195
velutina (Turcz.) Gardn. **94**, 189
Regelia, Barrens **94**, 189
Rhagodia 214
radiata Nees 13, **19**

Rhizanthella gardneri Rogers 198
Rhizophora mucronata Lam. 213
stylosa Griff. 215
Rhynchosia 216, 218
Ricinocarpos tuberculatus Muell. Arg. 201
Rose, Sturt's Desert 209
Yanchep **18**
Royal Robe **44**, 178
Rush, Jointed 13

Saltbush 208, 214
Berry 13, **19**
Spongy **154**
Salt-star, Yellow **122**
Samphires 13, 181, 208, 214
Sandalwood **123**, 198, 206
Santalum acuminatum (R.Br.) DC. 198, 206
spicatum (R.Br.) DC. **123**, 198, 206
Sarcostemma australe R.Br. **163**, 211
Sarsaparilla, Wild 177, 180
Scaevola 13, 44, 183, 189, 210, 213, 219
crassifolia Labill. 183, 213
nitida R.Br. 183
oxyclona F. Muell **141**, 204
phlebopetala F. Muell **98**
platyphylla Lindl. **45**, 178
pulvinaris (E. Pritzel) Krause **86**
spinescens R.Br. 204, 207, 213
striata R.Br. **44**, 178
Scallops **72**, 182, 185
Schizaea 183
Schoenia cassiniana (Gaud.) Steetz. **145**
Scholtzia 195
Scirpus 212
Sclerolaena 205, 207, 208, 214
Screwpine **172**, 218
Sea-heath 213
Sea Rocket 13
Sedge, Semaphore **31**
Selenothamnus helmsii (F. Muell. & Tate) Melville **154**, 208
Senna, Native **140**
Sesbania 214, 216
formosa F. Muell. **168**, 214, 216
Sheoak, Common 14, 16
Horned **88**
Scrub **21**
Sida 207, 211, 213, 217
inclusa Benth. 211
physocalyx F. Muell. 211
Smokebush, Blue **82**, 187
Blue-eyed **117**
Common 15, **26**, **96**, 193
Hooded **40**
Plume **106**, 193
Slender **36**
Stirling Range **71**
Summer 193
Tangled 182
Snakebush 13, **18**
Speckled **40**
Snottygobble **27**, 177
Solanum 162, 202, 211, 213
ellipticum R.Br. 211
gabrielae Domin 211
lasiophyllum Dun. 211
phlomoides A. Cunn. ex Benth. **162**, 211
sturtianum F. Muell. 211
Sorghum stipoideum (Ewart & White) Gardn. & Hubb. 215
Southern Cross **67**, 185
Lesueur **98**
Sowerbaea 27
laxiflora Lindl. **27**
Speargrass, Bunch 215
Sphaerolobium 195
Sphenotoma 77, 183, 185
capitatum (R.Br.) Lindl. 183
dracophylloides Sond. 183, 185
drummondii (Benth.) F. Muell. **77**, 185
gracilis (R.Br.) Sweet 183
Spiculaea ciliata Lindl. **134**, 201, 205
Spinifex hirsutus Labill. 13
longifolius R.Br. 13, 212
Spinifex **142**, **160**, 204, 208, 210, 214
Gummy 212
Spleenwort 180
Spongefruit **139**
Sporobolus virginicus (L.) Kunth. 213
Spurge, Broom 204
Stackhousia 36
brunonis Benth. **36**
dielsii Pampanini **104**
pubescens A. Rich **126**
Stackhousia, Downy **126**
Winged **36**
Yellow **104**
Staghorn Bush **97**, 195
Starbush, Yellow **116**
Starflower, Brush **74**
Pink **86**
Summer **23**
Superb **107** 194
Stemodia grossa Benth. **155**, 208, 214
viscosa Roxb. 214
Stemodia, Marsh **155**, 208, 214
Stenocarpus 217
cunninghamii R.Br. **170**
Sterculia viscidula W.V. Fitzg. **173**, 217
viridiflora W.F. Fitzg.
Stinkwood 217
Stipa **143**
Stirlingia latifolia (R.Br.) Steud. 15, **27**, 177
Sturt Pea **143**, **148**, 204, 205, 207, 210
Sturt's Desert Rose 209
Stylidium 33, 185, 202, 219
albomontis Carlquist 190
alsinoides R.Br. 212
bulbiferum Benth. **135**, 201
crossocephalum F. Muell. **99**
floodii F. Muell. **174**
galioides Gardn. 190
imbricatum Benth. 185
macranthum Carlquist **85**
pilosum Labill. **85**
preissii (Sond.) F. Muell. **95**
scandens R.Br. **62**, 185
utricularioides Benth. **33**
verticillatum F. Muell 185
Stypandra 131, 200
grandiflora Lindl. **131**, 200
imbricata R.Br. 200
Styphelia 21
tenuiflora Lindl. **21**
Sundews 14
Black-eyed **54**
Cone 198
Drummond's 199
Orange 199
Painted **28**, 198
Pearly 198
Pimpernel 14, **124**
A Pygmy **125**
Red Ink **28**, 198
Swainsona 142, 207, 210, 211, 214
colutoides F. Muell. **142**, 204
macullochiana F. Muell. 214
pterostylis (DC.) Bakh.f. 208, 214
stenodonta F. Muell. 211
Synaphea 65, 182
petiolaris R.Br. **65**
polymorpha R.Br. **65**
Synaphea, A. **65**
Albany **65**

Tail-flower, Sticky **61**
Tallerack **87**, 184, 187, 191, 194
Tamma 198
Tassel Flower **58**, 180
Tea-tree 15
Rottnest 13
Silver **89**, 188
Swamp 14
Tecticornia arborea Wilson **155**, 208
Templetonia retusa (Vent.) R.Br. 13, **20**
Tephrosia 210, 214, 216
Terminalia arostrata Ewart & Davies 217
Tersonia brevipes Moq. **99**, 196
Tetratheca 40
harperi F. Muell 204
hirsuta Lindl. **40**
Thelymitra 49, 189
campanulata Lindl. **108**, 196
crinita Lindl. **49**
sargentii Rogers **109**
variegata (Lindl.) F. Muell. **93**, 196
Themeda 214, 216
Thespesia 217
Thomasia 35
glutinosa Lindl. 16, **35**
Thomasia, Sticky 16, **35**
Thryptomene 182, 195, 204, 209
baeckeacea F. Muell. 210
saxicola (A. Cunn.) Schau. **132**
Timonius 217
Tingle, Red 180
Yellow 180
Tinospora smilacina Benth. 218
Tinsel Flower **120**, 198
Tomato, Wild **162**, 211, 213
Toothbrushes, Black **126**
Prickly **127**, 199
Red **80**
Toucan Flower **158**, 210
Trachymene hemicarpa (F. Muell.) Benth. **161**
ornata (Endl.) Druce **139**
Trianthema 214
oxycalyptra F. Muell. **153**
Tribonanthes 14, 200
Tribulus 149, 207
occidentalis R.Br. **149**, 207
Trichocline spathulata (A. Cunn. ex DC.) J.H. Willis **54**
Trichodesma zeylanicum (Burm.f.) R.Br. **166**, 212
Triggerplant 185, 219
Circus **135**, 201
Climbing **62**
Lizard **95**
Pink Fan **33**
Posy **99**
Silky **85**
Tile-leaved 185
Yellow Mountain 190
Triglochin procera R.Br. 13
Triodia 142, 207, 208, 210, 214, 215

pungens R.Br. 212
scariosa N.T. Burbidge 142, 204
Triumfetta 167
chaetocarpa F. Muell. **167**
Trumpets **55**
Trymalium spathulatum (Labill.) Ostf. 179
Tuart 13
Turpentine Bush **152**, 203
Twine-rush, Hoary 14, **34**
Twin-leaves 208
Typha domingensis Pers. 13, 212, 214

Upside-down Bush 208
Urchins **167**
Urocarpus 116
squamuligerus (Hook.) Wilson **116**
Utricularia 183, 219
chrysantha R.Br. **175**, 219
menziesii R.Br. 14, **33**

Vallisneria spiralis L. 219
Velleia 115, 207
foliosa (Benth.) Krause 185
panduriformis A. Cunn. ex Benth. 219
rosea S.Moore **155**, 207
Velleia, Pink **155**
Verreauxia 98
reinwardtii (De Vr.) Benth. **98**
Verticordia 111, 182, 184, 191, 194, 216
acerosa Lindl. **35**
brownii (Desf.) DC. **112**, 188, 194, 199
chrysantha Endl. **78**, 188, 194
chrysostachys Meisn. 194
cunninghamii Schau. **171**
etheliana Gardn. 194
fastigiata Turcz. 191
forrestii F. Muell **167**, 214
grandiflora Endl. **102**, 188
grandis Drumm. **102**
habrantha Schau. **62**, 182, 184
harveyi Benth. 191
huegelii Endl. **135**
minutiflora F. Muell 188
mitchelliana Gardn. **121**
monadelpha Turcz. **108**
muellerana E. Pritzel 194
multiflora Turcz. 182
oculata Meisn. 194
ovalifolia Meisn. 194
oxylepis Turcz. 191
picta Endl. **111**, 188, 199
plumosa (Desf.) Druce **134**
polytricha Benth. 194
pritzelii Diels **122**
roei Endl. **78**, 188
sieberi Diesing ex Schau. 188
staminosa Gardn et George **133**
Vetch 208, 214
Bladder **142**
Vigna 218

Waitzia acuminata Steetz. 207
Walnut, Native 214
Wandoo 16, **35**, 184, 197
Powder-bark 197, 198
Warrine **37**
Water Bush 177, 180
Water Currant 216
Water Nymph 212
Water Pincushions **176**, 219
Water-ribbon 13
Wattie 180, 181
Wattle **38**, **46**, **160**, 213
Baxter's **64**
Drummond's **73**, 183
Flat **94**, 191
Glowing **112**
Gregory's **166**, 213
Karri **57**, 179
Long-leaved **129**
Tan **137**, 203
Winged **50**
Wiry **43**
Wax, Geraldton 15, 195
Waxflower, Esperance 188
Large **88**
Weeooka 203
Wehlia 115
coarctata F. Muell **115**
White Dragon Tree **168**, 214
Whitewood 214
Wodjil 198
Woody Pear 177
Sandplain **114**, 177, 193, 198
Woollybush, Common 15, **31**
Woollybutt 216
Wrightia 218
Wurmbaea 131
tenella (Endl.) Benth. **131**, 200

Xanthorrhoea 114, **142**
brevistyla Herbert 196
gracilis Endl. **44**, 177
nana Herbert **114**
preissii Endl. **104**, 177, 196
thorntoni Tate 142
Xanthosia 67
rotundifolia DC. **67**, 185
var. *hypoleuca* Diels 185
tomentosa A.S. George **98**
Xanthostemon 171
paradoxus F. Muell **171**, 216
Xylomelum 193
angustifolium Kipp. **114**, 177, 192, 198
occidentale R.Br. 177, 193
Xyris 219

Yate, Bushy **94**
Flat-topped 181, 191, 197
Warted **79**, 188, 189, 191
Yulbah **158**, 207, 209, 216

Zamia **24**, 177
Zornia 216
Zygophyllum 208

INDIAN OCEAN
PORT HEDLAND
Yule R
Sherlock R
C Lambert
Dampier
Roebourne
Karratha
Pyramid Stn
Barrow I
Robe R
Cane R
Fortescue R
344 Mt Herbert
CHICHESTER
Millstream Stn
Onslow
Yarraloola Stn
North West Cape
Exmouth
Exmouth Gulf
Mt Hollister 315
CAPE RA
Yardie Cr
HAMERSLEY
DIVIDING RA
Wittenoom
Wittenoom G
Dale G
Mt Stuart Stn
Duck Cr
Ashburton R
Mt Brockman 1114
Mt Samson 1079
1236 Mt Bruce
1075 Tom Price Mine
Mt Tom Price
Hardey R
CAPRICORN RA
Winning Pool Stn
Lyndon R
Mt Palgrave 704
Ashburton Downs Stn
Turee Cr
Angelo R
TROPIC OF CAPRICORN
Minilya R
KENNETH RA
GODFREY RA
Lake MacLeod
Lyons R
Mt Vernon Stn
TEANO RA
KENNEDY RA
Mt Augustus 1105
Mt Phillips 780
WALDBURG RA
Mt Egerton 994
364
Gascoyne R
Mt Gascoyne 789
Bernier I
CARNARVON
Gascoyne Junction
Milgun Stn
Dorre I
ROBINSON
802 Peak Hil
SHARK BAY
Wooramel R
Murchison R
Peron Peninsula
Dirk Hartog I
Denham
Hope R
L Annean
20°
115°
25°
15
14
13
8